"THOU SHALT NOT STEAL"
Exodus 20:15 KJV.

PREPARE
THE WAY _____

PREPARE THE WAY

JOE ENGELKEMIER

**Author of
READY TO ANSWER
REALLY LIVING**

This book is published in collaboration with the Missionary Volunteer Department as an enrichment of the Morning Watch devotional plan.

**REVIEW AND HERALD
PUBLISHING ASSOCIATION
WASHINGTON, D.C.**

DEDICATION

To my wife, Gladys, to our three teen-agers,
Joetta, Marvin, and Eddie, and to those tens of
thousands of Adventist youth whom God is now
raising up to help "prepare the way" for a glorious completion of His work.

TO THE YOUTH OF THE CHURCH . . .

. . . AND TO ALL WHO WANT JESUS TO COME

DEAR FRIENDS:

A student at Andrews University recently observed that God must be "preparing the way for something wonderful to happen." On many Adventist campuses a new spiritual awakening and renewal has been taking place. "I will pour out my spirit upon all flesh," God has promised (Joel 2:28). Specifically mentioned are the youth of the church—sons, daughters, young men, servants, handmaids.

Envisioning such a time, the servant of God has written:

"I have been deeply impressed by scenes that have recently passed before me in the night season. There seemed to be a great movement—a work of revival—going forward in many places. Our people were moving into line, responding to God's call."—*Selected Messages,* book 2, p. 402.

Back in Nehemiah's time the unfinished task of his day had lingered on for year after year, when Nehemiah, with firm and eager purpose, threw himself into seeking a completed work. His consecration and enthusiasm were contagious, and within fifty-two action-packed crisis-filled days the task was finished!

Could the same consecration and enthusiasm today bring about similar results? Would each of you, at your schools and in your churches, be willing to become a Nehemiah?

You, the youth of the church, with your ardor, your enthusiasm, your generous devotion, are God's greatest hope for a swift completion of His work. Let there take place within your lives a revival of Bible study, of prayer, of living faith, of united effort, and your influence will be felt to the ends of the earth!

May God bless you as you help "prepare the way" for the promised outpouring of God's Spirit, which in turn will prepare the way for Jesus to come!

Yours for a great move forward to
finish the work of God,

JOE ENGELKEMIER

IF NOT NOW, WHEN?

"You shall receive power when the Holy Spirit has come upon you; and you shall be my witnesses in Jerusalem and in all Judea and Samaria and to the end of the earth." Acts 1:8, R.S.V.

Those at the dinner table, there at Southern Missionary College, had been discussing the second coming of Christ. "I want to see Jesus come," said one girl. "Nothing in this world can compare with what He has promised. I could turn my back on everything right now if Jesus would come."

"Why can't it be this generation?" asked a San Fernando Valley Academy student in a letter to *Insight.* "In other words, I'm sick of this world. How long do we have to stay? Let's work on heavenly things and strive to be one of the 144,000."

We should be celebrating this New Year's Day in the New Jerusalem. One of these New Years, by God's grace, we *will.* But there is a work to be done first—a task that can be completed only through the power of another Pentecost. To seek this, as we begin 1972, should be our very first purpose. In the words of another:

"The church must arouse to action. The Spirit of God can never come in until she prepares the way. There should be earnest searching of heart. There should be united, persevering prayer, and through faith a claiming of the promises of God."— *Selected Messages,* book 1, p. 126.

Will we, during 1972, arouse to action? Will we, through heart-searching, repentance, and persevering prayer, help prepare the way for a modern Pentecost?

It was in 1895 that the servant of God wrote:

"The descent of the Holy Spirit upon the church is looked forward to as in the future; but it is the privilege of the church to have it now. Seek for it, pray for it, believe for it. We must have it, and Heaven is waiting to bestow it."—*Evangelism,* p. 701.

Our privilege—*now!* Seek, pray, believe—*now!* Will we, *now,* this year?

If not now, when? If not you, who? And if not on your campus, in your church, in your home, where?

SEEKING HIM EACH MORNING

My voice shalt thou hear in the morning, O Lord; in the morning will I direct my prayer unto thee, and will look up. **Ps. 5:3.**

During the 1966-1967 school year, following a Bible conference at which the Holy Spirit had been markedly present, delegates from several academies began what they called the Seven and Seven Club. The idea was that at seven o'clock in the morning and at seven in the evening, or as close thereto as practicable, delegates would pause in whatever they were doing and offer a prayer for one another, and for an outpouring of the Holy Spirit upon their schools and upon God's youth everywhere. During the months that followed, lives were changed and remarkable conversions took place as God worked through some of these youth.

It was during the same school year, at the 1966 Autumn Council, that a stirring call was made for reformation and revival. Through the remainder of the sixties and into the seventies an emphasis on the need for revival has continued. God has blessed these earnest efforts. Wrote O. M. Berg, in the January, 1971, issue of *The Ministry:*

"We have seen some marvelous evidences of God's answer to our prayers as the work has gone forward in several areas with new power. We have experienced great revivals at Camp Berkshire and other ministerial gatherings and retreats; spiritual outpourings have come to churches, to academy and college campuses, and recently in rich measure to Andrews University. In these we rejoice, but we see in them but omens of a great tempest of power that must yet sweep through our ranks. We are quick to confess that the great outpouring of the Holy Spirit, destined to exceed even that of Pentecost, is still a future hope."

Elder Berg then asked, "How much longer must we wait? How much longer must *God* wait?"

A foremost influence on those campuses and at those meetings where revival has come has been the spirit of intercession that has prevailed. Could we at the beginning of this new year renew the plan of sending up a prayer at seven and seven for a mighty outpouring of God's Spirit?

THE LONG DELAY

The Lord is not slack concerning his promise, as some men count slackness; but is longsuffering to us-ward, not willing that any should perish, but that all should come to repentance. 2 Peter 3:9.

It was in 1755 that the first great sign of the return of Jesus— the earthquake foretold in Revelation 6:12—took place. Then came the dark day, May 19, 1780. Following this, in 1798, the 1260-year prophecy ended, marking the beginning of "the time of the end." Then, on November 13, 1833, the falling-star display predicted in Revelation 6:13 took place, followed by the beginning of the investigative judgment in 1844.

1755 . . . 1780 . . . 1798 . . . 1833 . . . 1844—each a solemn reminder that the return of Christ was drawing near.

Yet more than two centuries have now passed since the first of these signs appeared.

What has happened?

Wrote the servant of God, in 1868:

"The morning is deferred in mercy, because if the Master should come, so many would be found unready. God's unwillingness to have His people perish has been the reason for so long delay."—*Testimonies,* vol. 2, p. 194.

If it was already a long delay in 1868, what is it in 1972?

"It is not that the Lord is slow in fulfilling his promise, as some suppose," the *New English Bible* translates today's text, "but that he is very patient with you, because it is not his will for any to be lost." * God, because of His great love, has demonstrated an almost unbelievable forbearance. He does not want to lose you or me or anyone.

Through decade after decade after decade the gathering storm has been held back. Angels of God have kept watchful eyes on the darkening thunderheads, have refused to permit the rising winds to break forth into the howling fury of Armageddon. But is there a point beyond which there can be no more delay? Could it be that that point has almost been reached?

God help us to get ready!

---

* From *The New English Bible.* © The Delegates of the Oxford University Press and the Syndics of the Cambridge University Press 1970. Reprinted by permission.

THE LIMITS OF DELAY

But the day of the Lord will come as a thief in the night; in the which the heavens shall pass away with a great noise, and the elements shall melt with fervent heat, the earth also and the works that are therein shall be burned up. 2 Peter 3:10.

"The day of the Lord *will* come." Though the return of Christ has been postponed through decade after decade, there comes a point beyond which it can be delayed no longer. And that point may come, not so much through the exhausting of divine patience, as through the build-up of pressures within society itself. For example:

As the 1960's drew to a close, United Nations secretary-general U Thant warned, on May 9, 1969, that this world may have "perhaps ten years left" to solve its problems. Urging a global partnership to curb the arms race, to improve the environment, and to defuse the population explosion, he declared, "If such a global partnership is not formed within the next decade, then I very much fear that the problems I have mentioned will have reached such staggering proportions that they will be beyond our capacity to control."

At about this same time an authority on the population explosion, Stanford University biologist Paul R. Ehrlich, was asked, "How long can the world last at the present rate of population growth?"

His reply:

" 'Estimates vary between 1975 and 1984 as the time the end will come. These [estimates] are based on the point where the population growth exceeds the minimum diet available from food production.' "—*Signs of the Times,* March, 1969, p. 21.

This biologist conceded that with " 'very good growing years' " the end might be held off till somewhere between 1985 and 1990. But it is already too late, he contends, to keep millions upon millions of people from starving. " 'The battle to feed all of humanity is over,' " he warns, predicting that " 'hundreds of millions of people are going to starve to death in spite of any crash programs embarked upon now.' "—*Ibid.,* p. 18.

We do not set dates. But could it be that we are reaching the limits of delay?

10

AS THE SIGNS MULTIPLY

For nation shall rise against nation, and kingdom against kingdom: and there shall be famines, and pestilences, and earthquakes, in divers places. Matt. 24:7.

Dr. Paul R. Ehrlich, who has predicted that massive famines could bring the end between 1975 and 1984, was asked about birth control as a solution to the population explosion. Pointing out that India began such a program in 1951, he stated: "When the work program started, the population was about 330,000,000. After seventeen years of the birth-control program the population now stands at 540,000,000."—*Signs of the Times,* March, 1969, p. 21.

"Can we stem the tide?" a Ford Foundation adviser asked, concerning the problem of too many people.

"I think not," he said. "It's like the simple law of physics which says that momentum equals mass times velocity. In the case of population the bigger the population the faster it grows and the harder it is to slow down. It is a snowball effect."— San Jose *Mercury News,* April 13, 1969, p. 11.

So, also, in other problem areas. Violence, for example, tends to beget yet more violence. And even more ominous than the violence itself is the conditioning being effected—a conditioning which may cause people, in the words of one statesman, "to ask for dictatorship as a relief from anarchy."

Today's text also mentions earthquakes. On Tuesday morning, February 9, 1971, at 6:01 A.M., California's worst quake in forty years rocked the Los Angeles area. It was caused, not by the large San Andreas fault, but by an "unimpressive crack" not even found on some earthquake maps. God in His mercy has held back any really big shifting of the earth. Even "the elements of nature" such as earthquakes and tempests are mentioned as being "held by four angels" (*Testimonies to Ministers,* p. 444). But for how much longer will they be held?

Of February 9, 1971, one television newscaster said: "It was the day almost everybody in Los Angeles woke up at the same time."

As the signs multiply, would that God's people, as one, might awaken and seek Him with the whole heart!

11

MISSION '72

And upon the earth distress of nations, with perplexity; . . . men's hearts failing them for fear, and for looking after those things which are coming on the earth. **Luke 21:25, 26.**

Describing the aftereffects of the February 9, 1971, Los Angeles earthquake, one mother said concerning her eight-year-old daughter: "She's afraid to go to sleep, and she wakes up every time the bed moves. Her eyes get huge, and she quivers and shakes. Sometimes she walks in her sleep."—*Time,* March 8, 1971, p. 59.

Time mentioned adults as also suffering from earthquake jitters, and set forth Dr. Edward Stainbrook of the University of Southern California as saying that the adult's first response "is to think it's the wrath of God, maybe even the Apocalypse."

It is at this very hour that God's message of hope and security needs to go forth with unprecedented power. The year that has just closed has been a year of emphasis on lay evangelism. It has been a year that has seen the beginnings of revival, particularly on a number of campuses. In everything that has transpired the hand of God can be seen preparing the way for the final events. The week of February 5-12 of this year is to be a week for seeking greater revival throughout all of the church. Then, on March 4, MISSION '72 is to be launched, with a simultaneous evangelistic outreach all across North America.

If MISSION '72 is to accomplish all that God designs it should, a spirit of intercession must first take possession of the entire church. Inspiration declares that "not one" of the petitions arising for the descent of the Holy Spirit "has been lost." "Each prayer has been accumulating, ready to overflow and pour forth a healing flood of heavenly influence and accumulated light all over the world."—ELLEN G. WHITE, quoted in *Aflame for God,* p. 456.

In the words of N. R. Dower in the March, 1971, *Ministry* magazine, MISSION '72 should be "the beginning of a great advance that will not end until the work is finished and Jesus comes." Let us pray that this will indeed be a time that "a healing flood" of light will go forth!

JOYFUL NEWS

I go to prepare a place for you. And if I go and prepare a place for you, I will come again, and receive you unto myself; that where I am, there ye may be also. John 14:2, 3.

A Seventh-day Adventist minister, as he traveled, was reading his Bible. The passenger in the next seat, noticing the Bible, inquired, "Are you a minister?" Learning that he was, she exclaimed, "Sir, I believe that something has gone terribly wrong with the world."

"Would you like for me to tell you what the Bible says about our times?" the minister asked her.

"Please do," she replied.

Turning to John 14, he read the above promise of Jesus to come again. Then, step by step, he outlined from his Bible the conditions that would precede Christ's coming. Her interest grew as he talked, and she frequently interrupted to ask questions. As it dawned upon her that Jesus could come in this our day, she exclaimed, with tears in her eyes, "This is the most wonderful news I have ever heard!"

No one needs to be told, as this new year begins, that something has gone terribly wrong with this world. Yet it is at this very time that we are to "look up"—"for your redemption draweth nigh" (Luke 21:28). In the words of another:

"The Lord is coming. . . . This is the good, the joyful news which should electrify every soul."—*Evangelism,* p. 218.

And it is our privilege to hasten that coming. "By giving the gospel to the world it is in our power to hasten our Lord's return. We are not only to look for but to hasten the coming of the day of God."—*The Desire of Ages,* p. 633.

At a recent Bible conference a youthful delegate took the motto, "The Advent Message to All the World in This Generation," and, crossing out the "in this generation," penciled in the word "now."

"Behold, now is the . . . time" (2 Cor. 6:2). "God will do the work if we will furnish Him the instruments."—*Testimonies,* vol. 9, p. 107.

Would you during 1972 be willing to become *His* instrument?

PREPARING THE WAY

The voice of him that crieth in the wilderness, Prepare ye the way of the Lord. **Isa. 40:3.**

It was during my middle teens, while studying the Voice of Prophecy Bible lessons, that I first learned about Jesus' coming again. It was wonderful just to read, for the first time, the promises of His return. To discover that His coming was near was an even greater thrill.

A short time after starting these lessons, I found out about the Sunday morning broadcast, and tuned in whenever farm chores would permit. The dramatic words with which the broadcast begins—"This is the Voice of Prophecy, a voice crying in the wilderness of these latter days, Prepare ye the way of the Lord"—made an unforgettable impression.

"Prepare . . . the way." Prepare the way by helping take the gospel everywhere. But if we would make any impact at all "in this adulterous and sinful generation" (Mark 8:38), our message must be presented, "not as a lifeless theory, but as a living force to change the life" (*The Desire of Ages,* p. 826).

The gospel becomes this living, life-changing force only as its presentation is accompanied by the convicting power of the Holy Spirit. Never will the gospel proclamation be finished until it is attended, as on the day of Pentecost, by a mighty outpouring of God's Spirit. To seek this, to prepare the way for this, is our most urgent need.

The church has long looked forward to an outpouring of the Holy Spirit similar to that which is recorded in the book of Acts. It has always been anticipated as something future; about to come, perhaps, but still future. But could it be that we should stop anticipating it as being somewhat vaguely in the future, and start expecting it, and seeking for it, *now?*

We repeat, from our reading on the first day of this new year, the promise penned in 1895:

"The descent of the Holy Spirit upon the church is looked forward to as in the future; but it is the privilege of the church to have it now. Seek for it, pray for it, believe for it. We must have it, and Heaven is waiting to bestow it."—*Evangelism,* p. 701.

14

"HE'S COMING AGAIN!"

And that, knowing the time, that now it is high time to awake out of sleep: for now is our salvation nearer than when we believed. **Rom. 13:11.**

Back in 1967, as the time for the student Week of Prayer at Monterey Bay Academy drew near, a group of young people became deeply concerned because so many of their fellow students didn't seem to care about spiritual things. These students, searching their own hearts, began to seek the Lord most earnestly. Small groups, in planning the Week of Prayer, met frequently to pray together.

As the week progressed, and as the Friday night commitment service drew near, the prayer groups grew larger. On Friday some of these students, unbeknown to the faculty, also fasted, meeting together to plead with God for an outpouring of His Spirit upon the evening's service. And God wonderfully answered those prayers, bringing about a spiritual revival that transformed the whole campus.

Two or three months later some of these youth were presenting a program of testimony and song in various southern California churches and schools. After a Friday evening vesper program, as I drove several of them to the homes where they were staying, a senior girl asked, "Would you like to hear a chorus that has really become popular on our campus?" Assured that I would, they began, with vibrant enthusiasm:

> "The Lord is coming soon, prepare the way.
> The Lord is coming soon, O joyful day.
> Let's move forward hand in hand,
> Mighty youth at God's command,
> With the everlasting gospel."

"He's coming again, Christ is coming again," is the joyous and thrilling proclamation with which the chorus concludes.

What a message for God's church during 1972! Christ is coming! And *you* can help prepare the way!

"As a people we must prepare the way of the Lord under the overruling guidance of the Holy Spirit."—*Testimonies,* vol. 9, p. 96.

In the words of today's text—"It is high time!"

"THE HAPPIEST SABBATH"

The night is far spent, the day is at hand: let us therefore cast off the works of darkness, and let us put on the armour of light. **Rom. 13:12.**

At the close of the Week of Prayer mentioned yesterday, on Sabbath afternoon, as the sun was dropping behind the waves of the Pacific, a visitor on campus would have seen some 350 students hiking down to the beach, singing—and carrying paper sacks.

What had happened was this:

Following their Friday night commitment, several students had decided that if they were to begin a new life, some things in their rooms had to go. The outgrowth of this was that at the Sabbath afternoon MV meeting a student leader reviewed the bonfire recorded in Acts 19—when the Christians at Ephesus, determined to make a decided break with the past, committed to the flames some of their books. This young man then suggested that Monterey Bay Academy conclude their Week of Prayer with a similar service.

Paper sacks had been placed in the lobbies of the dorms, and at the close of the MV service there was opportunity for any who felt impressed to do so to go to their rooms, and put into a sack whatever they felt should be destroyed. A few minutes later those participating gathered in front of the cafeteria, from whence they hiked down to the beach a little over half a mile away.

As they gathered around the bonfire on the beach, the melodious notes of "I'll Be True, Precious Jesus, I'll Be True," floated out to mingle with the thunder of the breakers. A student leader made a few comments, and then scores of students filed quietly past the fire, throwing into the flames the paper sacks with their contents. A prayer of consecration concluded the service.

As the students hiked back up the hill to the campus, there were some with tears in their eyes—but these were tears of joy. "It was the happiest Sabbath we ever had on our campus," commented one girl.

Are there changes that ought to be made in your life, in your home? Why not now?

THE TWO RAINS

Then shall we know, if we follow on to know the Lord: his going forth is prepared as the morning; and he shall come unto us as the rain, as the latter and former rain unto the earth. **Hosea 6:3.**

In the land of Palestine, the showers of rain that fell at seed-time, and which sprouted the grain, were known as the early or former rain. Then, near the harvest, the latter rains came, filling out the grain, and assuring a bountiful harvest.

The Bible prophets have used these two times of rainfall as an illustration of the work of the Holy Spirit in this the gospel era. The prediction found in Joel 2, of a mighty outpouring of the Holy Spirit, was partially fulfilled on the day of Pentecost, as recorded in Acts 2. Peter, preaching on the day of Pentecost, quotes Joel's prophecy, and applies it to the events of that day (Acts 2:16-21).

This wonderful outpouring of God's Spirit at the beginning of the work of the gospel has become known as the early or former rain. Gracious manifestations of the Holy Spirit through all the years since, and the work of the Holy Spirit upon the hearts of individual believers, have likewise been understood to be manifestations of the former rain.

But near the close of earth's harvest there is to be another manifestation of the Holy Spirit's power which will be similar to that which came on the Day of Pentecost, except it will be with even greater power. This, coming just before the close of probation, is known as the latter rain, and will ripen earth's harvest.

Our preparation for the latter rain is in following "on to know the Lord"—seeking greater manifestations of His Spirit in our lives now; seeking, in Christ's strength, to "obtain the victory over every besetment, over pride, selfishness, love of the world, and over every wrong word and action" (*Early Writings,* p. 71).

Let us truly "follow on to know the Lord." Let us seek Him, and love Him, and walk with Him, *now.*

"I the Lord thy God," He promises, "will hold thy right hand, saying unto thee, Fear not; I will help thee" (Isa. 41:13).

LET IT BEGIN WITH ME

Ask ye of the Lord rain in the time of the latter rain; so the Lord shall make bright clouds, and give them showers of rain. Zech. 10:1.

The second chapter of Joel portrays the heartfelt seeking of the Lord, the heart-searching, repentance, and united and persevering prayer that prepares the way for the latter rain. Envisioning this time, the servant of God wrote:

"I have been deeply impressed by scenes that have recently passed before me in the night season. There seemed to be a great movement—a work of revival—going forward in many places. Our people were moving into line, responding to God's call."—*Testimonies to Ministers,* p. 515.

It is time—far past time—for the above scenes to be fulfilled. But revivals cannot be legislated. A revival takes place only when we as individuals really begin to seek the Lord, turning to His Word, taking time for prayer, repenting of our indulgences and sins—truly preparing the way.

The bestowal of heavenly power will never come upon those who neglect present opportunities for Bible study, for meditation, for prayer, for service. It will never come to those who, while sitting in idleness, wait for something miraculous to happen to them. The divine anointing comes only to those who seek it, and who make the most of present opportunities.

"Let us, with contrite hearts, pray most earnestly that now, in the time of the latter rain, the showers of grace may fall upon us. . . . As we seek God for the Holy Spirit, it will work in us meekness, humbleness of mind, a conscious dependence upon God for the perfecting latter rain. If we pray for the blessing in faith, we shall receive it as God has promised."—*Ibid.,* p. 509.

A revival has sometimes begun with just a single person. One person truly seeking the Lord, whether on a campus, or at his home church, will influence others. But it is to be more than one—for this work is to go forward "in many places."

"Lord, send a revival, and let it begin with me."

YOUTH AND THE LATTER RAIN

And it shall come to pass afterward, that I will pour out my spirit upon all flesh; and your sons and your daughters shall prophesy, your old men shall dream dreams, your young men shall see visions: and also upon the servants and upon the handmaids in those days will I pour out my spirit. Joel 2:28, 29.

Note the prominence of youth in this prophecy of the final outpouring of God's Spirit. Of the six groups mentioned—sons, daughters, old men, young men, servants, handmaids—five groups would be primarily young people.

As we seek the Lord for grace to finish His work, we do well to remember that "there is no other class that can do as much good as young men and young women who are consecrated to God. The youth, if right, could sway a mighty influence."—*Messages to Young People,* p. 204.

This "mighty influence" could be particularly far reaching in bringing about revival. There is something contagious about the ardor, the enthusiasm, the generous devotion, of youth who are consecrated to God.

"When divine power is combined with human effort," inspiration declares, "the work will spread like fire in the stubble."—*Selected Messages,* book 1, p. 118.

The illustration of fire is significant. A fire generally begins with a small flame. Let the fire be lighted, let the conditions be right, and it can spread very quickly.

In the April 8, 1971, issue of Andrews University's newspaper, *The Student Movement,* editor Roy Benton reviewed a new Inter-Varsity book entitled *Student Power in World Evangelism.* Mr. Benton wrote that "SDA students may be surprised to find that the most successful missionary movements stemmed from campus revivals, much like what we are experiencing now." He concluded his review with a quotation from the book that included this question: "Is it too much to believe that God, whose commands have not been withdrawn, may choose again to move upon the church through students?"

God has young people whom He is ready to use. Is it not time for all of us to seek the Lord together, that revival might spread throughout the entire world field?

A MIGHTY ARMY

Who knoweth whether thou art come to the kingdom for such a time as this? **Esther 4:14.**

The first union-wide Bible conference in the Pacific Union was held in the fall of 1967, when student leaders from more than twenty academies and the two colleges in the union, gathered at the Wawona youth camp. The chorus, "Prepare the Way," was the theme song. No one who attended will ever forget the enthusiasm with which these youth sang, their voices echoing out through the encircling pines, and up to the starry heavens. Angels, lingering near, must have rejoiced as they heard the enthusiastic proclamation, "The Lord is coming soon —prepare the way."

In the providence of God you who are the youth of the church could become the influence that would make MISSION '72 more than just another series of meetings. God wants to use your ardor, your enthusiasm, to help bring revival to the whole church. He wants you to set the example in witnessing. He will abundantly bless as you become His Spirit-filled instruments.

Wrote one academy student after the Wawona meetings, "I've always been afraid to witness for Christ, but now with the help of the Holy Spirit I'm going to witness in every way possible." She told how the very weekend the meetings closed, she had found opportunity to do so.

"Right here at this camp," she wrote, "I talked to a young man, a student body president. He told me that religion had really never meant much to him. I told him how much Christ meant to me, and when we had finished he said, 'You know, nobody has ever talked to me like that. You have really helped me. Thank you so much!'"

What would happen if hundreds followed her example?

"With such an army of workers as our youth, rightly trained, might furnish, how soon the message of a crucified, risen, and soon-coming Saviour might be carried to the whole world! How soon might the end come—the end of suffering and sorrow and sin!"—*Education,* p. 271.

A COVENANT TO SEEK THE LORD

And they entered into a covenant to seek the Lord God of their fathers with all their heart and with all their soul. **2 Chron. 15:12.**

During the three-day Bible conference mentioned yesterday the joyous message, "The Lord is coming soon," was heard again and again. The keynote address on Thursday evening by Elder John Loor underscored the solemnity of the times to which we have come. "We are seeing signs of the return of Christ fulfilled today on a scale that has no previous parallel," he said.

As he cited example after example, the conviction deepened that we are indeed on the very borders of the eternal world. The ever-increasing spirit of riot and violence, worsening storms, accidents, and earthquakes, an increasingly rampant and bold moral looseness, sharpening international tensions—all declare with an unparalleled urgency that something is about to happen.

Friday evening Dr. Leslie Hardinge, from Pacific Union College, spoke concerning our need to seek the Lord, calling attention to an experience of King Asa's time, when the people of God "entered into a covenant to seek the Lord God of their fathers with all their heart and with all their soul."

He then invited all who would like to enter into such a covenant to kneel and seek the Lord in prayer. Delegate after delegate did so, as the Spirit of God spoke to each heart.

Should it not be thus with each of us? Today is the third Sabbath of this new year. God has provided extra time for reflection, for heart-searching, for prayer. Let's make, or renew, a covenant to seek the Lord. It will doubtless mean some changes. As Elder Loor said at Wawona, we may need to go to our stereo sets and see whether there are not some records that need to be discarded. We may need to go to our bookshelves, and remove everything that offends. We may need to go to our kitchens, and make whatever changes are needed there.

Will you, this day, enter into this kind of covenant?

It could become for you, as it did for the Monterey Bay Academy students mentioned last Monday, the happiest Sabbath you have ever known!

DO YOU REALLY WANT JESUS TO COME?

Seeing then that all these things shall be dissolved, what manner of persons ought ye to be in all holy conversation and godliness, looking for and hasting unto the coming of the day of God. 2 Peter 3:11, 12, margin.

On several occasions within recent months we have asked groups of young people, How many of you expect that Christ will return within your lifetime? We generally invite them to indicate their response by standing. About 75 to 90 per cent usually stand.

The second question then is, How many of you expect that Christ may very likely come before the end of the 1970's? On this question the number who stand is always somewhat less.

The third and final question then is, How many of you would really want Christ to come during the 1970's? With this question the number who stand is generally, though not always, considerably less.

Do you, dear reader, really want Jesus to come? Would you be pleased if He would come within the next five years? What would be your reaction if you could know for a certainty that He was coming within the next twelve months?

None of us knows how much time is left. Those statesmen and scientists who express a fear that the end may come within the next five to fifteen years may or may not be right. There could be even less time left than they expect—or there could be more.

But this much we do know—whether or not the work of God is finished during the 1970's could well depend upon you, and others like you. Our text for today indicates that we are not only to look for but to hasten the coming of Christ. Comments inspiration:

"It is the privilege of every Christian not only to look for but to hasten the coming of our Lord Jesus Christ."—*Christ's Object Lessons,* p. 69.

But if you would really have any influence in hastening His coming, there is a question that you must answer:

Do you really want Jesus to come?
Do you? How about it?

THE BEGINNING OF ADVENTURE UNLIMITED

And, behold, I come quickly; and my reward is with me, to give every man according as his work shall be. Rev. 22:12.

To many people the thought that the coming of Christ is imminent is disturbing. There are too many things His coming would interrupt—plans for careers, for marriage, for building, for buying, for traveling, for luxuries.

Yet how shortsighted is such hesitation!

Is it travel that you long for? A trip to the moon would be as nothing compared to the space adventure that will begin at the coming of Christ. The trip out to the New Jerusalem, located in the region of Orion, will take seven days (*Early Writings,* p. 16). How awesome the thought that very shortly you could be on your way out there!

Is it social life that you enjoy? Inspiration speaks of "the harmonious social life" which will be enjoyed—with the angels, with "the faithful ones of all ages," with " 'the whole family of heaven and earth' " (*Education,* p. 306). John speaks of a great multitude "which no man could number" (Rev. 7:9) being there. Each will become a friend to you. Eventually, as you get acquainted, you will be drawn to each by a sacred, close fellowship.

Is it the absence of marriage that disturbs you? The changes in this order of things, whatever they are, will not make for less happiness, surely! And on this promise, from inspiration, you can rely:

"There the loves and sympathies that God has planted in the soul will find truest and sweetest exercise."—*Ibid.,* p. 306.

Is it learning, and exploration, and adventure, that challenge you?

There "every faculty will be developed, every capacity increased"—all without wearying the mind or exhausting the energies. There "the grandest enterprises may be carried forward, the loftiest aspirations reached, the highest ambitions realized; and still there will arise new heights to surmount, new wonders to admire, new truths to comprehend, fresh objects to call forth the powers of mind and soul and body."—*The Great Controversy,* p. 677.

NO MORE SUFFERING

And God shall wipe away all tears from their eyes; and there shall be no more death, neither sorrow, nor crying, neither shall there be any more pain. Rev. 21:4.

The author of the book *Education,* after mentioning the pain and suffering everywhere in this world, writes:

"In order to destroy sin and its results He gave His best Beloved, and He has put it in our power, through co-operation with Him, to bring this scene of misery to an end." Page 264.

"No more death." Velva Holt, writing in the *Review,* told of a bride who was killed in an automobile accident the day after being married. Mrs. Holt's husband had sung for this girl's wedding, and then, scarcely a week later, for her funeral.

And "no more . . . pain." War, any war, has always meant pain and suffering, with children as the keenest sufferers. Chandler Brossard, in an article in *Look* magazine (April 18, 1967) entitled "Vietnam's War-Ravaged Children," told of hundreds of thousands wounded in the war. "Tell me how one goes about rehabilitating a child whose arm has been blown off?" a U.S. psychiatrist asked.

War, in the Middle East, Indochina, Africa, or wherever, means refugees, too. In Vietnam hundreds of thousands of little ones have become refugees—most of them without fathers, some without either parent.

"What can it be like," asked *Look,* "to be five years old and without a mother or a father? What do these children dream of sleeping on a wet dirty floor?"

"It is unimaginable," said the author.

With modern medicines, and plenty to eat, most of us have known very little of pain or hunger. It is not that way for the more than 10,000 people who this very day will starve to death—or for the millions who, except for a miracle, will soon join them.

But what can you do? Simply this:

"He has put it in our power, through co-operation with Him, to bring this scene of misery to an end."—Education, p. 264. (Italics supplied.)

FOR LOVE OF HIM

Whom having not seen, ye love; in whom, though now ye see him not, yet believing, ye rejoice with joy unspeakable. 1 Peter 1:8.

A student of my acquaintance, though she professed to love Christ, seemed to resent very much the possibility that Jesus might be coming soon. This same girl had a fiancé who was overseas in the service of his country. Suppose she had said, "I love him very much. But I don't want him to come back soon. In fact, I would prefer that he not come back during my life-time."

It was not that way at all. As the time for him to return drew near, she could hardly wait for the days and hours to pass. When it was evident that his return was only hours away, she was almost overwhelmed with joy.

Shouldn't it be that way with the return of Jesus? There is nothing that can compare with what He has promised. Most of all, there is nothing that can compare with Him.

The apostle Peter, in today's text, mentions how, even though we have not seen Jesus, we love Him. "Though now ye see him not, . . ." he wrote, "ye rejoice with joy unspeakable."

But when Jesus comes, and we can be with Him personally, how much more it will be "joy unspeakable"!

Let your thoughts imagine that hour when you will stand in His presence—when you will be close enough to reach out and take His hand. What will impress you most? Will it be the sense of power that flows from His presence? Will it be the joy mir-rored in His eyes, the warmth in His smile? Will it be His noble stature? Will it be His voice? Or will it be His scars?

The scars will be there. "Our Redeemer will ever bear the marks of His crucifixion. Upon His wounded head, upon His side, His hands and feet, are the only traces of the cruel work that sin has wrought."—*The Great Controversy,* p. 674.

It can shortly be your joy to clasp the scarred hand of Christ. It will be a handclasp that will be firm, warm, kind—a handclasp welcoming you to His home—welcoming you with "joy un-speakable"!

ENDING GOD'S SUFFERING

In all their affliction he was afflicted, and the angel of his presence saved them: in his love and in his pity he redeemed them. **Isa. 63:9.**

Our text today indicates another reason, one seldom mentioned, why we should want to help hasten the return of Christ. As inspiration puts it:

"Those who think of the result of hastening or hindering the gospel think of it in relation to themselves and to the world. Few think of its relation to God. Few give thought to the suffering that sin has caused our Creator. All heaven suffered in Christ's agony; but that suffering did not begin or end with His manifestation in humanity. The cross is a revelation to our dull senses of the pain that, from its very inception, sin has brought to the heart of God."—*Education,* p. 263.

"It is one of Nature's rules," observed *Look* magazine, in its article on war-ravaged children, "that we cannot totally identify with the suffering of others. The function of this rule is to help us survive: life would be unbearable if our neighbor's broken leg became as real to us as it is to him. Paradoxically, while we survive by this rule, we are somewhat dehumanized by it: we are kept from fully participating in the humanness of another person."

Unlike us, God can and does identify with all our suffering. Wrote Isaiah, "In all their affliction he was afflicted." For six thousand years our heavenly Father has carried a burden of pain and suffering beyond comprehension. We cannot grasp, we "dare not allow even our thoughts to dwell upon" the pain and heartache in our world. "Did we realize it as it is, the burden would be too terrible. Yet God feels it all."—*Education,* p. 264.

"God feels it all."

We can't grasp it. Many of us, comfortable and complacent, are tempted to shrug, "So what? What can we do about it?"

Simply this:

"He [God] has put it in our power, through co-operation with Him, to bring this . . . to an end."—*Ibid.*

I CAN HARDLY WAIT!

And the ransomed of the Lord shall return, and come to Zion with songs and everlasting joy upon their heads: they shall obtain joy and gladness, and sorrow and sighing shall flee away. Isa. 35:10.

During the spring of 1970 tragedy came suddenly and unexpectedly to Southern Missionary College. In an automobile accident on a rain-slick road one stormy night, two of the dorm girls were killed. In the May 22, 1970, issue of the college paper, *The Southern Accent,* a fellow student and friend, Bonnie Iversen, wrote a tribute which she entitled "To Those We Lost."

Of the friendships they had formed, Bonnie said:

"We sang together and laughed and talked . . . and cried. But it was all a part of being friends. Good qualities, kindnesses, companionships are always appreciated; but they're not sensed with such vividness, such aching, until they are gone.

"If we could have known," Bonnie wondered, "—if we could have had one last moment together, knowing it was indeed the last, what would we have said?"

But there was, of course, no way of knowing.

"And suddenly . . . they were gone. They didn't come back. Our minds still argue unconvincingly with our hearts that they won't be back—at least not to room 260 or 237; not to Charlotte or Stone Mountain; not to these United States or to this old earth. But they *will* be back. That's for sure."

Looking forward to that time of reunion, Bonnie declared:

"We will see them again . . . we'll sing . . . we'll laugh—much harder than we ever could down here. We'll talk for years and years without running out of things to say; we won't have to discuss problems—there won't be any. And we won't cry—unless we cry tears of joy and thanksgiving: joy that we are once again with them; and thanksgiving for the love God gave us for others, whose deep-felt absence inspired us with determination to at last see them again.

"I can hardly wait!" the author concluded her tribute.

Would that all of us were that eager for Jesus to come!

27

A NOW GENERATION

This gospel of the kingdom shall be preached in all the world for a witness unto all nations; and then shall the end come. **Matt. 24:14.**

"Success in any line," declares inspiration, "demands a definite aim."—*Education,* p. 262.

"Such an aim is set before the youth of today. The heaven-appointed purpose of giving the gospel to the world in this generation is the noblest that can appeal to any human being."—*Ibid.*

The above words, penned in 1903, introduce the chapter in the book *Education* entitled "The Lifework." Succeeding paragraphs discuss the fact that God has put it into our power to hasten the return of Christ.

Let's face it. That generation has long since gone. The work was not finished in that generation, nor in the one following. Yet we still declare, as the motto of Advent youth, "The Advent Message to All the World in This Generation."

It was in the 1870's that the servant of God wrote, "We are now upon the very borders of the eternal world."—*Testimonies,* vol. 4, p. 306. Some would conclude that the pen of inspiration was in error in expressing words of urgency *then*—when, nearly a century later, we still haven't crossed over those borders.

But not so! What was written then was true then—and it is true now. We have been, all along, upon "the very borders of the eternal world." The problem is—we have been camping there!

The time has come to quit camping and start moving!

"You are the *now* generation," Elder Robert Pierson told the Zurich World Youth Congress. "You are insistent! You are impatient! You scorn procrastination and delay. You want things done *now!* So does God!"

Where do we begin, to get things moving?

We could begin with a revival of Bible study. We could begin with a revival of prayer. The Lord is more ready to pour out His Spirit upon us than parents are to give good gifts to their children. But we must first prepare the way.

Ought we not to begin—*now?*

A REVIVAL OF BIBLE STUDY

Man shall not live by bread alone, but by every word that proceedeth out of the mouth of God. **Matt. 4:4.**

"A revival in Bible study is needed throughout the world. Attention is to be called, not to the assertions of men, but to the Word of God. As this is done, a mighty work will be wrought."— *Evangelism,* p. 456.

As Kenneth H. Wood, editor of the *Review,* pointed out in the April 1, 1971, issue, the great Reformation of the sixteenth century was launched and powered by Scripture. The Advent awakening of the middle of the nineteenth century was likewise accompanied by a revival of interest in the Scriptures.

Both prayer and Bible study have always been a part of any revival movement that has had a lasting effect. The event that brought revival at Andrews University into prominence back in the fall of 1970 was a weekend retreat at which the main emphasis was prayer. Michael Stevenson, writing in the February, 1971, issue of *The Ministry,* said: "The topic of study at this retreat was prayer. The voluntary gathering of about ninety, mostly undergraduate students, simply did just that—they prayed."

As these students returned to campus, and as the influence of revival spread, one of the most noticeable effects was a new interest in Bible study. The college store was unable to keep the *Living New Testament,* one of the more popular Bibles being purchased, in stock, selling more than 1,000 copies within the first few weeks. By the middle of the spring quarter students had purchased from the college store and through the Pioneer Memorial church more than 6,000 *Living New Testaments* and 2,300 other Bibles. Thousands of these Bibles were used in personal witnessing. Often a student, in talking to someone, would give away his own well-marked Bible.

The God-given direction for revival is simple. We must take time to seek Him. And this seeking must include more than just talking about prayer and about Bible study—we need to really start praying and really start studying the Word.

A REVIVAL OF LIVING FAITH

So then faith cometh by hearing, and hearing by the word of God. **Rom. 10:17.**

"Every failure on the part of the children of God," we are told, "is due to their lack of faith."—*Patriarchs and Prophets,* p. 657.

Could it be that the failure of the church to finish God's work is also due primarily to a lack of faith? Could it be that one of our greatest needs in this new year, both as individuals and as a church, is for a greater faith?

How does one develop a stronger faith?

Faith, like anything else, strengthens as exercised. It grows by appropriating, by proving, the promises of God. "In order to strengthen faith, we must often bring it in contact with the word."—*Education,* p. 254.

The exercising of faith involves finding specific promises, and then appropriating these promises through prayer. In the words of inspiration, "We should now acquaint ourselves with God by proving His promises. Angels record every prayer that is earnest and sincere."—*The Great Controversy,* p. 622.

There is a lesson for us in Elijah's experience, when he prayed for rain. "As he prayed, his faith reached out and grasped the promises of Heaven."—*Prophets and Kings,* p. 157. His faith "grasped the promises." He believed, and, believing, persevered in prayer—laying hold on the promises.

"If thou canst believe," said Jesus, "all things are possible to him that believeth" (Mark 9:23).

There are conditions, of course, one of which is a willingness to have God's will fulfilled. (The book *Education,* in the chapter entitled "Faith and Prayer," discusses these conditions more fully.)

Where do we begin?

With the promises. We need to search out the promises. We need to meditate upon them. We need to talk to God about them. We need to thank God for them. We need to talk faith, and live faith.

What God has promised, He is "able also to perform" (Rom. 4:21).

HOW STRONG IS YOUR FAITH?

Now unto him that is able to do exceeding abundantly above all that we ask or think, according to the power that worketh in us. Eph. 3:20.

What a promise! He can do all that we ask . . . all that we ask or think . . . above all that we ask or think . . . abundantly above all that we ask or think . . . exceeding abundantly above all that we ask or think.

Following the first southern California Bible conference, a group of students at Glendale Academy launched a drive to collect 15 tons of canned goods for the Navajo Indians. On Halloween Eve about 100 students collected some 4,000 cans—or about two tons.

A freshman girl, that Halloween Eve, had gone to the home of an official of the Red Ball Trucking Company, who had volunteered to donate a truck to haul the food to Monument Valley. He also suggested, in a later telephone conversation, several food companies from which he thought we might possibly receive sizable donations.

None of these contacts seemed to develop into anything, but with the help of other schools, and the Pathfinders, we eventually gathered about seven tons of canned goods. Meanwhile, in daily noon-hour prayer bands, students frequently requested that we remember the food project as a special request.

Early in December the Red Ball truck delivered the seven tons of food, and the matter was considered closed. About two weeks later, however, an air-mail letter from a major food company said that they had some canned goods to donate if we could pick them up at their warehouse. Thus, in January, the conference truck delivered to the Holbrook Indian school in Arizona a truckload of 18,000 pounds of canned goods— bringing the total to 16 tons! We thanked God, and again considered the matter closed. But God sometimes does above what we ask—and a few months later the same company, without further solicitation, donated another nine tons of food. The following spring yet another truckload was given—bringing the total to more than 34 tons!

How strong, as you consider today's promise, is *your* faith?

31

"SUPERABUNDANTLY"

Ask, and it shall be given you; seek, and ye shall find; knock, and it shall be opened unto you. Luke 11:9.

We told you yesterday about how more than 34 tons of canned goods eventually came in for the Navajo work. That Halloween evening when we began, as the canned goods that had been solicited door to door were brought in, we stacked them in boxes along one side of the administration building hallway. I looked at all those boxes, after we figured that about two tons had been collected, and wondered how we ever permitted a group of student leaders to set a goal of 15 tons.

That same school year something else happened that reminded us that God is able "to do exceeding abundantly above all that we ask or think." The Voice of Prophecy offering that year was $50,000 short, and the summer months had showed a loss of another $50,000. This shortage, coming at the time the Voice of Prophecy was about to launch the "Nite-Owl" broadcasts, precipitated a crisis.

What to do? About December 9 Elder Richards sent out a letter to Voice of Prophecy friends, explaining the problem, and calling attention to the *Amplified New Testament* translation of Ephesians 3:20—how God is able to do "superabundantly" above our highest dreams. The staff, meanwhile, was praying most earnestly. And at the academy, a senior girl who had really found Christ at the Bible conference which we mentioned yesterday, frequently requested at our lunch-hour prayer bands that we join in these petitions.

God's answer was "superabundant." The March, 1967, Voice of Prophecy *News* told how first God "filled *to the full* the $100,000 Voice of Prophecy 'basket' to make up the losses. Then He filled it again with a *second* $100,000; and still a *third* time with an equal amount, plus another $33,000 above that! . . . Never in Voice of Prophecy history has there been such a swift and willing response to a call for funds, from tens of thousands of our broadcast friends. *And all this took place in the final three weeks of December.*"

"If ye have faith . . . nothing shall be impossible" (Matt. 17:20).

HOW MUCH MORE

If ye then, being evil, know how to give good gifts unto your children: how much more shall your heavenly Father give the Holy Spirit to them that ask him? Luke 11:13.

As we mentioned yesterday, God answered "superabundantly" the earnest prayers for funds at the time the Voice of Prophecy "Nite-Owl" program was ready to be launched. And, as we have also shared with you, efforts to secure 15 tons of food for use in Navajoland went far above the goal.

But there is something we need far more than funds or canned goods! We need an outpouring of God's Spirit "exceeding abundantly above" all that we might ask or think.

There is a work for us to do in preparing the way. Note, from inspiration, these prerequisites:

"Our heavenly Father is more willing to give His Holy Spirit to them that ask Him, than are earthly parents to give good gifts to their children. But it is our work, by confession, humiliation, repentance, and earnest prayer, to fulfill the conditions upon which God has promised to grant us His blessing. A revival need be expected only in answer to prayer."—*Selected Messages,* book 1, p. 121.

Along with confession, humiliation, and repentance—*a revival need be expected only in answer to prayer.*

We mentioned earlier this year the Seven and Seven prayer fellowship that was organized following a Bible conference. At one boarding academy many of the students were at breakfast by seven o'clock. Said one student, telling about it, "When seven o'clock came, you would see students at various tables pausing for a few moments to bow their heads and pray silently for a greater outpouring of the Holy Spirit."

Jesus reminds us in the words of today's promise how willing God is to give the Holy Spirit to those who ask. Are we taking time to ask? Are we praying daily for greater outpourings of God's Spirit? If you can't pause for a few moments at seven and seven, won't you find some time when you can truly pray?

Can't we, somehow, put first things first?

REVIVAL OF A FORGIVING SPIRIT

And forgive us our debts, as we forgive our debtors. Matt. 6:12.

Describing the gathering of the early believers preceding Pentecost, Luke writes that they "all continued with one accord in prayer and supplication" (Acts 1:14). They were not only united in coming together to pray, but by putting away differences and demonstrating a forgiving spirit they became one in heart.

We have, from inspiration, this inquiry:

"Shall we not, in our work in the future and in the gatherings we hold, be of *one accord?* Shall we not wrestle with God in prayer, asking for the Holy Spirit to come into every heart?"—*Testimonies,* vol. 8, p. 46.

After reviewing our need to put away our sins, and by repentance and confession to humble our hearts, God's servant notes:

"Floods of spiritual power are to be poured forth upon those prepared to receive it."—*Ibid.*

One of the biggest hindrances in our relationships with one another is that we are too slow to forgive. We need to forgive and forget. We too often keep a record, as teachers, of a student's last year's mistakes. We too often, as students, are just as unreasonable toward parents and teachers. We need a revival of a truly forgiving spirit!

In volume 5 of Heaven's special messages to the church, in a chapter entitled, appropriately, "Christian Unity," Mrs. White tells of receiving a letter from a certain lady. The lady described "a circumstance in which a brother had manifested indiscretion. Although it occurred years ago," said Mrs. White, "and was a very small matter, hardly worthy of a second thought, the writer stated that it had forever destroyed her confidence in that brother."—Page 246.

This woman, whoever she was, and whatever the indiscretion had been, was surely an example of an unforgiving spirit. Mrs. White commented that "if that sister's life should show upon review no greater errors, it would be indeed a marvel" (*ibid.*).

Too many of us, tragically, are too much like that letter writer! God help us to forgive—and to forget!

PUTTING GOD FIRST

But seek ye first the kingdom of God, and his righteousness; and all these things shall be added unto you. **Matt. 6:33.**

We know we need more faith. We know we should spend more time with God's Word. We know we need to pray far more than we do. Yet—so many things crowd in.

We need to recall, perhaps, the words of Jesus about putting God first.

Are you tempted, as a student, to let your school assignments crowd out Bible study time? Do you long to excel intellectually? Consider, then, this:

"As a means of intellectual training, the Bible is more effective than any other book, or all other books combined. . . . No other study can impart such mental power as does the effort to grasp the stupendous truths of revelation."—*Education,* p. 124.

Are you pressured doing so many good things, so many necessary details, so many things for the Lord, that you scarcely have time to pray before you begin the day? Do you fall into bed at night—often late at night—so utterly exhausted that you spend but seconds upon your knees? Consider, then, this:

"While we are to labor earnestly for the salvation of the lost, we must also take time for meditation, for prayer, and for the study of the word of God. Only the work accomplished with much prayer, and sanctified by the merit of Christ, will in the end prove to have been efficient for good."—*The Desire of Ages,* p. 362.

Glance back over this past year. How much of your work, by the above standard, was "efficient for good"?

Could one work diligently, provide almost everything for one's children, and yet find in the end that it has been for naught? Could one administer a school, or a conference, or pastor a church, and yet accomplish nothing for eternity? Could one run a dormitory, sacrificing oneself constantly yet not praying, and discover it has all accomplished exactly nothing that is lasting?

Shouldn't we make sure that we are putting first things first?

THEY DID NOT KNOW WHAT WAS HAPPENING

But as the days of Noe were, so shall also the coming of the Son of man be.
Matt. 24:37.

"The coming of the Son of Man will be like what happened in the time of Noah" (Matt. 24:37, T.E.V.).*

And how was it then?

Every imagination of man's heart was "only evil continually" (Gen. 6:5). The earth was "filled with violence" (verse 11). People were eating and drinking, marrying and giving in marriage, "up to the very day Noah went into the ark; yet they did not know what was happening until the Flood came and swept them all away. That is how it will be when the Son of Man comes" (Matt. 24:38, 39, T.E.V.).

They did not know what was happening!

So it will be again.

Every characteristic of Noah's day is seen in the world today. "Even now, in the present century, and in professedly Christian lands," wrote God's servant in 1890, "there are crimes daily perpetrated as black and terrible as those for which the old-world sinners were destroyed."—*Patriarchs and Prophets,* p. 102.

How much more true today!

Note the things already seen in 1890 which are far more evident today—an intense worldliness, extravagance, luxury and display, cold-blooded and causeless crimes, enslavement to lust, anarchy permeating the nations, pent-up fires of passion and lawlessness about to escape control. Is there a single one of these characteristics that has not, particularly within recent months, become noticeably more widespread and intense?

And yet there are those, even within the church, who apparently do not know what is happening!

Inspiration asks, "If the times in which we are living fail to impress our minds seriously, what can reach us?"—*Testimonies to Ministers,* p. 514.

Indeed, what can?

---

* From the *Today's English Version of the New Testament.* Copyright © American Bible Society 1966.

WHEN INIQUITY ABOUNDS!

And because iniquity shall abound, the love of many shall wax cold. But he that shall endure unto the end, the same shall be saved. Matt. 24:12, 13.

"Iniquity shall abound."

As the Holy Spirit is more and more withdrawn, evil has a field day. Sensuality becomes bolder, the popular music of the day more degenerate. Fashions become more lust-oriented—and more and more adopted and excused by church members. Violence intensifies, and crime multiplies.

"Thou shalt not follow a multitude to do evil," the Scriptures instruct (Ex. 23:2). But if a multitude—the crowd—does it, there are but few who will not go along.

The pressure of the crowd is one of the most irresistible pressures that there are. Back in Noah's time the pressure of "the now generation" was so great that out of the millions who apparently lived then, only eight had the courage to go into the ark. It may have been a ratio of less than one out of a million.

"The love of many shall wax cold."

Terrible and widespread apostasies are imminent. "Soon God's people will be tested by fiery trials, and the great proportion of those who now appear genuine and true will prove to be base metal."—*Testimonies*, vol. 5, p. 136.

Suppose hundreds of people, many whom you thought to be genuine, should depart. What will this do to your faith?

"He that endureth unto the end shall be saved."

There's a lot in that word *endure*. Such things as firmness. And resistance. And courage. And loyalty.

"To stand in defense of truth and righteousness when the majority forsake us, to fight the battles of the Lord when champions are few—this will be our test. At this time we must gather warmth from the coldness of others, courage from their cowardice, and loyalty from their treason."—*Ibid.*

Have you the courage *now* to stick by what you know to be right?

It will make it easier *then*.

A FATAL ASSIMILATION

Remember Lot's wife. Luke 17:32.

Why did Jesus, in discussing His return, include these terse words, "Remember Lot's wife"?

You remember the story. The guests who had come to her home had clearly demonstrated they were more than ordinary beings. During Sodom's final minutes they had accompanied her and her husband, and the only two children who would listen, to the edge of the plain outside the city. Their command, "Escape for thy life; look not behind thee," had been given with startling urgency. But she did look back, and perished. "While her body was upon the plain, her heart clung to Sodom, and she perished with it."—*Patriarchs and Prophets,* p. 161.

Her heart was in the wrong place. She had been assimilated into Sodom. Her investments were there. Her home was there. Her pleasures were there. Her heart, inevitably, was there too.

How is it with us? Have the pleasures of Sodom imperceptibly infiltrated our hours of leisure? Have we become fascinated by Sodom's entertainments? Have we adopted Sodom's fashions? Is the music of Sodom heard from our stereos?

Lot's wife has been characterized as "selfish" and "irreligious." This about sums up everything else—her unwillingness to deny self, her habits of indulgence, her craving for luxuries.

The Sodoms of today are sophisticated, affluent, sensual. Are we being assimilated into this sophistication? Are our thoughts more upon the luxuries and indulgences of Sodom than upon preparation for heaven? Does the call for revival fall upon deaf ears? Are we strangers to the deep movings of the Holy Spirit? Would we label an outpouring of God's Spirit fanaticism?

It has happened. It happened at Battle Creek, in 1893, when the Holy Spirit was striving with the youth and teachers there. The blessing that might have come was turned away. (See *Counsels to Teachers,* pp. 357-368.) Could it happen again? Are some of the attitudes of Lot's wife still with us?

DON'T FORGET LOT

And Lot went out, and spake unto his sons in law, which married his daughters, and said, Up, get you out of this place; for the Lord will destroy this city. But he seemed as one that mocked unto his sons in law. Gen. 19:14.

"Remember Lot's wife"—but don't forget Lot.

His tragic loss of his wife and of his married daughters, and the disgrace brought upon him by his conduct with his unmarried daughters, were largely the results of living in Sodom.

At first it was simply a matter of pitching his tent "towards Sodom" (Gen. 13:12). The wife and children could get to town more often. Then, attracted by Sodom's comforts, entertainments, and luxuries, they bought a home in town. Lot moved there with good intentions—he fully intended to keep himself free from iniquity, and to command his household after him.

It didn't work that way.

The influence of Sodom not only ruined his family but had an effect upon him, too. Subtly, steadily, his power of discernment was blurred, his power of decision weakened. A crisis came, and he hesitated, he lingered, he excused, he rationalized.

When finally he did flee, he left some of his family buried in the ruins of Sodom, and his wife a pillar of salt to erode away there on the plain. Making his way eventually to a mountain cave, he had opportunity, perhaps, for a backward glance.

As he stood there at the entrance of the cave, reviewing the past, what were his thoughts?

The decisions you have made—concerning Christ, your choice of where to live, your decisions concerning right and wrong—how will these appear when, at the second coming of Christ, you look back?

And the decisions you are now making—the friends you are choosing, your choice of leisure activities, your investments of time and money, your relationship to the needs of the work of God—how would these be evaluated in the blazing light of the return of Jesus?

Project yourself ahead, then look back.

FEBRUARY 3

IS IT NOT A LITTLE ONE?

Behold now, this city is near to flee unto, and it is a little one: Oh, let me escape thither, (is it not a little one?) and my soul shall live. Gen. 19:20.

Lot had been commanded to "escape to the mountain" (Gen. 19:17). But if Sodom must perish, why not find a smaller city? So he had pleaded for permission to go to Zoar. "It's close by," he argued, "and it's a little place. Please let me go there. Is it not a little one?"

He was given permission to go there, but he did not stay long. It was no better than Sodom. The people of Zoar undoubtedly had heard about the destruction of Sodom, but this knowledge had had no influence in curtailing their sensual depravity.

Sensuality—preoccupation with the sins of the flesh—has a benumbing effect. Paul, writing of some in his day who were "past feeling," notes that they had "given themselves over unto lasciviousness, to work all uncleanness with greediness" (Eph. 4:19). Perhaps in their utter sensuality the inhabitants of Zoar had so completely shut out the Holy Spirit that they had virtually committed the unpardonable sin. Shortly after Lot left, Zoar too was consumed (*Patriarchs and Prophets*, p. 167).

Possibly Lot had never been to Zoar. Or maybe he had, and was aware of the character of the inhabitants, but justified going there because of its smallness.

His argument, at any rate, is an example of rationalization. He makes his point, not once, but twice, about its being just "a little one."

Aren't we often the same way? Don't we excuse some deviations from God's expressed will as being of little consequence? Don't we argue, to ourselves at least, that even if it is sin, it's just "a little one"?

Eve used the same argument. "To Eve it seemed a small thing to disobey God by tasting the fruit of the forbidden tree." —*Patriarchs and Prophets*, p. 61. After all, what could be smaller than that? Yet what an awful train of events followed that which to her seemed such "a small thing." "Who can know, in the moment of temptation, the terrible consequences that will result from one wrong step?"—*Ibid.*

40

CAUGHT BY SURPRISE

But the same day that Lot went out of Sodom it rained fire and brimstone from heaven, and destroyed them all. Even thus shall it be in the day when the Son of man is revealed. Luke 17:29, 30.

Sodom, enriched by its commerce and famed for its unrivaled beauty and for its art, was a prestigious address. Its fertile soil, its luxuriant vegetation, its fragrant flowers, its rich harvests, its abundant flocks and herds, plus the wealth of its trade, made it a place where "the whole year seemed one round of festivity."

"This was the iniquity of . . . Sodom, pride, fulness of bread, and abundance of idleness," wrote the prophet Ezekiel (Eze. 16:49). Even a casual reading of Genesis 19 strikes one with the utter depravity of Sodom's inhabitants.

The things attempted on Sodom's last night were not new or unusual there. "That last night," remarks inspiration, "was marked by no greater sins than many others before it."—*Patriarchs and Prophets,* p. 159. For Sodom, though, their treatment of their divine guests that night marked the close of their probation. The following morning, as the rays of a rising sun fell upon its rich beauty, and as the city stirred to life, the end came. "Suddenly and unexpectedly as would be a thunder peal from an unclouded sky, the tempest broke."—*Ibid.,* p. 162. The palaces and temples, the luxurious homes, the gardens and vineyards, the gay crowds—all were destroyed.

"Even thus," said Jesus, "shall it be in the day when the Son of man is revealed." Gigantic chunks of ice, thundering down from the sky, will demolish every god that the worshipers of materialism have built for themselves (Rev. 16:21). Men's lordly palaces—their luxurious and extravagant homes—crumble to ruin before their eyes.

Will the owners of "lordly palaces" include some professed believers? Will those who have "lived deliciously" (Rev. 18:7) in the boldness of their sin include some who once professed Christ?

Will the return of Christ find your treasures, and your heart, still in Sodom? Or will you be wholly His?

"THIS IS IT!"

And it shall be said in that day, Lo, this is our God; we have waited for him, and he will save us: this is the Lord; we have waited for him, we will be glad and rejoice in his salvation. Isa. 25:9.

On the night of June 5, 1944, a villager in southern England went outside to shut up his chickens. While he was out, a nearby airfield came to life. Planes roared down the runway and came up over the elms in twos, in dozens, in scores. Climbing into the night sky, they went into formation, and were joined by hundreds of other planes from neighboring airfields.

The villager called to his wife to come outside. "This is it!" he exclaimed.

Down on the coast, British coast guardsman Percy Wallace, from his vantage point at St. Alban's Head, had watched that day as an armada of a thousand ships had moved out into the channel. He had looked down upon landing craft packed with troops, or carrying tanks. Farther out had been the mine sweepers, the destroyers, the heavy cruisers, the battleships. Out in the channel they had been joined by thousands of other ships. By evening they had all disappeared over the horizon, and then, as Mr. Wallace started home, he heard the planes.

"This is it!" he told his wife when he reached home.

The invasion of Europe, involving more than 4,000 ships and 11,000 first-line planes, was underway. Everybody in southern England, as they heard the noise in the sky that night, knew what it meant. Some were too awed to speak. Others silently prayed. Some simply breathed an excited "This is it!"

So it will be at the second coming of Jesus!

"Lo, this is our God!" the children of the Lord will exclaim. "The great day is come!" scream out those who are caught unprepared.

In other words—"This is it!"

Throughout the spring of 1944, as the invasion build-up progressed, a sense of expectancy pervaded southern England. So with us today. And shortly, with us too this sense of expectancy will become an excited "This is it!" Will you be ready?

THE DEPARTING OF THE HOLY SPIRIT

And the Lord said, My spirit shall not always strive with man. Gen. 6:3.

Toward the end of the past decade, as it became evident that marked changes were taking place in society, the *Saturday Evening Post* published an article entitled "Has This Country Gone Mad?" The author, discussing the violence and lawlessness abroad in the land, commented that "repeated reference to William Butler Yeats's poem *The Second Coming"* was emerging as a "symbol of the time."

The *Post* writer quoted several lines from Yeats's poem, about things falling apart, and about the loosing of "the blood-dimmed tide." Even more significant, though, was the very fact that the secular press would mention a poem entitled *The Second Coming* as a "symbol of the time."

Through decade after decade "the blood-dimmed tide" has been held back. It will not always be so. "There are forces now ready, and only waiting the divine permission, to spread desolation everywhere."—*The Great Controversy*, p. 614. As the Spirit of God is withdrawn, an unimaginable tide of lawlessness and violence will sweep the earth, until finally "the whole world will be involved in ruin more terrible than that which came upon Jerusalem of old" (*ibid.*).

Yet even as the Holy Spirit is being withdrawn from society, and as His restraining influence is being removed from the nations, the church is to seek most earnestly for that special outpouring of heavenly grace and power which will make possible the finishing of the work of God. As lawlessness increases, the lives of the people of God must be more and more Spirit controlled.

On Christian campuses and in our churches two distinct groups are becoming more and more evident. Those truly seeking to prepare for the coming of Christ are becoming more earnest about that preparation. Another group is becoming increasingly hardened.

To which group do you belong? Is the convicting, converting influence of the Holy Spirit welcome in your life? Or do you resist it?

A CALL TO REPENTANCE

Blow ye the trumpet in Zion, and sound an alarm in my holy mountain: let all the inhabitants of the land tremble: for the day of the Lord cometh, for it is nigh at hand. Joel 2:1.

Blow ye the trumpet in Zion!

There was something very sobering in Bible times about the blowing of a trumpet. It sometimes meant a call to war (Num. 10:9). Ten days before the Day of Atonement the "blowing of trumpets" (Lev. 23:24) was a call to ten days of heart searching and prayer.

Today's scripture, the beginning of the second chapter of Joel, is a call to repentance. As the day of the Lord—"great and very terrible"—draws near, there is need for a deep searching of heart, "with fasting, and with weeping, and with mourning" (Joel 2:12). Sin has separated the church from her God, and changes need to be made.

The prophet suggests in Joel 2:15, 16 that a solemn assembly be called. The whole congregation—the elders, the ministers, the newlyweds, even the children—are urged to come together to seek the Lord. Joel envisions at these gatherings a work of heart searching, thorough and deep. Differences are put away, sins made right, earnest prayers offered. As this is done, the Lord draws near. Sorrow turns to rejoicing, and the Lord, manifesting His presence, does "great things," causing to come down "the rain, the former rain, and the latter rain." The gospel goes forth with new power, bringing deliverance to "whosoever shall call on the name of the Lord."

And thus, through "the remnant whom the Lord shall call" (verse 32), the work of God is finished!

But before this refreshing from the presence of the Lord can take place, there must be a thorough work of repentance. Pentecost was preceded by ten days of heart searching, prayer, and putting away of differences.

Let there begin in the hearts of each of us this work of repentance! Let us pray specifically for a double measure of the spirit of repentance. If we will pray sincerely, seeking God on our knees and earnestly studying His Word, it is a prayer He will surely answer.

ARE THERE SOME CHANGES NEEDED?

Repent ye therefore, and be converted, that your sins may be blotted out, when the times of refreshing shall come from the presence of the Lord. **Acts 3:19.**

What are the sins that have barred the "refreshing" which comes from the Lord's presence among His people? Of what do we most need to repent?

In the words of Elder N. C. Dower at the 1970 General Conference we need to repent "of our worldliness and materialism, our lack of commitment and concern, our lukewarmness and self-satisfaction, our failure to preach the Word of God and to set the right example. . . . We need to repent . . . for our pride and self-seeking and prejudice. We need to repent because of our lack of love for Jesus Christ and for the souls for whom He died."—*The Ministry,* June, 1970, p. 6.

We need to repent of our indifference to the Holy Spirit. "This promised blessing, claimed by faith, brings all other blessings in its train."—*The Desire of Ages,* p. 672. Yet how often this gift has been ignored on our campuses, from the pulpit, and in our personal lives. "How rarely it is presented before the people, and its reception spoken of in the church," wrote the servant of God in 1891. "The promise of the Holy Spirit is casually brought into our discourses, is incidentally touched upon, and that is all."—*Testimonies to Ministers,* p. 174.

How about the schedules on most of our campuses? Study is emphasized, and work is provided for, and recreation and socials, and a formal attendance at meetings is generally required—but where, in most schedules, is there room for special study groups, special prayer groups, and seasons to voluntarily come apart and seek God?

Is the Holy Spirit in many places still just as casually regarded as back in 1891? Could that be why we are still here? Is there opportunity in your personal schedule or in your campus schedule or in the care of earning a living to go apart for real soul searching? Are there some changes that need to be made?

"Seek ye the Lord, all ye meek of the earth, which have wrought his judgment; seek righteousness, seek meekness" (Zeph. 2:3).

45

PREPARING TO RECEIVE THE HOLY SPIRIT

"Do not leave Jerusalem, but wait for the gift my Father promised, that I told you about. For John baptized with water, but in a few days you will be baptized with the Holy Spirit." Acts 1:4, 5, T.E.V.

Have you ever wondered why there was this period of waiting? Why was the Holy Spirit not poured out as soon as Christ ascended?

The disciples were not ready. For ten days they entered into a special season of heart searching and prayer, making things right with one another and with God. Reports inspiration:

"Putting away all differences, all desire for the supremacy, they came close together in Christian fellowship. . . . The disciples felt their spiritual need and cried to the Lord for the holy unction that was to fit them for the work of soul saving. They did not ask for a blessing for themselves merely. They were weighted with the burden of the salvation of souls. They realized that the gospel was to be carried to the world, and they claimed the power that Christ had promised."—*The Acts of the Apostles,* p. 37.

Thus it must be again. Note from the above paragraph these practical specifics:

First, we must feel our need—a need that will lead us to seek the Lord for "the holy unction" which alone can fit us for soul saving. "Since this is the means by which we are to receive power," the servant of God asks, "why do we not hunger and thirst for the gift of the Spirit? Why do we not talk of it, pray for it, and preach concerning it?"—*Ibid.,* p. 50.

Second, our seeking should lead us into heart searching and repentance, and into close fellowship with one another. All differences, all desire for supremacy, must be put away.

Third, we must have a burden for souls, and finally, we must begin to pray most earnestly, claiming the power Christ has promised.

Consider, for example, the third—having a real concern for people. Does it matter to you about people? Would a chance to speak to someone about Christ mean more to you than a grade, or a date, or money?

Will we in the weeks ahead *really begin to care?*

46

WONDERFUL CHANGES

Therefore also now, saith the Lord, turn ye even to me with all your heart, and with fasting, and with weeping, and with mourning: and rend your heart, and not your garments, and turn unto the Lord your God: for he is gracious and merciful, slow to anger, and of great kindness, and repenteth him of the evil. Joel 2:12, 13.

As we have noted, the book of Joel, and particularly chapter 2, is especially applicable to the church and its youth in these last days. Today's text, in the most solemn language, is a call to arouse from spiritual indifference and to seek the Lord in repentance and humility.

In a chapter entitled "An Appeal to Laymen," inspiration gives this description of scenes yet to be enacted:

"In the visions of the night, representations passed before me of a great reformatory movement among God's people. Many were praising God. The sick were healed, and other miracles were wrought. A spirit of intercession was seen, even as was manifested before the great Day of Pentecost. Hundreds and thousands were seen visiting families and opening before them the word of God. Hearts were convicted by the power of the Holy Spirit, and a spirit of genuine conversion was manifest. On every side doors were thrown open to the proclamation of the truth. The world seemed to be lightened with the heavenly influence. Great blessings were received by the true and humble people of God. I heard voices of thanksgiving and praise, and there seemed to be a reformation such as we witnessed in 1844."—*Testimonies,* vol. 9, p. 126.

As this great reformatory movement bears fruit, as a spirit of intercession grips the church, as hundreds and thousands go forth to share God's Word with neighbors and friends, the Spirit of God will come with unprecedented power. Hearts will be convicted, doors will be thrown open everywhere, and the whole world will be enlightened.

Note particularly that there will develop a spirit of intercession such as preceded the Day of Pentecost. Isn't that where, this very day, we could begin? Wouldn't it be possible through you for this vision to begin to be fulfilled on your campus, in your church, in your home?

"SEARCH ME, O GOD"

Search me, O God, and know my heart: try me, and know my thoughts: and see if there be any wicked way in me, and lead me in the way everlasting. **Ps. 139:23, 24.**

In today's scripture, David throws open his heart to the all-seeing eye of God.

As we seek the Lord for more of His Spirit in our lives, we do well to make David's prayer our own. As the Lord sends conviction upon us concerning changes that need to be made, and as we make these changes, we are truly preparing the way for greater manifestations of His Spirit.

Consider, from the book *Messages to Young People,* these words:

"There is nothing that Satan fears so much as that the people of God shall clear the way by removing every hindrance, so that the Lord can pour out His Spirit. . . . When the way is prepared for the Spirit of God, the blessing will come. Satan can no more hinder a shower of blessing from descending upon God's people than he can close the windows of heaven that rain cannot come upon the earth. Wicked men and devils cannot hinder the work of God, or shut out His presence from the assemblies of His people, if they will, with subdued, contrite hearts, confess and put away their sins, and in faith claim His promises."— Page 133.

Nothing—not the devils themselves—can prevent the descent of the Holy Spirit, if God's people "will, with subdued, contrite hearts, confess and put away their sins, and in faith claim His promises"!

Note, from inspiration, the emphasis of two things:

1. The confessing and putting away of sins.

2. A claiming, in faith, of Heaven's promises.

To both of these, during the days ahead, we want to give more than ordinary attention.

The disciples, we might recall, spent the ten days preceding Pentecost doing this very thing. What might be the results if the church today would unitedly spend ten days truly seeking the Lord?

Could we not, individually at least, start *now?*

48

THE HARDEST PRAYER YOU WILL EVER PRAY

And he went a little farther, and fell on his face, and prayed, saying, O my Father, if it be possible, let this cup pass from me: nevertheless not as I will, but as thou wilt. Matt. 26:39.

It was the most difficult prayer anyone has ever prayed. The submission was so anguished that Jesus sweat blood over it.

For us, too, the simple words, "Not as I will, but as Thou wilt," can be the hardest prayer we ever pray.

The decisions facing us are no comparison to the decision that Jesus faced there in Gethsemane. It was for Him a decision whether or not to go ahead to Calvary. The issue with us is probably the surrender of some favorite indulgence, some cherished sin. It may be for us the making of some changes that human nature would rather not make.

In preparation for Pentecost, 120 believers gathered together in one place to seek the Lord. The church today, some two million strong, could never meet together as they did. Probably we could never, as completely as they did, put everything aside for ten days, devoting the time to the putting away of differences, to heart-searching and prayer.

But could we not at least give prayerful thought to some of the changes we need to make in preparation for a modern Pentecost?

With us, as with them, the place to begin is with the death of self. "Self must die."—*Testimonies,* vol. 5, p. 219.

Note the *must.* "The only hope for us if we would overcome is to unite our will to God's will and work in co-operation with Him, hour by hour and day by day. We cannot retain self and yet enter the kingdom of God."—*Thoughts From the Mount of Blessing,* p. 143.

"Are we willing to pay the price required of us?" the pen of inspiration asks. "Are we willing to have our will brought into perfect conformity to the will of God?"—*Ibid.*

That's the issue to be settled. We cannot of ourselves change our desires. But if we are "willing to be made willing," God can and will. Are you willing to do anything God might ask? Are you willing to be made willing?

OF ONE ACCORD

And the multitude of them that believed were of one heart and of one soul.
. . . And with great power gave the apostles witness of the resurrection of the
Lord Jesus: and great grace was upon them all. Acts 4:32, 33.

The disciples had frequently argued among themselves. When James and John sought the highest place, the ten were angry. This was exactly what every one of them had wanted. Their self-seeking spirit continued right up to the eve of the crucifixion—and was probably still reflected to some extent in the anxiety of the disciples after the resurrection to know if Christ was about to set up His kingdom.

Then, there in the upper room their attitudes began to change. Who took the initiative we do not know, but of this we can be sure—there were some apologies offered. "Putting away all differences, all desire for the supremacy, they came close together in Christian fellowship."—*The Acts of the Apostles,* p. 37.

All differences put away! Self submerged in Christ so that all desire for supremacy was gone! How wonderful, then, the fellowship.

Would you be willing to do *anything* the Lord might ask?

Probably nothing is doing more to obstruct the outpouring of the Holy Spirit than differences among us. What if God asks you to take the initiative in putting away your differences with a fellow believer, or a neighbor, or a member of the family? What if He asks you to go to that person, as though you were the chief offender, humbly seeking reconciliation?

The fault may be largely the other person's. But it may be that the only way you can bring about reconciliation would be for you to go with the same humility with which you would if the fault were all yours. What if God impresses you to do this?

The hour is too late for children to be at odds with their parents, for church members or workers to be at odds with one another! It is too late for there to be rivalry or hard feelings between schools or institutions or workers! It is too late for there to be harshness anywhere among us! How about making things right *now?*

THE LOVE THAT UNITES

And above all things have fervent charity among yourselves: for charity shall cover the multitude of sins. **1 Peter 4:8.**

During the ten days of seeking the Lord which preceded Pentecost, the believers came close together in Christian fellowship. The outpouring of the Holy Spirit brought them even closer. Of their experience at this time inspiration records:

"They rejoiced in the sweetness of communion with saints. They were tender, thoughtful, self-denying, willing to make any sacrifice for the truth's sake. In their daily association with one another, they revealed the love that Christ had enjoined upon them."—*The Acts of the Apostles,* p. 547.

The obstacles from without are as nothing compared to the obstacles that exist within the church. It is the evils within that most hinder the progress of God's cause. Notes inspiration:

"There is no surer way of weakening spirituality than by cherishing envy, suspicion, faultfinding, and evil surmising. On the other hand, the strongest witness that God has sent His Son into the world is the existence of harmony and union among men of varied dispositions who form His church."—*Ibid.,* p. 549.

Are there envy and suspicion upon your campus or within your church? Is there faultfinding? Is there "evil surmising"? You don't know for sure that this person or that one is doing thus and thus, but you surmise it.

As young people do you ever find yourselves surmising evil concerning your parents, your teachers? Are they, to you, simply "the establishment"?

As parents, as teachers, has there been "evil surmising" against varied ones of your young people? Have you forgotten that suspicion demoralizes, creating the very evils you are guarding against?

These attitudes must go. We may not see all things alike. But remember, *the strongest witness you can give of the power of Christ is for there to be harmony and union among men of varied dispositions!*

Self must die! Are you willing?

51

WHEN THERE ARE DIFFERENCES

Hereby perceive we the love of God, because he laid down his life for us: and we ought to lay down our lives for the brethren. 1 John 3:16.

Think for a moment of the person with whom you have had the strongest differences. It could be a neighbor, an employer, a pastor, a student, a teacher, a fellow worker—or perhaps a member of the family. Would you be willing to lay down your life for that individual?

It may be someone who has sinned deeply. Not against you, necessarily, but against someone you know, or against the church, and against God.

Even so, if you have Christ within, if you love the way today's text says you ought to love, you will have no disposition to watch him, or to expose his errors. "Instead of seeking to accuse and condemn, it will be your object to help, to bless, and to save. In dealing with those who are in error, you will heed the injunction, Consider 'thyself, lest thou also be tempted.' Galatians 6:1. You will call to mind the many times you have erred and how hard it was to find the right way when you had once left it. You will not push your brother into greater darkness, but with a heart full of pity will tell him of his danger."— *Thoughts From the Mount of Blessing*, p. 128.

No matter how wrong he may be, not until you would be willing to lay down your life in order to save him are you truly prepared to help him.

And as for his wrongs, you might also remember this:

"Search thine own heart: what paineth thee
In others, in thyself may be."
—JEAN INGELOW

J. A. Hadfield writes: "It is literally true that in judging others we trumpet abroad our secret faults. Allow any person to give free vent to his feelings about others, and then you may with perfect safety turn and say, 'Thou art the man.' "

Won't you leave your critical feelings about others at the foot of the cross?

JUMPING TO CONCLUSIONS

Judge not according to the appearance, but judge righteous judgment. John 7:24.

Do you ever jump to conclusions? Have you ever condemned someone on the basis of circumstantial evidence? Could it be that you did not have all the facts?

Elder H. M. S. Richards relates this true incident:

A woman in Buffalo, New York, was shopping one day and thoughtlessly picked up an umbrella belonging to another woman and started to walk off with it. The owner stopped her, and the absent-minded shopper, with many apologies, returned the umbrella. The incident reminded her that she needed some umbrellas for her family. So she bought two for her daughters and one for herself, and went on about her shopping. Later in the day, when she was on the way home on the bus armed with her three umbrellas, she happened to glance up, and there, directly opposite her, was the very woman with whom she had had the unfortunate experience in the morning. The second woman stared very hard at the three umbrellas for several minutes. Then, with a significant smile she leaned forward and said in an icy tone, "I see you have had a successful morning."

The woman was innocent. But it would have been pointless to even try to explain.

Before allowing yourself to criticize another, turn and read again what Jesus has said about this, as found in Matthew 7:1-5. Then read the comments on these verses from the first several pages of *Thoughts From the Mount of Blessing,* chapter entitled "Not Judging, but Doing."

One of the sternest warnings Jesus ever uttered was directed to those who piled up endless rules and regulations as a barrier against sin—and then turned themselves into self-centered judges and petty spies, criticizing and condemning all who came short of their prescribed standard. "Judge not, that ye be not judged," He warned (Matt. 7:1).

Have we been critical of one another? Have our words been an obstacle in the Lord's way? Are there things we need to make right?

IF

If any man offend not in word, the same is a perfect man, and able also to bridle the whole body. James 3:2.

Someone has figured that the speech of an average person totals the equivalent of about fifteen notebook pages a day—a 105-page book in a week. Over a period of fifty years this would become a library of a quarter of a million pages.

How many tens of thousands of pages would it take to hold the record of the words of your life thus far? Upon how many of these pages would be found impatient words?

The sin that kept Moses out of the Promised Land was that "he spake unadvisedly with his lips" (Ps. 106:33). Do you find yourself speaking "unadvisedly"? Do you dwell upon the faults of others? How about the church members who come short of what you think they should be—do you criticize them? Suppose they are younger than you, with some pretty glaring faults—do you censure them?

Consider a startling truth:

"No one has ever been reclaimed from a wrong position by censure and reproach; but many have thus been driven from Christ and led to seal their hearts against conviction."—*Thoughts From the Mount of Blessing*, p. 129.

Are there those whose hearts you or I have sealed against conviction? Have we, by censuring them, driven them from Christ?

"Shall not the miserable spirit of faultfinding and mumuring be buried, never to have a resurrection?" asks inspiration. "Shall not the incense of praise and thanksgiving ascend from hearts purified and sanctified and glorified by the presence of Christ?"—*Testimonies*, vol. 8, p. 45.

There is no room in the upper-room experience for impatience, for sharp retorts, for censure, for criticism. "Set a watch, O Lord, before my mouth; keep the door of my lips" (Ps. 141:3). If each of us would make this our prayer, what a difference it would make!

If!

Let it begin with each of us. Let it begin with me. Keep, O Lord, the door of my lips.

WINNING ONE HUNDRED TIMES AS MANY!

"Take my yoke upon you, and learn from me; for I am gentle and lowly in heart." Matt. 11:29, R.S.V.

If the people of God during 1972 could win one hundred times more people to Christ than were won last year, we would probably conclude that the latter rain had begun.

Consider the following:

"If we would humble ourselves before God, and be kind and courteous and tenderhearted and pitiful, there would be one hundred conversions to the truth where now there is only one." —*Testimonies*, vol. 9, p. 189.

This promise was penned in 1905. Wouldn't it be just as applicable today?

"One hundred conversions . . . where now . . . only one"!

A congregation that has been winning fifteen people to Christ during a year's time would, under the blessing of God, begin winning closer to 1,500 a year! A conference that has been having three hundred baptisms a year would begin baptizing more like thirty thousand a year!

It would indeed be a latter-rain experience!

The conditions?

First, to truly humble ourselves before the Lord. It is not human wisdom or skill that wins people to Christ. A hundredfold more conversions could happen only by God's working mightily in behalf of His people. His church would have to prepare the way, through humbling of heart and through genuine repentance, so that God could safely bring into our midst these thousands and tens of thousands.

The second condition would be to manifest—in our homes, in the church, and in the world—the kindness and gentleness and courtesy of Jesus. Self-righteousness—so quick to see mistakes, to criticize, to accuse—would have to go. There are too many among us who "do not in their life make manifest the softening influence of the Saviour's love. They misrepresent the gentle, courteous spirit of the gospel and wound precious souls, for whom Christ died."—*Thoughts From the Mount of Blessing*, p. 125.

"Learn from Me," Jesus invites.

THE COURTESY THAT WINS

Be kindly affectioned one to another with brotherly love; in honour preferring one another. Rom. 12:10.

Would you like to see a hundredfold more conversions among the youth of the church? Would you, if you are a teen-ager, like to see hundreds of your fellow teen-agers brought to Christ?

Yesterday we discussed the promise that if we would humble ourselves before God, and manifest a kind and courteous spirit in our dealings with others, there would be a hundredfold more conversions.

Are there some changes you need to make?

Suppose in your home a six-year-old spills a glass of milk. Do you speak to him in just as courteous a tone of voice as you would if a visiting adult should have a similar accident?

Suppose on your campus a student worker in the cafeteria accidentally drops a tray of food while preparing dinner. With what tone of voice would he be spoken to? Would he be treated with the same courtesy that would be extended to another adult having a similar mishap?

"What Christ was in His life on this earth, that every Christian should be. He is our example, not only in His spotless purity but in His patience, gentleness, and winsomeness of disposition. He was firm as a rock where truth and duty were concerned, but He was invariably kind and courteous."—ELLEN G. WHITE, in *Review and Herald,* Aug. 20, 1959.

There are parents who pray daily that their children will be converted. There are teachers who complain of a lack of spirituality among youth. But could it be that one of the greatest obstacles to answered prayer has been our failure to manifest the patience and gentleness and winsomeness of Christ?

Firmness? Christ was "firm as a rock." But note also that "He was invariably kind and courteous."

Would you like to see genuine conversions multiplied among the children and youth in your church or on your campus? The place for this work to begin is in our own hearts.

Bring a change, Lord—and let it begin with me.

THOSE RESENTMENTS

Thou shalt not avenge, nor bear any grudge against the children of thy people, but thou shalt love thy neighbour as thyself. Lev. 19:18.

One time on a campus where I was a teacher, we were giving special attention to seeking the Lord, and the Spirit of God was manifestly working. One day, in several different Bible classes, we asked, "How many of you have no hard feelings in your heart against anyone? How many have no resentments against any teacher or parent or anyone?"

We asked for a show of hands. Not many hands were raised.

We had no chance to make the same inquiry of the teachers. But had we done so, how many of them would have been able to raise their hands?

The Spirit of God had blessed, and many during those days of special attention to spiritual things had gained victories. But how much greater could have been God's blessing if all the grudges and hard feelings and resentments could have been laid at the foot of the cross! The revival that we need and must have can never come until we put on that strength and humility which does not harbor resentment and grudges.

James writes, "Be ye also patient; stablish your hearts: for the coming of the Lord draweth nigh. Grudge not one against another, brethren, lest ye be condemned" (James 5:8, 9).

"The Lord's coming is very near," Phillips translates it. "Don't make complaints against one another in the meantime, my brothers—you may be the one at fault yourself." *

Suppose someone has terribly wronged you. Was Jesus ever wronged? When He was, did He carry resentments? What was it He prayed while being nailed to the cross? "Father, forgive them; for they know not what they do" (Luke 23:34).

If anyone could have avenged an injustice suffered, Jesus could have, there at the cross. Don't picture Him as One who had to take it. He didn't.

God help us to put away all resentments and grudges—*now!*

.* The Bible texts in this book credited to Phillips are from *The New Testament in Modern English,* © J. B. Phillips 1958. Used by permission of The Macmillan Company.

GETTING PERSONAL

Let this mind be in you, which was also in Christ Jesus. **Phil. 2:5.**

Self-centeredness, envy, suspicions, faultfinding, evil surmising, resentments—these are the sins that separate Christians from one another.

These things fall primarily within the area of human relationships. Let's consider now some of those things that are much more private matters—things such as eating habits, dress, and certain leisure-time activities.

This is really getting personal, but let's ask some questions. Can dress be an obstacle to the workings of the Holy Spirit? Can leisure activities? Can what you eat? Could it possibly be that eating habits could hinder the work of God in our midst?

The psalmist, after discussing at some length Israel's insistence upon food not for their best good (Ps. 78:17-40), notes that they "limited the Holy One of Israel" (verse 41). And today, within the context of an appeal to live our God-given health principles, we read: "The Lord does not now work to bring many souls into the truth, because of the church members who have never been converted and those who were once converted but who have backslidden. What influence would these unconsecrated members have on new converts? Would they not make of no effect the God-given message which His people are to bear?"—*Testimonies,* vol. 6, p. 371.

As for the influence of unChristlike fashions, consider this, penned at a time when "showy extravagant dress" was the thing hindering the witness of the church:

"Obedience to fashion is pervading our Seventh-day Adventist churches and is doing more than any other power to separate our people from God."—*Ibid.,* vol. 4, p. 647.

The solution, when issues such as these arise, is not found in blaming one another and criticizing one another, but in determining God's will and then doing it. As today's text puts it: "Let this mind be in you, which was also in Christ Jesus."

THE TEMPTATION OF FOOD

I keep under my body, and bring it into subjection: lest that by any means, when I have preached to others, I myself should be a castaway. 1 Cor. 9:27.

"Food is one of my biggest temptations," said one teen-ager.

There's no law against enjoying food. After God stocked Eden with an abundance of delicious things to eat, He pronounced them very good. And of the desires that we have labeled "appetites," inspiration remarks, "These appetites were given us for important purposes, for good, and not to become the ministers of death by being perverted and becoming warring lusts."—*Testimonies,* vol. 4, p. 244.

Our problem comes from eating too much, or at the wrong times, or from eating unhealthful things—and doing it even when our better judgment tells us we ought not. It is this—the indulgence of appetite—that hinders the work of the Holy Spirit in our lives. "The Spirit of God," we are told, "cannot come to our help, and assist us in perfecting Christian characters, while we are indulging our appetites to the injury of health."—*Counsels on Diet and Foods,* p. 57.

For a lot of us the reformation that must precede the outpouring of the Holy Spirit should begin at our tables. How can we overeat and then pray for the Holy Spirit? With the ever-increasing evidence from science as to the harmfulness of coffee, tea, and flesh food, and with all the counsel Heaven has given, how can we still use these things and then kneel down and pray for revival?

Too much is at stake to pass off the temptation of food with a jest. "The controlling power of appetite will prove the ruin of thousands, when, if they had conquered on this point, they would have had moral power to gain the victory over every other temptation of Satan."—*Ibid.,* p. 59.

Self-control in eating and drinking means clearer minds, more attractive bodies, calmer nerves, happier dispositions, and better health. Whatever changes are needed, why not make them now?

If not now—when?

CRIME AND HEMLINES

Women should adorn themselves modestly and sensibly in seemly apparel. 1 Tim. 2:9, R.S.V.

Modest, sensible, attractive. Could three guidelines be more reasonable?

"Girls' skirts," wrote ABC newscaster Paul Harvey, on April 14, 1970, "started creeping upward in 1964. . . . Simultaneously, however coincidentally, crimes against women began a dramatic increase.

"Is there a correlation?" he asked. "The consensus of law enforcement officers in 50 states is 'yes.'

"Women," said Mr. Harvey, "do not see miniskirts from the same point of view as men do. A girl accustomed to appearing in public in a swimsuit cannot comprehend the difference between that and the provocative promise of a possible view of intimate areas."

Mr. Harvey noted the claim of the designer of the miniskirt that "miniclothes are symbolic of those girls who want to seduce a man." Of the lawmen surveyed, he said, 83 per cent agreed that "a normally sexed young man will be more likely to think in the direction of overt sex activity by the strip-tease effects of a short skirt wearer, seated, than by any other public fashion in history.

"Yet many women," concluded Mr. Harvey, "cannot imagine that it could ever be improper—or even dangerous—to follow fashion."

To what extent has this "many" included professed daughters of God? How long after 1964, for example, was it before abbreviated skirts began appearing in church, and even on the platform? Was it proper that this "strip-tease effect" be brought into God's house?

A lot of teen-agers feel, and justly so, that they have been too much browbeaten about dress. But could it be, in the words of Mr. Harvey, that there are times when it is "improper—or even dangerous—to follow fashion"?

Would you be willing to make it a matter of prayer? Would you, in laying it before God, include a "not my will, but Thine, be done"?

OPPORTUNITY!

That ye may be blameless and harmless, the sons of God, without rebuke, in the midst of a crooked and perverse nation, among whom ye shine as lights in the world. **Phil. 2:15.**

I had stepped into the language lab at our school. An eleventh-grade girl was fixing a bulletin board. The scenes, of a European country, showed some very pretty girls very attractively dressed, with skirt lengths about to the knees.

The dean of women at our academy had just said something to the girls about dress lengths, and thus, as we stood there talking about the bulletin board, the subject of dress came up. This girl, with disarming frankness, commented, "I know I should wear my skirts longer. I guess I just don't want to be different."

I thought of what a youth leader had said some months earlier in commenting upon the unparalleled degeneracy that had come into the fashion world. "Perhaps the Lord has permitted this degeneracy," he said, "so that the witness of Christian young people will be even more striking. This contrast becomes one of the most telling aspects of a Christian's witness." It doesn't mean becoming a gazingstock. Suppose when dress lengths were climbing higher and higher the girls and women in our churches and on our campuses had kept theirs somewhere near knee length. Would this have made them repulsive?

Quite the opposite, if the words of a telephone repairman who came onto one Christian campus mean anything. Most of the girls he saw in the hallways were wearing moderate lengths. This repairman had just come from a public school campus, and commented that the contrast was striking. He liked the difference, and said so. He marveled to see so many good-looking and tastefully dressed teen-agers.

Fashions change, and skirt lengths probably will have changed too before this is in print. Other attention-getting styles will be devised. May God make His sons and daughters willing to be different if need be in order to represent Him—"blameless and harmless, the sons of God, without rebuke, in the midst of a crooked and perverse nation, among whom ye shine as lights in the world."

SHOW US CHRIST

For thou art an holy people unto the Lord thy God: the Lord thy God hath chosen thee to be a special people unto himself, above all people that are upon the face of the earth. **Deut. 7:6.**

What is it that makes God's people different? Isn't it the fact that they reflect Christ? We have discussed during the past few days some of the sins that have hindered God's blessing. We realize, without a lot being said, that appetite, immodesty, and pride separate us from God. We know that we should turn away from "the lust of the flesh, and the lust of the eyes, and the pride of life" (1 John 2:16). We know that changes need to be made in order to reflect Christ more fully.

But in order to reflect Christ we must first see Christ. Wrote a 23-year-old girl in a letter published in the February, 1971, issue of *The Ministry* magazine, "My greatest need, and that of my Seventh-day Adventist friends is Christ." "We know the seventh day is the real Sabbath. We know we should tithe. We know meat, cigarettes, liquor, and drugs are not good for us. We know a lot of things, but *we do not know Christ or God."*

Her letter is one which should be read by every teacher, every parent, every leader of youth. "Please preach and teach us about the character of God," she pleaded. "Show us, tell us, point Him out to us. . . . Show us from your personal experience. . . . We need more than anything else *to know God. We need Christ.* Can you—will you—show Him to us?"

In a few days, through MISSION '72, the church will be beginning the greatest evangelistic outreach in its history. That outreach should be to those among us who do not know Christ, to those who have become discouraged, as well as to the world. The plea of the above letter is also the unspoken plea of young people who have left the church, many of whom could be won back through the influence of MISSION '72, if we would show them Christ. And it is the plea of millions whom the church should reach during the coming months. If the way could be prepared for God to mightily intervene in behalf of His work, if we would truly reflect Christ, and uplift Him, thousands would rejoice to become a part of the special people mentioned in today's text. Are we ready? Do we know Christ?

COMING IN HIS NAME

And whatsoever ye shall ask in my name, that will I do, that the Father may be glorified in the Son. If ye shall ask any thing in my name, I will do it. John 14:13, 14.

During the precious instruction given to the disciples by Christ just hours before He was crucified, He repeatedly mentioned the privilege of our coming to the Father in His name, and our right to pray in His name. But what does it mean to pray in the name of Christ? Note the following:

"To pray in Christ's name means much. It means that we are to accept His character, manifest His spirit, and work His works."—*The Desire of Ages*, p. 668.

How is it that you accept His character? Isn't it through faith in His righteousness? Notice this beautiful explanation:

"In Christ's name His followers are to stand before God. Through the value of the sacrifice made for them, they are of value in the Lord's sight. Because of the imputed righteousness of Christ they are accounted precious. For Christ's sake the Lord pardons those that fear Him. He does not see in them the vileness of the sinner. He recognizes in them the likeness of His Son, in whom they believe."—*Ibid.*, p. 667.

Power in prayer, which we will be considering during the next few days in preparation for MISSION '72, is directly related to the confidence that comes from possessing the gift of Christ's righteousness. Then we know as we come to the Lord with our requests that He does not see in us "the vileness of the sinner." Instead, He recognizes in us "the likeness of His Son." Realizing this, we are able to "come boldly" (Heb. 4:16) with our requests.

We are invited as we think of MISSION '72 to "expect large things" (*ibid.*, p. 668). This expecting large things, this coming to God with "the very highest demands" (*ibid.*), is possible because of the confidence we can have in *His* righteousness. And how do we receive that righteousness? "The righteousness of God is embodied in Christ. We receive righteousness by receiving Him."—*Thoughts From the Mount of Blessing*, p. 18. It is as you have this experience that God will be able to use you in MISSION '72.

TEACH US TO PRAY

And it came to pass, that, as he was praying in a certain place, when he ceased, one of his disciples said unto him, Lord, teach us to pray. Luke 11:1.

Inspiration gives some added insights concerning this incident. One day Christ's disciples, after a short absence from Jesus, returned to find Him "absorbed in supplication. Seeming unconscious of their presence, He continued praying aloud. The hearts of the disciples were deeply moved. As He ceased praying, they exclaimed, 'Lord, teach us to pray.' "—*Christ's Object Lessons,* p. 140.

There are several things of interest here. First, as Jesus prayed He was completely absorbed in His praying. He didn't seem to notice that a dozen people had come there. Second, He was not at all ashamed to be found praying. And third, even though these were private devotions, He was praying aloud.

"I wish," said an academy student, "that prayer would be so natural on our campus that you would feel at ease stopping anywhere on campus to pray with someone."

There have been instances where, for some young people at least, prayer was that natural. On one occasion, as the result of students' actively working to win other students, a special student-directed commitment service was held during a school assembly. Many young people were influenced to make decisions for Christ, and at the close of that chapel service several dozen students lingered there in the chapel. I was standing in the aisle, quietly talking with several of them, when one of the fellows, nodding over toward one side of the chapel, said, "Carol is praying with someone. Let's pray too."

Carol, who had made the commitment call, had been talking to one of the girls who had not responded, and had knelt to pray with her. Mike had noticed it, and asked the several of us to pray too. We did, right there. There were still people around, but neither Carol nor Mike nor the others were ashamed to pray.

Should not the "spirit of intercession" which Heaven has foretold (*Testimonies,* vol. 9, p. 126) begin to be seen everywhere?

PRAYER AS A COMPANIONSHIP

Pray without ceasing. 1 Thess. 5:17.

We were reviewing a number of things in the office, when the associate pastor looked directly at Linda, one of our readers, and asked, "Do you know how to pray?"

"Yes," Linda replied without hesitation, "I just learned to—this school year."

"How do you pray?" she was asked.

"I just talk to Him," she said.

The simplicity of it, and Linda's sincerity and sureness, rang true. *Just talk to Him.* That's a beautiful discovery, I thought, that everyone ought to experience.

"Prayer," as you have often heard, "is the opening of the heart to God as to a friend."—*Steps to Christ,* p. 93. Does it mean that to you?

Yesterday we noticed that Jesus, even in His private devotions, sometimes prayed aloud. "Let your prayers be semiaudible," one current author suggests. "You are speaking to a person, and hearing your own voice will keep your thoughts centered on Him."

Count Zinzendorf, one of the Reformers, often did this. Sometimes while walking to some appointment, he would, if with a group, either drop behind or walk on ahead so he could talk aloud to Christ as he walked.

Communion can also be silent, however. The important thing is that you make your prayer life an experience in companionship. Today's scripture, "Pray without ceasing," becomes meaningful or possible only as it does become an experience in companionship. And, as with human friendship, it can sometimes be simply the silent communion of heart with heart. As inspiration so beautifully puts it:

"Cultivate the habit of talking with the Saviour when you are alone, when you are walking, and when you are busy with your daily labor. Let the heart be continually uplifted in silent petition for help, for light, for strength, for knowledge."—*The Ministry of Healing,* pp. 510, 511.

IS THERE A TREE SOMEWHERE?

Be still, and know that I am God. . . . The Lord of hosts is with us; the God of Jacob is our refuge. **Ps. 46:10, 11.**

The discussion topic that day, in an academy Bible class, was meditation. "It was evident," said the teacher, "that no one was doing much meditating." So he decided to give an assignment.

"Your assignment for the rest of today's class period," he told the class, "is to go out onto the campus and find a tree. Sit there, with your back to the tree, and spend thirty minutes just thinking. If anyone comes by, and tries to start a conversation, just tell him, 'I can't talk now; I'm doing an assignment.'

"And by the way," he added, "just one person to a tree!" There were thirty persons in the class, and he knew that there were at least thirty trees on campus.

One girl stopped by on her way out of the room, started to say something, and then began to cry. She did not want to be alone with her thoughts, even in full daylight.

Another student, the next day, told her Bible teacher: "I've had a problem for six months, and haven't known what to do about it. Yesterday I decided what I could do."

Have you noticed how many people have to have a radio or TV on almost constantly? While doing her housework, the wife has to have either the radio or TV going somewhere close by. Teen-agers, in their coming and going, carry along a transistor radio. A family goes camping, and, wouldn't you know it—the quietness of a forest retreat, the stillness of a camp beside a mountain stream, is interrupted by the loud blare of a portable radio!

The radio, or TV, you see, keeps you from having to think.

The Christian, if he would keep in touch with Christ, must have time to meditate, to think, to listen. He must give Christ a chance to be heard. There must be opportunity for the impressions of the "still small voice" (1 Kings 19:12) to get through.

How about it?

Is there a tree somewhere?

PART OF GOD'S PLAN

Ask, and ye shall receive, that your joy may be full. John 16:24.

We had already had the fall Week of Devotion at Auburn Academy, and Thanksgiving vacation was approaching, when our associate pastor suggested that we have a ten-day period voluntarily devoted to heart-searching and prayer, concluding with a festival of praise.

This emphasis began on Wednesday evening at the joint worship in the academy chapel. The Spirit of God was manifestly present, and most of the students remained for prayer groups. Voluntary discussion and study groups met a number of times thereafter. The second Friday of this ten days was a day of fasting and prayer, particularly during the lunch hour, when about one hundred students met in the chapel for a special prayer service.

It was not an ordinary season of prayer. After several hymns and a time for special requests it was suggested that we kneel in groups of two to four, but that we not feel rushed, and that we take time to pray two or three times if desired.

A spirit of intercession prevailed. It was my privilege to pray with a senior fellow and a sophomore girl, both of whom prayed several times, each time for a different fellow student. These prayers were not mere empty words, mere formal requests. The girl, with tears in her voice, and possibly her eyes too, pleaded that somehow a friend of hers might find Christ.

Even the most careless and indifferent student on campus could not help recognizing the presence of the Holy Spirit upon campus that day and in the commitment service that evening.

"It is a part of God's plan," we are reminded, "to grant us, in answer to the prayer of faith, that which He would not bestow did we not thus ask."—*The Great Controversy*, p. 525. Of those wonderful hours that mark the close of God's work, inspiration describes a "spirit of intercession" being seen—"even as was manifested before the great Day of Pentecost" (*Testimonies*, vol. 9, p. 126). Should not this very spirit be seen *now?* Could we put first things first, beginning *now* to really seek the Lord?

CAUSING SATAN TO TREMBLE

Every one who asks receives, and he who seeks finds, and to him who knocks it will be opened. **Luke 11:10, R.S.V.**

"The devil will let me do just about anything," commented a teacher at Andrews University, "rather than let me pray." And Satan will let the church develop just about any plan for evangelizing the world, if only he can somehow exclude a spirit of prayer and intercession.

If we would somehow only put first things first, what a difference it would make!

A youthful minister, speaking at an academy Bible conference, told how it was he learned the absolute necessity of taking time to pray. During his first year in the ministry, he said, he saw almost no conversions among those for whom he was working. He finally realized that he was keeping so busy doing God's work that he was not taking time to pray.

He decided that he would begin spending ten minutes a day interceding for others. That first morning he took off his watch, laid it on the bed, and began to pray. After praying for what seemed like a long time, he glanced at his watch. He had been on his knees for three minutes. He returned to his praying.

There is no merit, he was quick to point out, in just "putting in time." But as he took time, his prayers became more fervent. He began to notice a change in his ministry. Conviction came upon those with whom he was studying. Lives began to be changed. Opportunity after opportunity for bringing people to Christ opened up before him. The number who decided for baptism multiplied manyfold.

Are there specific persons you could be praying for in a similar fashion? Begin to think of several, asking God to lay upon you a spirit of intercession. Take time, this coming Sabbath in particular, to go apart and really pray for them. Continue throughout the coming week, and thereafter—and as you pray, remember this: "Satan cannot endure to have his powerful rival appealed to, for he fears and trembles before His [Christ's] strength and majesty. At the sound of fervent prayer, Satan's whole host trembles."—*Messages to Young People*, p. 53.

CONDITIONS FOR ANSWERED PRAYER

If my people, which are called by my name, shall humble themselves, and pray, and seek my face, and turn from their wicked ways; then will I hear from heaven, and will forgive their sin, and will heal their land. 2 Chron. 7:14.

Today's scripture brings out the conditions under which the Lord can work mightily in behalf of His people. These are that they (1) humble themselves, (2) pray, and seek His face, and (3) turn from their wicked ways.

We noticed earlier the promise that "if we would humble ourselves before God, and be kind and courteous and tenderhearted and pitiful, there would be one hundred conversions to the truth where now there is only one."—*Testimonies,* vol. 9, p. 189. The very first principle mentioned, as in today's scripture, is that we humble ourselves. We need to humble ourselves enough to make things right with God, and with one another. And "we need to have far less confidence in what man can do and far more confidence in what God can do for every believing soul."—*Christ's Object Lessons,* p. 146.

Then we are to pray, and seek God. If we are too busy to do this, if other things come first, the Spirit of God could be falling all about us without our even recognizing it. "It was by the confession and forsaking of sin, by earnest prayer and consecration of themselves to God, that the early disciples prepared for the outpouring of the Holy Spirit on the Day of Pentecost. The same work, only in greater degree, must be done now."—*Testimonies to Ministers,* p. 507.

"If I regard iniquity in my heart," wrote David, "the Lord will not hear me" (Ps. 66:18). At the lunchtime season of fasting and prayer mentioned a couple of days ago a freshman girl who came in to pray couldn't. As she knelt for the opening prayer, a quiz in which she had cheated came to mind. She left, hunted up the teacher in whose class she had cheated, and made it right. A few minutes later she was back, her face radiant. She joined one of the prayer groups—and this time she could pray with confidence.

God help us to search our hearts and forsake every cherished sin!

IT'S THE BELIEVING THAT MAKES THE DIFFERENCE

If thou canst believe, all things are possible to him that believeth. **Mark 9:23.**

It became the practice one year at Auburn Academy, where morning classes began at seven-ten, for a number of students to gather in the chapel at seven for voluntary prayer groups. The service was quite simple—a devotional thought, special requests, then prayer groups.

This opening thought was frequently brought by a former marine captain who had been converted as a result of the intercessory prayers of another person, and the challenge he presented to us one morning was this:

"It's the believing that makes the difference!"

So often, even though we are not aware of any cherished sin, and even though we pray, we don't seem to get any answers. Why? Could it be that we have not really believed? "Those who talk faith and cultivate faith," says inspiration, "will have faith, but those who cherish and express doubts will have doubts."—*Testimonies,* vol. 5, p. 302.

In other words—"It's the believing that makes the difference!"

"There can be no question in the heart of faith as to the power of God to perform His promises. . . . To abide in faith is to put aside feeling and selfish desires, to walk humbly with the Lord, to appropriate His promises, and to apply them to all occasions . . . ; it is to rely entirely, to trust implicitly, upon the faithfulness of God."—*Fundamentals of Christian Education,* pp. 341, 342.

"He staggered not at the promise of God through unbelief," the Scripture says of Abraham, "but was strong in faith, giving glory to God; and being fully persuaded that, what he had promised, he was able also to perform" (Rom. 4:20, 21).

True faith means not only to ask and believe but also to give thanks—knowing that if God has promised, and if we have complied with the conditions, the gift is ours and will be realized when we need it most.

Let us ask, then, and believe—and give thanks!

BEGINNING A WEEK OF SPECIAL REQUESTS

If two of you shall agree on earth as touching any thing that they shall ask, it shall be done for them of my Father which is in heaven. Matt. 18:19.

This promise is Heaven's encouragement for us to unite with one another in praying concerning a common request. We will mention for each day during this coming week a specific request concerning which God's people all around the world can unite their prayers. As we pray, let's put the Lord's promises to the test. He will more than fulfill the expectations of those who trust and obey Him.

Let's begin by praying most earnestly for our nearly 400,000 elementary, academy, and college youth throughout the world. What better place for revival to go forward than on Christian campuses? To make our requests specific, let us pray—

1. That God will help the teachers and administrators to have "understanding of the times, to know what Israel ought to do" (1 Chron. 12:32), so that they can help prepare the way for revival on their respective campuses;

2. That on every junior academy, academy, and college campus God will raise up consecrated youth who also will understand the need of the hour, and who will have conviction concerning what they can do to bring about a soul-winning revival on their campuses;

3. That God will remember His many children in public schools, and that He will open the way, as we put forth the effort, for these children and youth to have the privilege of a Christian education.

Inspiration has suggested that in our churches and on our campuses "companies be formed for service." "Why do not two or three meet together and plead with God for the salvation of some special one, and then for still another?" the Lord's servant inquires (*Testimonies,* vol. 7, p. 21). At one school where this was done there began to be seen changes even in some of the most indifferent students.

As faculties and students, why not do this?

"I WILL SAVE YOUR CHILDREN"

"Even the captives of the mighty shall be taken, and the prey of the tyrant be rescued, for I will contend with those who contend with you, and I will save your children." Isa. 49:25, R.S.V.

"How many of you," we have frequently asked academy student prayer groups, "have a member of the family who is not a Christian whom you would like to have remembered in prayer?" Generally almost every hand is raised—and in many instances it is for a brother or sister who has left the church.

In today's scripture, who is the "tyrant" who contends with us? Is it not Satan? And who are his "captives," his "prey"? Are they not our children, our loved ones, who have left the Lord?

Often we ourselves are responsible when our children lose interest in spiritual things. How can we permit unrestricted watching of TV, for example, and then ask the Lord to save our children? We need to make some changes first. But let's make those changes, and do what we can to redeem the mistakes we have made. God has promised to give us wisdom, and is pleased with the faith that takes Him at His word. And consider, as an encouragement, this example:

"The mother of Augustine prayed for her son's conversion. She saw no evidence that the Spirit of God was impressing his heart, but she was not discouraged. She laid her finger upon the texts, presenting before God His own words, and pleaded as only a mother can. Her deep humiliation, her earnest importunities, her unwavering faith, prevailed, and the Lord gave her the desire of her heart. Today He is just as ready to listen to the petitions of His people. . . . If Christian parents seek Him earnestly He will fill their mouths with arguments, and for His name's sake will work mightily in their behalf in the conversion of their children."—*Testimonies*, vol. 5, pp. 322, 323.

Let us with an earnestness and faith as great as that of Augustine's mother pray today for our sons and daughters (or brothers and sisters) who are not Christians—and also for those who are. We, like her, can claim specific promises, not forgetting also to thank God for His promise, "I will save your children."

72

THEY THAT SOW THE PRINTED PAGE

In the morning sow thy seed, and in the evening withhold not thine hand: for thou knowest not whether shall prosper, either this or that, or whether they both shall be alike good. **Eccl. 11:6.**

Today's text is especially appropriate as we think of the literature of the church. "Papers and books are the Lord's means of keeping the message for this time continually before the people. . . . The same ministry of angels attends the books that contain the truth as attends the work of the minister."—*Testimonies*, vol. 6, pp. 315, 316.

But the angels do not distribute these books and periodicals —that's our job. Recently our family had occasion to travel by car from the Seattle, Washington, area down to Los Angeles, then across to Oklahoma City and up to Michigan. We took a good supply of many types of literature to give out. We had dozens of opportunities to judiciously give away a booklet, a magazine, a book, or a Voice of Prophecy enrollment card. And as we left this literature, whether at a market near Columbia Academy, in Washington, or at a roadside park in Oregon, or at a service station in California, or to a roadside workman in New Mexico, or to another traveler in Kansas, we did so with the consciousness that the "ministry of angels" would attend these printed pages.

Why do we not use our literature more than we do? We need not travel to find such opportunities. If we were alert to recognize them, there would be contacts—providentially arranged— almost daily, where we could tactfully offer some kind of literature. It's an awesome thought that when you give a copy of this year's missionary book the ministry of the angels attends that book!

Let's pray today for everyone connected with the literature ministry—those who publish, those who write, and most of all, for those who go door to door as literature evangelists. And don't pray in generalities—pray for specific workers or publishing houses. Pray, too, that all around the world the conviction of the Holy Spirit will come upon church members, leading them to use more literature.

Why not through your own example begin to lead the way?

PRAY FOR GOD'S MINISTERS

The law of truth was in his mouth, and iniquity was not found in his lips: he walked with me in peace and equity, and did turn many away from iniquity. Mal. 2:6.

Today's scripture is from a passage in Malachi that portrays the opportunities and responsibilities of a minister. "He is the messenger," says the prophet, "of the Lord of hosts" (verse 7).

It was Peter, a minister of the gospel, through whom the Lord wrought so mightily on the Day of Pentecost. The Lord desires to do an even greater work today. But because the Lord's promise of His Spirit has not been appreciated as it should be, its fulfillment has not been seen as it might be. "Learning, talent, eloquence, every natural or acquired endowment," says inspiration, "may be possessed; but, without the presence of the Spirit of God, no heart will be touched, no sinner won to Christ."— *Testimonies,* vol. 8, p. 21.

"Why do we not hunger and thirst for the gift of the Spirit, since this is the means by which we are to receive power?" asks inspiration. "Why do we not talk of it, pray for it, preach concerning it?"

This suggestion is then made: "For the baptism of the Spirit every worker should be pleading with God. . . . Especially should men pray that God will baptize His missionaries with the Holy Spirit."—*Ibid.,* p. 22.

Let's make this the burden of our prayers today. Pray for God's missionaries, and for His ministers of the gospel, and for those who serve as administrators at the conference offices. Pray, too, for those who speak to millions at a time, through the Voice of Prophecy and Faith for Today. Pray that God Himself will be the answer to that longing for more of His presence. And let your pastor know you're praying for him.

Perhaps our greatest failing as ministers is that we do not take time to pray. A hundred things seem to press in—and communion with God is crowded out. Here's where a pastor's members can help by doing all they can to lessen the load—at Ingathering time, at the school, and in so many ways. Pray for your pastor—and do more than pray!

74

FOR THEY THAT HELP HEAL

And Jesus put forth his hand, and touched him, saying, I will; be thou clean. And immediately his leprosy was cleansed. Matt. 8:3.

The place—the Loma Linda Hospital. The time—evening. The occasion—a student nurse at the bedside of an elderly patient, offering a prayer for that patient.

The patient is not a member of the Seventh-day Adventist Church. But he has a warm spot in his heart for the church. The wonderful care he received during and following his surgery had a lot to do with creating his appreciation. And the thing that made the greatest impression of all was the fact that each evening a nurse took time to stop and pray for him.

Of the thirty-five recorded miracles of Jesus, twenty-three were healings. Today's scripture records how Jesus in healing a leper "put forth his hand, and touched him." It may have been years since that leper had felt the warmth of a human touch. He was unclean, shunned, feared—but Jesus touched him! And there was healing in that touch!

The medical work has been appointed by God Himself to help "prepare the way for our coming King" (*Medical Ministry,* p. 22). Let us remember, as our special request for today, the thousands of nurses and physicians and medical workers whose touch of love is helping prepare the way for the return of Christ. Pray that the ministry of heavenly angels will accompany the literature that is offered in the waiting rooms of hundreds of doctors' offices. Pray that an even greater "yearning for souls" (*ibid.,* p. 40) will be brought into the ministry of every medical worker. Pray that Christ will "be present in the sick room, filling the heart of the physician with the fragrance of His love" (*ibid.*).

Pray also for more workers, particularly in mission lands. There are so many vacancies that have not been filled, so many calls that have not been answered. Pray, yes, pray with intense earnestness that there will be hundreds and thousands more who will say, "Here am I; send me" (Isa. 6:8). Let's pray, too, for our hospital administrators, who are being confronted with ever-increasing perplexities and problems.

PRAYING FOR REPENTANCE

The sacrifices of God are a broken spirit: a broken and a contrite heart,
O God, thou wilt not despise. **Ps. 51:17.**

Revival, to be effective, must be accompanied by a deep conviction of sin—conviction that leads to changed lives. One great revivalist suggested that the most appropriate prayer for revival is, "Search me, O God, and know my heart: try me, and know my thoughts: and see if there be any wicked way in me, and lead me in the way everlasting" (Ps. 139:23, 24).

We need to pray, then, that the Spirit of God will be manifested through deep heart-searching and repentance. "We can no more repent without the Spirit of Christ to awaken the conscience than we can be pardoned without Christ. . . . Every desire for truth and purity, every conviction of our own sinfulness, is an evidence that His Spirit is moving upon our hearts." —*Steps to Christ,* p. 26.

Our heart-searching and praying should be combined with the study of God's Word. Men whom God has mightily used have sometimes spent hours in prayer. But such prayer is not a mere repeating of words over and over again. It is often prayer that has grown out of Bible study. One begins searching the Scriptures, and meditating—which leads to confession, or to thanksgiving, or to intercession, or to supplication.

Would that we might give ourselves as never before to seeking the Lord in prayer! Would that a great wave of repentance might sweep through the church! "When the message of truth was first proclaimed," wrote the servant of God, "how much we prayed. How often was the voice of intercession heard in the chamber, in the barn, in the orchard, or the grove. Frequently we spent hours in earnest prayer . . . ; often the sound of weeping was heard and then the voice of thanksgiving and the song of praise. Now the day of God is nearer than when we first believed, and we should be more earnest, more zealous, and fervent than in those early days. . . . We need now to be imbued with the spirit of Christ, and we should not rest until we receive it."—*Testimonies,* vol. 5, pp. 161, 162.

A DAY OF FASTING AND PRAYER

And he said unto them, This kind can come forth by nothing, but by prayer and fasting. Mark 9:29.

I had never given much thought to fasting, until one day in New Testament class a sophomore girl called this scripture to our attention. The fasting of the Pharisees, an external humiliation, was ignored by Jesus. Today's scripture reminds us that there is a place for fasting, however. It is not always total abstinence from food, but eating sparingly, and of simple food.

Nearly six years ago the 1966 Autumn Council sent forth, with a new urgency, a call for reformation and revival. God has blessed, but had we during these years prepared for the kind of outpouring of His Spirit that God desires to send, the work could have been finished by now. Our great need this day is to open our Bibles to Joel 2, and to seek the Lord with the kind of earnestness portrayed there.

"From the secret place of prayer," we read, "came the power that shook the world in the Great Reformation. There, with holy calmness, the servants of the Lord set their feet upon the rock of His promises."—*The Great Controversy*, p. 210. During the Augsburg struggle, Luther, it is reported, " 'did not pass a day without devoting three hours at least to prayer, and they were hours selected from those the most favorable to study' " *(ibid.)*.

We have given attention this past week to specific requests concerning the work of God. Let us make this Sabbath a day of special intercession with one specific request—that the Lord will set in motion those events that will make possible a mighty outpouring of His Spirit everywhere. Let us pray that in His providence such an outpouring can especially take place on our campuses. And that we may know that such prayers do have an effect, note the following:

"Satan is enraged at the sound of fervent prayer, for he knows that he will suffer loss."—*Testimonies*, vol. 1, p. 295.

"At the sound of fervent prayer, Satan's whole host trembles."—*Ibid.*, p. 346.

"Ask, and it shall be given you" (Matt. 7:7).

HOW TO GET PEOPLE TO CHANGE

But we all, with open face beholding as in a glass the glory of the Lord, are changed into the same image from glory to glory even as by the Spirit of the Lord. 2 Cor. 3:18.

Let us suppose that you recognize the need for removal of things that hinder the working of the Holy Spirit—but the one whom you are trying to help does not. Suppose he doesn't seem to care. What then?

People "are changed . . . by the Spirit of the Lord" as a result of beholding "the glory of the Lord." It is a law of the human mind that by beholding we become changed. As the Saviour is uplifted, a desire is awakened to become like Him—and the Spirit of God changes the beholder "into His likeness" (2 Cor. 3:18, R.S.V.).

It is as we uplift Christ, then, that we give the Holy Spirit the fullest opportunity to influence those we are trying to help. "The cross of Christ—teach it to every student over and over again," urges inspiration. "Turn the minds of your students from the glory of everything save the cross of Christ."—*Counsels to Parents and Teachers,* p. 23.

It is also our privilege, through the Word of God, to help educate the conscience. Consider from inspiration this counsel concerning how to help people to dispense with flesh food:

"In all cases educate the conscience, enlist the will, supply good, wholesome food, and the change will be readily made, and the demand for flesh will soon cease."—*The Ministry of Healing,* p. 317.

First, the conscience must be educated, giving opportunity for the Spirit of God to work. Second, the will must be enlisted—or anything we impose will be thrown off just as soon as our authority is removed. Third, we must provide something better. Whether the changes we seek involve diet, dress, amusements, or whatever, should we not utilize all three of these principles?

"The great motive powers of the soul," we are reminded, "are faith, hope, and love."—*Education,* p. 192. Let love for Christ be awakened, let faith in Him be encouraged, let the conscience be educated, and there is no habit that cannot be changed!

BEGIN WITH THE HEART

And I, if I be lifted up from the earth, will draw all men unto me. John 12:32.

Men are drawn to Christ—never driven. No one has ever become a true Christian under compulsion. You can require teen-agers to be in church every Sabbath, you can require students to attend half a dozen religious meetings every weekend —but this will not make them Christians. Unless love is there, unless the cross is uplifted, unless the services are vitalized by the presence of the Holy Spirit, one will secure, at best, only a hollow profession—and all too often, at the end, rebellion.

One can impose certain standards—and every home, every school, ought to have the highest standards—but unless love is manifested, unless the cross is uplifted, unless the Spirit of God is in what you do, you will accomplish little except to arouse a more determined resistance.

"Christianity," says inspiration, "proposes a reformation in the heart. What Christ works within, will be worked out under the dictation of a converted intellect. *The plan of beginning outside and trying to work inward has always failed, and always will fail.* God's plan with you is to begin at the very seat of all difficulties, the heart, and then from out of the heart will issue the principles of righteousness; the reformation will be outward as well as inward."—*Counsels on Diet and Foods,* p. 35. (Italics supplied.)

And what is it that appeals to the heart? The gripping spectacle of Jesus Christ "lifted up from the earth"—dying on the cross.

> "Lift Him up, this precious Saviour,
>   Let the multitude behold;
> They with willing hearts shall seek Him,
>   He will draw them to His fold;
> They shall gather from the wayside,
>   Hastening on with joyous feet,
> They shall bear the cross of Jesus,
>   And shall find salvation sweet."

MAY E. WARREN

(No. 520, *Church Hymnal*)

"JESUS CHRIST, AND HIM CRUCIFIED"

For I determined not to know any thing among you, save Jesus Christ, and him crucified. **1 Cor. 2:2.**

Before coming to Corinth, the apostle Paul had labored in Athens, where, in seeking to win the worldly-wise Athenians, he had "met logic with logic, science with science, philosophy with philosophy" (*The Acts of the Apostles,* p. 244). His work in Athens, however, had accomplished little, and as Paul thought and prayed about it he decided that in Corinth he would change his approach. He determined "not to know any thing" among the Corinthians, "save Jesus Christ, and him crucified."

Moral laxity was the accepted thing in Corinth. The favorite deity was the goddess of fertility, and her worship was accompanied by wild orgies. Gross immorality was permitted and even encouraged as a part of religion, and the Corinthians "seemed to have little thought or care beyond the pleasures and gaieties of the hour" (*ibid.*).

In spite of these influences Paul's success in Corinth was much greater than what it had been in Athens. "Many of the Corinthians hearing believed, and were baptized" (Acts 18:8). A "large church" was established. Some of those converted were from among "the most dissipated of the Gentiles and became monuments of the mercy of God and the efficacy of the blood of Christ to cleanse from sin" (*ibid.,* p. 252).

What the gospel did in Corinth, it can do today—if we will but remember that it is not eloquence or doctrinal argument that convicts and converts people, but the power of the cross of Christ.

"You can tell people about the second coming of Christ," said Emilio Knechtle at a youth rally, "and many will continue on their way totally unconcerned. You can talk of heaven, and people will say, So what? But the awful spectacle of God upon a cross breaks hearts that could be reached in no other way."

Everywhere around us are the careless and indifferent, yes, and the hardened and depraved. They will not be won by denunciation, nor by threats, nor by argument. But some of them can and will be saved if we like Paul will lift up "Jesus Christ, and him crucified." The appeal of the cross wins!

CRUCIFIED WITH CHRIST

I am crucified with Christ: nevertheless I live; yet not I, but Christ liveth in me: and the life which I now live in the flesh I live by the faith of the Son of God, who loved me, and gave himself for me. Gal. 2:20.

What does it mean to be crucified with Christ?

"We are commanded to crucify the flesh, with the affections and lusts. How shall we do it? Shall we inflict pain on the body? No; but put to death the temptation to sin. The corrupt thought is to be expelled. Every thought is to be brought into captivity to Jesus Christ. All animal propensities are to be subjected to the higher powers of the soul."—*The Adventist Home,* pp. 127, 128.

The words "flesh" or "fleshly" or "carnal lusts" refer to the lower, corrupt nature—for the body of itself cannot act contrary to the will of God. "I die daily," said Paul (1 Cor. 15:31). The inclination to sin must be put to death daily. And self, as all of us know so well, does not give up easily—it keeps coming back.

Self is easier to crucify, however, if it has not been made fat and strong by being well fed, pampered, indulged. Our two natures are in constant conflict. "The flesh lusteth against the Spirit, and the Spirit against the flesh: and these are contrary the one to the other," writes Paul (Gal. 5:17).

Suppose two wrestlers encounter each other daily. Then, let's say that you begin to starve one of them, while feeding the other one well. Will not the well-fed one soon be winning out every time?

And what is it that feeds the carnal nature? How about some of the TV programs we have been watching? "Walk in the Spirit," urges Paul, "and ye shall not fulfil the lust of the flesh" (Gal. 5:16). Let the mind be filled with the things of God—His promises, His words, the things that attract the heart heavenward.

Here, also, is another wonderful suggestion: "The surrender of all our powers to God greatly simplifies the problem of life. It weakens and cuts short a thousand struggles with the passions of the natural heart."—*Messages to Young People,* p. 30.

81

IN WHAT DO YOU GLORY?

But God forbid that I should glory, save in the cross of our Lord Jesus Christ, by whom the world is crucified unto me, and I unto the world. Gal. 6:14.

Some glory in things. "A man's life consisteth not in the abundance of the things which he possesseth," Jesus said (Luke 12:15). Yet a lot of us have a compulsion for more and more things—more luxuries, larger homes, more expensive furniture, more extras on the car, and on, and on, and on.

"The smell of a new Oldsmobile may be more of a deterrent to the Spirit of God than a few puffs of tobacco," remarked one speaker. None of us would deny the harm done to the body by smoking—yet could it be that our glorying in things is just as great a hindrance to the work of God?

Others glory in their indulgences. And many, far too many, glory in a reputation. "How many are lost by their effort to keep up a name! If one has the reputation of being a successful evangelist, a gifted preacher, a man of prayer, a man of faith, a man of special devotion, there is positive danger that he will make shipwreck of faith when tried by the little tests that God suffers to come. Often his great effort will be to maintain his reputation."—*The SDA Bible Commentary,* Ellen G. White Comments, on Rev. 3:1, p. 958.

The disciples, during the years they spent with Christ, certainly had not learned to glory in the cross. When Jesus began to tell them of His coming death on the cross, Peter tried to rebuke Him for even mentioning such a thing. But after the crucifixion, awed by the wonder of it all, they readily exclaimed, "God forbid that I should glory, save in the cross of our Lord Jesus Christ!"

We know the result. As they proclaimed the message of a crucified and risen Saviour, and as the Spirit of God was poured out upon their efforts, thousands were won to Christ. The church saw converts "flocking to her from all directions" (*Testimonies,* vol. 8, p. 19).

In what do you glory? Is the cross of Christ the all-absorbing interest of your life? Or is there something else that comes first?

YOU MUST POSSESS HIM TO CONFESS HIM

And we have seen and do testify that the Father sent the Son to be the Saviour of the world. Whosoever shall confess that Jesus is the Son of God, God dwelleth in him, and he in God. 1 John 4:14, 15.

"We have seen." We "do testify." The kind of testimony of which John speaks is a personal testimony. It is the testimony of the one who knows from personal experience what Jesus can do and is doing in his life.

Does your life confess that Jesus is the Son of God? In the words of another, "In order to confess Christ, we must have Him to confess."—*Testimonies,* vol. 1, p. 303. This observation, appropriately enough, is from a chapter entitled "Family Religion." "I was shown," the author wrote, "the necessity of opening the doors of our houses and hearts to the Lord. . . . I was shown that merely observing the Sabbath and praying morning and evening are not positive evidences that we are Christians. These outward forms may all be strictly observed, and yet true godliness be lacking."—*Ibid.,* p. 305.

And what is this "true godliness"? What is a genuine confession of Christ?

"The fruits of the Spirit manifested in the life are a confession of Him."—*Ibid.,* p. 303.

The author mentions how the husband, who so often is almost totally unacquainted with a mother's cares and burdens, is too quick to find fault if things do not go just as he feels they should. He needs to be more tender, needs to speak kind, cheerful, encouraging words.

And often, from the wife, there are fretfulness and unnecessary complaining. The husband comes home from work weary and perplexed, and "meets a clouded brow instead of cheerful, encouraging words. He is but human, and his affections become weaned from his wife" (*ibid.,* p. 307). Then, far too often, temptations from outside enter the picture—temptations that would have had no power if there had been more cheerfulness and affection shown in the home.

Love, joy, patience, kindness, gentleness, self-control—may these fruits of the Spirit be seen in our lives today!

THE TIME OF THE HOLY SPIRIT'S POWER

The kingdom of heaven is like unto a merchant man, seeking goodly pearls: who, when he had found one pearl of great price, went and sold all that he had, and bought it. Matt. 13:45, 46.

The precious pearl is Christ. Christ and His love and our privilege of possessing Him is the theme upon which we need to dwell. In the words of inspiration:

"The time of the Holy Spirit's power is the time when in a special sense the heavenly gift is sought and found."—*Christ's Object Lessons,* pp. 118, 119.

But what does it mean to "in a special sense" find Christ? How does one do it?

Joel 2 suggests special assemblies for seeking the Lord. It is when the regular routine is put aside and special thought and preparation are given to the things of God that the Spirit of God can come in with more than usual power.

This has happened so wonderfully on Bible conference weekends, when the youth who choose to go have known ahead of time that it is to be a commitment weekend. Generally the Thursday evening keynote address sets the atmosphere. It is emphasized from the beginning that Saturday evening will be a commitment service, and each person, youth and adult alike, is urged to give much thought and prayer concerning what his response will be.

The late Elder Wilton O. Baldwin, associate educational secretary of the Pacific Union, told of his impressions of the work of the Holy Spirit at a union-wide student leaders' Bible conference. In a report in the Pacific Union *Recorder* in the fall of 1969 he wrote that what he saw and heard seemed the very fulfillment of Joel's prophecy.

There must be, in our homes, on our campuses, and in our churches, deep movings of the Holy Spirit. Let Jesus be exalted as "a Prince and a Saviour, for to give repentance . . . and forgiveness of sins" (Acts 5:31), and God's Spirit will be there in power.

Let us continue to pray that God's Spirit will be able to work mightily everywhere!

HOW COULD HE DO IT?

And as Moses lifted up the serpent in the wilderness, even so must the Son of man be lifted up: that whosoever believeth in him should not perish, but have eternal life. John 3:14, 15.

It was at this night interview with Nicodemus, some three years before Calvary, that Jesus first said anything to anyone about the manner of His death. Nicodemus didn't even begin to get the full impact of what Christ said. But do we, these many centuries later?

Jesus, during His youth, had doubtless known of and possibly even seen criminals put to death by crucifixion. Rome, with ruthless efficiency, used this most agonizing of deaths to impress upon conquered peoples the fate of anyone who incurred the displeasure of the government. Explaining the agonies of such a death, Dr. Howard A. Matzke, professor of anatomy at the University of Kansas, has said that besides the pain of hanging on the nails through the hands, the stretch on chest and arm muscles prevented normal breathing. The impaired breathing, causing a decreased oxygen supply to the muscles, would result in severe muscle spasms comparable to cramps.

"To alleviate the pain of severed nerves and the muscle spasms," wrote Dr. Matzke, "the victim would try to push himself up by using the nails through his feet as a brace. Within a few minutes, the pain in the feet would become unbearable, and the body would sag again."—Quoted in Glendale *News-Press,* April 13, 1968, p. 4-A.

How could Jesus calmly, purposefully, go forward to such a death? How can we ever appreciate the magnitude of His sacrifice?

Let us at least try. Encouraging us to spend some time each day thoughtfully contemplating Christ's life, inspiration suggests: "We should take it point by point, and let the imagination grasp each scene, especially the closing ones. As we thus dwell upon His great sacrifice for us, our confidence in Him will be more constant, our love will be quickened, and we shall be more deeply imbued with His spirit."— *The Desire of Ages,* p. 83. As we approach the time of year when the world, however superficially, remembers His death, may we pause often at the cross.

UNTO JERUSALEM—TO BE KILLED

From that time forth began Jesus to shew unto his disciples, how that he must go unto Jerusalem, and suffer many things of the elders and chief priests and scribes, and be killed, and be raised again the third day. Matt. 16:21.

The incident mentioned in today's scripture evidently took place during the latter part of the summer of A.D. 30, some eight or nine months before the crucifixion in the spring of A.D. 31. Jesus and the disciples had gone to the vicinity of Caesarea Philippi, about 25 miles north of the Sea of Galilee. It has been suggested that they had spent the night in the open, somewhere in the foothills of Mount Hermon, and that Jesus had "either devoted the night to prayer or had risen early and gone apart from the disciples for a season of prayer in some quiet, secluded place" (*The SDA Bible Commentary,* on Matt. 16:13).

Jesus was about to tell the disciples, for the first time, of His coming death, and He was deeply burdened that they might be prepared to receive His words.

When He told them they were appalled. How could something like this ever be? Peter took Jesus, evidently somewhat to one side, and began to rebuke Him. "This shall not be," Peter emphatically stated. But Jesus did not allow Peter to finish. Speaking, not merely to Peter, but to Satan, Jesus commanded, "Get thee behind me, Satan."

It was one of the most severe rebukes ever spoken by Jesus. "The command means, literally, 'Get away from me!' or more freely 'Go away!' or 'Get out of my sight!' "—*Ibid.,* on Matt. 16:23. Jesus would allow nothing to turn Him aside from His intended plan to give His life for us.

Jesus knew what He was headed for. He saw it all before leaving heaven. Every bit of the insult and pain "was open to His view before He laid aside His crown and royal robe, and stepped down from the throne, to clothe His divinity with humanity. The path from the manger to Calvary was all before His eyes. He knew the anguish that would come upon Him."— *The Desire of Ages,* p. 410. Yet He was willing to do it—and would have done it for you alone.

How could He love us so much?

PASSIVELY INTERESTED?

And being in an agony he prayed more earnestly: and his sweat was as it were great drops of blood falling down to the ground. Luke 22:44.

Most Seventh-day Adventist academies and colleges require three written recommendations before considering the application of a prospective student. On these recommendation blanks there is a place to describe the religious attitude of the student. One of the several items that could be checked reads, "Passively interested." And how often on a recommendation blank this is what has been checked!

Would that such a one might go to Gethsemane!

Can you picture the scene described by today's scripture? The moon is full, the night chilly. The Saviour prays, not kneeling, as the artists so often picture, but prostrate on the ground— His arms outstretched, His fingers digging into the soil. A bloody sweat oozes from the pores and runs down onto the ground.

What is this superhuman agony? What is this "mysterious, shuddering dread?"

It is the anguish of separation from God—a separation caused by the awfulness of sin, which Christ has voluntarily taken upon Himself as our Substitute. And, also, it is the anguish of rejected love, which the devil drove home with fiendish urgency. "What are You going to gain by all this suffering?" the enemy sneered. "One of Your disciples is going to betray You. Another will deny You. All will forsake You. Your own nation is going to murder You."

"And," Lucifer might have added, "all down through the centuries ahead, very few will care. Down in the last generation, most of the people for whom You have done so much will reject You. Even some who profess to serve You will be only passively interested."

That those whom Christ loved so much should care so little pierced His heart as He lay prostrate there in Gethsemane. But did His anguish end there? Ponder, again, this:

"All heaven suffered in Christ's agony; but that suffering did not begin or end with His manifestation in humanity."— *Education*, p. 263.

Just passively interested? How can we be?

87

WHAT FAULT DO YOU FIND IN HIM?

Then said Pilate to the chief priests and to the people, I find no fault in this man. Luke 23:4.

"I find no fault in this man," said Pilate.

How about you? What about those of you, if there be such, who are only "passively interested"? What about those of you who are too ashamed of Him to say grace in a restaurant or cafeteria? What about those of you who are rejecting Him? What fault do you find in Him?

Have you pictured Jesus as some kind of soft, ethereal, even emaciated weakling who effeminately pleads for our hearts?

Some of the reasons for such distorted concepts are that religious artists have frequently pictured Jesus as somewhat effeminate. Authors of the theological volumes have so often pictured Him in a dull, dry way. The average religionist in telling of Him often does so with little enthusiasm. Emotionalists, going to the other extreme, have many times caused others to see Him in a distorted way.

But the artists are wrong. The authors are wrong. The average religionist has been wrong. The emotionalist has been wrong. If this is what you think, you are dead wrong. That Man standing before Pilate was a strong, sun-tanned outdoor Man who loved people so much that He was willing to pay any price to save them. Let's get a different picture. In the words of Peter Marshall:

"We have had enough of the emaciated Christ . . . the pale, anemic, namby-pamby Jesus. . . . Let us see the Christ of the gospels . . . striding up and down the dusty miles of Palestine . . . sun-tanned, bronzed, fearless."—CATHERINE MARSHALL, *A Man Called Peter,* p. 301.

This bronzed, fearless Man didn't have to be crucified. He was not some religious weakling who was unable to help Himself. With a single snap of His fingers He could have laid all his tormentors in the dust. But He had the self-control not to— because of love for you.

If you are one of those who have not given themselves to Christ, what is there about Him that you don't like? What fault do you find in Him? How would you want Him to be any different?

88

CHRIST—OR BARABBAS?

And they had then a notable prisoner, called Barabbas. Therefore when they were gathered together, Pilate said unto them, Whom will ye that I release unto you? Barabbas, or Jesus which is called Christ? Matt. 27:16, 17.

The Saviour had been stripped to the waist, and scourged. The blood was flowing freely down His back, staining His garments and the floor.

"Behold the Man!" Pilate exclaimed.

The whips with which He had been lashed—His back had been lacerated—may have ripped into His face, too. His face, at any rate, was stained with blood. And yet, there was no hate there. There was no lust for revenge in His eyes. There was exhaustion, and there was pain, but also there were gentleness and pity—"no cowardly weakness, but the strength and dignity of long-suffering" (*The Desire of Ages,* p. 735).

Then Barabbas was brought out. The lines on his face were hard and cruel. The glare in his eyes was fierce. He had shed blood, he had murdered—and there was hate in his face.

Barabbas and Christ—standing side by side. Barabbas, the representative of Satan. Christ, the representative of God. Representatives of two different kingdoms, two different ways of life.

And, inevitably, we are choosing one or the other. There is no middle ground. No choice is yet a choice. "It is not necessary for us deliberately to choose the service of the kingdom of darkness in order to come under its dominion. We have only to neglect to ally ourselves with the kingdom of light. If we do not co-operate with the heavenly agencies, Satan will take possession of the heart, and will make it his abiding place. The only defense against evil is the indwelling of Christ in the heart through faith in His righteousness."—*Ibid.,* p. 324.

"We must inevitably be under the control of the one or the other of the two great powers that are contending for the supremacy of the world."—*Ibid.*

The human race, every day, is choosing. You, today, will be manifesting your choice.

Christ—or Barabbas? Which will it be?

LOVE CAN TAKE A LOT

And when they had platted a crown of thorns, they put it upon his head, and a reed in his right hand: and they bowed the knee before him, and mocked him, saying, Hail, King of the Jews! And they spit upon him, and took the reed, and smote him on the head. Matt. 27:29, 30.

Matthew twice mentions that "they spit in his face" (Matt. 26:67; 27:30). A modern journalist envisioned it as having been like this:

"They bound him by the wrists to a post in the courtyard of the barracks and took turns lashing his bare back with a whip. It was a special kind of whip called a scourge, made of leather straps weighted with bits of metal. It bit into the flesh with every lash. . . .

"One barracks wit took off his scarlet legionnaire's cloak and put it over the prisoner's shoulders, in imitation of a king's royal purple robe. Another plaited a crown of sharp briars to thrust down on his head. A third put a reed in his hand to resemble a scepter. Then they hailed him: 'Long live the King of the Jews.'

"One by one they approached his blood-spattered 'throne,' kneeling before him in mock homage, then rising to spit in his face."—LOUIS CASSELS, Glendale *News-Press,* April 13, 1968, p. 4-A.

As you try to let your imagination "grasp each scene," it will help, perhaps, to remember that it was the last of March or the early part of April. The time of day when this mockery took place was probably around eight o'clock in the morning. The anguished prayer in Gethsemane may have lasted for about two hours, with the arrest by the mob coming about midnight. Between His arrest and Peter's denial at dawn, possibly about 5:30 A.M., Jesus was arraigned before Annas, and then before Caiaphas and the Sanhedrin. He was taken to Pilate, then sent to Herod, then back to Pilate, at which time the scene in today's scripture took place. Jesus was strong physically, but the agony in Gethsemane had almost killed Him. He had had no sleep, had been slapped about, scourged, and spit upon.

It is now about 8:00 A.M.—with the worst yet to come.

But love can take a lot.

THERE THEY CRUCIFIED HIM

And when they were come to the place, which is called Calvary, there they crucified him. **Luke 23:33.**

Have you ever run a thorn into your arm, or a large splinter under your fingernail? You know, if you have, the pain of a single such thorn or splinter. But what would it be like to have a crown of thorns pressed down into the tender skin of the forehead?

You quickly removed the thorn or splinter. But what would it be to have your hands tied, and a crown of thorns penetrating into the skin, remaining there to burn as fire burns?

It was, I suppose, a hundred pounds of wooden cross which was laid upon His shoulders. The scourging had left His back bloody and raw. It was probably after eight o'clock as they started toward Calvary. As they left the place of scourging there must have been left at every step stains on the pavement. When they arrived at the place of execution it was, Mark records, "the third hour"—or 9:00 A.M. "And they crucified him" (Mark 15:25).

Have you ever stepped on a nail? It hurts, it aches with an agonizing ache. You jerked away as quickly as possible. But for Christ it was a spike through one palm, then a spike through the other, then a spike through both feet. And there could be no jerking away.

Have you ever thought of some sin as small, as so inconsequential? Go to Calvary. "Behold the patient Sufferer! Upon His head is the thorny crown. His lifeblood flows from every lacerated vein. All this in consequence of sin!"—*Testimonies,* vol. 2, p. 207.

The chapter from which this description is quoted is entitled simply, "The Sufferings of Christ." If you haven't read it, you should—quietly, thoughtfully, prayerfully.

"That Christ, so excellent, so innocent, should suffer such a painful death, bearing the weight of the sins of the world, our thoughts and imaginations can never fully comprehend. . . . The contemplation of the matchless depths of a Saviour's love should fill the mind, touch and melt the soul, refine and elevate the affections, and completely transform the whole character."—*Ibid.,* p. 213.

91

"FORGIVE THEM"

Then said Jesus, Father, forgive them; for they know not what they do.
Luke 23:34.

The hill called Calvary was just a short distance outside the city wall. The time was about nine o'clock in the morning. The sun had been up for about three hours or so. Since it was about the first of April, there may have been a lingering trace of coolness, of morning freshness, still in the air. Perhaps above the surrounding hills there were white clouds. The previous night had apparently been perfectly clear, with a full Passover moon. Except for the executions about to be enacted there on the hill, it could have turned out to be just another lovely spring day.

The thieves were fastened to their instruments of torture first, cursing and struggling, wrestling with their executioners. Then it was Jesus' turn.

Can you see them? The Saviour is roughly thrown down onto the cross. There is very likely a soldier holding down each arm, another at each foot, each gripping an ankle perhaps, or the calf of the leg. A fifth soldier brings the spikes and the hammer. This time there is no struggle, no cursing. There is no word from the victim except a quiet, "Father, forgive them; for they know not what they do."

The cross was lifted by several men, and violently dropped into place. It was nine o'clock. The final six hours had now begun.

One journalist mentions that the Roman author Cicero, who witnessed numerous crucifixions, wrote that the victims often became raving madmen long before they were mercifully released by death. It was sometimes necessary, Cicero adds, to cut out a victim's tongue to stop his terrible screams and curses.

This youthful victim, instead, prayed for the forgiveness of His murderers. That prayer included us. "Upon all rests the guilt of crucifying the Son of God. To all, forgiveness is freely offered. 'Whosoever will' may have peace with God, and inherit eternal life."—*The Desire of Ages,* p. 745.

Forgiveness—freely offered to all. Peace—for whosoever will.

MORE THAN A KING

And Pilate wrote a title, and put it on the cross. And the writing was, JESUS OF NAZARETH THE KING OF THE JEWS. John 19:19.

Luke adds that this superscription was in three languages—Greek, Latin, and Hebrew (Luke 23:38).

During a student Week of Devotion at Auburn Academy it was arranged for the chapel to be open during the lunch hour for half an hour so that any student or teacher who desired to stop in for quiet meditation or prayer could do so. There was only a subdued light that came through some stained windows, with a single slide on the screen throughout the half hour. One such slide portrayed just the top part of a cross, with this sign, in its three different languages, fastened to it. Even though one could not read these languages, one knew what the sign said.

In the quiet of that chapel the significance of it all began to sink in. It was a King who hung on that cross—the King of an infinite number of milky ways. One might flash onto the same screen a picture of Andromeda, or of Orion, or of any other portion of the heavens, to try to portray a tiny fraction of His kingdom. But the vastness of it all, who could have pictured—and who would have been able to grasp it?

A King—and more than a King. He was also God. A cross is not where you expect to find any god, even a small god. Certainly not the God of all creation. On a throne, perhaps. Or passing from star to star, from milky way to milky way, superintending all. Or being worshiped. Or maybe in Eden. But not on a cross.

"Oh, what love! What amazing love! that brought the Son of God to earth to be made sin for us, that we might be reconciled to God, and elevated to a life with Him in His mansions in glory. Oh, what is man, that such a price should be paid for his redemption!"—*Testimonies,* vol. 2, pp. 211, 212.

"Such a price!" When, before long, you can travel out through the galaxies, when you see firsthand some of the glory of His kingdom, you'll understand a little better. But fully? Never!

WHY WAS HIS DEATH NECESSARY?

The Lord hath laid on him the iniquity of us all. Isa. 53:6.

In our academy Bible classes the question has sometimes come up, "Why did Christ have to die?"

God is love. When someone has sinned, and is repentant, why couldn't that person be forgiven without someone having to die?

"If I were a father," said a student, "and my son did wrong, and was truly repentant, I would just forgive him. I wouldn't expect him or anyone else to have to die for that wrong. Why does God require such an awful price?"

It's a good question. What would you answer? Why was the cross necessary?

George H. Morrison, the well-known Scottish Presbyterian pastor, answered it this way:

"God is more than a private person; God is the moral ruler of the universe. A father forgives his child freely if the child is penitent; but if the father is a judge he cannot forgive a criminal like that, even though the criminal is his child; it is his duty to uphold and administer the law in the highest interests of the state, and if he pardoned the criminal on the ground that he was penitent, the country would lapse into lawlessness and chaos." —Quoted in *Decision* Magazine, Dec. 1964, p. 12.

When Adam and Eve sinned, there was more at stake than just this planet. How God would deal with this problem would affect the future of the whole universe.

What would you have done? A wrong decision could have lessened the confidence of the watching universe in that justice which is the foundation of His government. It could have led to the ultimate disintegration of law and order elsewhere in the universe. How could God forgive, as His heart ever yearns to do, and at the same time maintain His law?

There was only one possible solution. Through the death of Christ both mercy and justice could be maintained. Pardon could be freely given, without the law being belittled. But what a price had to be paid! Do we even begin to appreciate such wonderful love?

WATCHING GOD DIE

And sitting down they watched him there. Matt. 27:36.

The previous verse tells that they crucified Him, and then parted His garments. Then—"sitting down they watched him there."

Who were the "they"? The soldiers, no doubt. Possibly, after a time, some of the Pharisees and priests. And perhaps some of the idly curious. Those who loved Him were probably standing in small groups, or singly, but as close to the cross as they dared. Their hearts were breaking. It is not likely that they would be among those who would simply sit down and watch.

But all of them, whether seated or standing, were watching the most incredible event of all ages—the God of all creation, the One whose goings forth had been "from the days of eternity," dying there on a cross.

There were other watchers. The whole universe was watching. And how did they regard it?

"Heaven viewed with grief and amazement Christ hanging upon the cross, blood flowing from His wounded temples, and sweat tinged with blood standing upon His brow. From His hands and feet the blood fell, drop by drop, upon the rock drilled for the foot of the cross. The wounds made by the nails gaped as the weight of His body dragged upon His hands. His labored breath grew quick and deep, as His soul panted under the burden of the sins of the world. . . . What a sight for the heavenly universe!"—*The Desire of Ages,* p. 760.

What a sight! Let the imagination grasp this scene. Can you, in your mind's eye, see "the rock drilled for the foot of the cross"? Will you watch, as drop by drop, the blood drops stain that rock?

The blood of a good man? Yes, but more than that. The blood of a great King? Yes, but more than that. For this is the blood of God—the blood of the One Isaiah called, "The mighty God, the everlasting Father, the Prince of Peace" (Isa. 9:6).

Del Delker sings so beautifully, "Each drop of blood bought me a million years." And so it has. A million years—and more.

If only we will reach out by faith and accept it!

FOR OUR HEALING

But he was wounded for our transgressions, he was bruised for our iniquities: the chastisement of our peace was upon him; and with his stripes we are healed. Isa. 53:5.

Mark records that as Jesus hung there on the cross, "when the sixth hour was come, there was darkness over the whole land until the ninth hour" (Mark 15:33). This darkness apparently descended quite suddenly. Inspiration mentions cursing and reviling ceasing "in the midst of half-uttered sentences," with men, women, and children falling to the earth (*The Desire of Ages*, p. 754). As the darkness falls, "the silence of the grave" descends upon that hill. Then, after a time there is some whispering, and then others, wailing in fear, try to grope their way through the darkness back toward the city.

Again, let your imagination grasp the scene. "Vivid lightnings occasionally flashed forth from the cloud, and revealed the cross and the crucified Redeemer."—*Ibid.*

What did Jesus think about as He hung there? Or was the pain so intense that He found it difficult to think? It wasn't just physical pain that wrenched His soul and body. It was the darkness of His separation from God. Sin is so offensive that He fears this separation will be eternal. "So great was this agony that His physical pain was hardly felt."—*Ibid.*, p. 753.

Did He think for a moment of the power He had laid aside—power to speak worlds, solar systems, milky ways, the universe, into existence? Could He have heard again, far off, the reverberating notes of a creation hymn? Did there pass before His vision the splendor of the galaxies He had left behind, and risked losing for always—the flung-out glory of millions of suns and stars and milky ways all circling His throne? Or would His mind have lingered more on the peace and love of His heavenly home, and upon the grateful loyalty of His numberless realms of adoring subjects? We do not know, but this we do know:

"The blows that fell to him have brought us healing" (Isa. 53:5, Moffatt).*

---

* From *The Bible: A New Translation* by James Moffatt. Copyright by James Moffatt 1954. Used by permission of Harper & Row, Publishers, Incorporated.

THOSE STAINS

For God loved the world so dearly that he gave up his only Son, so that everyone who believes in him may have eternal life, instead of perishing. John 3:16, Moffatt.

The darkness surrounding Calvary lifted just before Jesus died, and the light of heaven encircled His head, causing His face to shine like the sun. With clear, trumpetlike tones He exclaimed, "It is finished." "Father, into thy hands I commend my spirit." He breathed a last breath, His head slumped forward—and He was gone.

You know the rest of the story—how two wealthy and heretofore undeclared friends came forward to give Him a decent burial, how His body was taken down, how it was carefully wrapped in a linen sheet, and how it was borne, late that Friday afternoon, to its place of rest.

While the shades of evening are gathering, let's go back up to the spot where He was crucified. As we climb toward it, we see the crosses are still there, outlined against the clouds of the evening sky. Arriving, we find the crowds gone, the Pharisees gone, the curiosity-seekers gone. We stand there in the silence, alone.

It's still light enough to see, and we gather about the center cross. Before night falls, before that cross disappears into history, there is something we ought to see. It's the stains. Notice the stains on the rock first. It's the blood of the eternal God that made those stains. Can you grasp that?

Then step back a foot or two and look at the crossbars, where His hands were fastened. There are stains there too. Note the upright, where the back would have rubbed. There are stains there too. Finally, glance down to where the feet had been spiked to the rough wood. The feet bled too—likewise staining the wood.

The sun is about to sink beyond the stormy horizon. There is red upon the clouds. The Sabbath is about to begin. It will be a grandly beautiful sunset.

The stains will fade into the twilight, into oblivion. The cross will be taken down, perhaps used again, eventually cast aside. But don't forget the message of those stains. It's John 3:16.

AN UNFORGETTABLE SABBATH

And they returned, and prepared spices and ointments; and rested the Sabbath day according to the commandment. **Luke 23:56.**

What a Sabbath!

The men responsible for the death of Christ went to church, of course. The courts of the Temple were filled with worshipers. The high priest, splendidly dressed, who had led out in the murder of Christ, was at the service. The choir and the trumpets and the musical instruments were as loud and clear as usual.

Yet there was a strangeness about everything. For one thing, the heavy tapestry that formed the veil which had shielded the Most Holy Place had been mysteriously ripped from top to bottom—doubtless by an angel hand. A sense of dread, a feeling of impending calamity, pervaded many hearts.

There was no happiness that day among the worshipers. The priests did not find victory sweet. They could not put the uncomplaining Sufferer out of their minds. They feared that at any moment He might stand before them, and, like their father the devil, they believed and trembled. As for Satan and his host of evil angels, they would try desperately to keep the Saviour in the tomb, but they must have realized it wouldn't work.

What a contrast to this was the feeling in the courts of heaven! The One who had lived in the shadow of the cross from the days of eternity was quietly sleeping. The price of sin had been paid, and He was at rest. God's law had been vindicated, Satan's administration exposed, and the ultimate destruction of sin assured.

It was as if the cross had two sides to it, one side the side of shadows, the other side blazing with glory. And it was as if eternity itself could be divided into two parts, with the shadow of the cross stretching all the way back into the infinite past, and the glory of the cross shining all the way into the infinite future. And the Prince of Sufferers had just passed from the side of the shadow to the side of joyous light.

Well might the watching universe rejoice!

"HE IS RISEN"

And entering into the sepulchre, they saw a young man sitting on the right side, clothed in a long white garment; and they were affrighted. And he saith unto them, Be not affrighted: Ye seek Jesus of Nazareth, which was crucified: he is risen; he is not here: behold the place where they laid him. Mark 16:5, 6.

These words of Scripture are among the most descriptive in all the Bible. The women, tears in their eyes, have made their way through the early morning freshness to the tomb. As soon as they arrive they discover to their horror that the stone has been removed. An angel in the form of a young man invites them to enter the tomb. In fear and wonderment they step inside, to find another young man there. "Do not be frightened," he says. "You seek Jesus; He is not here. He is risen." Then, pointing to the ledge where the body of Jesus had lain, the young man invites, "Behold the place where they laid Him."

Enter that tomb, in your imagination, while the angel and the women are still there. See the ledge where for some thirty hours His body had lain. Then, stepping back outside to a few yards distant, behold the stone that has been rolled away.

Had you been there earlier, while it was still dark, you could have seen the one hundred Roman troops as they stood guard. As you watched in the early morning darkness you would have seen heaven's mightiest angel descending, parting the darkness before him. "As soon as his feet touched the ground it quaked beneath his tread. . . . The angel approached the grave, rolled away the stone as though it had been a pebble, and sat upon it." — *The SDA Bible Commentary,* Ellen G. White Comments, on Matt. 28:2, p. 1110.

Another angel entered the tomb, and unwound the graveclothes. The angel who had removed the stone then spoke, "Thy Father calls Thee; come forth." Moments later the Saviour stood in the entrance, proclaiming, "I am the resurrection, and the life." The angels and the Saviour departed, leaving the guards to tell the story.

And what a story!

THE RELIGION OF THE OPEN TOMB

For I delivered unto you first of all that which I also received, how that Christ died for our sins according to the scriptures; and that he was buried, and that he rose again the third day according to the scriptures. 1 Cor. 15:3, 4.

Some years ago Dr. Harry Rimmer, while carrying on business in the Middle East, had occasion to do some negotiating with an important officer of the Egyptian Government. As he talked with this officer, a refined and cultured gentleman, the conversation turned to religion.

"We believe that God has given to man three revelations of Himself," said Dr. Rimmer.

"We too believe that," said the officer, who was a Moslem.

"We believe that God has revealed Himself in the works of creation," Dr. Rimmer stated.

"We too believe that."

"We believe that God has revealed Himself in a Book, the Holy Bible," Dr. Rimmer went on.

"We believe," said the officer, "that God has revealed Himself in a book, the Koran."

"We believe that God has revealed Himself in a man, and that man is Jesus Christ," continued Dr. Rimmer.

"We believe that God has revealed Himself in a man, and that man is the prophet Mohammed," was the officer's reply.

"We believe that Jesus died to save His followers."

"We believe that Mohammed died for his people," said the officer.

"We believe," said Dr. Rimmer, "that Jesus is able to substantiate His claims because He rose from the dead."

Here the Moslem official hesitated. Then his eyes fell, and finally he replied, "We have no information concerning our prophet after his death."

Christianity, as Elder H. M. S. Richards puts it, is the religion of the open tomb. And for us, though "the wages of sin is death, . . . the gift of God is eternal life through Jesus Christ our Lord" (Rom. 6:23).

A MOMENT OF SILENCE

Your life is hid with Christ in God. When Christ, who is our life, shall appear, then shall ye also appear with him in glory. Col. 3:3, 4.

The Los Angeles *Times* recently described a battlefield memorial at El Alamein, Egypt, where one of the decisive battles of World War II was fought. It was here that the allies under General Montgomery defeated the forces led by Field Marshal Erwin Rommel. Concerning this battlefield, lying between "the turquoise sea and the desert," the *Times* said:

"In the spring, with the desert wild flowers in bloom, El Alamein is a strangely beautiful place, an unearthly landscape where lie the bones of about 12,000 soldiers. The overpowering impression for the visitor is one of silence, loneliness, and an emptiness under the blue-white sky, and a deep sense of futility."

Except for Christ, we might all share that futility. To many people, including most teen-agers, death is a subject that one just doesn't mention. If possible, one doesn't even think about it. But to the Christian the resurrection of Christ is an assurance that death need not be feared. Here, from the chapter in *The Desire of Ages* entitled "The Lord Is Risen," is what is probably the most beautiful passage ever penned concerning death:

"To the believer, death is but a small matter. Christ speaks of it as if it were of little moment. 'If a man keep My saying, he shall never see death,' 'he shall never taste of death.' To the Christian, death is but a sleep, a moment of silence and darkness. The life is hid with Christ in God, and 'when Christ, who is our life, shall appear, then shall ye also appear with Him in glory.' John 8:51, 52; Col. 3:4."—Page 787.

That which is only "a moment of silence" is not something to be feared. As the same author words it, "Jesus lives, and because He lives, we shall live also. From grateful hearts, from lips touched with holy fire, let the glad song ring out, Christ is risen!"—*Ibid.*, p. 794.

THE FOLDED LINEN

Then cometh Simon Peter following him, and went into the sepulchre, and seeth the linen clothes lie, and the napkin, that was about his head, not lying with the linen clothes, but wrapped together in a place by itself. John 20:6, 7.

What was the incident behind this folded napkin, and the linen wrappings left there in the tomb of Jesus? The author of *The Desire of Ages* gives this interesting insight:

"The graveclothes were not thrown heedlessly aside, but carefully folded, each in a place by itself. . . . It was Christ Himself who had placed those graveclothes with such care. When the mighty angel came down to the tomb, he was joined by another, who with his company had been keeping guard over the Lord's body. As the angel from heaven rolled away the stone, the other entered the tomb, and unbound the wrappings from the body of Jesus. But it was the Saviour's hand that folded each, and laid it in its place."—Page 789.

"Let all things be . . . in order," wrote Paul (1 Cor. 14:40). Is not this incident an illustration of the principle Paul mentions? Even at this dramatic moment, when He had just been called forth from the dead, the Saviour did not overlook the importance of neatness, but carefully folded the graveclothes.

What kind of order was your room left in this morning? If you have just arisen, or perhaps are reading this morning watch thought while yet in bed, will you take time to make your bed, and straighten up your room before leaving for school or for work?

It has been my privilege to organize dozens of camping trips and ski outings for teen-agers. On a number of occasions this has involved renting a portion of a lodge or dorm facility. The facility was neat when we arrived, and we managed to make sure we left it that way. But during the course of our stay, what disarray there sometimes was in many of the rooms—the contents of suitcases strewn about, clothes left lying around, towels not hung up.

Why did John mention this apparently insignificant detail about the folded napkin? Is Heaven encouraging us to be just as neat and orderly?

JESUS DREW NEAR

And it came to pass, that, while they communed together and reasoned, Jesus himself drew near, and went with them. Luke 24:15.

It is late Sunday afternoon on the day of Christ's resurrection. Let us join two of the friends of Christ as they leave Jerusalem to return to their home in Emmaus, about eight miles away. They had heard earlier that day that the body of Christ was no longer in the tomb, and had also gotten the report that certain of the women had seen Him. But they were slow to believe. Utterly disheartened, they have decided to return home. As they walk along, they talk over the crucifixion and the events of the day.

They have not gone far when a Stranger joins them. The disciples, barely glancing toward Him, continue their conversation. As they recount to themselves the crucifixion, they cannot restrain their grief, and tears fill their eyes. At this point, the Stranger interrupts. "What are you discussing, that you are so sad?" He asks.

Amazed at this Stranger's ignorance, they tell Him of the crucifixion, and of their crushed hopes. This gives Jesus the opportunity He has been waiting for. As they walk along, He opens to them the Scriptures and explains the various prophecies about the sufferings of Christ.

They are thrilled at His words, but do not suspect who this Stranger is. They assume He is someone who has been at the Passover and is now returning home. He steps as carefully as they over the rough stones on the mountain road, and, like them, pauses to rest now and then. The sun sets about six-thirty, and by the time they reach Emmaus, it is dark.

You know the rest of the story—how this Stranger is constrained to spend the night with them, and how, as He lifts His hands to bless the food, they see the nailprints. They rise to cast themselves at His feet, but He vanishes out of sight. The food untasted, their weariness forgotten, they rise, and though it is now probably eight o'clock, they start back to Jerusalem with the good news.

"Jesus himself drew near." He will draw just as near to walk with you this day if you invite Him.

"DID NOT OUR HEART BURN WITHIN?"

And they said one to another, Did not our heart burn within us, while he talked with us by the way, and while he opened to us the scriptures? Luke 24:32.

Have you ever wondered whether Jesus was all He claimed to be? Was He truly the Son of God?

The miracles of Christ are a proof of His divinity. But an even stronger proof that He is the world's Redeemer is found in comparing the prophecies of the Old Testament with the history of the New Testament.

We do not know what scriptures Jesus explained as He walked along with these two friends on their way home to Emmaus that Sunday evening. He certainly must have included Isaiah 53, which so vividly foretells the sufferings of Christ, giving details about His death that no mere human writer living centuries before Christ could have known. And none can deny that Isaiah *was* written long before the time of Christ. The Dead Sea scrolls have silenced the critics on this point.

When these two disciples discovered who the Stranger really was they had walked along with, they could scarcely contain their joy. This was so fantastic, so wonderful, it was beyond words.

So with us. We can know that it *was* the Son of God who walked with these men that Sunday evening. His resurrection really did occur. Nothing else can explain the power of early Christianity. Nothing else can explain what it was that so transformed these early believers. At the death of Christ the handful of people who had been following Him lost all hope. They were so depressed, so fearful for their lives, that the better known among them hid behind locked doors. Then a few days later this same handful of people radiated courage and enthusiasm. Nothing could stop them—not the hatred of their own nation, not the armies of Rome, not death itself. Their witness concerning Christ, in the words of their enemies, "turned the world upside down" (Acts 17:6).

Only the resurrection of Christ can account for it! As we realize all this means, our hearts, too, should burn within us. And we like the apostles should be radiating courage and enthusiasm!

YOU ARE MY WITNESSES

Thus it behoved Christ to suffer, and to rise from the dead the third day: and that repentance and remission of sins should be preached in his name among all nations, beginning at Jerusalem. And ye are witnesses of these things. **Luke 24:46-48.**

After the two disciples at Emmaus finally recognized the Saviour, and He had suddenly vanished, they left immediately to return to Jerusalem. Apparently it is about eight o'clock as they start up that eight-mile-long mountain path, and the moon is not yet up. Some parts of the road are not safe, and there are times when they slip on the smooth rocks as they climb over the steep places. Sometimes they lose the path completely, and have to find it again.

What they do not know is that the One who had walked with them down that path a couple of hours earlier is still with them, and they have His protection. "Sometimes running, sometimes stumbling, they press forward, their unseen Companion close beside them all the way."—*The Desire of Ages,* p. 801. The moon has risen as they enter Jerusalem, and they make their way to the same upper chamber where Jesus had spent that last evening before His death. They know this is where they will find the disciples. After they give their names, and the door is unbarred, they enter, and Another, unseen, enters with them.

They discover a surprised excitement in the room. "The Lord is risen indeed, and hath appeared to Simon," they are told (Luke 24:34). Then these two travelers, still almost breathless from their trip, tell their story. They have scarcely finished, when they see Jesus standing there in their midst.

Again, you know the rest of the story. Jesus impresses upon them that they are His witnesses, and that the good news is to be taken to all nations. We do not know what time the meeting broke up, but we can imagine that none of them slept very much that night. There was so much to talk about, and so much to praise God for.

What we do know is that the commission given that evening there in that room is now ours. As He asks, "Whom shall I send?" are you ready to answer, "Here am I; send me" (Isa. 6:8)?

"LOVEST THOU ME MORE THAN THESE?"

Simon, son of Jonas, lovest thou me more than these? John 21:15.

Do you love Jesus more than *anything* else?

This was the question Jesus pressed home to Peter that morning. Seven of the disciples had gone fishing, but though they had toiled all night they had caught nothing. As they were coming in, just at dawn, a lone Watcher there on the shore had inquired of their success. Upon their reply that they had caught nothing, He bade them cast their net on the right side of the ship. This they did, and were not able to draw it in for the multitude of the fishes.

It was then that they recognized the Stranger as the Lord, and discovered when they reached the shore that He had built a fire and had breakfast cooking. After the fish have been brought in, and the preparation for breakfast is completed, Jesus invites them to come and eat. It is then, while they are eating together there by the seaside, that Jesus looks directly at Peter, and asks, "Lovest thou me more than these?"

For us, the "these" might be other individuals, or it could be things, or both. If you had to choose between Him and some cherished dream, some favorite indulgence, some possession, which would it be? Suppose He should ask you, for His sake, to discard every record, every book upon which you could not ask God's blessing. Which would it be—your records, or Him?

In your imagination go back to that April morning there by the lake. Join them there for breakfast. As you eat, imagine the expressive, clear eyes of Jesus looking directly at you. He lifts a palm, with its still very noticeable scar, and with a light sweep of the hand, as if to indicate whatever it is that might come between you and Him, He asks, "Lovest thou me more than these?"

What would your answer have been?

For you, as for Peter, there is a work He wants you to do. It may mean feeding His sheep, or it may be the more gentle work of caring for His lambs. But whatever or wherever it is, the first qualification is that you love Jesus more than anything else.

BEGINNING AT JERUSALEM

And he said unto them, Go ye into all the world, and preach the gospel to every creature. Mark 16:15.

The disciples were to take the good news to "all nations, beginning at Jerusalem" (Luke 24:47).

A Seventh-day Adventist girl in her late teens, noticing an elementary-age neighbor boy up the street, invited him to come to Sabbath school. And she did more than just give an invitation—she arranged for him to ride with her family each week. His parents were not the least interested in religion, for the boy's father operated a liquor outlet. But the boy continued to attend, off and on, through many months.

Then this older friend began to talk to him about someday attending a Seventh-day Adventist academy. Again, she did more than talk. She began to work on the problem of finances, and eventually he went off to boarding school. While there he was baptized, and he is now in a Seventh-day Adventist college.

Suppose this teen-age girl hadn't taken a personal interest in her neighbor. What likelihood is there that he would ever have found Christ? "Many have gone down to ruin who might have been saved if their neighbors, common men and women, had put forth personal effort for them."—*The Desire of Ages,* p. 141.

How many are there on your street who might find salvation if someone would take a personal interest in them? What are Christ's feelings when we neglect this work? "Would we know how Christ regards it?" asks inspiration. "How would a father or mother feel, did they know that their child, lost in the cold and the snow, had been passed by, and left to perish, by those who might have saved it? Would they not be terribly grieved, wildly indignant? Would they not denounce those murderers with wrath hot as their tears, intense as their love? The sufferings of every man are the sufferings of God's child, and those who reach out no helping hand to their perishing fellow beings provoke His righteous anger."—*Ibid.,* p. 825.

You would, surely, try to help someone lost in the snow. Should not our efforts be just as earnest for those lost in sin?

WHAT! US?

And unto the angel of the church of the Laodiceans write; These things saith the Amen, the faithful and true witness, the beginning of the creation of God; I know thy works, that thou art neither cold nor hot: I would thou wert cold or hot. Rev. 3:14, 15.

Ever taste a lukewarm bottle of 7Up? It's an illustration, perhaps, of God's distaste for lukewarmness in our attitude toward Him and toward the needs of our neighbors.

Early Sabbathkeeping Adventists did not think of themselves as being Laodiceans. But in 1856 messages began to come through Mrs. White that it was *we,* not our neighbors, who were the church of the Laodiceans. (See *Testimonies,* vol. 1, pp. 141-146, 186.) As Elder Arthur W. Spalding puts it, "This message shocked the believers. What! they Laodiceans? But under the conviction of the Holy Spirit the message was accepted, at least by some, and a new birth of humility and zeal resulted."—*Review and Herald,* July 26, 1951, p. 4.

Elder Spalding then relates how as the years passed, the old subtle temptation to look to the works of the law rather than the grace of Christ again prevailed. Then came the 1888 General Conference, with the issue squarely put: Shall we trust to our keeping of the law for righteousness, or to the grace of Christ? Again, a new birth came to the church, and in 1892 the servant of God wrote, "The loud cry of the third angel has already begun in the revelation of the righteousness of Christ."—*Selected Messages,* book 1, p. 363. But, again, human self-sufficiency got in the way, and the fullness of the loud cry that might have been did not develop.

When will we be humble enough to be used of God for the full and final display of His mercy, His grace, and His love? To bring us to the place of this humble trust and submission is the purpose of the Laodicean message. This message is not to be used to tear down, but to build up.

The "faithful and true Witness" knows your spiritual needs, and He knows mine. He sees our lukewarmness, and offers to us a remedy. Let our hearts be thrown open to Him, that He may correct and heal.

THE HUMILITY LAODICEA NEEDS

For thus saith the high and lofty One that inhabiteth eternity, whose name is Holy; I dwell in the high and holy place, with him also that is of a contrite and humble spirit, to revive the spirit of the humble, and to revive the heart of the contrite ones. Isa. 57:15.

A key problem of Laodicea, according to the true Witness, is an attitude of "I am rich, and increased with goods, and have need of nothing" (Rev. 3:17).

An attitude of self-sufficiency makes it impossible for the Spirit of God to work with mighty power. This self-sufficiency is not always founded on an increase of goods, either. It is based all too often on a subtle spiritual pride in which one looks at the failings of others, and then congratulates himself that he is not like them.

It may be done ever so unconsciously. But in such a heart the love of Jesus is absent. And no amount of skill, no amount of knowledge, no amount of eloquence, no amount of zeal in upholding the standards, no amount of money given, can compensate for the lack of the love of Jesus. Without this tender, compassionate love, the more zealous our efforts, the more we will misrepresent God.

The lack of this love explains why the latter rain has not come. When a person is self-sufficient, when he is in any way harsh toward others, it would be disastrous to entrust him with the power of the Holy Spirit. As Elder A. Graham Maxwell put it at the 1970 General Conference: "We speak confidently of the coming of the latter rain. But will the Holy Spirit give us energy and influence to misrepresent God?"—*General Conference Bulletin,* No. 8, June 21, 1970, p. 16.

We should thank God every day of our life for the promise in today's scripture. And it should influence our attitude toward others. In a short two-page message concerning the straying sheep, the servant of God, before quoting Isaiah 57:15, pleads, "If you see one whose words or attitude shows that he is separated from God, do not blame him. It is not your work to condemn him, but come close to his side to give him help."—*Testimonies,* vol. 6, p. 125.

This kind of humbleness God will surely bless!

THE GOLD LAODICEA NEEDS

I counsel thee to buy of me gold tried in the fire, that thou mayest be rich; and white raiment, that thou mayest be clothed, and that the shame of thy nakedness do not appear; and anoint thine eyes with eyesalve, that thou mayest see. Rev. 3:18.

What is this gold? What is the white raiment, and the eyesalve?

James speaks of those who are "rich in faith" (James 2:5). White raiment, throughout the Bible, is symbolic of purity, and in many instances, of the righteousness of Christ. The eyesalve, one would conclude, would have to do with one's vision, one's discernment.

It is thus inspiration defines these. "The gold . . . is faith and love. . . . The white raiment is purity of character, the righteousness of Christ imparted to the sinner. . . . The eyesalve is that wisdom and grace which enables us to discern between the evil and the good, and to detect sin under any guise."—*Testimonies,* vol. 4, p. 88.

"Buy of me gold," Christ invites. It is not purchased with money. Heaven's riches are "without money and without price" (Isa. 55:1). It is a purchase made by earnest desire, through the surrender of self, so that there can be an infilling of God's Spirit—through whom "the love of God is shed abroad in our hearts" (Rom. 5:5).

It is through faith and love that God is enabled to do mighty works in our behalf. Why, for example, do we not see more healings? Consider this: "The power of love was in all Christ's healing, and only by partaking of that love, through faith, can we be instruments for His work. If we neglect to link ourselves in divine connection with Christ, the current of life-giving energy cannot flow in rich streams from us to the people. . . . Unbelief separates the church from her divine Helper. Her hold on eternal realities is weak. By her lack of faith, God is disappointed, and robbed of His glory."—*The Desire of Ages,* p. 825.

God is looking for instruments who, recognizing their need, will partake of this love, and who, through faith, will bring the power of His presence among us. Will you become such a one?

You will then, through Him, become rich indeed!

THE RAIMENT LAODICEA NEEDS

And this is his name whereby he shall be called, THE LORD OUR RIGHT-EOUSNESS. Jer. 23:6.

"I counsel thee to buy of me . . . white raiment, that thou mayest be clothed, and that the shame of thy nakedness do not appear" (Rev. 3:18). This raiment, as we have noted, "is purity of character, the righteousness of Christ imparted to the sinner."

Many young people, and a lot of older ones as well, do not understand righteousness by faith. They think that they must do something to earn salvation. But salvation is not earned. It is a gift. You accept it by accepting Christ. "If you give yourself to Him, and accept Him as your Saviour, then, sinful as your life may have been, for His sake you are accounted righteous. Christ's character stands in place of your character, and you are accepted before God just as if you had not sinned."—*Steps to Christ*, p. 62.

What more could you ask? Christ's character in place of your character. Accepted before God just as if you had not sinned. This is justification by faith. Once young people can see this they no longer feel that it is no use trying. They see that victory *is* possible.

And God does more than justify a person. Through the Holy Spirit, He changes your heart. Day by day, as you cooperate with Him, He changes you. You will make mistakes, but unless you turn your back upon Christ, His character still stands in place of your character. At any point along the way, and at every point, you can continue to be "accepted before God just as if you had not sinned."

The very moment you confess a sin and make it right, that sin is forgiven. No matter how unworthy you feel, you are forgiven. By God's grace you can leave both your sin and your guilt feelings at the foot of the cross. What a glorious new enthusiasm for life this truth can produce! No matter what your mistakes of yesterday, today is a fresh, glorious new day. Christ is your righteousness.

I need to pause and remind myself of this wonderful truth frequently. It brings new hope, new courage, to the heart!

111

THE EYESALVE LAODICEA NEEDS

Give therefore thy servant an understanding heart to judge thy people, that I may discern between good and bad. 1 Kings 3:9.

The youthful Solomon, shortly after coming to the throne, held a great festival of thanksgiving at Gibeon, a little town about five miles northwest of Jerusalem. It was there that "the Lord appeared to Solomon in a dream by night: and God said, Ask what I shall give thee" (1 Kings 3:5).

Suppose God should come to you, giving you opportunity to ask for anything you might wish. For what would you ask?

Solomon asked for "an understanding heart"—a heart that would be able to "discern between good and bad." Would you desire above all else that you might have the ability to tell the difference between good and bad?

"Anoint thine eyes with eyesalve, that thou mayest see," Laodicea is urged (Rev. 3:18). This eyesalve is defined as "that wisdom and grace which enables us to discern between the evil and the good, and to detect sin under any guise" (*Testimonies,* vol. 4, p. 88).

This wisdom is the fruit, as Solomon's request so well puts it, of "an understanding heart." But how does one develop an understanding heart? Read sometime the one hundred and nineteenth psalm, and notice how many times David mentions "understanding." He clearly indicates from whence this understanding comes. "The entrance of thy words giveth light; it giveth understanding unto the simple" (verse 130).

Can you "detect sin under any guise"?

Some of us may be finishing income tax reports tonight. Have we left any income unreported? Would our report pass the inspection of heavenly auditors? And in our leisure-time activities can we "detect sin under any guise"? How about our social relationships? Would a heavenly escort be acceptable to us at every place and at any time? Has every absence excuse written for our children been completely honest? Has every business transaction been "as transparent as sunlight"?

"Through thy precepts," wrote the psalmist, "I get understanding: therefore I hate every false way" (verse 104).

HOW TO BE A "SUCCESSFUL" DEVIL

For we are not ignorant of his [Satan's] devices. 2 Cor. 2:11.

I have sometimes told my Bible classes that we should offer a religion course in our schools entitled "How to Be a Successful Devil." Its purpose, of course, would not be to add to the forces of the enemy, but to study the enemy's devices—to understand and see through the techniques he uses to mislead and destroy.

In war probably nothing disturbs an enemy more than for the opposition to be aware of his every device. And nothing disturbs Satan more than for us to understand his devices. So put yourself momentarily in Satan's place. How would you go about getting people to sin?

Let's review a few principles of temptation, a few techniques and devices a successful devil would use. Then, by God's grace, may we have the "eyesalve," the spiritual discernment, to detect —and avoid—"sin under any guise."

A devil would quickly discover that his most effective allurements are those appealing to the physical nature of man. He would do well, then, to create an atmosphere where sensuality flourished—using every entertainment and communication medium possible. For individuals not readily ensnared, he would need to apply the "one wrong step leads to another" principle—beginning with little indiscretions, little departures from purity and uprightness.

A successful devil should do everything possible to encourage man's inclination to call attention to himself. He should exploit the tendency towards skepticism, planting seeds of doubt wherever possible. He should encourage men to rationalize. The old argument, "I don't see anything wrong with it," would often work. Keep your subject so blinded that he can truly say, "I don't *see.*" And specialize in using halfhearted Christians—their noncommittal position will lead many astray. A lukewarm Christian is the devil's best ally.

Have we stimulated some thought? Read at your first opportunity the chapter in *The Great Controversy* entitled "The Snares of Satan." May God give you the discernment to see and avoid Satan's devices.

THE REPENTANCE LAODICEA NEEDS

As many as I love, I rebuke and chasten: be zealous therefore, and repent.
Rev. 3:19.

In our academy Bible doctrines class we generally spend several days on Revelation 2 and 3, where the messages to the seven churches are recorded. We discover in our study, or course, that these messages, while they had some local application, also cover seven periods of church history—from the time of the apostles right down to the second coming of Christ. We discover that these messages to the seven churches generally have four parts, namely, (1) praise, (2) reproof, (3) counsel, and (4) a promised reward. Two churches, however, receive no praise. One of those two is Laodicea, the period which began in 1844 and reaches down to the coming of Christ. Laodicea has a high opinion of herself. "I am rich, and increased with goods, and have need of nothing," she says (Rev. 3:17). "You are not rich," God tells her. "You are wretched, and miserable, and poor, and blind, and naked—and don't even know it!"

"Repent," the Lord urges. "I love you, or I wouldn't bother to rebuke and chasten you." "Be zealous therefore, and repent."

And of what does Laodicea need to repent? We discuss this in Bible doctrines classes. Almost always we arrive at the conclusion that Laodicea's problem could be summed up in one word—lukewarmness.

Repentance, Webster says, is to turn from sin and dedicate oneself to the amendment of one's life. Genuine repentance leads to changed lives. Indifference is replaced by concern, pride gives way to humility. Self-righteousness is stripped away, and a healthy self-distrust takes its place. There is a resolute turning away from evil. Most of all, love for Jesus and a desire to win others become the motive powers of the soul.

Repentance itself is a gift (Acts 5:31). Would you be willing to pray for a spirit of repentance? Pray that God will show you yourself as you really are. Open His Word with a prayer that He will send to you conviction, and repentance, with a fuller view of your Saviour.

It's a prayer He will answer—and it will mean some changes!

REPENTANCE—A GIFT

Him hath God exalted . . . to be a Prince and a Saviour, for to give repentance to Israel, and forgiveness of sins. **Acts 5:31.**

Have you asked God to give you repentance? It will not make you comfortable. One of the first things the Holy Spirit does is to "convince the world of sin" (John 16:8, R.S.V.).

A student once lingered after class to ask her Bible teacher, "How can we know when we have God's Spirit?"

"Have you ever felt utterly unworthy, and deeply aware of your shortcomings?" the teacher inquired. "Yes, often," she replied.

"That was the Holy Spirit convicting you," said the teacher. "It is His first work to convict of sin. Do not get discouraged when you feel unworthy, but rejoice, for God is drawing you closer to Himself. The time to get frightened about yourself is when you feel that you are a pretty good person."

Paul spoke of himself as the chief of sinners. "The closer you come to Jesus, the more faulty you will appear in your own eyes. . . . This is evidence that Satan's delusions have lost their power; that the vivifying influence of the Spirit of God is arousing you."—*Steps to Christ,* pp. 64, 65.

But it is also the work of the Holy Spirit to "convince . . . of righteousness" (John 16:8, R.S.V.). "A view of our sinfulness drives us to Him who can pardon; and when the soul, realizing its helplessness, reaches out after Christ, He will reveal Himself in power."—*Ibid.,* p. 65. As He reveals Himself, we will ever have a humble estimate of ourselves, and at the same time we will possess that joy which comes from the consciousness of sins forgiven. It is thus that joy becomes the very keynote of one's Christian experience.

Such joy must be shared. It cannot be kept to oneself. "You just have to tell others what He's done for you!" exclaimed one academy girl who had found Christ at a Bible conference. And there is no more effective witness than this. Give the church thousands of youth who can give this kind of witness, and the world, once again, will be "turned . . . upside down" (Acts 17:6).

TIME FOR A CHANGE

So then because thou art lukewarm, and neither cold nor hot, I will spew thee out of my mouth. **Rev. 3:16.**

Would it be possible for every Seventh-day Adventist to win one person to Christ before the end of this year? To do so would mean the doubling of our world membership within less than a year's time. Some among us for various reasons might be unable to win anyone, but others could win more than one. As the Spirit of God moves, "triumph always follows decided effort" (*Testimonies,* vol. 7, p. 30).

One person who attended the 1970 General Conference, Pastor Eduardo Castro, of Bolivia, won 702 people to Christ during 1969. And there are others who by God's grace and "decided effort" on their part have won more than one hundred people within a year's time. But how many of us put forth any kind of "decided effort" to bring even one person to Christ?

At the same 1970 General Conference, Elder Neal Wilson reported that in the North American Division a total of 94,836 people came into the church by baptism and profession of faith during the 1966-1969 quadrennium. Commented Elder Wilson, "This is hardly the full result that should be expected from a working force numbering 27,000 in North America when combined with the labors and witness of the members of our 3,398 churches."—*General Conference Bulletin,* No. 3, June 15, 1970, p. 30.

That's about seven new members per year per church. But at least some of those seven would be children from our own families, so that new members won from among our neighbors would be considerably fewer than seven per church.

This report represented a field where many influences make it difficult to interest the majority of our neighbors in spiritual things. But are all indifferent?

Does my lukewarmness contribute to the lack of real soul winning among us? Does yours? Would we be willing to pray *now* that God would lead us to some contact that could result in someone's being won to Christ this year? Could you? Would you?

116

THE FELLOWSHIP LAODICEA NEEDS

Behold, I stand at the door, and knock: if any man hear my voice, and open the door, I will come in to him, and will sup with him, and he with me. Rev. 3:20.

It is the King of kings who stands there knocking. He invites you to fellowship with Him. Eating together, visiting together, suggests a very real, a very meaningful fellowship.

"If any man hear." Many young people do not hear Him knocking. There are too many other distractions, too much noise. And some of them couldn't care less anyway. So, also, with too many adults.

It is those who do hear, who do invite Him in, who do know Him, who are Laodicea's hope of revival. Their witness—the witness of a personal experience—is far reaching. The July 25, 1970, issue of the Southwestern Union *Record* reported the influence of Texas' AYA team. This AYA (Adventist Youth in Action) team was organized at the close of the 1969-1970 school year, rehearsing during the week of June 7-12 at Jefferson Academy, and spending much time in prayer. Shortly thereafter they began meeting a number of appointments in the Galveston-Houston area. At one of these appointments they presented their program at a large Protestant church. Representatives from several other churches were also present.

Following the regular program an after-meeting was held, to explain how a witness group such as this might be organized. During this time these youth had opportunity to give their testimonies. At the close the pastor of the church came to the group leader with tears in his eyes as he said, "You are standing in one of the most beautiful churches in the Galveston-Houston area. A tremendous amount of money has been spent here. The only thing we lack is what your young people have." He extended to them an invitation to come back to take an eleven o'clock service in his church.

We must possess Christ before we can share Him. Do you? Is His forgiveness a reality in your life? Has He been invited to come in and fellowship with you? Won't you do so *now?*

NOTHING TO WEAR

Behold, I come as a thief. Blessed is he that watcheth, and keepeth his garments, lest he walk naked, and they see his shame. **Rev. 16:15.**

Today's scripture is starkly vivid. It would be terribly disconcerting to be out walking—the text implies it's in public —and suddenly discover that you have nothing on.

The 1964 Alaskan earthquake happened Friday afternoon. An off-duty policeman in Anchorage apparently was taking a shower when the earthquake hit. In the excitement and confusion he went out into the street to help untangle a traffic jam, wearing only a towel about his waist. Told about it later, he wouldn't believe that he had been wearing only a towel—until he was shown a picture someone had snapped.

But at least he had a towel on. What would be one's embarrassment, if during an earthquake one dashed from a shower to the outdoors wearing nothing? And what would it be to be out in public walking naked and not know that you were naked? This is the condition of some in Laodicea. "Thou . . . knowest not that thou art . . . naked" (Rev. 3:17).

Can you picture anyone going to church in that condition? A very religious man, in the story Jesus told of the Pharisee and the publican, did this very thing. Complacent and self-satisfied, he stood before God and presented his recommendations. "God, I thank thee," he says, "that I am not as other men are, extortioners, unjust, adulterers, or even as this publican" (Luke 18:11).

The publican, a sinner and well aware of his sinfulness— others wouldn't have let him forget it even if he could have— stood there in bitter anguish and self-abhorrence. He was overwhelmed with a sense of guilt. His cry, "God be merciful to me a sinner," was the cry of utter self-despair. But of him Christ said, "This man went down to his house justified" (verse 14).

There is nothing in us—no good deeds of any kind—with which we can clothe the nakedness of the soul. We have nothing to wear—unless, like the publican, we seek and find Christ's righteousness.

THIRSTING FOR RIGHTEOUSNESS

Blessed are they which do hunger and thirst after righteousness: for they shall be filled. Matt. 5:6.

The very first step in approaching God is to know and believe that He loves us, and the first chapter of the much-read *Steps to Christ* is, appropriately, "God's Love for Man." (The title given in the *Real Happiness Is* edition, "Someone Cares," is equally appropriate.)

The very next step is to recognize our need. Chapter two, "The Sinner's Need of Christ," discusses this. There must be awakened in our soul a sense of need. The Lord can do absolutely nothing to help us until, stripped of our self-sufficiency, we hunger and thirst for His righteousness.

Attending a Christian school will not make you a Christian. A theoretical knowledge of the Bible does not make you a Christian. Saying prayers—the Pharisees loved to say prayers standing on street corners—certainly does not make one a Christian. Doing missionary work or giving large offerings does not make one a Christian. Strict adherence to a check list—the prodigal son's older brother kept all the rules—does not make one a Christian, either.

To be a Christian, one must be righteous in God's sight— and none of the above things can make one righteous. How does one become righteous? There is only one way. One must receive Christ. One receives righteousness by receiving Him. "The price of heaven," says the author of *The Desire of Ages,* "is Jesus" (p. 385). The good works then follow, not as the source of righteousness, but as fruit.

The price of heaven is Jesus—this is our message. In 1890 in the *Review and Herald* the servant of God wrote, "Several have written to me, inquiring if the message of justification by faith is the third angel's message, and I have answered, 'It is the third angel's message in verity.' "—April 1. Earlier she had indicated that "there is not one in one hundred who understands for himself the Bible truth on this subject" (*ibid.,* Sept. 3, 1889).

"The price of heaven is Jesus." This makes it so simple. Do you know it by personal experience?

119

THE GREATEST DECEPTION

Except your righteousness shall exceed the righteousness of the scribes and Pharisees, ye shall in no case enter into the kingdom of heaven. Matt. 5:20.

No one likes to be deceived. When someone puts something over on you, generally you are disgusted with the person who deceived you—and even more disgusted with yourself.

The most serious deceptions have to do, not with things, but with spiritual truths. In a comment on today's scripture, the servant of God says, "The greatest deception of the human mind in Christ's day was that a mere assent to the truth constitutes righteousness."—*The Desire of Ages,* p. 309. She notes that it was some very orthodox people—people who "thought themselves the greatest religionists of the world" (*ibid.*)—who crucified Christ.

Could the power of this same deception concerning what constitutes righteousness still be an influence today? Would any Seventh-day Adventists, had we lived then, have helped crucify Christ?

At the 1970 General Conference, Elder A. Graham Maxwell was discussing how our relationship with God should be one of love, trust, and admiration. There were those at the 1888 Minneapolis Conference, when righteousness by faith was brought to the forefront, who preferred "a more arbitrary, vindictive Deity." Elder Maxwell related how Ellen White went so far as to say of some of the delegates to the 1888 conference, " 'The same spirit that actuated the rejectors of Christ, rankles in their hearts, and had they lived in the days of Christ, they would have acted toward Him in a manner similar to that of the Godless and unbelieving Jews.' "—*General Conference Bulletin,* No. 8, June 21, 1970, p. 16.

What is the lesson in this for us? Simply this: "Men may profess faith in the truth; but if it does not make them sincere, kind, patient, forbearing, heavenly-minded, it is a curse to its possessors, and through their influence it is a curse to the world."—*The Desire of Ages,* p. 310.

We need more than the righteousness of the Pharisees, lest we deceive ourselves into thinking that we are better than they.

THE TEST OF A RELIGION

For he hath made him to be sin for us, who knew no sin; that we might be made the righteousness of God in him. 2 Cor. 5:21.

Have you ever noticed how often Paul writes concerning righteousness by faith? What a miracle of God's transforming grace that a bigoted Pharisee became the apostle of righteousness by faith!

In writing to his own Hebrew people, Paul uses Cain and Abel as an illustration. "By faith," he said, "Abel offered unto God a more excellent sacrifice than Cain" (Heb. 11:4).

Cain's was a religion of salvation by works. He wanted nothing to do with the blood of a lamb. He would present *his* fruits, the products of *his* labors. And there are Cains in the world today, "for nearly every false religion has been based on the same principle—that man can depend upon his own efforts for salvation" (*Patriarchs and Prophets,* p. 73).

Cain's religion has been the blight of the church from his day till now. It is a religion that breeds intolerance and hardheartedness on the part of those who possess it. It is a religion that creates a feeling of "What's the use?" in the hearts of those who when the Spirit of God is drawing them encounter orthodoxy's all-important check list instead of the Lamb of God. It is a religion that quenches spirituality, a religion where love is suppressed and mercy ignored.

Paul, again writing of his own people, noted their zeal. Yet this very zeal set them into opposition to the Lord Himself— "for they being ignorant of God's righteousness, and going about to establish their own righteousness, have not submitted themselves unto the righteousness of God" (Rom. 10:3).

Cain's religion permitted murder. Abel's led him to a martyr's grave. Cain's religion led to jealousy and hatred, Abel's produced meekness and a humble firmness in defending the goodness of God.

And today, as then, the test of a religion is the kind of people it produces.

KNOCKING . . . AND KNOCKING . . . AND KNOCKING

But we are all as an unclean thing, and all our righteousnesses are as filthy rags; and we all do fade as a leaf; and our iniquities, like the wind, have taken us away. Isa. 64:6.

If any Bible text can strip a man of his feelings of self-sufficiency, today's scripture ought to be able to do so. We are unclean. Our goodness is a filthy rag. Our iniquities whip us about like the wind would a faded leaf fallen off a tree.

Jeremiah does not help matters any, either, when he says, "The heart is deceitful above all things, and desperately wicked: who can know it?" (Jer. 17:9).

We would like to apply these texts to unbelievers. But Isaiah uses the pronoun "we"—speaking of himself and Judah. And Jeremiah's message is specifically concerning "the sin of Judah" (verse 1).

What, then, can we do?

We can renounce all self-sufficiency. Like Jeremiah, we can pray, "O Lord, I know that the way of man is not in himself: it is not in man that walketh to direct his steps" (chap. 10:23). With Peter we can claim the promise of salvation through "the precious blood of Christ, as of a lamb without blemish and without spot" (1 Peter 1:19). We can, like Paul, determine to be able to say, "I count everything as loss because of the surpassing worth of knowing Christ Jesus my Lord. . . . That I may gain Christ and be found in him, not having a righteousness of my own, based on law, but that which is through faith in Christ, the righteousness from God that depends on faith" (Phil. 3:7-9, R.S.V.).

It is so easy for a Laodicean Christian, moderately religious and comfortable, to think the reproof given to Laodicea is more for his brethren than for him. I am in a fairly good condition spiritually, he thinks. These sharp words do not mean me. I do not have all the fervor of some, but I believe the truth. This message is for my brethren. I think some of them need it.

What can words say? What can God Himself do? Nothing more than what He has been doing through all these years of delay. "Behold," He says, "I stand at the door, and knock."

SATAN'S POWER BROKEN

Ye are complete in him. Col. 2:10.

In today's scripture Paul puts the whole gospel of righteousness by faith into five words. Inspiration, commenting upon this wonderful truth, in *Messages to Young People,* says:

"Through faith in Christ, every deficiency of character may be supplied, every defilement cleansed, every fault corrected, every excellence developed."—Page 252.

Take today's scripture and this one-sentence commentary with you as you go through today. Let your mind keep coming back to this wonderful truth. Ponder what it means. "Every deficiency . . . supplied." "Every defilement cleansed." "Every fault corrected." Do you have any defilements that need cleansing away? Do you have any faults that need correcting? The blood of Christ is your cleansing, the power of Christ your help.

And do you long to be a better person, to see His excellencies reproduced in you? Christ, through His Spirit, will do this, too. Let those who fear that an exalting of the righteousness of Christ will lower the standards consider the significance of the words, "Through faith in Christ . . . every excellence developed."

God help us to believe it! If we would only do so, Satan's power in our lives would be broken. If righteousness by faith would be clearly taught and fully received upon our campuses Satan's power would be broken there, too. And what a foretaste of heaven a school campus would become, if only Satan's power could be broken!

Here's the assurance:

"The thought that the righteousness of Christ is imputed to us, not because of any merit on our part, but as a free gift from God, is a precious thought. The enemy of God and man is not willing that this truth should be clearly presented; for he knows that if the people receive it fully, his power will be broken."—*Gospel Workers,* p. 161.

The alternative is doubt and unbelief and darkness. For too long these have prevailed. Shouldn't there be a change—*now?*

CLEANSED!

If we walk in the light, as he is in the light . . . the blood of Jesus Christ his Son cleanseth us from all sin. 1 John 1:7.

We were discussing in the office that day the problem of guilt. I tried to point out that when we come to Christ in sincere repentance, guilt feelings can and should be left at the foot of the cross. This is true no matter how terribly we have sinned. We tend to carry such feelings, day after day, until time finally deadens the vividness and shame. But God does not want us to do this. He invites us to bring our guilt to the cross and leave it there.

A young woman, a college student, listened intently, then suggested that a failure to understand this is one of the biggest reasons young people give up in discouragement. "We find it impossible to live with guilt," she said. "You get so that you try to push these feelings aside. But this does not really solve the problem, and you end up deciding that there is no use even trying to be a Christian."

How many thousands of Adventist youth have given up in discouragement? How many thousands have left the church because in the agony of guilt they felt there was no longer any use to try?

It need not be that way. The very moment we confess our sins and sincerely turn away from them, we are forgiven. At that very moment we should banish all feelings of guilt. God does not put us on probation, to see if we really mean it. He accepts us immediately. Let us accept His forgiveness just as immediately.

"The blood of Jesus Christ . . . cleanseth us from all sin" (1 John 1:7). How wonderful to be clean—to step forth from a shower, refreshed and alert! How wonderful that somebody invented soap, so that dirt and grime can be cleansed away! Yet what illustration from the physical world can portray the sense of relief and peace and spiritual alertness that comes when the guilt of one's sins has been cleansed away?

Today's scripture is for you! Believe it!

THE "MORE THAN THIS"

For it is God which worketh in you both to will and to do of his good pleasure. Phil. 2:13.

Two girls were talking in a high school corridor. "What is sin?" one of them asked the other. Her friend thought for a moment, shrugged her shoulders, and replied, "I don't know for sure. I think it has something to do with Adam and Eve."

Our definition of sin need not be hazy. "Sin is the transgression of the law" (1 John 3:4). The same author who pointed out that a clear understanding of and a full receiving of the truth of righteousness by faith will break the power of Satan also said, on the same page, "If we would have the spirit and power of the third angel's message, we must present the law and the gospel together, for they go hand in hand."—*Gospel Workers*, p. 161.

The righteousness of Christ is not a cloak beneath which one can conceal cherished sin. The doctrine of justification by faith is that when you accept Christ as your Saviour "you are accounted righteous. Christ's character stands in place of your character, and you are accepted before God just as if you had not sinned."—*Steps to Christ*, p. 62. But this assurance has a "more than this." Here it is:

"More than this, Christ changes the heart. He abides in your heart by faith. You are to maintain this connection with Christ by faith and the continual surrender of your will to Him; and so long as you do this, He will work in you to will and to do according to His good pleasure."—*Ibid.*, pp. 62, 63.

The "more than this" is what Paul promises in today's scripture. And it returns to that most difficult of all problems—the problem of a surrendered will. But even here, God will be at our side to help. He works "in you . . . to will." You have complete freedom of choice. He will not dominate your will. But if you find human nature shrinking back from a full surrender, ask Him to "make you willing to be willing." He can, and will.

Have you claimed the "more than this"?

THE SECRET OF COMMANDMENT KEEPING

For this is the love of God, that we keep his commandments: and his commandments are not grievous. 1 John 5:3.

We aren't always sure, in the book of 1 John, whether the expression "the love of God" stands for God's love for us or for our love for Him. The context would indicate that in today's scripture it is our love for God. Phillips translates this verse, "Loving God means obeying his commands, and these commands of his are not burdensome." "To love God is to keep his commands," *The New English Bible* puts it.

Loving God and keeping His commandments go together. "If ye love me, keep my commandments," Jesus said (John 14:15). The receiving of the righteousness of Christ and obedience likewise go together. The robe of Christ's righteousness can never be used as a cloak for any kind of cherished sin. To put on that robe means "obedience unto righteousness" (Rom. 6:16).

The apostle James makes so clear that "faith without works is dead" (James 2:26). That so-called faith that requires "no self-denial, no divorce from the follies of the world" is a dead faith. Equally worthless is that obedience which is "a mere outward compliance" given without love.

Do you really love God? Have you accepted the robe of Christ's righteousness? Then there will be seen within your life "obedience unto righteousness." You will still make mistakes, but you will not cling to any known wrong. As you seek an experience like this, consider the following:

"Supreme love for God and unselfish love for one another—this is the best gift that our heavenly Father can bestow. This love is not an impulse, but a divine principle, a permanent power. The unconsecrated heart cannot originate or produce it. Only in the heart where Jesus reigns is it found."—*The Acts of the Apostles,* p. 551.

"We love him, because he first loved us" (1 John 4:19). The secret of keeping His commandments—and these commandments "are not burdensome"—is to behold that love and to respond to it by inviting Him to reign within our hearts.

HEART WORK

Bringing into captivity every thought to the obedience of Christ. 2 Cor. 10:5.

Is it possible to develop a Christian experience where your highest desire is to do the will of God? Is it possible to come to the place where obedience becomes your natural impulse?

Notice today's scripture in its context as expressed in *The Living Bible:*

"I use God's mighty weapons, not those made by men, to knock down the devil's strongholds. . . . With these weapons I can capture rebels and bring them back to God, and change them into men whose hearts' desire is obedience to Christ" (2 Cor. 10:4, 5).*

Thoughts are not easy to control. Jesus said that it is in our thoughts that sin originates. "For from within, out of the heart of man, proceed evil thoughts, adulteries, fornications, murders, thefts, covetousness, wickedness, deceit, lasciviousness, an evil eye, blasphemy, pride, foolishness" (Mark 7:21, 22).

Take a second look at that list. Are there any of these things in your life? Notice how many of them have to do with the lust of the flesh. Remember the words of Jesus, that "whosoever looketh on a woman to lust after her hath committed adultery with her already in his heart" (Matt. 5:28).

What are the "mighty weapons" that can change sinners "into men whose hearts' desire is obedience to Christ"? Are they not God's Word, and the transforming power of His Spirit?

Is it possible to reach a place where obedience is a natural impulse? Consider this:

"It was heart work with Christ. And if we consent, He will so identify Himself with our thoughts and aims, so blend our hearts and minds into conformity to His will, that when obeying Him we shall be but carrying out our own impulses. The will, refined and sanctified, will find its highest delight in doing His service. . . . Through an appreciation of the character of Christ, through communion with God, sin will become hateful to us."—*The Desire of Ages,* p. 668.

---

* The texts in this book so credited are from *The Living Bible,* Tyndale House, Publishers, Wheaton, Illinois. Used by permission.

THE FIRST OF MAY

Consider the lilies of the field, how they grow; they toil not, neither do they spin: and yet I say unto you, That even Solomon in all his glory was not arrayed like one of these. Matt. 6:28, 29.

In many parts of the world new life has burst forth everywhere. It's springtime again! Flowers are in bloom, and a fresh new green adorns trees that stood stark and bare during the winter. As I think back to my childhood on an Oklahoma farm, one of my fondest memories is of my mother going with us to find the first wildflowers out in the pasture in the springtime.

"Consider the lilies," Jesus invited. There were children and youth listening as He spoke these words. In one of the most descriptive word pictures I have found, inspiration portrays the occasion like this:

"Jesus plucked the beautiful lily, and placed it in the hands of children and youth; and as they looked into His own youthful face, fresh with the sunlight of His Father's countenance, He gave the lesson, 'Consider the lilies of the field, how they grow [in the simplicity of natural beauty]; they toil not, neither do they spin: and yet I say unto you, that even Solomon in all his glory was not arrayed like one of these.' "—*Christ's Object Lessons,* p. 19.

Can you picture the scene? It is early enough in the day that the dew still clings to the flowers. Jesus, as He teaches the people, notices a cluster of wildflowers at His feet and picks several lilies, handing them to some of the children and youth who have pressed in close to Him. As He does, they look into His youthful face, filled with the sunlight of His Father's countenance. Gently, earnestly, He urges these children and youth and the gathered multitude of people to "consider the lilies of the field, how they grow."

The flowers teach us so many things! We are encouraged not to worry. We are reminded, from how the lily grows, of the simplicity of natural beauty. There comes to us, gently and almost unconsciously, the thought that God would have us cultivate purity and simplicity. And there is written upon each blossom the assurance that God is love.

A BILLION TIMES OVER

For lo, the winter is past, the rain is over and gone. The flowers appear on the earth, the time of singing has come, and the voice of the turtledove is heard in our land. S. of Sol. 2:11, 12, R.S.V.

The California poppy has been called "The Cup of Gold." Its orange blossoms are first seen early in the spring along the southern slopes of the lower hills. Then, in the words of the book *Our Wonderful World*, "it flames along the meadow in countless millions and millions of brilliant golden cups, fairly covering the earth with its red-gold sheen" (p. 162). It is the California State flower, and grows wild throughout the State. It can readily be cultivated in your garden as well.

When we moved from California to Auburn Academy in the State of Washington, we took along some California poppy seed. The vacant lot across the street from our house was an eyesore of weeds and grass. We got permission from Dr. Peters, the principal, to have it plowed, and then we planted our poppy seed along the side next to the campus. By the second summer thousands of blossoms made that side of the vacant lot a mass of orange color. Each individual blossom lasts for several days, opening when the sun is out, and closing when it is cloudy or when evening comes.

How many billions of these cups of gold does a single season produce? Add all the lupine, the shooting stars, the violets, and all the other wildflowers of a whole season—how many would you have? Then include all the cultivated flowers of earth, and consider this:

"Every opening bud and blossoming flower is an expression of God's love for His children."—*Medical Ministry*, p. 233.

This truth has made such a deep impression upon me that I recall it almost every time I see flowers anywhere. I think of the irises, the marigolds, and the dahlias that we grew in that same vacant lot there in Washington, and the rhododendrons all about the campus. I think of those brilliant "cups of gold"—and of the wildflowers one sees throughout the country. Every blossom, every bud, is a message from God of His love for each of us. How could He say it more clearly?

LINGERING ON THE SHORES

O the depth of the riches both of the wisdom and knowledge of God! how unsearchable are his judgments, and his ways past finding out! **Rom. 11:33.**

Those who have grown up near an ocean probably do not realize the feeling of awe that comes to someone who, having never seen the ocean, stands before it for the first time. My wife and I grew up in the Middle West. Neither of us during our teen-age years had opportunity to see an ocean. Upon my graduation from college, we moved to the Los Angeles area, where I was to teach at Glendale Academy. Shortly after our arrival we had the opportunity to stand for the first time on the shore of the Pacific Ocean. How vast it seemed!

Glendale is inland some twenty-five miles from the ocean, and though we lived there for fourteen years, we did not get down to the ocean often enough for it ever to become common to us. A sense of awe would always fill our hearts when we would pause or stand along its shore.

There is a vastness, an infinitely greater vastness, to the love of Christ. "In the contemplation of Christ we linger on the shore of a love that is measureless. We endeavor to tell of this love, and language fails us. We consider His life on earth, His sacrifice for us, His work in heaven as our advocate, and the mansions He is preparing for those who love Him, and we can only exclaim, O the height and depth of the love of Christ!"—*The Acts of the Apostles,* pp. 333, 334.

"Language fails us."

Sometimes, watching the mighty waves of the Pacific Ocean break against the shore, I would think of the illustration of the song writer and try to picture those waves and that ocean as being all ink, and "every man a scribe by trade." A whole ocean of ink and an innumerable company of writers could not tell the story of God's love.

Linger if you will upon the shore of God's love—gazing into depths that are measureless. Let the softening, subduing influence of such contemplation be felt and seen in your life. And as you ponder, may your heart go out in love to Him.

BUT HOW?

And thou shalt love the Lord thy God with all thine heart, and with all thy soul, and with all thy might. Deut. 6:5.

Moses repeatedly urged that the people of God should "love the Lord." He mentions it three times in a single chapter (Deut. 11:1, 13, 22). Jesus spoke of this as "the first and great commandment" (Matt. 22:38).

But how, as many students have so often asked, do you love someone you can't see?

A counselor, one time discussing a question similar to this in *The Youth's Instructor,* pointed out that love for God is not a feeling, as is much of human love. The Greek word used when we are told to love God is *agapaō,* which means "that one sees value in the one loved. This is love and respect from principle rather than feeling." Another New Testament word for love is *phileō*—which "more nearly means human love, tender affection. This word is never used in the Bible to command men to love God. One loves God, not with tender affection, but with respect, gratitude, and complete submission" (April 17, 1962, p. 23).

This same counselor said that we shouldn't try to love God in the same manner that we love earthly friends. As we realize His love for us our hearts will go out to Him in gratitude and appreciation. "Do not mistake feeling for love," he wrote. "They are not the same. Nevertheless, deeper religious feeling will come with a closer acquaintance with God. Do not try to force it. Commune with Him, give Him the opportunity to speak to you, and a more certain sense of His love will surely come."— *Ibid.*

Paul speaks of "the love of God" being "shed abroad in our hearts" by the Holy Spirit (Rom. 5:5). And what is it that gives the Holy Spirit opportunity to influence you? Is it not the result of your turning your eyes toward an uplifted Saviour? Contemplate the cross, and you cannot help loving Him.

And love, like knowledge, is progressive. The more you learn of God, the greater will be your admiration and love.

LOVE IS FOR SHARING

Thou shalt love thy neighbour as thyself. Matt. 22:39.

A love for God grows as it is shared. And if it is not shared, it will soon grow cold. This is why missionary work should have a prominent place in Christian education. There are numerous opportunities to help others right on campus, but beyond this there should also be off-campus missionary activities.

In the home, likewise, it is not enough simply to attend church, and have worship. Both eventually become an almost mechanical routine unless there is opportunity to help others.

The story is told of a man who, traveling one winter day through deep, drifted snow, became benumbed by the cold. His will to continue was almost imperceptibly being chilled away, when he heard the moans of another traveler, who was perishing with cold. He rubbed the limbs of this almost frozen traveler, finally getting him to his feet. But the poor man could not stand. There was nothing to do but to try to carry him. This he did, bearing him on his shoulders through the very drifts that he had thought he could never get through himself. As he got his fellow traveler to a place of safety, he realized that in saving his neighbor he had saved himself also. His earnest efforts to save another had quickened the blood that was freezing in his own veins, creating a healthful warmth in limbs that had been becoming numb with the freezing cold.

Jesus illustrated today's scripture with the story of the good Samaritan, showing that our neighbor is anyone who is in need. And there are needs everywhere. There are those in our own community from whom hope has departed—to them we can take sunshine. Many have lost courage—to these we can speak words of cheer, and we can pray for them. There are those who have physical needs—with them we can share some of our bounty. There are those whose hearts would open to the Word of God—if only we would take it to them. There are those who will listen to the story of Jesus and His love—if only we will tell them.

Love is for sharing. Are we doing it as much as we might?

A REVIVAL OF LOVE

**This is my commandment, That ye love one another, as I have loved you.
John 15:12.**

When the church is filled with this kind of love, both for those who are our brethren within the church, and for all those without, it will have a power that will be felt everywhere. The next to last chapter of *The Desire of Ages* is entitled "Go Teach All Nations." It is in this chapter that we are reminded that "the power of love" was in all of Christ's healing—and that "only by partaking of that love, through faith, can we be instruments for His work" (p. 825). Only through "the power of love" can our gospel witnessing become that revival through which "the riches of His mercy, His grace, and His love, are to appear in full and final display" (*ibid.,* p. 680).

"Our church needs a revival, a reawakening, a resurgence of power," wrote H. J. Harris in the May 29, 1969, issue of the *Review and Herald.* This revival needs to include, he said, "a revival of love for people—all kinds of people, red and yellow, black and white, educated and uneducated, refined and crude. When I speak of love I do not mean mere tolerance or acceptance or an ecumenical spirit. I mean the love that registers concern for the soul of the man across the street, in the office next to ours, the man who runs the service station, or the waitress at the café where we eat our noonday lunch. What do they know about Christ? How much of the Bible and its teachings do they understand? Is there anyone who loves them, anyone who cares whether they live or die?"

"We need," he says, "love that understands and forgives, love that cares and is concerned, love that communicates, love that loves when all others have ceased to care. We need a revival of love."

We must have "the power of love" in our intercessory prayers, in our speaking, in our witnessing, in all that we do. It needs to become a "current of life-giving energy" (*The Desire of Ages,* p. 825). And it will when, kneeling at the foot of the cross, your heart is broken in repentance and gratitude—and when, in faith, you seek and find the infilling of His Spirit.

ABOVE ALL THINGS

And the Lord make you to increase and abound in love one toward another, and toward all men, even as we do toward you. 1 Thess. 3:12.

Wrote Elder R. R. Bietz, back in 1960:

"The full and final display of God's love will be manifested first of all within the church. And if it is manifested in the church, it will permeate throughout the entire neighborhood. Then this love will be seen in a full and final blaze of glory throughout the entire world. Thus the church will fulfill its mission of bringing the Adventist message to every nation, kindred, tongue, and people."—*Review and Herald,* May 19.

Paul mentions in today's scripture that the believers at Thessalonica were to "increase and abound," first of all, "in love one toward another." Then, "toward all men."

One finds throughout the New Testament much emphasis upon the need for believers to have love for one another. Peter wrote, "And above all things have fervent charity among yourselves: for charity shall cover the multitude of sins" (1 Peter 4:8). And Paul, writing to the Colossians, urged, "And above all things put on charity, which is the bond of perfectness" (Col. 3:14).

The apostles recognized the tendency for church members to criticize one another, and to drift apart. These men knew that unless the believers could "abound in love one toward another," their power for witnessing would be greatly weakened.

Love abounding one toward another can wonderfully transform a home, a church, a campus. At one academy during a student Week of Prayer, the Spirit of God came in, and differences were swept away. Teachers and students alike participated in making things right with God and with one another. One teacher, who had tended to be too sharp in how he said things, apologized to the students he had hurt. Students went to teachers, making things right. There was a revival of love, bringing an atmosphere onto that campus which was a foretaste of heaven.

Thus it could be, and must be, everywhere!

A HEAVENLY FIRE

Lo, this hath touched thy lips; and thine iniquity is taken away, and thy sin purged. Isa. 6:7.

The youthful Isaiah, possibly still in his late teens, was standing in the temple, meditating upon the condition of his people. Uzziah's prosperous reign was drawing to a close, and the Assyrian armies were soon to invade the land of Judah. And the danger from without, overwhelmingly serious as it was, was less perilous than the dangers from within. The outward prosperity had not been accompanied by a corresponding spiritual growth, and pride and formality had gradually taken the place of humility and sincerity. With wealth had come a love of display, a spirit of revelry, and iniquitous practices of every kind.

When Isaiah, under these conditions, had been called to be a prophet the situation seemed impossible. As he had stood in the temple thinking and praying, the Lord came to him in the vision that has been recorded in Isaiah 6. A seraph brought a coal and touched Isaiah's lips, with the promise that God would be with him on his mission. Throughout his ministry of more than sixty years Isaiah never forgot this vision. A prophet of hope, he waxed bolder and bolder in his predictions of the final triumph of the church.

We have not, like Isaiah, a commission spanning out over sixty years—for God's work will be "cut . . . short in righteousness" (Rom. 9:28). But our lips, like Isaiah's, must be touched by a coal from Heaven's altar. Of the one who has been thus anointed, inspiration says: "Those who hear him know that he has drawn near to God in fervent effectual prayer. The Holy Spirit has rested upon him, his soul has felt the vital, heavenly fire. . . . Hearts are broken by his presentation of the love of God, and many are led to inquire, 'What must I do to be saved?' "—*The Acts of the Apostles,* p. 329.

Whether to a stranger, or to friends, or within the family, or as a witness in public from a pulpit, should not our words show that we have felt the touch of this "vital, heavenly fire"? Shouldn't we pray for a greater anointing of this fire upon God's people everywhere?

135

KEEPING IT ALIVE

Nevertheless I have somewhat against thee, because thou hast left thy first love. Rev. 2:4.

What causes someone to lose his first love? Why is it that young people who really love the Lord sometimes begin to change, and grow cold and indifferent? What causes new converts to leave the church?

There are many factors that can cause the loss of one's first love. Cherished sin can come in and separate one from the Saviour. One can neglect God's Word, or let prayer get crowded out. Criticism of one another or feelings of resentment can eat away our devotion to God.

One of the most common causes, however, is a failure to share with others one's love for Christ. This has sometimes been illustrated by comparing the Sea of Galilee with the Dead Sea. The Sea of Galilee receives to give again. But the Dead Sea has no outlet. It receives, but does not give. The Sea of Galilee is fresh, sparkling, alive. The Dead Sea is dead.

Inspiration, noting our need to work for others, states:

"It is because this work is neglected that so many young disciples never advance beyond the mere alphabet of Christian experience. The light which was glowing in their own hearts when Jesus spoke to them, 'Thy sins be forgiven thee,' they might have kept alive by helping those in need. The restless energy that is so often a source of danger to the young might be directed into channels through which it would flow out in streams of blessing. Self would be forgotten in earnest work to do others good."—*The Desire of Ages,* pp. 640, 641.

We need to reread the chapter entitled "True Education a Missionary Training," in *The Ministry of Healing.* It, too, mentions the "superabounding" energy of youth—energy that must find some outlet. Unless we as parents and teachers direct this energy toward doing good, it will almost inevitably be turned toward evil. Helping youth become involved in efforts for others will disrupt some routines—but is not such ministry the very purpose of Christian education?

WHERE MORE LOVE IS MOST NEEDED

Thy gentleness hath made me great. Ps. 18:35.

The place where a revival of love is most needed is in our own homes. How can we have an influence, through "the power of love," upon others, if that same power is not at work in our own homes? How can we speak words of compassion to a neighbor in need if we are speaking impatient, cross words at home?

Someone has said that home is the place where we treat the worst those whom we love the best. But do we really love them the best if we speak impatiently and unkindly to them?

Can you picture the mother of Jesus speaking to her Son impatiently? Can you imagine her yelling at Him?

Suggested the mother of four boys:

"Fathers and mothers, speak kindly to your children; remember how sensitive you are, how little you can bear to be blamed; reflect, and know that your children are like you. That which you cannot bear do not lay upon them. If you cannot bear censure and blame, neither can your children, who are weaker than you and cannot endure as much. Let your pleasant, cheerful words ever be like sunbeams in your family. The fruits of self-control, thoughtfulness, and painstaking on your part will be a hundredfold."—*The Adventist Home,* p. 442.

For an interesting study, secure a copy of *Child Guidance* by Ellen White, and using the index in the back of the book, look up all the references under "Scolding." Of the suggestions you will find, here's one: "When an emergency arises, ask, Lord, what shall I do now? If you refuse to fret or scold, the Lord will show you the way. He will help you use the talent of speech in so Christlike a way that peace and love will reign in the home." —Pages 478, 479. There is a time for punishment, of course— but never in anger or sharpness.

Does love reign in your home? Is there the peace of Christ there? Is there, along with firmness, gentleness?

"Thy gentleness," said the psalmist, "hath made me great."

137

THAT PRAYER BE NOT HINDERED

If a man say, I love God, and hateth his brother, he is a liar: for he that loveth not his brother whom he hath seen, how can he love God whom he hath not seen? 1 John 4:20.

Is there someone in the church whom you just can't stand? If there is, how can you pray with confidence? In 1 John 3:21, 22 the apostle writes, "If our heart condemn us not, then have we confidence toward God. And whatsoever we ask, we receive of him, because we keep his commandments, and do those things that are pleasing in his sight."

One of those commandments is that we love one another the way Christ has loved us. No matter how wrong the other person may be, nor how unlovely he may appear to you, you are to love him as Christ has loved you. If you can't stand him, then there will be, consciously or unconsciously, a sense of guilt in your own heart, and you will not be able to pray with confidence and power. You may or may not hurt him by harboring your resentments, but you surely hurt yourself.

One author, in the book *Prayer—Conversing With God,* suggests, "I will love God only as much as I love the person I dislike the most." The author goes on to explain, "The kind of love God commands us to have is a genuine caring about what happens to the other person. It doesn't necessarily mean being attracted to him" (p. 64).

"Love one another; as I have loved you," Jesus commands (John 13:34). But how poorly we do it! "In the church of God today," inspiration indicates, "brotherly love is sadly lacking" (*The Acts of the Apostles,* p. 550).

We need to demonstrate "the power of love" both in our homes and in the church before that love will move the world. In the words of God's servant, "Christians are all members of one family, all children of the same heavenly Father. . . .Very close and tender should be the tie that binds them together."— *Ibid.*

It has been said that an examination of the quality of a man's love for his brethren will reveal much concerning the genuineness of his love for God.

How is it, my friend, with you?

HANDLING PROBLEMS COMPASSIONATELY

And Jesus . . . was moved with compassion toward them . . . : and he began to teach them many things. Mark 6:34.

Have you ever been, or are you, a dormitory hall monitor? Or are you, perhaps, a parent? Or do you have administrative responsibilities?

How do you deal with the people problems that arise?

A teacher serving in the mission field was having some problems—problems primarily of her own making. It became necessary for the principal to talk to her. Embarrassed and discouraged, she was ready to quit. But she had a principal who knew how to correct in love. Listen in, as she tells about it:

" 'Don't feel so discouraged,' I heard the principal's voice say. 'You didn't realize what you were doing. It isn't so bad as that. You're doing all right. Just try to do better next time.' "

"On and on he sought to strengthen me. At last he said, 'Why don't we pray about it?'

" 'All right,' I agreed. 'You pray first.'

"He did pray first. It was a humble, quiet prayer. I liked the sound of his voice. Then his voice broke; the words would not come for a moment. Then he continued. My bitterness gradually disappeared. I prayed.

"When I opened my eyes . . . I looked into my friend's face and really saw it for the first time that night. There were tears in his eyes as he whispered something about courage and told me good night.

"I went home to bed, but not to sleep. Again and again I could hear his voice and see his face. . . . Was this the way Jesus looked when He looked upon people with compassion? I wondered."—*The Youth's Instructor,* July 17, 1962, p. 3.

When difficulties arise, we can, as parents, or as a dean, simply "lay down the law." By so doing we may for a while secure compliance. But is there some way we can enlist the will of the offender? Can we encourage and inspire as well as correct? Will you deal with today's problems, whatever they are, with compassion?

139

DEALING WITH THE UNREASONABLE

Be not overcome of evil, but overcome evil with good. **Rom. 12:21.**

How do you get along with someone who is unreasonable? What do you do when someone deliberately tries to provoke?

A man who had just purchased a farm was out walking around the boundary of his newly acquired property, when he met his neighbor. "Don't look now," said his future neighbor, "but when you bought this piece of ground, you also bought a lawsuit with me. Your fence is ten feet over on my land."

The new owner smiled. "I thought I'd find some friendly neighbors here," he said, "and I'm going to. And you're going to help me. Move the fence where you want it, and send me the bill. You'll be satisfied, and I'll be happy."

The fence was never moved.

We need to remember that we are not yet in heaven. We are not associating with angels, but with human beings liable to error. And some of them can at times be unreasonable. We can tell them how wrong they are, but inspiration suggests a better way. Here it is:

"We may never know until the judgment the influence of a kind, considerate course of action to the inconsistent, the unreasonable, and unworthy. If, after a course of provocation and injustice on their part, you treat them as you would an innocent person, you even take pains to show them special acts of kindness, then you have acted the part of a Christian; and they become surprised and ashamed, and see their course of action and meanness more clearly than if you plainly stated their aggravated acts to rebuke them."—*Medical Ministry,* pp. 209, 210.

Have you the courage to do it? Will you sincerely perform some special act of kindness for the person who deliberately tries to provoke you? Try it, whether the offender be an older (or younger) brother or sister who is simply teasing, or whether it's a real enemy.

WHAT BROUGHT HIM BACK?

I will arise and go to my father. **Luke 15:18.**

The story of the son who went off to the far country has been duplicated in thousands upon thousands of homes within recent years. The far country may be Haight-Ashbury or Greenwich Village or Sunset Strip or Big Sur or any one of dozens of other places. But "the precious years of life, the strength of intellect, the bright visions of youth, the spiritual aspirations" (*Christ's Object Lessons,* p. 200), can be just as surely consumed in these modern far countries as in the one to which the Bible prodigal departed.

What can bring a departed son or daughter home? What was it that brought the son in the Bible story home? He "came to himself" (Luke 15:17), Jesus said. He saw the folly of "riotous living." Yet for all that he could have stayed away in despair, sinking lower and lower, but for one thing—he knew he was loved. It was love that drew him homeward. It is "the goodness of God" that leads to repentance (Rom. 2:4).

It is estimated that in one large metropolitan area there are up to twenty thousand used-to-be church members, many of whom left the church during their teen-age years or shortly thereafter. What can be done to win these back to God?

It will take much prayer, and much personal interest. In the Bible story the son came home on his own. We today may need to go after the ones we would win. Julia W. Wolfe expressed it well when she wrote in *These Times* "Concerning a Prodigal":

Common Sense said: "Let him suffer;
Firmly let the black ox tread."

Grace said: "If he comes, I'll give him
Welcome, yes, with board and bed."

Long stood Kindness in the doorway,
Hoping he might chance to pass.

Love went after him to the world's end,
Barefoot over broken glass.

Are there those whom you could go after? Will you?

141

THE OTHER PRODIGAL

And he said unto him, Son, thou art ever with me, and all that I have is thine. **Luke 15:31.**

The parable that we have called the story of the prodigal son is really the story of two prodigals—one lost away from home, and the other just as lost right at home.

The boy who left home had developed a bad attitude toward his father. He was tired of rules, and was determined to get away where he could do as he pleased. He didn't want to wait until his father died to get his share of the estate. He wanted it now, asked for it, and got it. Then he went off to a far country and spent it on pleasure and prostitutes.

You couldn't have a much worse attitude than that. Or could you?

The other son stayed at home. He didn't run around. His life, in fact, was "circumspect" (*Christ's Object Lessons*, p. 208). But in many ways he was worse off than his profligate younger brother. He was hardhearted, coldly speaking of his returning brother to his father as *"thy* son." "The elder son, in his selfishness and jealousy, stood ready to watch his brother, to criticize every action, and to accuse him for the least deficiency. He would detect every mistake, and make the most of every wrong act."—*Ibid.*, p. 210.

How would you rate his attitude?

What was his problem, anyway? The answer is found in his proud words to his father. "Lo, these many years do I serve thee" (Luke 15:29). If you read between the lines, you can hear him saying, "I have *earned* your favor." His was a salvation by works, encasing his heart in an impenetrable self-righteousness. His father's tender reply also implies the elder son's problem. "All that I have is thine," he said. It's not something you have to earn. It's yours, not as wages, but as a gift.

Did "the other prodigal" ever repent of his self-righteous, hardhearted ways? We don't know. Jesus left the story unfinished.

Both prodigals needed Jesus. So also do we today.

FROM THE FAR COUNTRY

I have loved thee with an everlasting love: therefore with lovingkindness have I drawn thee. Jer. 31:3.

In the August, 1970, *These Times,* Paul Harvey notes that God, like parents, cannot force His children to love Him. In trying to picture what God is like, Mr. Harvey used this illustration:

"I remember hearing of a preacher's son who grew up keen and clean and wholesome. At high school age he fell in with a brilliant but foulmouthed and atheistic adult. His admiration for the man's brilliance encouraged him to emulate his hero otherwise. At home he became sullen, irritable, unmanageable, contemptuous of his parents.

"One midnight the preacher with a heavy heart stole softly into his son's bedroom. The air was filled with the stale stench of overindulgence.

"He found the boy's mother kneeling by his bed, stroking his hair, kissing his forehead, weeping. Through her tears she said, 'He won't let me love him when he's awake.'

"That," said Mr. Harvey, "is what God is like."

Today there are thousands upon thousands of prodigals—sons and daughters who have left the faith of their childhood, and who must, if possible, be won back. To each of them God is saying, "I have loved thee with an everlasting love: therefore with lovingkindness have I drawn thee."

This is the only thing that will ever win them back. Rebuke will not do it. Sternness will not do it. But for some, lovingkindness and the assurance of forgiveness will.

There are many hindrances, not the least of which are those professed Christians who are stern and unloving. Like the prodigal son's elder brother, they are quick to criticize, quick to detect every mistake, quick to make the most of every wrong act.

Think again of the story of the prodigal son as Jesus told it. There is the father. And there is the elder brother. Which are you and I like?

"He that loveth not knoweth not God; for God is love" (1 John 4:8).

DOES IT MATTER TO YOU?

For the Son of man is come to seek and to save that which was lost. **Luke 19:10.**

How well do we follow the example of Jesus in seeking to save those who are lost? "Every year millions upon millions of human souls are passing into eternity unwarned and unsaved. From hour to hour in our varied life opportunities to reach and save souls are opened to us. These opportunities are continually coming and going. God desires us to make the most of them."— *Christ's Object Lessons,* p. 373.

"Millions upon millions" passing into eternity "unwarned and unsaved." Could you have reached at least one or two of these? Did God in His providence cause at least one or two of them to cross your path? Will someone cross your path to-day? Will you be prepared to take advantage of the opportunity?

Does it matter to you about the children on your block? Have you ever tried to do anything to share Christ with your milkman, or with the postman, or with the various ones who come to your door? How about those with whom you work? One man in less than a year's time was able to get more than a dozen of his fellow employees interested in taking the gift-Bible lessons. Could more of us follow his example? Could you?

"Is it nothing to you, all ye that pass by?" the prophet asks (Lam. 1:12). Perhaps you enjoy the services of religion. Perhaps you enjoy hearing the gospel preached. You enjoy the church for its social opportunities, for its fellowship, for its status. But these "millions upon millions"—are they nothing to you?

" 'To how many have you spoken regarding their salvation? How many have heard from your lips earnest appeals to accept Christ as a personal Saviour? How many have been led by your words to turn from sin to the service of the living God?' "— *Testimonies,* vol. 7, p. 117. These questions were directed by "One in authority," not to ministers, but to restaurant workers. Could it be that they are directed this day to *you?*

WOULD $1,000 MAKE A DIFFERENCE?

And the Lord said unto him, What is that in thine hand? Ex. 4:2.

In talking to a conference evangelist, I asked him what percentage of the church members he found out giving Bible studies as he went from community to community to hold meetings. "Would there be about 10 per cent out doing this?" I asked.

"Generally not even one per cent," he replied.

Giving Bible studies is not the only kind of witnessing, obviously. But what per cent of the membership in any given church does any kind of missionary work? "Not one in a hundred among us is doing anything beyond engaging in common, worldly enterprises," wrote the servant of God in 1895. "We are not half awake to the worth of souls for whom Christ died."—*Testimonies,* vol. 8, p. 148.

How much has the situation improved since 1895?

Gift Bible Evangelism makes it possible for almost any layman, any teen-ager, to take Bible studies to neighbors and friends. It is a method, simple and effective, that could help fulfill the vision of "hundreds and thousands . . . seen visiting families, and opening before them the word of God" (*ibid.,* vol. 9, p. 126).

But how many of us have even attempted to use this tool that God has placed in our hands?

Suppose that each time you would return home from successfully delivering a gift-Bible lesson to someone, or from giving a Bible study, an angel would meet you as you got back to your front door, and would reward you with a thousand-dollar bill. Would you somehow, someway, find time to give at least one Bible study a week?

And suppose, as you take your vacation this coming summer, you would be rewarded with one thousand dollars for each piece of literature left with contacts made along the way. Would you somehow manage to find room for some literature in your car? Would you use it? Could it be that we would do for money that which we have not been doing from love?

God has given us all kinds of tools for helping to hasten His coming. But no tool is of any value unless it is used.

"What is that in thine hand?"

145

THE WORTH OF ONE WON

I will make a man more precious than fine gold. Isa. 13:12.

Let's imagine that you have an unlimited bank account, and that you determine that you are going to buy all the real estate in your county. We'll suppose that you live in the city, and decide to begin by purchasing all the property in your block. You take your checkbook, make your offers attractive enough that no one turns you down, and after a day or so of negotiating, you have purchased every property on your street.

What would be the worth at this point of your holdings?

You employ others to assist you, and keep at it until eventually you own everything in your city—homes and industries alike. Then you and your agents begin writing checks for all the rural properties, and for the properties in the other cities of your county, until you actually own a whole county.

What would be the worth of your holdings now?

Since you have an unlimited bank account, you decide to keep at it until you own your whole State or province, and after that—the whole country. If you live in the United States, what might your assets now be worth?

Back in 1967 an article in the *Saturday Evening Post* said: "The aggregate assets of America, tangible and intangible, have never been inventoried. The best estimate of these assets, prepared by Dr. John Kendrick, of the National Bureau of Economic Research, is $4.5 trillion."—Dec. 30, 1967, p. 18.

Our illustration has become too preposterous to continue, but how would the worth of your holdings compare with the worth of a person won to Christ?

A whole continent would not be an adequate comparison. "One soul is of such value that, in comparison with it, worlds sink into insignificance."—*The Desire of Ages*, p. 578.

"Worlds" is plural. Who could compute, in dollars, the worth of even one planet? What is the worth, then, of someone redeemed by the blood of Christ?

"I JUST WANT TO LOVE HER"

Let us not love in word, neither in tongue; but in deed and in truth. 1 John
3:18.

Many years ago in *These Times,* Caris Lauda related the
story of a country schoolteacher, Miss Miller, who lay near
death out in a little village hospital in west Texas. As doctors
and nurses were working urgently to fan the spark of life into
a flame, a gentle knock was heard on the door. A lad of six,
one of Miss Miller's kindergarten pupils, stood there holding a
bouquet of flowers he had gathered from the prairie that spring
morning. When the nurse told him no visitors were allowed,
he told her, "I don't want to talk to her. I just want to love her."

The door was just being closed when the doctor, who heard
these last words, said, "Nurse, we have done all we can. Science is
helpless. I believe in love. Let the lad in."

The nurse quickly called the sobbing boy back. Seating him
in a chair by the bed, she put his hand, with the flowers, into
the open palm of Miss Miller's limp hand. This caused Miss
Miller to move slightly. "Miss Miller," said the six-year-old,
"I don't want to talk to you. I just want to love you."

The nurses heard nothing more for nearly an hour. When
they did open the door, the boy and his teacher were talking
together. This six-year-old's touch of love had brought life
with it.

A love like that of this six-year-old "is of God" (1 John
4:7). It is practical and thoughtful, and, like the love of Christ,
"is a vitalizing power" (*The Ministry of Healing,* p. 115).

When everything seemed to be going wrong, David
lamented that "no man cared for my soul" (Ps. 142:4). How
many are there in your very neighborhood from whom hope
has departed? Could you not search out someone who is discouraged, who is battling against great odds? In every town
there are the elderly, and widows with small children. A bouquet
of flowers and a few kind words would bring new hope and
cheer. And if they have physical needs, do we not have an obligation to demonstrate a *practical* love that can see and care for
those needs?

147

THE GREATEST THRILL

For what is our hope, or joy, or crown of rejoicing? Are not even ye in the presence of our Lord Jesus Christ at his coming? **1 Thess. 2:19.**

Would you like to find a diamond worth a half million dollars?

The Los Angeles *Herald-Examiner* told of a woman who did. Mrs. Ernestine Ramoboa, in Angola, Africa, "sifted sand in her husband's small claim and came up with a 601-carat diamond the size of a golf ball—worth more than a half million dollars" (Jan. 1, 1968, p. B-5).

It would be quite a thrill, wouldn't it, to suddenly find yourself a half million dollars richer?

Your chances of ever finding any kind of diamond are pretty remote. But there is a thrill that far surpasses finding even a half-million-dollar diamond—and that is the thrill of being the instrument in helping to win someone to Christ.

Larry was rooming with a fellow who was not a Christian. He had been praying for his roommate, but without any noticeable effect. Then during the student Week of Prayer, Larry asked others to pray too. One day he and his roommate were in the room talking when there was a knock on the door, and his roommate was called out. It was a friend. He had been impressed to come to see Larry's roommate, and he came right to the point. "Would you like to be baptized?" he asked.

"You know," Larry's roommate replied, "I've got a funny feeling that someone has been praying for me."

"You're right!" he was told. "There are fellows all over the dorm praying for you."

"I can't hold out any longer," Larry's roommate said. "I'll do it."

Telling about it, Larry said, "You've never known the greatest happiness there is until you see someone you have been praying for go down into the water to be baptized."

What will it be worth, in eternity, to see someone there because of your interest and your prayers? Could any thrill be greater?

BEAUTIFUL FEET

How beautiful upon the mountains are the feet of him that bringeth good tidings, that publisheth peace; that bringeth good tidings of good, that publisheth salvation; that saith unto Zion, Thy God reigneth! Isa. 52:7.

I was talking to about 60 Bible doctrines students, when I paused, then asked, "How many of you have beautiful feet?"

The whole class looked up, with amused smiles, wondering what their Bible teacher was getting at. I turned to Isaiah and read today's scripture.

Do *you* have beautiful feet?

For the thousands of you who are academy and college students, school will soon be out. Have you given any thought to spending the summer as a literature evangelist?

At the close of the 1968-1969 school year about ten students from Auburn Academy who had decided to spend the summer as literature evangelists began work right there within a twenty-mile radius of the school. The youngest, and one of the most successful, had just completed his ninth-grade year. He did not yet have a driver's license, and could not have afforded a car anyway, so he went by bicycle. He stayed with a family in a nearby town, and made contacts both within the city and country areas. He returned to school financially ahead and spiritually enriched—with the satisfaction of having left literature in homes that will be a seed unto eternal life.

Attending the weekly get-togethers of these young people and hearing their experiences would have thrilled anyone. Two of the graduating seniors made a contact which, a few months later, resulted in two baptisms.

As you go forth in this work you will have the companionship of angels. "Thousands upon thousands, and ten thousand times ten thousand angels are waiting to co-operate with members of our churches in communicating the light that God has generously given."—*Testimonies,* vol. 9, p. 129.

You could not ask for better help.

THE HIGHEST HONOR

Now then we are ambassadors for Christ, as though God did beseech you by us: we pray you in Christ's stead, be ye reconciled to God. 2 Cor. 5:20.

Have you ever pictured yourself as an ambassador? The position suggests important responsibilities, travel, and honor. Few of us have ever dreamed of having such a position.

Yet you have been thus honored. "We are ambassadors for Christ," Paul wrote.

An ambassador is defined, by secular usage, as "a diplomatic officer of the highest rank, the representative of one nation at the court of another. In this capacity he is expected to support the interests and dignity of his own state."—*Encyclopedia Americana* (1959 ed.), vol. 1, p. 470d. The root word has the idea of "one sent."

An ambassador from one state to another is an officer of "the highest rank." But there is an office even higher—that of being a "laborer together with God." "This is the highest honor, the greatest joy, that it is possible for God to bestow upon men."—*Steps to Christ,* p. 79. As the final crisis develops, many of you will have an ever-expanding influence. Dedicated youth, and others, "will yet stand in legislative assemblies, in halls of justice, or in royal courts, as a witness for the King of kings" (*Education,* p. 262).

You do not need to wait until the final crisis to become an ambassador, however. You may go forth as one today. When you took upon yourself the royal name of "Christian," you became an ambassador for the courts of heaven. And like your secular counterpart you are to support the interests of your state.

What are these interests? Are they not, above all else, the winning of people to Christ? "Be ye reconciled to God" is your message. And as you live for Christ today, and as you speak for Him when opportunities arise, you have the cooperation and help of ten thousand angels of God. You represent a great country, a noble cause, and the resources provided are infinite.

Go forth then with courage and dignity.

THE WITNESS THAT WINS

Go home to thy friends, and tell them how great things the Lord hath done for thee, and hath had compassion on thee. Mark 5:19.

The sun was rising over the Sea of Galilee as a small group of men were stepping out of their boat onto the sandy beach. Suddenly, from among some nearby tombs, wild screams broke the stillness of that early morning. Startled, the men on the beach turned to see two madmen rushing toward them. Their eyes glared out through their long hair, and these onrushing demoniacs looked more like beasts than men.

The disciples turned and ran up the beach. Then, noticing that Jesus was not with them, they paused long enough to look back. They saw Jesus, His hand raised, calmly standing there by the boat while the madmen raged furiously but helplessly before Him.

Speaking with authority, Jesus bade the demons depart. A marvelous change came over these men. Their eyes sparkled with intelligence, and with glad voices they praised God. Later in the morning, as Jesus was about to depart, they begged to go with Him. But Jesus saw there were more important things for them to do. "Go home to thy friends," He said, "and tell them how great things the Lord hath done for thee."

They did exactly that. They had never heard a single sermon, but they simply told what Christ had done for them. People listened, and were deeply impressed. When Jesus returned to that region nine or ten months later, thousands flocked out to hear Him.

This is the kind of witness for which the Lord calls today. "As witnesses for Christ, we are to tell what we know, what we ourselves have seen and heard and felt. If we have been following Jesus step by step, we shall have something right to the point to tell."—*The Desire of Ages,* p. 340. And as the experience of these two men illustrates, there is no more effective way of winning others to Christ than this. You need not be a public speaker to talk about Christ. You can begin by telling your friends about Him—and about what He has done for you.

151

ALERT FOR OPPORTUNITIES

And the angel of the Lord spake unto Philip, saying, Arise, and go toward the south unto the way that goeth down from Jerusalem unto Gaza, which is desert. Acts 8:26.

This was not Philip the apostle, but Philip the deacon, a layman in the church. He had been preaching Christ in Samaria, when he was instructed by an angel to go down to Gaza. Meanwhile, an Ethiopian official who had been in Jerusalem was traveling toward Gaza, beginning the long journey back to his homeland. One route from Jerusalem to Gaza runs along the coast, and was the more traveled route. Another, less traveled, went through the desert country, and it was the latter road the Ethiopian had chosen to travel. It was this route to which the angel directed Philip.

The Ethiopian was probably accompanied by a sizable escort, and Philip apparently joined the group, walking along with them, when he was impressed to come up close to the chariot in which the Ethiopian was riding. This Ethiopian was reading aloud from Isaiah 53, when Philip tactfully inquired if he understood what he was reading.

You know the rest of the story, how Philip explained the Scriptures to him, and how a baptism resulted. There is a very instructive point in this story for us today. This contact was providentially arranged. An angel guided Philip to one who was seeking for more truth.

So it can be today, too. Angels will guide the footsteps of those who in their coming and going are prepared to take advantage of a providential contact. It may be on a plane, or at a local grocery store, that the Lord will bring someone seeking truth into contact with fellow beings who know the truth. The only reason it doesn't happen more often is that we are not prepared to take advantage of the opportunity—or else fail to recognize an opportunity when it does arise. If we were prepared, with appropriate literature, or simply in our conversation, to share a knowledge of God, we would be surprised how often opportunities would arise. Perhaps today, even.

"PREACHED UNTO HIM JESUS"

Then Philip opened his mouth, and began at the same scripture, and preached unto him Jesus. **Acts 8:35.**

It is apparent that some doctrinal instruction must have also been brought into what Philip said. For one thing, the Ethiopian was baptized. He was either told of or already understood the significance of this. He must have known of the Sabbath and other scriptural teachings. But that which he needed most, and that which brought conviction, was what Philip did— he "preached unto him Jesus."

"This is life eternal," said Jesus in a prayer, "that they might know thee the only true God, and Jesus Christ, whom thou hast sent" (John 17:3). This is the knowledge that above all other we so much need.

The speaker one Sabbath morning had an interesting talk. But very little was said about Christ. It was more a classroom lecture than a message of salvation. What the speaker did not know was that among his listeners was a former Seventh-day Adventist and his family, who seldom attended any church. Their great need that Sabbath morning was to hear someone preach unto them Jesus.

It is a mistake all of us have made, whether as speakers or as church members in our community. Contacts arise as providential as that of Philip with the Ethiopian, but we hesitate, nothing is said—and the opportunity is gone.

As we have noted, the Philip of today's scripture was a layman in the church. It is not just the ordained minister who is to go out and seek souls. "It is a fatal mistake," declares inspiration in comment upon this story in Acts 8, "to suppose that the work of soul-saving depends alone upon the ministry."—*The Acts of the Apostles,* p. 110. Laymen too are to go forth and preach Jesus —not only by the lives that they live, but by endeavors as active as the ministry of Philip, when he explained the Scriptures to the Ethiopian. God has long waited for a spirit of service to possess all the members of the church. If all of us would be as alert as Philip and as faithful, how quickly the work could be finished!

SOWING GOD'S WORD

He that goeth forth and weepeth, bearing precious seed, shall doubtless come again with rejoicing, bringing his sheaves with him. **Ps. 126:6.**

"The seed," Jesus said, "is the word of God" (Luke 8:11). Hundreds and thousands of literature evangelists go forth each day, sowing the precious seed. Angels of heaven watch over the seed that is sown, and the time is coming when "more than one thousand will soon be converted in one day, most of whom will trace their first convictions to the reading of our publications" (*Colporteur Ministry,* p. 151).

Has God ever impressed you that you ought to go into the literature ministry? Have you given any further thought, those of you who are students, to going forth this summer?

At the close of the 1969-1970 school year seventeen of the graduating class at Union Springs Academy, in New York, went out as student literature evangelists. When I saw their pictures, along with others, in the July 21, 1970, issue of the Atlantic Union *Gleaner,* I thought, We surely ought to thank God for them, and ought to especially pray that the angels of heaven will abundantly bless their ministry.

For those who work regularly as literature evangelists, and for those who will be working this summer, today's scripture is your assurance of success. There will be times of discouragement, but look beyond the things that discourage to the promise that you will *doubtless* come again with rejoicing, bringing with you to eternal life some whom you have helped. And all of us, whatever our work, need to remember that "if you fail ninety-nine times in a hundred, but succeed in saving the one soul from ruin, you have done a noble deed for the Master's cause (*Christian Service,* p. 101).

"Pray one for another," James 5:16 suggests. We can think of this as God's special invitation to each one of us to pray today for all of the students who will be going out this summer as literature evangelists. And if you are personally acquainted with any literature evangelists, pray for them by name too.

AS YOU PLAN A VACATION

Now thanks be unto God, which always causeth us to triumph in Christ, and maketh manifest the savour of his knowledge by us in every place. 2 Cor. 2:14.

In His ministry to mankind Jesus "took advantage of the opportunities to be found along the great thoroughfares of travel" (*Prophets and Kings*, p. 73). He had no home of His own, but in His journeys to and fro He spent considerable time at Capernaum, which came to be known as "his own city" (Matt. 9:1). Capernaum, located on the shores of the Sea of Galilee, was situated on the highway from Damascus to Jerusalem and Egypt, and people from many lands passed through the city, or tarried there to rest. Here Jesus met people of all nations, who took with them some of the things that He taught.

This kind of missionary work has frequently been neglected by God's people. In Solomon's time, for example, the missionary spirit was supplanted by commercialism. The land of Israel was strategically located, so that many travelers journeyed through it—but "through the cupidity and shortsightedness of those to whom had been committed the oracles of God, the countless multitudes who thronged the highways of travel were allowed to remain in ignorance of Jehovah" (*ibid.*, p. 72).

The people of God today have even greater opportunities to manifest a missionary spirit. With the close of school, the thoughts of many are turning toward vacation trips. As we travel God is ready to provide opportunities that could set in motion a chain of circumstances that could eventually lead someone to find eternal life. "In this our day the opportunities for coming into contact with men and women of all classes and many nationalities are much greater than in the days of Israel. The thoroughfares of travel have multiplied a thousandfold."—*Ibid.*, p. 73. Vacation trips, particularly when you camp out, could provide numerous providential contacts—if you were prepared to take advantage of the opportunity God gives to you.

Why not take with you several copies of our current missionary book, and other literature? Why not let there be manifest through you "the savour of his knowledge . . . in every place"?

SHARING WHEN YOU TRAVEL

I am the Lord thy God . . . which leadeth thee. **Isa. 48:17.**

I was walking across the parking lot at O'Hare Field in Chicago, to continue a journey back to Auburn, Washington, after a trip to Mississippi. As I walked, I prayed silently that the seating on the plane would work out in a way to give opportunity to share some more literature. I had left home with a brief case full, knowing that in the providence of God several opportunities to share it might arise. We scarcely had left the ground at the beginning of the trip when I was able to start a conversation with an Air Force man returning from Vietnam to his home in Oklahoma City. "What do you think is the solution in Vietnam?" I had asked him. "There is no solution," he had replied—which led into a discussion of world events. During this discussion I had opportunity to introduce him to the book *The Great Controversy,* which he began to read. When we parted I told him he could keep the book, and he assured me he would read it all.

The course of the trip had provided several similar opportunities. On the way up from New Orleans to Chicago, I made the acquaintance of a physician and his wife who are associated with the Mayo Clinic. Learning that she had taught a Sunday school class, and that he was active in church work, I gave them a copy of *Positive Christian Living*—the missionary book for that year. They thanked me, mentioning Maplewood Academy and how impressed they had been with the work done at the bookbindery there.

But now, on the final stretch of the trip, I still had some literature left. My seatmate was a young man in uniform, but he was not very talkative, so I took out some work. A few minutes later he inquired, "Are you a teacher?" I told him that I taught several religion classes. As we chatted, I discovered he had just told his family good-by, and was on his way to Vietnam. It turned out that he had trained with some Adventist young men and was very interested in religion, and in the Sabbath. I gave him three books.

God will lead you in your coming and going to similar opportunities. Why not travel prepared?

THOSE OFTEN FORGOTTEN

Pure religion and undefiled before God and the Father is this, To visit the fatherless and widows in their affliction, and to keep himself unspotted from the world. James 1:27.

On this Memorial Day we appropriately remember those who have given their lives for their country, and all of our dead. It might also be appropriate, on the basis of today's scripture, to give some thought as to how we could be a greater blessing to those who have been the bereaved, particularly those who are widows. In an article in the Los Angeles *Herald-Examiner,* Gay Pauley reported that in the United States there are eight million widows, an "often lonely, often tragic, often pessimistic group" who "either give up to grief or struggle to rejoin the human race" (April 19, 1968).

For Seventh-day Adventists who are widows there is much courage in reading the biographical account left by Ellen White concerning the difficult days when she lost her husband (*Testimonies,* vol. 1, pp. 105-112).

The rest of us should be reminded that in Israel the rights of widows and orphans were specially guarded, and a tender regard for them was enjoined. The book of Deuteronomy, in particular, frequently mentions widows and the compassion that should be shown to them. The pen of inspiration likewise, as a check under the word "widow" in the Spirit of Prophecy *Index* will quickly show, gives considerable attention to our responsibilities concerning widows.

One interesting suggestion is that youth should do what they can to help widows. "Young men and women to whom God has given health can obtain a great blessing by aiding the widow and the fatherless in their affliction."—*Ibid.,* p. 190.

The eight million widows of the United States, and the millions in other parts of the world, are probably one of our most neglected groups as far as missionary work is concerned. Why not, in your church, organize a youth service group whose missionary responsibility would be to watch the papers concerning bereavements—and then at an appropriate time make a visit to see what ways you might help.

"THE BEST WAY"

I . . . have shewed you, and have taught you publickly, and from house to house, testifying both to the Jews, and also to the Greeks, repentance toward God, and faith toward our Lord Jesus Christ. Acts 20:21, 22.

"We have found that the best way to win others is by house-to-house visitation," reported Chafic Srour, from Lebanon, in the March 6, 1969, issue of the *Review and Herald.*

Such visitation does not always need to be a Bible study. One Sabbath afternoon when out with a group of students, we came across a home where the wife had been bedfast for some time. The next day we stopped by with a potted plant and get-well card from the church. The contact did not result in Bible studies, though we left some literature on a later visit. This elderly couple, who had known very little of Seventh-day Adventists, were most appreciative.

"Our Saviour," we read, "went from house to house, healing the sick, comforting the mourners, soothing the afflicted, speaking peace to the disconsolate. He took the little children in His arms and blessed them and spoke words of hope and comfort to the weary mothers. With unfailing tenderness and gentleness, He met every form of human woe and affliction."—*Gospel Workers,* p. 188.

Paul, as today's scripture indicates, also went from door to door in seeking souls. Inspiration, commenting concerning Paul's house-to-house labor, urges, "Do not neglect speaking to your neighbors, and doing them all the kindness in your power, that you 'by all means may save some.' We need to seek for the spirit that constrained the apostle Paul to go from house to house pleading with tears, and teaching 'repentance toward God, and faith toward our Lord Jesus Christ.' "—*Christian Service,* p. 116.

A fire chief lived for seventeen years within two blocks of a Seventh-day Adventist church, and for eight years next door to one. Finally, someone called on him with gift-Bible lessons. Today he is a Seventh-day Adventist. But how is it that it took so long for someone to invite him? Could there be thousands more like him?

A MARVELOUS BOOK

O Lord, how manifold are thy works! In wisdom hast thou made them all: the earth is full of thy riches. Ps. 104:24.

Let's say that you are looking for a good book for yourself or for your children. You find one that is not merely good—it's marvelous! It has among other things, all the following qualities: (1) it holds the interest of everyone from small children right up to the most highly educated adult; (2) it invigorates the spirit, drawing out the affections toward God and instilling an attitude of reverence and awe; (3) it has a refining, subduing effect, causing anxiety to subside, restlessness to be calmed, and vanity to be diminished; (4) it tends to break the spell of fashion; and (5) it leads the soul away from sin and worldly attractions, and toward purity, peace, and heaven.

By now you have guessed what book we are talking about— the book of nature. We have become more and more a people of the cities and suburbs, but, as with Lot, many of us may be paying too high a price. The child deprived of contact with the works of God tends to become absorbed with the artificial and the false. And with adults and children alike, the ear that seldom hears nature's utterances is less likely to hear the still small voice. Eyes that never look upon meadows and mountain peaks and starry skies are more easily enamored by the sights and sounds of sin.

Inspiration speaks of the "refining, subduing influence in nature" (*Fundamentals of Christian Education*, p. 423). The music of running streams, the beauty of flower-gemmed meadows, the simple grandeur of a countryside, waves lapping against the beach, the influence of open skies and mountains— these subdue not only restlessness and anxiety, but unholy thoughts as well. "The beauty of nature leads the soul away from sin and worldly attractions, and toward purity, peace, and God." —*Counsels to Parents and Teachers,* p. 186.

It is an influence all of us need. Especially do small children need the blessings of daily contact with the great outdoors. Are they and we getting it?

OUT IN THE GARDEN

And I will bring again the captivity of my people of Israel, and they shall build the waste cities, and inhabit them; and they shall plant vineyards, and drink the wine thereof; they shall also make gardens, and eat the fruit of them. Amos 9:14.

Had Israel followed God's plan, the whole land of Palestine would have become virtually another Garden of Eden. The prophecies that describe the fruitfulness that could have prevailed in the land of Israel will ultimately be fulfilled in the earth made new.

Meanwhile, one of the greatest blessings that can come to a child of God is to be able to grow his own garden. Wherever we have lived we have tried to have at least a little space for vegetables and flowers. A couple of times we have utilized a vacant lot, and in a third instance rented some space up the street. One's garden need not be large. Too much space we have discovered can make it drudgery trying to keep ahead of the weeds. A small plot that one can really enjoy caring for is better than getting bogged down.

Children, especially, benefit from being able to help grow plants and flowers. "In cultivating carefulness, patience, attention to detail, obedience to law, it [the care of plants] imparts a most essential training. The constant contact with the mystery of life and the loveliness of nature, as well as the tenderness called forth in ministering to these beautiful objects of God's creation, tends to quicken the mind and refine and elevate the character."—*Education*, p. 112.

God would have us utilize the lessons taught by the flowers in the training of our children. "He is a lover of the beautiful," we read in *Steps to Christ*, "and above all that is outwardly attractive He loves beauty of character; He would have us cultivate purity and simplicity, the quiet graces of the flowers."—Page 85.

With children particularly, thoughts of God are readily associated with growing things, and with the flowers. It can become natural for them to see in the lovely blossoms reminders of God's love. The flowers remind us, too, of the Garden of Eden, now in heaven. Soon, by God's grace, we will be walking its pleasant paths.

REFLECTING HIS GRANDNESS

Which by his strength setteth fast the mountains; being girded with power.
Ps. 65:6.

One weekend we accompanied a group of young people on a climb up Mount Whitney. On Friday we hiked up to above ten thousand feet and made camp on the shores of Mirror Lake. That evening, awed by the starry heavens above and by the surrounding ridges and peaks which seemed to reach up almost to the stars, we found it natural to talk of God. During that evening and throughout the Sabbath this sense of reverence deepened.

Sunday morning we hiked on up to Whitney's 14,501-foot summit. There one can see along the crest of the Sierras, peak after peak rising out of the distant blue mists, and at the same time look down upon a sweeping desert valley lying some ten thousand feet below. Of this top-of-the-world spot Geologist Francis Matties once said, "Upon it I have never set foot without a certain sense of reverence."

The benefits of our climb were more than recreation and fellowship. Minds accustomed to the sights and sounds of Los Angeles stirred to new thoughts. The Friday evening by the lake, the seeming nearness of the stars, the quietude of the trails, the mountain vastness—all began to have an effect. Said one student later, "For a long time I had been yearning for a sports car, but as I hiked up the trail I had time to think and to see things as they really are. Some things I had thought were so important no longer seemed so."

The book *Fundamentals of Christian Education* has an article entitled "The School of the Ancient Hebrews." We would do well to review it. If we would preserve our children from the spell that the world so quickly casts over so many of the youth from Christian homes, we need all the help we can get. Nature can be part of that help. "As we behold the beautiful and grand in nature, our affections go out after God; while the spirit is awed, the soul is invigorated by coming in contact with the Infinite through His works."—Page 443.

The mountains, the prairies, the streams, the forests, the starry heavens—all reflect His greatness.

IN AWE BEFORE HIM

Let all the earth fear the Lord: let all the inhabitants of the world stand in awe of him. **Ps. 33:8.**

We lay in our sleeping bags at the bottom of the Grand Canyon, watching a full moon come up over the rim. All was quiet except for the rustle of cottonwood leaves and the splashing of Bright Angel Creek a few yards away.

There were twenty-one of us—three Glendale Academy teachers and eighteen students—out to spend spring vacation seeing what we could of this immense canyon. The moon as it rose higher began to play hide-and-seek with the clouds floating across the sky. The cliffs surrounding us towered up in more distinct immensity as the light of the moon penetrated down into the canyon depths. As we tried to take it all in, the awe mentioned in today's scripture was ours.

The Grand Canyon, a mile deep, four to eighteen miles wide, and 217 miles long, encompasses a thousand square miles. An Empire State Building or Washington Monument could be neatly tucked out of sight behind some cliff, or among some of the hundreds of mountain peaks that rise out of its depths. "The Grand Canyon of Arizona fills me with awe," wrote Theodore Roosevelt. "It is beyond comparison—beyond description; absolutely unparalleled throughout the wide world."

How much more true of God's greatness! Look up into the starry heavens on a clear night. The whole earth is as nothing compared to the immensity out there. "Let all the inhabitants of the world stand in awe of him," David wrote of the Creator. One need not hike into the Grand Canyon to sense His greatness—it is displayed in some form wherever one turns out in the world of nature.

"The study of God's character as revealed in His created works," says inspiration, "will open a field of thought that will draw the mind away from low, enervating pleasure."—*The Youth's Instructor,* May 6, 1897, p. 138. It is an influence we much need. Even "the frivolous and pleasure-seeking," it is suggested, cannot but be "filled with reverence," if they will but dwell upon the things of God as revealed in the world of nature.

162

A RIVER CRYSTAL CLEAR

And he shewed me a pure river of water of life, clear as crystal, proceeding out of the throne of God and of the Lamb. Rev. 22:1.

When one hikes into the Grand Canyon by taking the Bright Angel Trail from the South Rim, you follow along the Colorado River for some two miles before crossing over the river to the north side. We have taken student groups on pack trips into this canyon on two different occasions, and both times one of the most awesome things for me has been hiking along that two-mile stretch of trail that follows along the edge of this swift-flowing river.

On our first of these two trips one of the teachers sprained her ankle while at the bottom, and we had to call for a mule for her to ride out upon. I waited, on the day we climbed out, until the mule train had arrived, then struck out to catch the group. As I hiked alone along the Colorado River, noticing an occasional wildflower, or glancing beyond the red cliffs to the blue sky above, God seemed very close. As I hiked I thought of the river of life, and how different it would be from the turbulent Colorado.

Draining 300,000 square miles, the Colorado is the second longest river in the United States, and until the Glenwood Canyon Dam was finished, it was one of the fiercest in the world. At Lava Falls it would roar down a 25 per cent grade for some two hundred yards at speeds up to thirty miles an hour, churning up billows nearly fifteen feet high. Its treacherous rapids have claimed the lives of many would-be explorers.

Its muddy waters were once described as "too thick to drink and too thin to plow." Let your thoughts go in contrast to the river described in today's scripture. Its "clear as crystal" waters, beginning at the throne of God, will flow through the New Jerusalem, then out across the vast plains of the earth made new. Inspiration speaks of waving trees casting their shade over "the paths prepared for the ransomed of the Lord"—and of wide-spreading plains swelling into hills of beauty, beyond which "the mountains of God rear their lofty summits" (*The Great Controversy*, p. 675).

What will it be to hike along those trails?

PRESSING UPWARD

I press toward the mark for the prize of the high calling of God in Christ Jesus. Phil. 3:14.

Whichever of the two trails you take down from the South Rim into the Grand Canyon, the hike out is an unforgettable experience. The Kaibab Trail, the shorter of the two, is seven miles from Yaki Point down to the Phantom Ranch at the bottom. It is, in the words of one hiker, "seven miles down and seventy-seven miles out."

The 6,870-foot elevation of the South Rim of the canyon is higher than any point in the eastern States. The elevation down at the river is 2,500 feet. In hiking into the canyon the drop is equivalent climatically to a journey of some three thousand miles from the Canadian border all the way down into Mexico. The weather can vary from a snowstorm on the rim to semitropical conditions at the river. Both of our pack trips into the canyon with student groups were made during spring vacation—and both times it rained on us while we were at the bottom, and snowed on the top.

On our second trip down the biggest storm of the season dumped an inch of rain on us at the bottom, and a foot of snow on the families camping on the rim. We hiked out the day following this storm, taking the steeper Kaibab Trail. For the first two or three miles we slushed through the mud. Then the mud gradually became snow, so that as we finally neared the top we were breaking our way through a foot of snow on the trail.

One student mentioned as we kept pushing upward that it made him think of the song, "I'm Pressing on the Upward Way." Our packs were heavy, and the trail challenging, but we made it. And so in spiritual things. "By taking one step after another, the highest ascent may be climbed, and the summit . . . reached at last."—*Messages to Young People,* p. 46.

> I want to scale the utmost height,
>   And catch a gleam of glory bright;
> But still I'll pray till heaven I've found,
>   "Lord, lead me on to higher ground."
>   JOHNSON OATMAN, JR.

ARE YOU AWARE OF ANGELS?

Are they not all ministering spirits, sent forth to minister for them who shall be heirs of salvation? Heb. 1:14.

Are you aware of the angels in your life? We've quoted Bible verses about them. We say we believe they exist. But are they really a recognized and appreciated influence in our lives?

A lot of people would put angels into the same category as Santa Claus. They can scarcely imagine that there is an unseen but very real army of heavenly beings all about us.

Angels are specifically mentioned in thirty-five of the sixty-six books of the Bible. The word for angels is used 106 times in the Old Testament, and 170 times in the New. We find angels speaking with Abraham and Lot, with Gideon and Daniel, with Zacharias and Mary, and with Paul. These were not occasions when they came in a dream. They came as visible, physical beings. They have often communicated with men and women in dreams, too, as Gabriel did to Joseph before the birth of Christ. And they have wrought deliverances, as with the destruction of the Assyrian army, without being seen at all.

We need to understand better than we do the mission of the angels. "It would be well," suggests inspiration, "to consider that in all our work we have the cooperation and care of heavenly beings. Invisible armies of light and power attend the meek and lowly ones who believe and claim the promises of God."—*Christ's Object Lessons,* p. 176.

Could the curtain that separates the seen from the unseen world be drawn aside, what would we see? Here's one description:

"Amid the busy activity of our great cities, amid the multitudes that crowd the thoroughfares and fill the marts of trade where from morning till evening the people act as if business and sport and pleasure were all there is to life, where there are so few to contemplate unseen realities—even here heaven has still its watchers and its holy ones. There are invisible agencies observing every word and deed of human beings."—*Ibid.*

Do you really believe this?

HEAVEN'S SECRET SERVICE

The angel of the Lord encampeth round about them that fear him, and delivereth them. Ps. 34:7.

At the time Vice-President Lyndon Johnson found himself suddenly thrust into the Presidency of the United States, nineteen-year-old Lynda Johnson was a sophomore at the University of Texas, living with eight hundred other women students in a university-operated dormitory.

A story in the Glendale *News-Press* on December 3, 1963, reported that on that tragic Friday afternoon when President Kennedy was slain, she was taken from her dormitory by Secret Service agents to the governor's mansion in Austin for protection. Following the funeral services in Washington, she returned to school. Thereafter, the Associated Press reported, at least one Secret Service agent was with her wherever she went in public. Inside the dormitory the Secret Service set up an office in a glass-walled room that commanded a full view of the lobby and main entrance. Extensive telephone circuits were set up in the office.

Lynda was taking a nineteen-hour class load of English, Latin, history, government, chemistry, and Bible. Of the Secret Service agent who accompanied her to class, she reportedly told a friend, "He sits in class and seems very interested. He's learning things too."

Heaven has its secret service agents too—the ones mentioned in today's scripture, who encamp "round about them that fear him" to deliver them. "In all ages, angels have been near to Christ's faithful followers. The vast confederacy of evil is arrayed against all who would overcome; but Christ would have us look to the things which are not seen, to the armies of heaven encamped about all who love God, to deliver them. From what dangers, seen and unseen, we have been preserved through the interposition of the angels, we shall never know, until in the light of eternity we see the providences of God."—*The Desire of Ages*, p. 240.

Then we shall understand. We shall look back and wonder how we could have been so slow to discern. But let us at least try, even now, to appreciate what the angels are doing.

ALWAYS ON DUTY

He shall give his angels charge over thee, to keep thee in all thy ways.
Ps. 91:11.

Lora Clement years ago shared this story:

The evangelist baptized a woman whose husband was angry because his wife had become a Christian, and swore that he would kill the evangelist come next prayer meeting. He knew the custom, how that after the singing all knelt with bowed heads and closed eyes to pray. The preacher would be in front, near the door. It would be easy to slip in and lop off his head.

And so on prayer meeting night this man stood outside the hall in which the service was being held. His bolo was in his hand, sharp and ready. As the people knelt in prayer, he stepped in silently. All heads were bowed. Not an eye saw him. Then suddenly he dropped his bolo and turned and fled. Later he told why.

As he approached the kneeling leader an angel with wings outspread stood facing him, piercing eyes fixed upon him! He could not lift his knife, and terrified, he ran away.—In "Let's Talk It Over," *The Youth's Instructor,* March 3, 1942, p. 2.

"He shall give his angels charge over thee," the inspired Word promises, "to keep thee in all thy ways."

Nor is such assurance given without need. Enemies far more powerful, more malignant, more determined than an angry bolo knife carrier are on our track constantly. But for Heaven's Secret Service, we would be at their mercy.

"We carefully secure our houses with bolts and locks to protect our property and our lives from evil men," notes inspiration; "but we seldom think of the evil angels who are constantly seeking access to us, and against whose attacks we have, in our own strength, no method of defense."—*The Great Controversy,* p. 517.

Would that those who feel no need of God could see things as they really are! And how thankful we should be for the fact that the angels of heaven "excel in strength"! "Those who follow Christ are ever safe under His watchcare. . . . The wicked one cannot break through the guard which God has stationed about His people."—*Ibid.*

167

MORE PROTECTION THAN REALIZED

Hast not thou made an hedge about him, and about his house, and about all that he hath on every side? Job 1:10.

This complaint, made by Satan to God, illustrates how much the heavenly angels have to do with our secular affairs, and with the protection of even our property. That which protected Job from loss was the "hedge about him, and about his house, and about all that he hath." When this hedge was temporarily withdrawn, loss followed loss, and tragedy followed tragedy, with overwhelming rapidity.

It was not that Job had been unfaithful in his financial stewardship or in any other way. Satan had challenged God's right to establish such a hedge. He argued that Job served the Lord simply because God had "blessed the work of his hands, and his substance is increased in the land" (Job 1:10). To refute this argument, God allowed Job to be tested. Once Job had passed the test, the hedge was again fully re-established as a shield against disaster and loss.

If permitted, the same agencies that brought such loss to Job could "distract our minds, disorder and torment our bodies, destroy our possessions and our lives" (*The Great Controversy,* p. 517).

Do you ever pause to consider that God's protection extends even to your material possessions?

But, you may ask, are there not many non-Christians who prosper? David noticed the same thing—that some have "more than heart could wish" (Ps. 73:7). "I was envious . . . when I saw the prosperity of the wicked," he had exclaimed—until he remembered that their prosperity can become desolation "as in a moment" (verses 3, 19).

And, drawing aside the veil that separates us from the invisible world, inspiration points out this:

"A silent witness guards every soul that lives, seeking to draw that soul to Christ. As long as there is hope, until men resist the Holy Spirit to their eternal ruin, they are guarded by heavenly intelligences."—*Testimonies,* vol. 6, pp. 366, 367.

Heaven's involvement in this world is surely far greater than we have realized!

DISGUISED AS MEN

And he lift up his eyes and looked, and, lo, three men stood by him: and when he saw them, he ran to meet them. Gen. 18:2.

In this scripture the three men whom Abraham met were two angels and Christ in human form. Ministering angels sometimes disguise themselves as human beings when they converse with men.

Such was the case when Elder Starr, Elder Farnsworth, and two other ministers were conducting a tent meeting at Oskaloosa, Iowa. The four of them were at the tent one morning. Elder Starr and another young man were talking together, Elder Farnsworth was sitting at a table writing, and the fourth minister was walking about, when a tall stranger entered. As the fourth minister met him at the tent door, the stranger inquired as to the meaning of the tent, whereupon he was told, "This is a religious meeting. We are Seventh-day Adventists. We believe the Lord Jesus is coming soon and we are working to prepare a people."

The stranger replied, "I am very much interested in that, and would like to talk with you about it." The minister invited the stranger to be seated, and the visitor asked how they thought Jesus would come. The minister who had greeted him at the door gave an explanation—and then followed the usual questions as to what would happen to the living, the resurrection of the righteous, et cetera. As the conversation continued, the minister, for no reason—for the inquiries were very courteous—assumed an argumentative attitude. After about an hour the stranger arose and told the minister, "You are no minister of Jesus Christ, you are a controversialist, sir."

The minister laughed and said, "Oh, you can't meet the argument." The visitor told this minister the same thing a second and third time, concluding, "I bid you good day," and left.

When Elder Starr shared this incident with Mrs. White, she told him, "Why, Brother Starr, that was an angel of God." She herself, as it turned out, had already told this minister that the Lord had sent an angel to rebuke him for his controversial ways.—*Notes and Papers Concerning Ellen G. White and the Spirit of Prophecy,* Ellen G. White Publications, 1966, pp. 17, 18.

SOMETHING TO THINK ABOUT

And the angel of the Lord appeared unto him, and said unto him, The Lord is with thee, thou mighty man of valour. Judges 6:12.

Gideon did not recognize this stranger as an angel until after they had talked together for some time. It was only after the angel had put forth the staff in his hand, causing the food which Gideon had set before him to be consumed, that Gideon realized to whom he had been talking. And at this point the angel disappeared.

"Ministering angels," wrote the servant of God, "frequently disguise themselves in the form of human beings, and as strangers converse with those who are engaged in the work of God." —*The Review and Herald,* Nov. 22, 1898.

She writes that many people "have listened to the voices of the inhabitants of other worlds. Time and again they have been the leaders of armies. They have been sent forth to cleanse away pestilence. They have eaten at the humble board of families, and often have they appeared as weary travelers in need of shelter for the night."—*Ibid.*

Notice that angels "frequently" disguise themselves as human beings, that "time and again" they have been the leaders of armies, that "often" they have appeared as weary travelers. Could it be, as the work draws to a close and as angels become even more active in the affairs of men, that you might personally have occasion to talk with a stranger who in reality is an angel of God? And even if you never see them visibly until Jesus comes, remember this: "In every assembly for business or pleasure, in every gathering for worship, there are more listeners than can be seen with the natural sight."—*Christ's Object Lessons,* p. 176.

Have there ever been angels disguised as strangers at your Sabbath school or at your church services? Perhaps not—but their presence there is just as real as if they had assumed human form. Would we go into God's house with a greater sense of awe, with greater reverence, if we fully realized this?

It is indeed something to think about!

A HUNDREDFOLD MORE

But the word of God grew and multiplied. Acts 12:24.

Since the beginning of the dollar missionary book plan, sales of the book selected for a particular year have generally been between one hundred thousand to five hundred thousand books. The book *The Desire of Ages* was one of the most popular, with 557,000 copies of the missionary edition being sold. Sales of *The Great Controversy* the year it was a missionary edition were 344,747.

Only eternity will reveal the results of the seed that has been sown through the dollar missionary book plan. This seed is watched over by heavenly beings, and as today's scripture assures us, it will grow and multiply.

The membership of the church in the North American Division, where the missionary edition is primarily used, is now above 425,000. What would happen if each church member in this division would determine, with God's help, to use at least one of the dollar missionary books a month? We would be using over five million of these books annually instead of half a million or less!

We ought to be doing all that and more. Said one man to his Seventh-day Adventist neighbor, "If I really believed what you say you believe, I'd be shouting it from the housetops."

The dollar missionary book is a plan better than shouting! And the opportunities that would come if we were prepared to take advantage of them would require far more than a dozen books a year. In the words of inspiration: "Golden opportunities occur almost daily where the silent messengers of truth might be introduced into families and to individuals; but no advantage is taken of these opportunities by the indolent, thoughtless ones. Living preachers are few. There is only one where there should be a hundred."—*Testimonies,* vol. 4, p. 389.

In the context of these words, written before our present literature evangelism program was developed, there is an appeal for literature evangelists. But the "almost daily" opportunities come to all of us. Could we indeed be doing a hundredfold more? Could *you?*

WITH ALMOST IMPATIENT EAGERNESS

Herein is my Father glorified, that ye bear much fruit. John 15:8.

In the *Index to the Writings of E. G. White* there are more than nineteen pages of references under the heading of "Angels." Many of these references have to do with the ministry of angels to human beings—and of these some of the most impressive have to do with the eagerness of the angels to assist in our missionary endeavors. Consider, for example, this:

"Heavenly angels have long been waiting for human agents —the members of the church—to co-operate with them in the great work to be done. They are waiting for you."—*Testimonies,* vol. 9, pp. 46, 47.

If we would only begin to show the same eagerness, wonderful things would begin to happen. "When the reproach of indolence and slothfulness shall have been wiped away from the church, the Spirit of the Lord will be graciously manifested. Divine power will be revealed. The church will see the providential working of the Lord of hosts."—*Ibid.,* p. 46.

At the 1970 General Conference the delegates and ministers pledged the church to the baptism of one million new members by the time of the next General Conference in 1975. If we really believe what we say we believe—and with the angels of God so ready to help—shouldn't two million people be able to win two million people within just one year?

The chapter from which the above quotations are taken is entitled "The Need of Earnest Effort." If you want your heart to be deeply stirred, turn and read it, and also the two preceding chapters, "Home Missionary Work," and "Called to Be Witnesses." There is an impelling eloquence of appeal in these three chapters unequaled anywhere. Will we get the message? The angels are waiting. God is waiting. What will it take to awaken us to earnest soul-winning effort? At Pentecost "the church beheld converts flocking to her from all directions" (*The Acts of the Apostles,* p. 48). Could the same thing happen again before 1975? It partly depends upon *you.*

ONE BILLION CHILDREN

Suffer little children, and forbid them not, to come unto me: for of such is the kingdom of heaven. Matt. 19:14.

In December of 1969 a UNESCO Space Communication conference was held in Paris. One of the speakers estimated that "there are about one billion children of school age on this planet."—*Clear Channel,* August-September, 1970 issue, p. 5.

One billion children of school age! The speaker didn't indicate what grades this encompassed, but could we estimate that in the lower grades there are upwards of eighty million at each grade level?

Eighty million six-year-olds! How many of them will have favorable opportunities to learn of salvation? How many of them, during their impressionable years, will be taught anything from the Word of God? Millions of six-year-olds, and seven-year-olds, and five-year-olds are getting such a steady diet of junk TV programs that by the time they are in their early teens they will be so hardened that the gospel will have little chance in their hearts. Yet if only they could be put under Christian influences while they are still impressionable, many of them would eventually accept eternal life.

But what can we do? It seems utterly impossible that the majority of the children of the world will ever have strong Christian influences in their young lives. But if we could help even one or two, it would be better than doing nothing. We can at least take one neighbor child to Sabbath school, and we can support vacation Bible schools this summer. Jesus in His teaching came down to the level of the children, for "He knew that these children would listen to Him and accept Him as their Redeemer far more readily than would grown-up people. . . . He planted in their minds the seeds of truth, which in after years would spring up, and bear fruit unto eternal life. It is still true that children are the most susceptible to the teachings of the gospel; their hearts are open to divine influences, and strong to retain the lessons received."—*The Desire of Ages,* p. 515.

Is there a child in your neighborhood whom you could help?

CAN WE SLEEP WHEN PEOPLE DIE?

When wilt thou arise out of thy sleep? **Prov. 6:9.**

A chapel speaker told how he and his wife, with their eight-year-old son, were traveling through hilly country when the road was wet. A car going in the same direction passed them at a high rate of speed. As they came over a hill they saw that car again, just as it was skidding over into the other lane of traffic. Coming from the other direction was another car also traveling at high speed. A collision was inevitable, and within moments the highway was littered with debris and with the broken bodies of the occupants of both cars.

The eight-year-old saw it all. He became as pale as a sheet. He did not speak a word during the rest of the trip. No one did.

When they arrived at their destination, the boy's concern did not lessen. His parents put him to bed. Ten o'clock came, then eleven, then twelve, and still the boy remained awake.

His father went in and sat on the bed beside him. "Sweetheart, won't you try to sleep?" he said.

The little fellow broke into tears. "Daddy," he said, "when people die, can we sleep?"

The Jewish people, as God's special vineyard, had all kinds of blessings bestowed upon them. But they appropriated these advantages for their personal use, caring little for the millions upon millions whom they should have helped. Ingratitude to God, the neglect of opportunities and blessings, the selfish appropriation of God's gifts—these were their sins.

How is it today? "Multitudes are perishing. But how few of the professed followers of Christ are burdened for these souls. The destiny of a world hangs in the balance; but this hardly moves those who claim to believe the most far-reaching truth ever given to mortals. . . . There is a stupor, a paralysis, upon the people of God, which prevents them from understanding the duty of the hour."—*Christ's Object Lessons,* p. 303.

How can we sleep when souls are in peril? *How can we?*

174

THE SIN OF HELP NOT DELIVERED

Moreover it is required in stewards, that a man be found faithful. **1 Cor. 4:2.**

Today's scripture is generally associated with thoughts of financial stewardship. This it certainly includes, but stewardship is more than financial faithfulness. Peter mentions, for example, that we have been made "stewards of the manifold grace of God" (1 Peter 4:10).

Consider an illustration:

Let us suppose that back in the time when the sun never set on the far-flung British Empire a distant colony is in great distress because of famine and threatened war. Even as thousands are dying of starvation, a powerful enemy is gathering on the frontier. The government at home is stirred to action. Supplies are gathered, and public charity pours forth. A fleet of ships is loaded and is sent to the distant colony, accompanied by the prayers of many.

For a time the fleet sails directly for its destination, but after a time the ardor of those entrusted with delivering the supplies cools. A group of islands lies in their course, at which they decide to stop. They find advantages for buying and selling, and those in charge of the fleet of ships are persuaded to discontinue their trip. Remaining on the islands, they take the supplies entrusted to them and use these materials for personal gain. The starving multitudes in the distant colony are forgotten and left to perish. The relief never reaches its destination.

Could something like this ever happen?

The inspired writings, from which the above illustration has been taken and abbreviated, draw this parallel: "It is difficult for us to realize that man could be guilty of so terrible a sin. Yet I am instructed to say to you, my brother, my sister, that Christians are daily repeating this sin."—*Testimonies,* vol. 8, p. 25.

The sin lies not alone in financial unfaithfulness but in a failure to share the "manifold grace of God." It is the bread of life that has been hoarded and not delivered to those needing it.

Are *you* fulfilling *your* stewardship responsibilities?

WITH JOY

Neither count I my life dear unto myself, so that I might finish my course with joy, and the ministry, which I have received of the Lord Jesus, to testify the gospel of the grace of God. Acts 20:24.

Paul's burden and that of the early believers was not how much they could get, but how much they could give. "In their work the disciples constantly encountered privation, calumny, and persecution; but they counted not their lives dear unto themselves and rejoiced that they were called to suffer for Christ. Irresolution, indecision, weakness of purpose, found no place in their efforts. They were willing to spend and be spent."—*The Acts of the Apostles,* p. 595.

A number of years ago Elder A. H. Roth, of the Inter-American Division, told of a church member who was out doing house-to-house visitation, such as Paul so frequently did. One day he was severely beaten by a mob, but "instead of fleeing to another village, he started out again the next day to continue his house-to-house visitation program.

"The village church bell rang, and soon a mob formed. Once more he was beaten and left for dead. He recovered, however, and again the next day began his work. For the third time he was attacked, beaten severely, and rendered unconscious by stoning. But his life was spared, and just as soon as he was able he began visiting again.

" 'Do you want us to kill you dead?' one of the villagers cried.

" 'No. I have come to tell you about Jesus and His love. But I am ready to die if it will save you,' our faithful lay missionary replied.

"This so impressed the family that he was invited in. Eleven of the neighbors also became interested, and one week later he organized a Sabbath School. Today nine ringleaders of the mob are lay preachers."—*Review and Herald,* Nov. 15, 1956, p. 5.

What means the most to you—personal gain and comfort, or the work of God? Do you count your life dear unto yourself, or would you be willing to suffer if need be to win others to Christ?

Paul thought of himself as belonging completely to Christ. Personal interests were put aside, and God's work came first.

How is it with you?

MY BED IS TOO COMFORTABLE

"Cry aloud, spare not, lift up your voice like a trumpet; declare to my people their transgression, to the house of Jacob their sins." Isa. 58:1, R.S.V.

This scripture is perhaps one of the most misused in all the Bible. So often an admonition to do better in keeping our standards is prefaced with a "Cry aloud, spare not, lift up your voice like a trumpet." But that is not what Isaiah is talking about at all. Read the rest of the chapter and you discover that the sin Isaiah is crying aloud against is the sin of neglecting the spiritual and physical needs of the afflicted.

Isaiah's message from God is this:

"Is not this the fast that I have chosen? to loose the bands of wickedness, to undo the heavy burdens, and to let the oppressed go free, and that ye break every yoke? Is it not to deal thy bread to the hungry, and that thou bring the poor that are cast out to thy house? when thou seest the naked, that thou cover him; and that thou hide not thyself from thine own flesh?" (Isa. 58:6, 7).

This same emphasis is brought by Mrs. White. Young people sometimes think that her main burden was "don'ts" in the area of amusements and dress. But in her writings Isaiah 58 is quoted more than any other Old Testament chapter except Isaiah 53 and Exodus 20. Her burden is that we might forget ourselves in earnest efforts to help relieve the suffering and needs of others.

"When I visit our leper colonies," writes Elder Robert Pierson, "I can't sleep at night—my bed is too comfortable; my blankets are too clean; I am too warm. Somehow, those shivering, scantily clad dark bodies sitting or sleeping on the cold, hard earth without adequate blankets haunt my fitful slumber. Those scaly stubs where fingers once had been, those missing toes, those puffy cheeks, those appealing, blood-shot eyes— how can I ever forget them? These people need our prayers, it is true, but they also need our *money* to provide them with blankets and good food!"—*Review and Herald,* Jan. 27, 1966, p. 7.

IN HIS MASTER'S STEAD

The silver is mine, and the gold is mine, saith the Lord of hosts. Haggai 2:8.

We sometimes conclude that after we have paid tithe and set apart a portion for offerings, the Lord has nothing to do with the balance of our income. But today's scripture indicates that every penny is the Lord's. We are stewards. "A steward identifies himself with his master. He accepts the responsibilities of a steward, and he must act in his master's stead, doing as his master would do were he presiding."—*Counsels on Stewardship,* p. 113.

Fritz Kreisler, a well-known violinist, put it this way: "I never look upon the money I earn as my own. It is public money. It is only a fund intrusted to my care for proper disbursement. I am constantly endeavoring to reduce my needs to the minimum. I feel morally guilty in ordering a costly meal, for it deprives someone else of a slice of bread—some child, perhaps, of a bottle of milk. My beloved wife feels exactly . . . as I do. You know what I eat; you know what I wear. In all these years of my so-called success in music, we have not built a home for ourselves. Between it and us stand all the homeless in the world!"

A single performance would bring him more than most of us would make in several months. How would you or I spend our money if we had a similar income? Would we too shun even a costly meal?

Have you ever read *Counsels on Stewardship?* Consider the following:

"My brethren and sisters, practice economy in your homes. . . . Give up your selfish pleasures. Do not, I beg of you, spend means in embellishing your houses; for your money belongs to God, and to Him you must give an account for its use. Do not use the Lord's money to gratify the fancies of your children. . . . Do not lavish it upon those who need it not. . . . If you have extravagant habits, cut them away from your life at once."—Page 37.

Do we, like Fritz Kreisler, try to keep personal needs to a minimum? What would Christ do? What was His example?

178

JUNE 21

HAVE YOU BEEN ROBBING YOURSELF?

*Ye looked for much, and, lo, it came to little; and when ye brought it home,
I did blow upon it. Why? saith the Lord of hosts. Because of mine house that
is waste.* Haggai 1:9.

A housewife whose husband was earning an above-average income complained:

"I get to worrying so much about money—the lack of it—that I am afraid it will drive me out of my mind. There just isn't enough cash left out of the weekly paycheck to make ends meet."

"He that earneth wages earneth wages to put it into a bag with holes" (Haggai 1:6). "Ye brought it home, and I did blow upon it."

Inflation, then, is not necessarily the only reason why the money does not go around.

Our obligation to God—the support of His house and of His work—is specified as "tithes *and* offerings." Robbery of God has to do with both tithes and offerings (Mal. 3:8).

Withholding from the Lord, be it tithes or offerings, hinders the forward progress of the gospel. But the one doing the withholding is also hurt. Notes inspiration:

"When they robbed God in tithes and in offerings, they were made to realize that they were not only robbing Him but themselves, for He limited His blessing to them just in proportion as they limited their offerings to Him."—*Testimonies,* vol. 3, p. 395.

Not enough money to live on even though you are paying tithe? Could it be that you have been too limited in your offerings?

Could it be that Heaven's blessing is being restricted by your neglect of the church budget? Could it be that you have not been helping with the building funds? Might it be that God's blessing has been limited "just in proportion" to what you have been giving for Sabbath school?

Could it be that as a family you have been robbing yourselves?

179

LEAVE IT TO GEORGE?

He which soweth sparingly shall reap also sparingly; and he which soweth bountifully shall reap also bountifully. **2 Cor. 9:6.**

Whose responsibility is the church budget in your church? Should teen-agers help? Should you? You have a lot of expenses. So do others.

For many years I gave very little thought to church expense. We helped with it, somewhat regularly, but without any keen feeling of responsibility. Then along with teaching we assumed the additional responsibilities of pastoring a church of two hundred fifty plus members. We met in an academy chapel, along with several hundred academy students, so we had no janitorial expense as a church. Even so our church expense needs, counting the subsidies to the elementary school, averaged six hundred to seven hundred dollars a month. I became very keenly aware of church expense! And it is a matter of no small concern that in so many of our churches scarcely half the tithe-paying membership helps with the church budget.

The January 1, 1970, issue of the *Review and Herald* carried a thrilling story that a lot of folks probably missed. It related the budget problems at a large church in the Martinique mission. The frequent appeals from the pulpit became tiresome and ineffective. Various things were tried, but did not solve the problem. Finally, a well-prepared program organized by the mission's stewardship department came in to help. An education of the conscience took place and a spirit of revival took hold, as people began to put God's promises to the test.

One member, working as a servant in a home, pledged an amount equal to one fourth of her salary. One month she needed a new pair of shoes, yet she realized that after she paid her tithe and pledge, she would not be able to buy shoes too. She decided to put her pledge first, and somehow get along. At the end of the month her mistress added an additional 50 frs. (US$9) to her usual wages.

Such instances were multiplied. God does have a care for the local church needs, and for those who help meet these needs.

Shouldn't *all* of us have the blessing of helping?

"ALL YOUR NEED"

My God shall supply all your need according to his riches in glory by Christ Jesus. Phil. 4:19.

Said George I. Butler, one-time president of the General Conference, concerning tithing:

"We have watched this matter quite closely for twenty-five years. We have never seen that those who pay tithe grow poor in doing so. We have never seen them in the poorhouse or objects of charity. But we have seen many who dodged tithing become paupers and in deep affliction, helpless and most needy."— *Why Christians Tithe,* p. 14.

When His children pay a faithful tithe, God makes "their nine tenths worth more to them than the entire amount without His blessing" (*Testimonies,* vol. 3, p. 404). It has ever proved thus.

One caution, though, in this day of easy credit, concerning debt. Let us not think that the payment of a faithful tithe will save us from the results of unwise spending. It is easy through a multitude of installment purchases to become overcommitted financially. The Scriptures promise, "God shall supply all your need" (Phil. 4:19). Heaven does not say, God shall supply all your wants.

Some, though they pay a faithful tithe, have very little to give beyond that, and often they get behind on things such as church school obligations simply because they do not manage wisely. Their downfall, all too often, is in the area of installment purchases and charge accounts.

An excellent suggestion, made to youth but equally applicable to all of us, would be this: "When they really desire an article of dress, or some ornament or convenience, do they lay the matter before the Lord in prayer to know if His Spirit would sanction this expenditure of means?"—*Messages to Young People,* p. 357.

This suggestion, if followed, would not only lessen our financial pressures but would also enable us to have larger offerings as well.

And how much greater is one's peace of mind when one is not being constantly plagued with unpaid bills!

INVESTMENT OPPORTUNITY

Lay up for yourselves treasures in heaven, where neither moth nor rust doth corrupt, and where thieves do not break through nor steal. Matt. 6:20.

How would you like to invest seven dollars and get back one million dollars?

Someone has estimated that seven dollars invested in the Ford Motor Company back in the early 1900's would now be worth well in excess of one million dollars. That would be a return of more than $133,000 for each dollar invested.

Let's imagine that such an opportunity should become available today, but that because of increased living expenses you simply do not have seven dollars available to invest. Would you be willing to skip desserts, chewing gum, and similar things in order to secure the seven dollars?

Wouldn't we probably economize on a lot of other things too? We would probably save every dime, every penny, and invest not merely seven dollars, but every possible dollar we could spare!

But in thinking of investments, consider this:

"Let it be considered that every dollar may represent a soul, for someone might be brought to a knowledge of the truth through the use of that dollar in the missionary work."—*Testimonies to Ministers,* p. 179.

Due to inflation the dollar has decreased in value since this was written. Yet the missionary book of the year can be purchased for a single dollar! A subscription to *Message* magazine, *These Times,* or *The Signs of the Times* has brought more than one person to Christ! Yet how often we neglect to give as many of these as we might simply because "we can't afford it."

How much is a person won to Christ worth? "One soul is of more value than the entire world."—*Evangelism,* p. 324. If there is the slightest chance that a dollar, or a hundred dollars, or a thousand dollars might win a person to Christ, shouldn't we put forth every effort to make this kind of investment? Shouldn't we even be willing to dispense with some luxuries in order to do this?

A JOYOUS PRIVILEGE

Ye ought . . . to remember the words of the Lord Jesus, how he said, It is more blessed to give than to receive. Acts 20:35.

"It is . . . blessed to give."

So great is this privilege that the faces of God's people might well "light up with joy when the cause of God appeals to their liberality" (*Counsels on Stewardship*, pp. 155, 156).

Have you ever thought of it that way? Is stewardship to you a burden? Or is it a joyous privilege? What was the message on your countenance when the offering was taken last Sabbath? Did your face "light up with joy" as the offering plate started down your row?

Of the early Christians we read:

"Unselfish liberality threw the early church into a transport of joy; for the believers knew that their efforts were helping to send the gospel message to those in darkness."—*The Acts of the Apostles*, p. 344.

"It was not necessary to urge them to give; rather, they rejoiced in the privilege of denying themselves even of necessary things in order to supply the needs of others."—*Ibid.*, p. 343.

They did not need to be urged! It was a privilege to deny themselves "even of necessary things" in order to give!

"Give, and it shall be given unto you," Jesus promised; "good measure, pressed down, and shaken together, and running over" (Luke 6:38).

Notice the way Jesus worded this promise. He is saying, literally, that you cannot outgive God. His giving is not merely financial blessings, for there are spiritual blessings far greater than any monetary consideration. Yet the financial is not forgotten. One time when I was encouraging more people to help carry the church expense load in our church, a man and his wife decided one Sabbath that they would begin paying church expense regularly. A few days later he came to see me. The very next day, he said, he had made one of the largest sales he had ever made. He considered it to be a favor from the Lord as a direct blessing on his decision to help with church expense.

183

THE SPIRIT OF THE APOCALYPSE

For the love of Christ constraineth us. 2 Cor. 5:14.

"The movies are on to something big—the end of the world." Thus began a *Newsweek* magazine film review about two years ago (April 27, 1970). The reviewing editor didn't think much of the end-of-the-world movies that he had seen, but he suggested that "the very worst of these movies, and even the exultant ads that accompany them, strike a responsive chord in our souls. . . . We know as well as they do," he wrote, "that things can't go on much longer as they're going. . . .

"It doesn't take much," he said, "to get with the spirit of the apocalypse these days."

"In the last extremity," says inspiration, "before this work shall close, thousands will be cheerfully laid upon the altar. Men and women will feel it a blessed privilege to share in the work of preparing souls to stand in the great day of God, and they will give hundreds as readily as dollars are given now."—*Counsels on Stewardship*, p. 40.

The last extremity, though, will be very late. At that time will come a decree that "no man might buy or sell" except by government permission (Rev. 13:17). Will not many of God's people, even as they bring their gifts, find that they have waited too long?

The need is now. The time for Adventism's message of hope and courage to go forth as a loud cry is now. Imagine the results, if in our mission giving, and in evangelism, and in Christian education, hundreds were to be given as readily as dollars have been before! How the proclaiming of the gospel could be accelerated if for every dollar now given to the Voice of Prophecy and Faith for Today hundreds were to pour in!

Impossible? Not really. "If the love of Christ were burning in the hearts of His professed people, we would see the same spirit manifested today."—*Ibid.*

Today! Called for decades ago! Why wait any longer?

YOU'VE GOT TO BREATHE

Continue in prayer, and watch in the same with thanksgiving. Col. 4:2.

The Voice of Prophecy speaker relates that an old Indian teacher met a young convert and asked him if he was praying regularly. He answered, "I am a Christian, but I have no time to pray."

"Then you have no time to breathe," said the teacher.

"Oh, I have to take time for that, so as to live," was the reply.

"Then," said the teacher, "it is just as important to pray as to breathe."

We sometimes share this story in our Bible classes when we are discussing spiritual growth. Before telling it, we put on the blackboard or overhead projector these four essentials for physical life: breathing, nourishment, exercise, and rest. "What would you say are the parallel needs for spiritual life?" we then ask the class.

It is readily seen that the nourishment, or food, is the Word of God. Working to win others to Christ can be compared to exercise. Even our secular work responsibilities, when fulfilled "as to the Lord" (Col. 3:23), can also become a means of increasing spiritual strength. And the Sabbath, of course, is a day for rest and worship—refreshing one both physically and spiritually.

But what about the breathing? "Prayer," we read in *Messages to Young People,* "is the breath of the soul" (p. 249).

The comparison with physical breathing may not be exactly the same in every respect, but let's ask some questions. How long can you live physically without breathing? How long can you stay alive spiritually if you quit praying?

Remember that prayer need not always be words. On the same page of *Messages to Young People* is this suggestion:

"While engaged in our daily work, we should lift the soul to heaven in prayer. These silent petitions rise like incense before the throne of grace; and the enemy is baffled. The Christian whose heart is thus stayed upon God cannot be overcome."

185

THAT WE SLIP NOT

Hold up my goings in thy paths, that my footsteps slip not. Ps. 17:5.

We were just completing a seventy-mile pack trip in the high country of Yosemite National Park. Part of our group decided that before returning to the valley we would climb Half Dome. We wanted to see a sundown from the top of this mile-high piece of granite, and arrived at the summit just as the sun was dipping below the western horizon.

The last several hundred feet of the climb is up a steeply sloping apron of smooth rock, and one uses cables in order to make the climb safely. Going up isn't bad, but coming down can be more unnerving if one is at all bothered by heights. We watched the sun go down, just as the moon was becoming visible in the east. I thought of that steeply sloping granite, and a text of Scripture came to mind. I could not recall where it was found, but I knew it said something about footsteps slipping not. We paused just before we began the descent for a prayer together, at which time I mentioned this particular promise, assuring these young people that as soon as we got back to where we had left our packs I was going to try to find it in the pocket Bible I had along.

We made it down safely, and I located the text—our promise for today. Every time I read it I think back to that steep granite, and how careful we were. The same carefulness in our spiritual life would save many from a fatal fall.

Another promise that we have frequently discussed in Bible class is this one from *Messages to Young People:*

"When you rise in the morning, do you feel your helplessness, and your need of strength from God? and do you humbly, heartily make known your wants to your heavenly Father? If so, angels mark your prayers, and if these prayers have not gone forth out of feigned lips, when you are in danger of unconsciously doing wrong, and exerting an influence which will lead others to do wrong, your guardian angel will be by your side, prompting you to a better course, choosing your words for you, and influencing your actions."—Page 90.

ENJOYING YOUR FOOD

Thy words were found, and I did eat them; and thy word was unto me the joy and rejoicing of mine heart. Jer. 15:16.

Prayer is the breath of the soul, and God's Word is its food. And while you can go longer without eating than without breathing, sooner or later you must eat or perish. Some birds, we are told, can go nine days without food, a dog twenty days, a turtle five hundred days, some snakes eight hundred days, some fish a thousand days, and some insects even twelve hundred days. But eventually all living creatures must eat or they will die.

We profess to be a people of the Book. In many of our homes one would find up to a dozen Bibles or more. But are they being read? We pack a Bible when we travel, for example, then scarcely open it. Students home from academy and college sometimes go all summer without looking into a Bible, even once.

One thing is for sure—just having a Bible on our desk is not enough. Sometimes I have taken a loaf of bread to class, and putting it on the desk, have asked, "How much good will this bread do me if I just look at it, or just talk about it?"

The students get the point. The Word of God must be eaten, must be assimilated. And eating it should not be a burden or a duty. It ought to be a pleasure!

Earlier we mentioned the need for a revival in Bible study. Earnest Bible study and lukewarmness cannot coexist. Any Laodicean Christian, if he would overcome his spiritual malaise, must have a desire to eat. He needs to begin to enjoy his food.

Pastor Richards tells of a young woman who illustrated devotional Bible reading like this:

"I received a letter this morning from one I dearly love and to whom I am engaged. Well, I confess I have read his letter over five times already—not because I did not understand it the first time or because I wanted to gain his good will by reading it more frequently. It wasn't a question of duty, but simply one of pleasure and joy."

Should not the Word of God bring us pleasure too?

EXCEEDING GREAT PROMISES

Whereby are given unto us exceeding great and precious promises: that by these ye might be partakers of the divine nature, having escaped the corruption that is in the world through lust. **2 Peter 1:4.**

Elder J. N. Loughborough found in his Bible a total of 3,573 promises. He broke them down like this: Old Testament promises for the present, 2,253; for the future, 791. Total Old Testament promises, 3,044. New Testament promises for the present, 276; for the future, 253. Total New Testament promises, 529. Grand total of all promises—3,573.

Of the more than 2,500 promises for the present, how many have you tested and proved true during this past year? How many new ones will you discover during the year ahead?

Someone has suggested, "Tarry at a promise until God meets you there." As the angels of heaven draw near to open the understanding, and as the Holy Spirit impresses the heart, each new promise discovered can become a wonderful thrill. We have sometimes tried to illustrate this for our Bible classes by taking to class a Bible in which we have placed, next to a Bible promise, a twenty-dollar or even a fifty-dollar bill. We will read a promise, such as Jude 24, "Now unto him that is able to keep you from falling, and to present you faultless before the presence of His glory with exceeding joy." Then, taking from the Bible the fifty-dollar bill, we ask, "Suppose that every time you found a promise like this you were to be rewarded with a fifty-dollar bill. Would you spend more time with your Bible than you do now?"

The students generally conclude that there would be a real "revival" of Bible reading on campus!

But who could compress into a fifty-dollar bill the worth of even one promise from God's Word? How slow we are to see the worth of the things that really count! "Keep your Bible with you," inspiration suggests. "As you have opportunity, read it; fix the texts in your memory. Even while you are walking the streets, you may read a passage, and meditate upon it, thus fixing it in the mind."—*Steps to Christ*, p. 90.

You would, wouldn't you, if you were finding fifty-dollar bills?

PRACTICAL RELIGION

All scripture is given by inspiration of God, and is profitable for doctrine, for reproof, for correction, for instruction in righteousness: that the man of God may be perfect, throughly furnished unto all good works. **2 Tim. 3:16, 17.**

Suppose you have a car for sale. It's a stick shift, and the clutch started slipping when you were pulling a heavy load the other day. You have been thinking of buying a new one anyway, and now seems the time to do so before you have to start spending a lot of money on the old one. So you put an ad in the paper.

Do you tell a prospective buyer about the clutch? He probably wouldn't notice it around town for a while at least. And after he's bought it the problem is all his.

What would you do? What would Jesus do? Is your religion practical enough to make you completely honest?

Paul indicates that the Scriptures were given, not only for doctrine, but "for instruction in righteousness." It is the influence of a practical religion that gives genuine Christian witnessing its power.

"The Bible must be studied," urges inspiration, "not alone for the doctrines it teaches, but for its practical lessons."— *Review and Herald,* July 1, 1884. This principle has influenced the new Bible Doctrines teaching materials that will soon be available for use in teaching academy Bible Doctrines courses. Not only will the doctrines be covered, but important practical lessons will also be included.

In both 1 and 2 Thessalonians, for example, Paul writes much concerning the second coming of Jesus. Within that context he also emphasizes the importance of honest work. Thus, in a study of the Second Coming, a discussion of work habits can appropriately be included. "A religion which is not practical," we read in *Messages to Young People,* "is not genuine. True conversion makes us strictly honest in our dealings with our fellow men. It makes us faithful in our everyday work."—Page 72.

"Christianity," the same book brings out, "is always intensely practical."—Page 200.

A BUSINESSMAN'S EXAMPLE

Then the presidents and princes sought to find occasion against Daniel concerning the kingdom; but they could find none occasion nor fault; forasmuch as he was faithful, neither was there any error or fault found in him. Dan. 6:4.

Many Seventh-day Adventist youth train for responsibilities in the field of business, both within and without the church. Others go into various trades. Many of their parents serve both God and the community in the field of business.

There are many pressures. As one advertising man summed it up, "In the pursuit of the dollar, anything goes." However guarded we may be in resisting the temptation to dishonest practices, we live and work in a world where such pressures are prevalent.

These very pressures provide Seventh-day Adventist businessmen with some of their finest witnessing opportunities, for it gives them opportunity to demonstrate a *practical* religion— one that works during the week in the business world just as much as on Sabbath.

Daniel not only had to work with godless, prevaricating, unscrupulous men—he was supervisor of 120 of them. How did he get along?

"The experience of Daniel as a statesman in the kingdoms of Babylon and Medo-Persia reveals the truth that a businessman is not necessarily a designing, policy man, but that he may be a man instructed by God at every step. . . . His business transactions, when subjected to the closest scrutiny of his enemies, were found to be without one flaw. He was an example of what every businessman may become when his heart is converted and consecrated, and when his motives are right in the sight of God."—*Prophets and Kings,* p. 546.

For youth going into business, as well as for businessmen, two sources of practical instruction and inspiration are the book of Proverbs and the chapter in the book *Education* entitled "Business Principles and Methods." It is an interesting reading exercise to go through the book of Proverbs and underline every thought that could have an application in the business world. Why not try it?

WHAT WOULD YOU HAVE DONE?

Every one that doeth evil hateth the light, neither cometh to the light, lest his deeds should be reproved. But he that doeth truth cometh to the light, that his deeds may be made manifest, that they are wrought in God. John 3:20,21.

We were on a snow ski trip. One of the fellows in purchasing his ticket was accidentally given two tickets, so closely stuck together that the clerk did not notice her error. This student, instead of returning the extra ticket, gave it to a friend who was thus able to ski that day without purchasing a ticket.

Had you received the extra ticket, what would you have done? Had you been the friend, would you, knowing what had happened, have accepted the extra ticket?

On another ski trip we were eating breakfast at a café. One of the senior girls, in paying for her breakfast, gave the waitress a dollar. The waitress somehow mistook it for a twenty-dollar bill, and gave back nineteen dollars and some cents in change. The amazed girl took the change, started to leave, thought better of it, and returned the extra nineteen dollars to the waitress.

What would you have done?

Would you like to know one of the reasons why there has been so much lukewarmness among us? "Dishonesty is practiced all through our ranks," said the servant of God, "and this is the cause of lukewarmness on the part of many who profess to believe the truth."—*Testimonies,* vol. 4, p. 310.

One can understand that dishonesty would indeed produce a lukewarm church member! One could hardly be enthusiastic about his religion, or be very eager to win others to it, while practicing dishonesty in his financial dealings or in any other way.

Observes one church administrator, "One member practicing dishonesty does more harm than a score of honest members can repair in years." Members of the remnant church, of all people, should pay their just obligations and be completely aboveboard in their dealings.

God help us to come to the light and make any changes needed!

"I KNOW ADVENTISTS"

Providing for honest things, not only in the sight of the Lord, but also in the sight of men. 2 Cor. 8:21.

When the exam schedule came out, Hal knew he had a problem. The French exams were scheduled for Saturday. After careful and prayerful consideration, he went to the French professor's office. He explained to his professor that he could not take the exam on Saturday, even if it meant waiting another year in the hope that the timetable would be different.

Hal had no idea what the professor's reaction would be, but what happened was certainly not what he would have expected. "Yes," the professor said, "my mother is a Seventh-day Adventist and my sister teaches in your schools. I was brought up for the greater part of my youth as an Adventist, though I do not follow the church now. I am sure we can find a way through your problem.

"I would be quite willing," he continued, "for you to take the exam home on Friday in a sealed envelope. You can keep the envelope till Saturday night and then sit down and do the exam by yourself."

"But, Professor," Hal replied, "surely I couldn't do anything like that."

"I know Adventists. If you gave your word not to look at the papers or phone anyone on Saturday, such a plan would be all right with me. I see no difficulties at all, but perhaps you had better see the registrar first and check with him."

As it turned out, the registrar said No. The first of the next week, however, the registrar's office changed the schedule, and the French exam was postponed until the following Tuesday.

"I know Adventists," the professor had said. His words were a compliment. Is it always thus? Are the business dealings of church members such that they can always be trusted? Are our bills always paid? Can our word be depended upon?

"We require," said a sign in a service station, "a 50 per cent deposit from customers we don't know, and 100 per cent deposit from some we do know."

God forbid that any of us should ever be among the latter group!

AS TRANSPARENT AS SUNLIGHT

We have wronged no man, we have corrupted no man, we have defrauded no man. 2 Cor. 7:2.

Paul's statement is one every Christian should be able to declare with equal conviction. Can you?

D. A. Delafield shares the following story:

One January a man who was building a new home purchased twenty spruce trees, each five or six feet tall, from a trucker who was passing through town. He paid $4.50 apiece for the trees, considering that price a real bargain.

The trucker said to him, "Now, don't tear off the burlap from the ball of soil around the base of each tree, but plant each tree just as it is." So the trees were planted according to instructions. For several months everything seemed fine. The evergreens remained green. The man who bought them watered them conscientiously. Then suddenly they began to turn brown in the warmer weather.

One of his neighbors came over and said to him, "Say, you're watering your trees more than you should. They're all dying." Then without thinking, he took hold of one of the trees and pulled. The spruce came out of the soil, and on the bottom they were amazed to see the trunk neatly sawed off, with a wooden Christmas tree stand attached. They discovered that every one of the twenty trees was in the same condition.

We wouldn't pull a trick like this, but what about lesser things? How about things we borrow and neglect to return? Do we ever loaf on the job? Have we ever concealed goods from a customs check? Do we have any old school bills from years ago that we have neglected to pay? Have we ever damaged an employer's property by carelessness and then tried to conceal the damage? Have we ever "fudged" on expense accounts? Or on time sheets?

"Everything that Christians do should be as transparent as the sunlight."—*Thoughts From the Mount of Blessing,* p. 68. In their life, as in their speech, should be found "no guile" (Rev. 14:5).

Are all your dealings that transparent?

NO WATERMELONS IN THE WAY

And herein do I exercise myself, to have always a conscience void of offence toward God, and toward men. Acts 24:16.

A college student, taking summer school, got behind in the outside reading for one particular course. No written summaries were required—just a weekly report of the total pages read that week. It came time for the final report, when he would be leaving campus for another State, and he still lacked about one hundred pages. On this final report he included that one hundred pages, and then completed the reading within the following couple of weeks.

It seemed like a small thing—but didn't quite qualify for "a conscience void of offence." It took a letter of explanation and an apology to the teacher concerned to achieve that.

The past three or four days we have been thinking about the need for complete honesty. If it is still true that "dishonesty is practiced all through our ranks" and is a major cause of many people's lukewarmness, it is appropriate that we have done so. And one thing I know—to prepare devotional readings on a subject such as this leads one into some personal re-examination!

For example, I came across this illustration: John Quincy Adams' son was reaching for some paper to write on. It was paper belonging to the government. John Adams told his son not to use that paper, but to take some from another drawer, which belonged to him personally. I recalled having done some nonschool literary work at my school office, using the paper at hand. Conscience reminded me that the school should be paid for this paper.

A woman received a dollar for a watermelon stolen from her father's farm years earlier. The sender, in going toward heaven, had found the watermelon blocking his way.

Inspiration speaks of professed Christians coming up to the time of trouble with sins unconfessed. Little deviations from honesty, which now seem so small, will then loom up before one as insurmountable obstacles. And it will then be too late to make things right!

Let's make sure there are no watermelons in our way!

THE FIRST REQUISITE

Take heed, and beware of covetousness: for a man's life consisteth not in the abundance of the things which he possesseth. **Luke 12:15.**

When Solomon was seeking a master workman to superintend the construction of the Temple on Mount Moriah, he secured, not a consecrated workman from Israel, but a man from Tyre, Huram by name, who though he had great skill was covetous. Huram was actually a descendant on his mother's side of Aholiab, to whom God had given special skill for the construction of the tabernacle. But his father was a man from Tyre, and Huram apparently grew up in Tyre, serving the god of this world—mammon. Because of his unusual skill, Huram demanded and received large wages. Those working under him, comparing his wages with their own, gradually lost the spirit of self-denial. They demanded higher wages, too, which were granted. The wrong influences thus set in operation permeated the whole nation, bringing luxury and extravagance on the one hand, and oppression on the other.

The spirit of seeking for the highest position and for the highest wage is completely foreign to the example of Christ. We are invited, in following Christ, not to high wages, but to self-denial and sacrifice. "Unselfish devotion and a spirit of sacrifice always have been and always will be the first requisite of acceptable service."—*Prophets and Kings,* p. 65.

The Seventh-day Adventist Church today employs more than 64,000 workers in various denominational programs. These workers, in almost every case, could secure higher wages elsewhere. And yet, in spite of commitment to the work of God, covetousness sometimes creeps in, and except we guard against it, could become as baleful an influence in our day as it was in Solomon's time.

Do those of us who are denominational workers ever complain about our wages? Do we ever find ourselves putting on pressure in an effort to secure a higher salary? Suppose one does complain—what will be the influence of one's words and actions upon others? Are not "unselfish devotion and a spirit of sacrifice" still "the first requisite of acceptable service"?

195

THE CHARM OF PATIENCE

Here is the patience of the saints: here are they that keep the command-ments of God, and the faith of Jesus. **Rev. 14:12.**

I have sometimes asked a classroom of teen-agers, "How would each of you grade yourself on patience? Would you give yourself a C for average? Could you rate a B or even an A? Or would you have to give yourself a D or an F?"

Patience is one of the most practical fruits of genuine Christianity. Patience, consistency, and love on the part of a follower of Christ "will make an impression on hearts that sermons fail to reach" (*Gospel Workers,* p. 204). And, on the other hand, "a lack of courtesy, a moment of petulance, a single rough, thoughtless word, will mar your reputation, and may close the door to hearts so that you can never reach them."—*The Advent-ist Home,* p. 38.

But how does one cultivate patience? In the same way one cultivates other Christian graces—through watchfulness, through prayer, and through the power of an indwelling Christ. God will often use your own home as a classroom—for once you learn to be patient at home you will generally be patient elsewhere.

Healthful living makes it a lot easier to be patient. If we overwork, things upset us easier. Fresh air, physical exercise, plenty of rest, a good diet, trust in divine power—these are the things that help make us patient, loving, and lovable Christians.

A judge whose circuit took him through a certain Western town was somewhat annoyed by the sneering remarks of a law-yer living there. One day a friend asked the judge why he didn't take action against the fellow.

"Up in our town," said the judge, "there lives a widow who has a dog which whenever the moon shines, goes out on the steps and barks and barks away at it."

A pause followed the story. Finally the questioner asked, "Well, Judge, what about the dog and the moon?"

"Oh," said the judge, "the moon keeps on shining, that's all."

So be it with us all!

THE POWER OF KINDNESS

Inasmuch as ye have done it unto one of the least of these my brethren, ye have done it unto me. Matt. 25:40.

C. L. Paddock relates how an elderly man came to President Lincoln concerning a son who had been convicted for some offense and sentenced to death. Lincoln wrote a few lines on a sheet of paper and handed it to the weeping father. It read, "Job Smith is not to be shot until further orders from me. Abraham Lincoln."

The father read it with a look of disappointment. "I thought it was a pardon," he said. "You may order him to be shot next week."

"My friend," replied the President, "I see you are not well acquainted with me. If your son never dies till orders come from me to shoot him, he will live to be a great deal older than Methuselah."

Earlier in Lincoln's career, a fellow lawyer had charged an aged poverty-stricken widow of a Revolutionary soldier two hundred dollars as a fee for securing a four-hundred-dollar pension for her. Lincoln went to court for her, won the case, and returned the two hundred dollars—and also paid her hotel bill and bought her a ticket home.

Seventh-day Adventists should be noted for being the kindest and most thoughtful people in the community. Kindness should prevail in our homes, and in our relationships with one another. "Duty, stern duty," says God's servant, "has a twin sister, which is kindness. If duty and kindness are blended, decided advantage will be gained; but if duty is separated from kindness, if tender love is not mingled with duty, there will be a failure, and much harm will be the result. Men and women will not be driven, but many can be won by kindness and love."— *Testimonies,* vol. 3, p. 108.

Are you, as a parent or teacher, loved by your youth? Are you, as a pastor or administrator, loved by the people you serve? As teen-agers, are you loved by younger brothers and sisters?

Perhaps your religion, to be more practical, needs more kindness blended into it.

TOO RELIGIOUS TO HELP

He hath shewed thee, O man, what is good; and what doth the Lord require of thee, but to do justly, and to love mercy, and to walk humbly with thy God? Micah 6:8.

The papers carried a story some time ago of a woman on her way to church one Sunday morning. A newsboy's papers were being scattered by the wind. When he asked for help, she refused, telling him that she must hurry and get to church.

It was almost that way in the incident with the priest and the Levite who passed by the wounded stranger on the road from Jerusalem to Jericho. They were the religious ones in the story; they were the ones who were especially to represent what God is like, having "compassion . . . on them that are out of the way" (Heb. 5:2). But when he came to the wounded man, the priest didn't even stop—he merely glanced toward the wounded man. The Levite, curious, stopped and looked. Convicted of what he ought to do, he wished he had taken another route. He persuaded himself the wounded man was no concern of his, and went on.

Then came the despised Samaritan. He did not ask if the wounded man were Jew or Gentile. The Samaritan well knew that were the condition reversed, the man probably would have spit in his face and gone on. But he did not hesitate because of this. He only noticed that here was someone in need, someone suffering, someone whom he could help. And help he did.

The story illustrates the practical nature of true religion— that it "consists not in systems, creeds, or rites, but in the performance of loving deeds, in bringing the greatest good to others, in genuine goodness" (*The Desire of Ages,* p. 497).

We are eager to get the gospel to the whole world. The Lord's work must get done. But could we sometimes be neglecting those responsibilities that lie close at hand? Are there neighbors whom we could help? By "neighbor" Christ does not mean "merely one of the church or faith to which we belong. It has no reference to race, color, or class distinction. Our neighbor is every person who needs our help."—*Ibid.,* p. 503.

198

THE LITTLE MINISTRIES

For who hath despised the day of small things? Zech. 4:10.

In our work for God we tend to attach too much importance to position and prestige, to big assignments, overlooking the little ministries, which in the end may prove more fruitful for good than some of the apparently bigger things.

It was May, 1940. Hundreds of thousands of British troops had been forced onto the sands of Dunkirk. Behind them was the enemy, ahead the ocean, and from above enemy planes rained death upon them. Escape seemed impossible.

Fifty miles across the English Channel, the Admiralty put out a call for every available craft. Word spread quickly. Three hundred London businessmen with yachting experience quietly reported for duty. All along the south coast of England, and even up to Scotland, little boats congregated for one of the most daring operations of the war. Under cover of darkness, they set out for Dunkirk.

Early the next morning, a Friday, the stranded troops saw out in the mists the strangest fleet ever to sail. Hundreds of tiny craft hovered near the shore—rowboats, canoes, pleasure steamers, lifeboats, even rafts.

With admirable discipline, the men formed in groups, and waited their turn, even as enemy fire rained down upon them. Back and forth ferrying troops to larger ships went these small boats, ignoring the danger, until more than 338,000 troops were safe in England!

What if there had been no small craft available?

It is the individual personal ministry within the home, the neighborhood, that is often the most productive for good. Jesus mentions the giving of a glass of water as an influence for good.

If you have a flower garden, why not make it a point to give away as many bouquets of flowers as you can this summer to shut-ins and others who would appreciate them? An appropriate piece of literature, such as *Real Happiness Is,* could accompany the gift. Or you could attach a card, indicating you are sending a year's subscription to one of our missionary magazines.

WHAT KIND OF NEIGHBOR ARE YOU?

Bear ye one another's burdens, and so fulfil the law of Christ. Gal. 6:2.

What kind of recommendation would your religion get from your neighbors? Do you know anything about their burdens and needs? Have you ever helped someone up or down the street, or at a neighboring farm, to bear his burdens? If every Christian were just like you, how much of neighborly helpfulness would be seen in your community? If every Adventist teenager were just as thoughtful as you—no more and no less—what kind of youth would the church have?

A *Review* editorial shared this experience. John Kareth, a barley farmer in the upper Sacramento Valley, had been in the hospital to receive treatment for a lingering illness. It was November, the time for barley planting, and Mr. Kareth, though home, was still confined to bed.

The planting season wore on. Then came dawn of the twenty-first of November. Neighbors began to arrive at his 650-acre ranch, until there were one hundred of them—with twenty-one heavy tractors equipped with disks and harrows. As Mr. Kareth watched from his modest home, the hilly surfaces of his ranch were prepared for sowing. Then an airplane appeared and crisscrossed the fields, sowing the barley. By nightfall all 650 acres had been planted, and all but fifty harrowed, with the few remaining acres being finished the following morning.

It was a demonstration of caring in a very practical way!

Today's scripture asks us to think of another's burdens as also being our own. We are to do all we can to relieve these burdens—and not just for those who could repay our kindness. Even the publicans, said Jesus, love those who love them.

Do any of your neighbors have burdens you could help bear? Even a word of courage can help. "Kind words, looks of sympathy, expressions of appreciation, would be to many a struggling and lonely one as the cup of cold water to a thirsty soul. A word of sympathy, an act of kindness, would lift burdens that rest heavily upon weary shoulders."—*Christian Service*, pp. 189, 190.

THE INFLUENCE OF TV

Do men gather grapes of thorns, or figs of thistles? Matt. 7:16.

Nell L. Weidenbach, in *Christian Life,* relates this illustration: Erich and Mark, aged five and seven, had spent two years in Europe, where their father was on a diplomatic assignment for the United States Government. These little boys while there were shielded from any form of entertainment that stressed violence. As they were returning to America, they saw a shipboard movie featuring Kirk Douglas in a lusty, brawling role as a prize fighter.

The younger child began to scream, "Daddy, Daddy! Make them stop!" And he buried his face in his father's lap. The older boy, pale and shaken, quickly said, "I'm sleepy; I think I'll go to bed." He hurriedly left the room.

Some months later their father recalled the incident. "Do you know how they react to shows like that now?" he asked. " 'Call me when the shooting starts!' they say."—September, 1965, p. 46.

Back in 1959 a Los Angeles newsman estimated that by the time an average child is thirteen years old he has seen 13,000 killings on television. Children often do not distinguish between the real and the make-believe. What is the effect of this mass exposure to slaughter upon their impressionable minds? We have a generation now coming onto the scene of action that has been raised on this kind of entertainment. Should we be surprised at the increase of violence that we are seeing? Could it be that we have sown the wind and are reaping the whirlwind?

The emperor Nero found "satanic delight" in the anguish and suffering of others (*The Great Controversy,* p. 667). Could we, by default, be permitting our children to develop a callousness that though less in degree will so harden them that God could not safely take them to the New Jerusalem? Will some of our own children, through the influence of TV, end up as the associates of Nero in the attack on the City of God?

"It is a law of the human mind that by beholding we become changed."—*Patriarchs and Prophets,* p. 91. There is no statement we as Adventists have quoted more often. But don't we need to do more than quote it?

201

THAT THIRD PARENT

I will set no wicked thing before mine eyes. Ps. 101:3.

Columnist Henry J. Taylor, in the February 29, 1968, issue of the Los Angeles *Herald-Examiner,* wrote that television has become a third parent. "Millions of impressionable children," he wrote, "spend more time at the feet of this third parent, TV, than they do listening to their actual parents. When you realize the repetition, repetition, repetition of the TV diet of murder, violence, mayhem, criminal action and dramatized filth, morning, noon and night, years on end, how can parents safely permit this third parent to take over?"

What can we do about it? Mr. Taylor suggests that we simply turn off all violent programs. "The children may fuss," he says. Such programs are made "as dramatic and mind-gripping as possible. That's what makes the third parent so dangerous. But we as parents who love our children are entitled to put up a fight for their minds and dreams."

We have three children in our family, ages 18, 16, and 12 at the time of this writing, and our solution to the TV problem has been to never get a TV set. We have missed some good programs and some worth-while entertainment. But there have also been many advantages. This past summer, for example, our youngest read several dozen books. Had there been a TV set in our home he probably would not have read a single one.

In some homes the TV set is doubtless well controlled. In many it is not. It is my studied conclusion, after having taught on the elementary, junior high, and academy levels, that more Seventh-day Adventist children and youth will probably lose eternal life in consequence of unwise TV viewing than from any other cause. Even in Mrs. White's day there were professed Christians whose minds were so oriented to impurity that they were no more prepared for the coming of Christ "than Satan himself" (*The Adventist Home,* p. 328). How much greater the danger with the "dramatized filth" Mr. Taylor mentions!

"Parents should endeavor," Heaven urges, "to keep out of the home every influence that is not productive of good."—*Ibid.,* p. 411. In your home would this include the TV set?

202

GUARDING THE THOUGHTS

Now these things were our examples, to the intent that we should not lust after evil things, as they also lusted. . . . Neither let us commit fornication, as some of them committed, and fell in one day three and twenty thousand. 1 Cor. 10:6-8.

To what extent can the people of God be influenced by the standards and customs and amusements of the world?

The children of Israel were camped right on the borders of the Promised Land. On the eastern side of the Jordan there was a plain, several miles in width, and extending for some distance along the river. The climate of this sheltered valley was that of the tropics. While the Israelite leaders were busy with plans for entering Canaan, the people found this camping spot a pleasant place to relax after the hardships of the way. There was a danger here, though, more deadly than the armies they had just encountered. On every side were places noted for idolatry and licentiousness, and as the minds of the people became familiar with the thoughts of impurity constantly suggested, the way was prepared for the apostasy which later took place—an apostasy that led to the loss of thousands of men, many of whom were princes in Israel.

As the people of God again stand on the borders of a promised land—the heavenly Canaan—Satan has redoubled his efforts to prevent them from entering therein. "And he employs the same agents now as he employed three thousand years ago. By worldly friendships, by the charms of beauty, by pleasure seeking, mirth, feasting, or the wine cup, he tempts to the violation of the seventh commandment."—*Patriarchs and Prophets,* p. 458.

The same conditioning has also been going on. Every possible agency has been used to educate the mind to familiarity with evil. Unless we profit from the lessons of the past, many today will likewise fall. The inspired chapter which provides a commentary upon today's scripture—the one in *Patriarchs and Prophets* entitled "Apostasy at the Jordan"—could well be reviewed by all of us. And let the thoughts ever be guarded—for before there can be *acts* of impurity there must first be *thoughts* of impurity.

WHOSE RESPONSIBILITY?

But I say unto you, That whosoever looketh on a woman to lust after her hath committed adultery with her already in his heart. Matt. 5:28.

One day we were having a discussion in Bible class about these words of Jesus and the commandment not to commit adultery. One student suggested that boys and men have a lot more trouble with wrong thoughts than girls do. And evidently they do. But does not much of the responsibility for preventing such thoughts fall directly upon the girls and women? The seventh commandment "forbids not only acts of impurity, but sensual thoughts and desires, or any practice that tends to excite them" (*Patriarchs and Prophets,* p. 308).

Examine this as God sees it. What are the things that tend to excite sensual thoughts and desires? Mention has been made of the results of a survey that indicated that a normal young man "will be more likely to think in the direction of overt sex activity by the strip-tease effects of a short skirt wearer, seated, than by any other public fashion in history." And various other dress styles through the years have been a factor in awakening in men sensual thoughts. But what are some of the other things besides dress that are an influence toward the same end?

A failure to be circumspect and properly reserved can have the same effect. "Thoughts are awakened that would not have been if woman had kept her place in all modesty and sobriety. She may have had no unlawful purpose or motive herself, but she has given encouragement to men who are tempted, and who need all the help they can get from those associated with them." —*The Adventist Home,* p. 332.

Girls have sometimes objected, in class discussions, that men should keep their thoughts where they belong. David should have, too. But Bathsheba should also have been more careful about where she bathed. Would any Christian girl by indiscreetness or by her manner of dress want to cause someone who is weak to think sensual thoughts? Would not Christian love make her want to help keep even the weakest David from looking with lust?

WHEN LUST CONCEIVES

When lust hath conceived, it bringeth forth sin: and sin, when it is finished, bringeth forth death. James 1:15.

"Sin, however small it may be esteemed, can be indulged in only at the peril of infinite loss. What we do not overcome, will overcome us, and work out our destruction."—*Steps to Christ,* pp. 32, 33.

S. D. Gordon, in his book *Quiet Talks on Personal Problems,* tells of a man taking a walk along the seashore in the old province of Brittany, that juts out into the sea on the west of France. The sky was blue, the sun shining, the air invigorating, and the view very beautiful. As the man walks leisurely along, he thinks only of the beauty of his surroundings. Absent-mindedly, he does not notice that his feet sink into the sand somewhat. Then they begin to sink a little more, until he begins to think it strange. All at once it flashes upon him that the tide is out, and he has strayed into a bed of quicksand.

With the instinctive dread of a native he knows what this means, and instantly turns toward the mainland. But his quicker, more intense movements make his feet sink in deeper, up to the ankles. He plunges madly this way and that, screaming wildly for help. He pulls frantically to the left, then to the right, but he only sinks down deeper into the smooth, slippery sand. Soon the sand is up to his knees, then to his loins. He sinks lower, wildly waving his arms and shrieking for help. Then only his head is above the sand, then but his eyes, and a tuft of hair. And then there is only a smooth stretch of sand, a blue sky, a laughing sea.

"That," comments S. D. Gordon, "is the working of nature's laws."—Page 25.

The spiritual laws of God's universe are equally inexorable—and one of those laws is, "What we do not overcome, will overcome us."

If "the lust of the flesh" or "the lust of the eyes" (1 John 2:16), like quicksand, is pulling us down, there is a nail-pierced hand stretched out to save. But don't hesitate to reach out for it! For lust, conceived, brings sin—and sin, finished, brings death!

KEEP THYSELF PURE

Keep thyself pure. 1 Tim. 5:22.

Of all the letters of Paul, the ones he wrote to the youthful Timothy contain the words *pure* or *purity* more than any other. Timothy is to be an example of the believers in purity (1 Tim. 4:12). The younger women are to be regarded "as sisters, with all purity" (chap. 5:2). "Neither be partakers of other men's sins," Paul cautions, urging Timothy to keep himself pure (chap. 5:22).

How is such a life possible, when there is so much sin all about us? How does one keep from being affected?

When Mrs. White was in Australia, she wrote concerning something she had at one time called to the attention of her son as a kind of object lesson. "In America," she said, "we have the fresh water lilies. These beautiful lilies come up pure, spotless, perfect, without a single mar. They come up through a mass of debris. I said to my son, 'I want you to make an effort to get me the stem of that lily as near the root as possible. I want you to understand something about it.'

"He drew up a handful of lilies, and I looked at them. They were all full of open channels, and the stems were gathering the properties from the pure sands beneath, and these were being developed into the pure and spotless lily. It refused all the debris. It refused every unsightly thing, but there it was developed in its purity."

Applying her point, she indicated that the minds of youth are to be centered upon God, and Christ, and upon the sacrifice Jesus has made in our behalf. "Let them draw the purity, the virtue, the grace, the courtesy, the love, the forbearance; let them draw it from the Source of all power."—*Child Guidance,* p. 58.

In coming to Christ for help, we are coming to Someone who understands. He "was in all points tempted like as we are" (Heb. 4:15). He grew up in a village proverbial for its wickedness. And He did so "without sin." He is able to help us to do the same. "Watch ye and pray," He urges, "lest ye enter into temptation" (Mark 14:38). As we do so, He will hold us by a hand that will never let go.

IN WHAT DO YOU TRUST?

Some trust in chariots, and some in horses: but we will remember the name of the Lord our God. Ps. 20:7.

Curtis Quackenbush shared through the *Review* an experience that came to him when an Eastern Air Lines four-motored plane crashed not far from his home near Bainbridge, Maryland. He was at the scene of the crash within minutes after it happened. All fifty-three aboard had been killed instantly. When he arrived he found two fires still burning, a motor, and a broken suitcase with half of its contents spilled out. He was able to stamp out this smaller fire, recovering a Bible lying nearby, with its edges badly burned. As he stood there in the midst of that scene of death, he opened the partially burned Bible. On the flyleaf was the name of a woman. Under the flyleaf was a savings bond for ten thousand dollars.

In what, he wondered, had the owner of that bond been trusting at the moment of her death? In the promises of her Bible? Or in that ten thousand dollars, and the things money can buy? Was she ready to meet her God?

In what do you trust? Your skills? Your reputation? Your bank account? Your hard work? The rich man who pulled down his barns to build greater ones was apparently a hard worker. He had provided an abundance of material things for himself and his family. He was well thought of—"honored by his fellow townsmen as a man of good judgment and a prosperous citizen" (*Christ's Object Lessons*, p. 258). "Men will praise thee, when thou doest well to thyself" (Ps. 49:18).

Yet he had been living for self alone. The wealth entrusted to him had become his god. There was no thought for the afflicted, nor for the God of heaven. Suddenly, it was all over— and he was bankrupt for eternity. His trust had been in the wrong thing.

Today you will be working, shopping, visiting, playing, studying. It will be easy to become absorbed in the routine— and forget that which is important above all else. How much time will you be taking for God? Is everything right between you and Him?

BEING READY

Therefore be ye also ready: for in such an hour as ye think not the Son of man cometh. Matt. 24:44.

A new freeway was being put in just down the street a few blocks from where we lived in Glendale, California. It was being built as an overpass above Chevy Chase Drive, one of the main traffic arteries in that part of town. In hauling the countless tons of dirt required to build up the elevation, giant earthmovers were frequently crossing Chevy Chase, and flagmen were kept stationed there to stop the traffic as required.

One day a woman motorist was talking to a passenger and completely ignored the flagman. She cruised past his red flag and hand-held stop sign right into the path of a roaring giant. The operator slammed on the brakes, geared down, and dropped the machine's scraper into the ground. It stopped in a cloud of dust and exhaust smoke just five feet from the car. The woman, still talking to her friend, kept going and apparently never knew she had come within an instant of death.

All of us have had narrow escapes on the highways—some of them our own fault, some the result of another person's carelessness. We would not dwell on the shortness and uncertainty of life, but we are more foolish than this careless woman motorist if we do not give some quiet thought to being ready. Today's text is generally used in connection with the second coming of Christ, and that, of course, is what Jesus was talking about. But if we should be taken by a heart attack or accident today, the very next thing for us would be the second—or third—coming of Christ. Even if we are not awakened until the third coming of Christ, it will seem like just a moment.

Is your life completely in the hands of Christ? Will you, before going to sleep tonight, have left every sin at the foot of the cross? It is as a comment upon today's scripture that inspiration says, "Go to your rest at night with every sin confessed."—*Testimonies,* vol. 9, p. 48. An eccentric Scottish pastor would sometimes drop in on his parishioners unannounced. He would walk in without knocking, asking the startled member, "What if I were death?" Then he would be gone.

Eccentric? Perhaps. But he asked an appropriate question.

IF THIS NIGHT

God said unto him, Thou fool, this night thy soul shall be required of thee: then whose shall those things be, which thou hast provided? Luke 12:20.

"Since men could not do away with death," the philosopher Pascal once observed, "they decided not to think about it."

To some extent even Seventh-day Adventists seem to share this reluctance, though for the Christian death will be but "a moment of silence." Such reluctance can sometimes be criminal negligence.

A pastor of a large church recently called to the attention of his people this observation made in 1893: "It is a solemn statement that I make to the church, that not one in twenty whose names are registered upon the church books are prepared to close their earthly history, and [many] would be as verily without God and without hope . . . as the common sinner."—*Christian Service,* p. 41.

How much have conditions changed since 1893? And has it been for the better? I thought of the nearly two thousand of us who heard this pastor that Sabbath, and wondered how many of us would have been ready if, as in today's scripture, our probation suddenly and unexpectedly closed?

The things that would have made so many unready in 1893 included a "half-and-half" service, an "unsubdued spirit," perverted tastes, and "lustful practices" (*ibid.*). Can not each of us, through Christ, gain a complete victory over these things *now?*

Salvation, full and complete, is freely available. "Christ Jesus came into the world to save sinners" (1 Tim. 1:15). Not one person need be lost. Yet many will be lost, simply because of indifference and delay. "Beware of procrastination," we are urged. "Do not put off the work of forsaking your sins, and seeking purity of heart through Jesus. Here is where thousands upon thousands have erred, to their eternal loss."—*Steps to Christ,* p. 32.

As God's servants, we need first of all to deal truly with our own souls. Then as "Ministers of our God" (Isa. 61:6)—which every Christian is—we need to help others not only to get ready, but to *be* ready.

REST IN GOD

Rest in the Lord, and wait patiently for him. Ps. 37:7.

I had finished high school. If I wanted to go to a Christian college, it would be up to me to find a way. I had been baptized a year earlier at the Oklahoma camp meeting, and during the course of that camp meeting—my first—I had attended some of the meetings of the literature evangelists. These had deeply impressed me, and I decided to try to earn a scholarship by selling literature. The way had been worked out in the providence of God and through the generosity of a friend of youth for me to have transportation, and I began my work in north central Oklahoma, living at home.

I attended Sabbath school and church at Ponca City, Oklahoma, where a group of about thirty-five members were meeting in an upstairs hall above a place of business. One week an order of books I had been expecting did not come. I had a three-hundred-dollar delivery the following Monday, and though I went to Sabbath school as usual, I kept thinking about those books that had not arrived. My anxiety, I am sure, must have shown in my face. Between Sabbath school and church, a visitor, a stranger I did not know, walked over to me and pulled out a copy of *Steps to Christ*. He opened it, turned to a three-word sentence, and read it to me. It was this: "Rest in God."— Page 72. He said a few words, and read it to me again. That was all. But my anxiety was relieved.

Early the following Monday morning the publishing secretary drove into our farmyard. He had the books! He had decided to come to help me deliver them, though somehow word had not gotten to me, and this was why the books had not come by mail.

I have never forgotten the words from *Steps to Christ* called to my attention that Sabbath morning. *Rest in God.* How we need to! "Commit the keeping of your soul to God, and trust in Him. Talk and think of Jesus. Let self be lost in Him. Put away all doubt; dismiss your fears. . . . Rest in God. He is able to keep that which you have committed to Him. If you will leave yourself in His hands, He will bring you off more than conqueror through Him that has loved you."—*Ibid.*

210

THE GLORIES OF THE MORNING

It is a good thing to give thanks unto the Lord, and to sing praises unto thy name, O most High: to shew forth thy lovingkindness in the morning, and thy faithfulness every night. Ps. 92:1, 2.

It is indeed a good thing to give thanks unto the Lord! There are so many things for which to praise His name—and not the least of these are the glories of the early morning. Go out, a little after dawn, or whenever you arise, and just stand and take in the freshness, the beauty of the new day. "Let the fresh glories of each new morning awaken praise in your hearts for these tokens of His loving care."—*Testimonies,* vol. 5, p. 312.

Let this expression—"the fresh glories of each new morning" —be vividly impressed upon you. I came across it in my reading several years ago. To go out in the early morning and see the colors of the sunrise, or the dew on the grass, or perhaps a light mist lying low over a valley, almost invariably brings this expression back to mind. To sense the freshness of the air in the early morning, or to see growing things, also serves as a reminder of these words.

In spite of the scars of sin, we can see all about us the works of a Master artist. "The heavens declare His glory; and the earth, which is formed for the happiness of man, speaks to us of His matchless love. Its surface is not a monotonous plain, but grand old mountains rise to diversify the landscape. There are sparkling streams and fertile valleys, beautiful lakes, broad rivers, and the boundless ocean. God sends the dew and rain to refresh the thirsty earth. The breezes, that promote health by purifying and cooling the atmosphere, are controlled by His wisdom."—*Ibid.*

Have you ever stood on a hill on a summer day, and let the breeze blow through your hair? Did you thank God for that breeze? Man is rapidly polluting the earth, but without the breezes, the rains and dew, conditions would be a thousandfold worse.

Let's praise God every morning! Then, as night falls, let us also remember to thank Him for the faithfulness He has shown to us during the day. If we should try to number His blessings, who could count them?

211

JULY 24

AS SCHOOL DAYS APPROACH

Where is the flock that was given thee, thy beautiful flock? Jer. 13:20.

With the summer vacation more than half gone, thoughts will soon be turning to school again. Are you as parents making plans to send your children to church school? Those of you who are youth of academy and college age, are you planning on going to a Christian school?

Your decision concerning this may make more difference than anything else you ever decide.

A study done in the Pacific Union a few years ago, based upon 48,000 individuals reared in Seventh-day Adventist homes, "provided dramatic evidence on the relationship between Seventh-day Adventist education and church membership." For example, if ten children from Seventh-day Adventist homes do not get any Christian education during their first twelve years of schooling, only three of that ten will ever join the church. On the other hand, "twelve grades of Adventist education will result in a 97 per cent likelihood that the individual will join the church and 87 per cent probability that he will remain in the church."—*Pacific Union Recorder,* Aug. 15, 1966, p. 6.

Christian education, to have a maximum influence, needs to begin with the first grade. A Southern Baptist pastor, disturbed over a loss of faith among Baptist youth, urged the establishment of more Baptist elementary schools. Baptist colleges alone, he urged, are not enough—the religious training, to be effective, must be begun in the early years.

We, too, know this. Are we planning accordingly? We have been entrusted with a "beautiful flock." "Every shepherd should realize that the sheep under his care cost an infinite sacrifice. He should regard them each as of priceless worth, and should be unwearied in his efforts to keep them in a healthy, flourishing condition."—*Patriarchs and Prophets,* p. 192.

"Each as of priceless worth"!

In what pastures will your flock be feeding, come September?

A GREAT RESPONSIBILITY

While men slept, his enemy came and sowed tares. Matt. 13:25.

To what do you attribute the fact that up to half of the children born in Seventh-day Adventist homes eventually leave the church? Does the secular education that so many of them receive for part or all of their school years have anything to do with it?

"In the schools of today the conclusions that learned men have reached as the result of their scientific investigations are carefully taught and fully explained; while the impression is distinctly given that if these learned men are correct, the Bible cannot be. Skepticism is attractive to the human mind. The youth see in it an independence that captivates the imagination, and they are deceived. Satan triumphs. He nourishes every seed of doubt that is sown in young hearts."— *The Ministry of Healing,* p. 439.

Seventh-day Adventists have not been alone in recognizing the devastating influence of an all-secular education. Said Dr. Charles C. Morrison, former editor of *Christian Century:* "For every adult convert won through preaching, ten of the church's children succumb to the secularist influence of the public-school system."—Quoted in *Review and Herald,* Aug. 4, 1955, p. 9.

"All the youth," urges God's servant, "should be permitted to have the blessings and privileges of an education at our schools."— *Testimonies,* vol. 6, p. 197. "If ever we are to work in earnest," she says, "it is now. The enemy is pressing in on all sides, like a flood. Only the power of God can save our children from being swept away by the tide of evil. The responsibility resting upon parents, teachers, and church members, to do their part in co-operation with God, is greater than words can express."—*Counsels to Parents and Teachers,* p. 166.

To train a jet fighter pilot for combat duty requires an investment of more than a quarter million dollars, and the training of a B-52 pilot requires almost half a million dollars. The amount put into giving a child a Christian education is considerable, as all of us with children in Christian schools know so well, but it is far less than these. And the consequences are so infinitely more important!

213

UNLESS

Let not the wise man glory in his wisdom, neither let the mighty man glory in his might, let not the rich man glory in his riches: but let him that glorieth glory in this, that he understandeth and knoweth me, that I am the Lord which exercise lovingkindness, judgment, and righteousness, in the earth. Jer. 9:23, 24.

One journalist has listed "the attributes of life most men desire" as these: good looks, money, power, success, love, and fame. Are you hoping to get out of your education, if not good looks, at least as much as possible of the rest of the things in this list?

What makes one's education a success? Is it a matter of earning top grades? Is success measured by one's ability to make money? Is the successful graduate the one who as the result of his training can acquire, along with money, power and fame?

Men glory in intellectual attainment. They glory in power. They glory in riches. Yet these are the very things the Scriptures urge us not to glory in. And inspiration, speaking of what constitutes success in education, declares: "Upon the mind of every student should be impressed the thought that education is a failure unless the understanding has learned to grasp the truths of divine revelation, and unless the heart accepts the teachings of the gospel of Christ."—*Counsels to Parents and Teachers,* pp. 12, 13.

"A failure . . . unless the heart accepts . . . the gospel of Christ"!

By this standard how could one possibly get a successful education in any public school? Many Adventist youth, because it costs less, are going to public colleges. But if they graduate with an education that "is a failure," what have they gained for the years expended?

Even in a Christian school far too many do not take advantage of their opportunity to accept the teachings of Christ. In our homes as in our schools we need to remember that apart from Christ any knowledge or power or wealth we may attain is as nothing. God help all of us to understand what constitutes true success!

NEVER MORE NEEDED THAN NOW!

When the enemy shall come in like a flood, the Spirit of the Lord shall lift up a standard against him. Isa. 59:19.

"Our schools were never more needed than they are today," declared Dr. T. W. Walters, of the North Pacific Union, near the end of the 1968-1969 school year. He went on to predict that the expense of operating schools in America would double by 1975, adding, "We better know why we are in the business if we are going to continue."

As for his prediction that education costs would double by 1975, we still have three years to go on that—though we have seen the trends. But as for Christian schools never being more needed than now—the evidence has multiplied on that!

Take the crucial need to maintain decent moral conduct, for example. Concerning the attitude of "many university administrators" toward cohabitation by unmarried students, a recent leading magazine had this comment: "The policy now, says an assistant dean at a Big Ten university, 'is one of letting sleeping coeds lie.'"

The article indicated that "on scores of campuses, curfews, sign-outs and dormitory living requirements have been dropped or are enforced halfheartedly." A matronly university housemother was quoted as saying, "Girls used to sneak in through the kitchen door. Now they don't even bother to sneak out any more." At one college "some coeds list their boy friend's address when signing out overnight." At another school an estimated one thousand unmarried couples had set up housekeeping together.

Never has this caution from Heaven been more timely:

"It is a terrible fact, and one that should make the hearts of parents tremble, that in so many schools and colleges to which youth are sent for mental discipline and culture, influences prevail which misshape the character, divert the mind from life's true aims, and debase the morals."—*Counsels to Parents and Teachers,* p. 220.

God grant that Christian schools, in the power of the Holy Spirit, may indeed be a refuge from lawlessness, immorality, and violence!

HOW MUCH DOES IT TAKE?

Knowing this first, that there shall come in the last days scoffers, walking after their own lusts, and saying, Where is the promise of his coming? for since the fathers fell asleep, all things continue as they were from the beginning of the creation. 2 Peter 3:3, 4.

It is inevitable that in an educational system where God is excluded a spirit of unbelief will generally flourish. *Christianity Today* puts it this way: "The student in an institution in which secularism prevails will discover that in many courses, particularly in the humanities and social sciences, religion in any form is held in low regard. The general anti-religious tenor is set by the instructor, and few students dare challenge it. Since Christianity looms largest among the religions of Western civilization, it is likely to receive the most anti-religious barbs."— Page 3, Jan. 15, 1965.

Bill Melden, a senior in a public college, was taking a class called Introduction to the Bible. Writing in the May 6, 1970, issue of *The Presbyterian Journal,* he told what it was like. The first day of class the professor entered the room and threw a Bible on the floor. "I just want to show, class," he said, "that lightning will not strike simply because I'm not showing 'proper respect' to this book." Picking up the Bible, he opened it and ripped out a few pages, adding, "See, class? Still no lightning!"

He spent first semester attacking the inspiration of the Scriptures. Second semester consisted of attempts to undermine confidence in Christ as the Son of God. "Please do not," he told his class, "either in discussion or on a test, refer to this man as 'Jesus Christ.' He was not the Christ. He was merely a rather inspiring historical figure—a minor seditionist who was completely misunderstood by his peers." Such examples, said Bill Melden, "could go on endlessly—the Darwinian biology professor who pointedly sneers at the Genesis account of Creation, the psychology professor who goes out of his way to explain conversion experiences as self-induced delusions . . ."

How much of this kind of thing does it take to undermine faith?

DEATH IN THE CLASSROOM

And all thy children shall be taught of the Lord; and great shall be the peace of thy children. Isa. 54:13.

Would that all our children were being taught of the Lord! Estimates vary according to locality, but there are places where up to 50 per cent of God's youth are in public schools. In some cases there are no church schools available. But in the majority of cases this is not the reason.

An editor of *America,* a Catholic journal, sickened by the numbers of Catholic youth who were leaving the church through the influence of secular education, compared it to the slaughter on American highways. "Their mangled souls," he said, "do not lie on slabs in the morgue. Perhaps if Catholic parents could see that ghastly sight; could see the victims being brought in; brought in from the lower schools; brought in from the colleges and universities; laid in rows, long rows of young souls, dead to the heaven-born faith that once pulsed through their beings; dead after breathing in the noxious gases of atheism and materialism poured forth in countless classrooms throughout the United States—perhaps that might give Catholic parents pause. It might. One can never tell."

He illustrated with some case histories that could have been attached to the victims lying in this spiritual morgue. "There is John J. Blank, twenty-three years old. Born a Catholic. Both parents Catholic. Went to parochial school, to a Catholic high school. Then his parents said: 'He has a good foundation in the faith now. We will send him to the university. The courses are better there; he will make finer social and business contacts than he could in a Catholic college.'

"Here is Marie Doe, twenty-four years old. Born a Catholic. Both parents Catholic. Went to public high school, then to the university. Lost her faith in the second year."

Each tag, he says, tells the same story. "Spiritual death walked into the classroom with them; sat beside them; never left them afterward."

It's a vivid portrayal. But then, to what does one compare the tragedy of losing one's faith in Jesus Christ?

THE POCKETBOOK PINCH

And God is able to make all grace abound toward you; that ye, always having all sufficiency in all things, may abound to every good work. **2 Cor. 9:8.**

The May 19, 1969, issue of *U.S. News & World Report* had an article discussing what it called "the pocketbook pinch." The magazine reported that, while incomes were "at all-time highs," soaring prices were "straining family budgets." A housewife, telling how there just wasn't enough money left out of the weekly paycheck to meet all the bills, said, "We're going to have to cut back somewhere, but I honestly don't know where."

The temptation to some Seventh-day Adventists has been to do the cutting back by leaving out Christian education. Attending a church school, or going to an academy or to a Christian college, it is argued, has become just too expensive.

Has it?

A study in the Pacific Union, reported in 1966, showed that "in 1933 the tithe per capita in the Pacific Union Conference was $26.16, academy tuition was $10.00 per month, and boarding school students earned 18c per hour. . . . In 1933 it required 1755 hours of student labor to meet the expenses of one year in a boarding school. In 1966 it costs about 1230 [hours]." To compare it another way, the per capita tithe increase between 1933 and 1966 was 800 per cent, student wages increased 700 per cent, and boarding school costs went up 500 per cent. (*Pacific Union Recorder,* Aug. 15, 1966.)

If the increases since 1966 have been at about the same ratio, as they apparently have, Christian education costs considerably fewer hours of student labor now than what it did in 1933. Students can seldom work all their way, of course, but as we do our best, God has promised to see that we have "all sufficiency in all things," that we "may abound to every good work." We may need to cut back on some luxuries our affluent society has come to take for granted, but how can we even think of budgeting out Christian education?

KEEP ON PRAYING

And she was a widow of about fourscore and four years, which departed not from the temple, but served God with fastings and prayers night and day. Luke 2:37.

Some commentators understand today's scripture to mean that Anna had been a widow for 84 years. According to the previous verse, she had been married for seven years before losing her husband. If she had been a widow for 84 years, this would make her close to 110. But whether 84 or 110, she was still serving the Lord through her prayers.

A letter in the May 15, 1969, *Review and Herald* began with this comment and question:

"Well do I remember how earnestly in my younger years Elders Spicer and Daniells urged a revival and a reformation. Years have passed, and I am past my fourscore years, and still we are not ready for Jesus to come. What is wrong?"

Many are the devoted hearts who would echo this question. The church has wandered in the wilderness far longer than anyone would have dreamed possible. But let us never forget that in spite of the delay, "not one" of the prayers that have risen to God's throne for the descent of the Holy Spirit "has been lost" (Ellen G. White letter 96a, 1899). Each prayer has been "accumulating, ready to overflow and pour forth a healing flood of heavenly influence and accumulated light all over the world" (*ibid.*).

The Spirit of God can do much through the elderly. The day that Anna saw the infant Jesus at the Temple, another elderly servant of God was also there. Simeon, noted as one who was "just and devout," was moved by the Spirit of God to speak words of blessing and prophecy. Both Anna and Simeon are reminders of the service those who are senior citizens can yet give to God. We need, most of all, your prayers concerning the promised outpouring of God's Spirit. Begin to pray now for the new school year that will be beginning in a few weeks. He can use your prayers, as senior citizens, to help bring conviction and conversion to many youth. Let us pray most earnestly that the new school year will be a year of the Holy Spirit's power.

A LIGHT IN THE COMMUNITY

Ye are the light of the world. Matt. 5:14.

Of the Holy City it is written, "The glory of God did lighten it, and the Lamb is the light thereof" (Rev. 21:23). Thus it should be also in our homes. It is God's purpose that Christian homes should be a light in the community. But only as Christ "is the light thereof" can a home give forth light.

Elder H. M. S. Richards, relating on a Voice of Prophecy broadcast the influence of his Christian home upon him as a boy, said:

"As the speaker on this broadcast, I can never tell you all that home has meant to me. First of all, there were the love and care and example of my father and mother; kind words, care day and night, and love shown in actions and expressed in words. In our home there was little money, but lots of love; not much furniture, but a great deal of affection; not many dishes, but a good many books. The pictures on the walls were painted by mother herself.

"Then there was the family worship every morning—how can my brother and I ever forget those times? The Friday evening worship at the beginning of the Sabbath, and those wonderful Sabbath days when we would hear dear father preach, and then mother would always have something special for dinner! We loved to see the Sabbath come. The least I can do is to thank God for placing me in such a home."

Elder Richards told also of the impressions made upon him by the Christian homes of both sets of grandparents. His grandfather on his mother's side of the family had been a pioneer in the early days of the West, and a man of God. "What days we had with him on the farm and in the mountains!" he said. "What deep impressions we received as we saw him read the Scriptures silently to himself with tears trickling down his cheeks!"

God grant us more such homes, more such parents and grandparents! "One well-ordered, well-disciplined family," we read, "tells more in behalf of Christianity than all the sermons that can be preached."—*The Adventist Home,* p. 32.

May your home be this kind of influence!

"WE ARE SO HAPPY!"

And the Lord God said, It is not good that the man should be alone; I will make him an help meet for him. Gen. 2:18.

Notice that today's scripture does not say *helpmeet* or *helpmate,* but that it is two words—a help *meet* for him, *meet* being a Middle English word meaning "fit" or "suitable" for him.

During courtship individuals naturally put on their best behavior—so much so, sometimes, that courtship can become deceptive. "During the average courtship," says Dr. George R. Bach, "the two people con each other. They put on false fronts."

Somehow those contemplating marriage need to take a realistic look at each other—which means, for one thing, seeing the prospective partner in as many situations as possible. What is he or she like when the going gets rough? What are his or her family like? How does he treat his mother? What are her attitudes toward housework?

Looking beyond glamour and physical attractiveness, what are the qualities that make for a good wife? Inspiration suggests, among others, these: (1) she should be one fitted to bear her share of life's burdens, (2) she should be one whose influence will refine and ennoble her husband, (3) she should be one who will make him happy in her love.

Among the qualities to be sought in the prospective husband the following are suggested: (1) he should possess pure, manly traits of character, (2) he should be diligent, aspiring, and honest, and (3) he should be one who loves and fears God.

Perhaps one of the best safeguards against an unhappy marriage is to build in yourself, with God's help, the kind of character you would want your partner to have. "Like attracts like" —and to win someone with high ideals one should himself possess the same high ideals.

"We have been reading *The Adventist Home* for our family worship," a bride of six months wrote home, "and after reading the chapters dealing with choosing a mate, we think we have done a very good job. We are so happy." The qualities mentioned by inspiration should assure that after six years or sixty years a couple could still exclaim, "We are so happy!"

221

A LOVE THAT LASTS

And be ye kind one to another, tenderhearted, forgiving one another, even as God for Christ's sake hath forgiven you. **Eph. 4:32.**

If one were to suggest to newlyweds a book of the Bible that could mean a lot in their married life, it would be the Epistle to the Ephesians. This Epistle, plus the chapters in *The Ministry of Healing* on the home, could appropriately be the first worship material read together by a couple in their new home.

I have sometimes suggested to academy seniors that newlyweds could well take a copy of *The Ministry of Healing* along on their honeymoon, planning enough leisure to read or reread its chapters concerning the home. This suggestion usually brings smiles, or looks of "Don't be silly." But let those who would know all that married love can include especially consider the chapter entitled "The Builders of the Home." Of its many suggestions, here is just one:

"Determine to be all that it is possible to be to each other. Continue the early attentions. In every way encourage each other in fighting the battles of life. Study to advance the happiness of each other. Let there be mutual love, mutual forbearance. Then marriage, instead of being the end of love, will be as it were the very beginning of love. The warmth of true friendship, the love that binds heart to heart, is a foretaste of the joys of heaven."—Page 360.

"Continue the early attentions." Do we? You've heard the story of the old farmer whose wife had just died. The pastor came to comfort him. "You must have loved your wife very much," he said. "Yes, replied the farmer, "I almost told her so once."

And "determine to be *all* that it is possible to be to each other." Do we? Will we? Or will we, after six months or a year of marriage, get so absorbed in earning a living that neglect of each other begins to creep in?

The tenth year of married life can be better than the first, and the twentieth better than the tenth. And ahead is eternity —where "the loves and sympathies that God has planted in the soul will find truest and sweetest exercise" (*Education*, p. 306).

AVOIDING ARGUMENTS

The meek will he teach his way. **Ps. 25:9.**

A newspaper reporter covering the golden wedding anniversary of two of the senior citizens in his town asked, "To what do you attribute your longevity and apparent good health?"

"When my wife and I were first married," answered the husband, "we made a pact that would ensure harmony. We decided that if we ever became involved in an argument I would leave the house and go for a walk to give us both time to cool down.

"So," sighed the husband, "I guess I'd have to attribute my health and longevity to a vigorous outdoor life."

How do you handle conflicts in your family?

In the booklet "Is Your Marriage Headed for the Rocks?" the author suggests: "Perhaps the most sensitive test point for a marriage is not sex or money but the handling of conflict. Conflict comes into all marriages. It is inevitable that two human beings living together will have their differences. Much depends on how the differences are handled."—Quoted by Martin P. Simon, "Forgiveness in the Home," *Moody Monthly,* September, 1964, p. 24.

Differences, ideally, should be prayerfully and calmly examined in the spirit of Christ. There is no need to lash out at each other with the tongue, and argue and fight. Even if you win the argument, people are seldom, if ever, changed by force of argument.

But suppose the other member or members of the family simply will not even try to see things your way—what then? And what does one do when someone has been completely unfair? "We would better suffer wrongfully a hundred times," God's servant suggests, "than wound the soul by a spirit of retaliation, or by giving vent to wrath."—*Testimonies,* vol. 2, pp. 426, 427.

Can you let yourself be wronged a hundred times without retaliating? Do you wonder how such a spirit could ever be developed? "There is strength to be obtained of God. He can help. He can give grace and heavenly wisdom."—*Ibid.* When in the relationships between two people even one has the meekness of Christ, there can be no argument. Why don't *you* be that one?

CHRIST MAKES THE DIFFERENCE

They are no more twain, but one flesh. What therefore God hath joined together, let not man put asunder. Matt. 19:6.

The present divorce rate is such that one sociologist has suggested that more polygamy exists in the United States "than ever exists in such notorious places as ancient Baghdad." The only difference, he says, is that we practice what sociologists call "serial polygamy"—only one wife at a time, but several over a period of time.

There is only one Bible reason for getting a divorce and then remarrying—and that is in the case of the innocent party when unfaithfulness has occurred. Often there is no true "innocent" party, however, for the attitudes and habits of the so-called "innocent" one may have been a major factor in the guilty one's seeking affection elsewhere.

More of the religion of Christ is our great need. Taylor Bunch, in his book *Secrets of a Happy Marriage,* reported that one study showed that while the national average was one divorce in every four marriages, in families where the members regularly attended church together, the ratio was only one divorce in fifty-seven marriages, and that in homes where there was family prayer together and a vital Christian experience, there was only one divorce in five hundred marriages.

"I know of scores of homes which were almost on the rocks," says Billy Graham, "that have become happy homes because Christ abides in them." This same truth is emphasized in the book *The Adventist Home:* "Christ abiding in the heart of the wife will be at agreement with Christ abiding in the heart of the husband."—Page 120.

In our academy Bible classes this is one truth I have tried to emphasize over and over again. *Christ abiding in the heart of the wife will be at agreement with Christ abiding in the heart of the husband.* If the Holy Spirit reigns in the home, there will be no talk of divorce. As individuals demonstrate tenderness, forbearance, and love, they will find this same spirit will be returned—and through Christ within, there will be harmony in the home.

"More and more of Thee"—let this be our prayer.

INVITED TO PRESIDE

He shall give you another Comforter, that he may abide with you for ever.
John 14:16.

"I suppose you wouldn't know how things began to be as they are now," the letter could have begun. "Not any one thing was to blame. It was a dozen things, then a hundred. Wanting more things than your money could buy, you went neck-deep in debt. You worried, and so did your wife. You both became edgy and nervous and resentful about life. You got on each other's nerves. You criticized each other. You complained and she nagged. You began to disagree about how the children should be trained or reprimanded. You found fault with her appearance; she found fault with your relatives."

One doesn't need much imagination to continue. Even without divorce, happiness had fled from this home. One marriage in four ends in divorce, and of the remaining three only one is happy, according to a Baltimore lawyer who has written several books on marriage. The other two are merely tolerated.

Compare this to the experiences of the couples you know fairly well. How many in the twenty-thirty age bracket are happily married? How many in the above thirty age group? Would there be one in four in either group who, as far as you can tell, are genuinely happy?

With opportunity to evaluate with deeper insight, the servant of God has written: "There is not one marriage in one hundred that results happily, that bears the sanction of God, and places the parties in a position better to glorify Him."— *Testimonies,* vol. 4, p. 504.

It need not be this way. Marriage can be all that a couple dreams and more, if the Spirit of God is present. "The sweetest type of heaven," we are told, "is a home where the Spirit of the Lord presides" (*The Adventist Home,* p. 15). The key, as we have so often discussed in our senior Bible classes, is the word *preside.* The Holy Spirit must *preside*—preside over the financial affairs, over the words spoken, over the choice of leisure activities, over the intimate aspects of married life, over the training of the children, over everything.

Has He been invited to *preside* in your home?

THE KIND OF HUSBAND NOT TO BE

Likewise you husbands, live considerately with your wives, bestowing honor on the woman as the weaker sex, since you are joint heirs of the grace of life, in order that your prayers may not be hindered. **1 Peter 3:7, R.S.V.**

When we study the unit on the home in our academy senior Bible classes, it is generally our practice to read and discuss the book *The Adventist Home,* taking it a section at a time. When discussing the section on the husband and father, we use the material in the book to characterize various kinds of husbands. We put on the blackboard the following six kinds not to be:

The unreasonable type. He is exacting, never helps about the house, finds fault if the meals are not on time, and thinks of his wife more as a housemaid than as a companion.

The dictatorial type. He insists upon his way in every particular, is completely unyielding and vicelike, and never admits he is wrong.

The fretful, querulous type. He is like a grownup who is still a child, frequently whining and complaining.

The selfish, morose type. He is morose and gloomy, overbearing, frequently cutting in his words, too selfish ever to speak a word of approval to the members of his family.

The egotistical, intolerant type. He has a high opinion of himself, takes extreme positions, does not consider his wife's opinion, scolds too much, does not give affection and sympathy.

The stern, discourteous type. He considers it beneath his dignity to speak gently and lovingly to his wife. He thinks it unmanly to be tender and sympathetic, or to perform deeds of kindness.

"If you had to be married to one of the above six types," I then ask the girls, "which type would you take?" A lot of the girls conclude that they would just forgo ever getting married.

A little self-examination on the part of all husbands might be in order. "Live considerately with your wives," Peter urges. Such consideration would do much to eliminate the unhappy traits listed above.

THE GOOD WIFE

Most of Proverbs 31 is a discussion of the qualities of a good wife. To facilitate class discussion, we usually put on the blackboard a list of the things this chapter mentions, somewhat as follows:

She is trustworthy. "Her husband doth safely trust in her" (verse 11).

She is not afraid of work. "She . . . worketh willingly with her hands" (verse 13).

She gets up in time to fix breakfast. She riseth also while it is yet night, and giveth meat to her household" (verse 15).

She knows something about business matters. "She considereth a field, and buyeth it" (verse 16).

She shops wisely. "She perceiveth that her merchandise is good" (verse 18).

She can sew. "She layeth her hands to the spindle. . . . She is not afraid of the snow for her household. . . . She maketh herself coverings of tapestry" (verses 19-22).

She helps the needy. "She stretcheth out her hand to the poor; yea, she reacheth forth her hands to the needy" (verse 20).

She speaks kindly. "In her tongue is the law of kindness" (verse 26).

She manages the children well. "She looketh well to the ways of her household" (verse 27).

She loves the Lord. "A woman that feareth the Lord, she shall be praised" (verse 30).

As we have mentioned, these discussions concerning the home are during the senior year of academy Bible. And as you can imagine, a list such as the above sparks considerable discussion. The idea is not that we go around with a check list, but that we review the ideal. By the time a girl is a senior, these traits should be manifesting themselves. Wherein there may still be a lack, God can become her help and strength in developing yet-needed skills or in making changes.

A FAR-REACHING TRUTH

Now therefore beware, I pray thee, and drink not wine nor strong drink, and eat not any unclean thing. Judges 13:4.

This instruction from God, given to the mother of Samson, and then repeated to her husband, has to do with prenatal influence. It comes as a surprise to many that prenatal influence affects not only the physical strength of a child but also his "mental and moral power." And the father as well as the mother can transmit "dispositions and appetites" (*Patriarchs and Prophets,* p. 561).

For years it was generally accepted in scientific circles that the unborn child was not affected by the habits and mental state of the mother. Only within the past two or three decades has evidence to the contrary been seriously considered. In 1968 the Los Angeles *Herald-Examiner* published a report entitled "Life Seen Influenced Before Baby's Birth." One medical researcher concluded concerning prenatal and early after-birth influences that "many effects of such early influences appear irreversible."

Mrs. White first mentioned prenatal influence in 1865 when she stated that "the tone" of a mother's morals would "in a great measure be represented" in her offspring (in *How to Live,* chap. 2, p. 37). Then, in *The Ministry of Healing,* in 1905, she clearly stated concerning the mother: "If before the birth of her child she is self-indulgent, if she is selfish, impatient, and exacting, these traits will be reflected in the disposition of the child. . . . But if the mother unswervingly adheres to right principles, if she is temperate and self-denying, if she is kind, gentle, and unselfish, she may give her child these same precious traits of character" (pages 372, 373).

A realization of this truth, when we discuss it in our academy senior Bible unit on the home, makes considerable impact on some of the girls! Almost invariably somebody says, "I don't believe it!" But the scientific confirmation of this truth grows stronger, and it is a wise teen-ager who, thinking ahead to parenthood, begins to develop those traits he or she would like to see in his or her children.

For this is indeed a far-reaching truth!

ANGELS IN THE KITCHEN

That they may teach the young women to be sober, to love their husbands, to love their children, to be discreet, chaste, keepers at home, good, obedient to their own husbands, that the word of God be not blasphemed. Titus 2:4, 5.

We had taken the sophomore class at Glendale Academy to Cedar Falls, the conference youth camp, for a weekend outing. After a delicious Sabbath dinner, about a dozen of the sophomore girls were in the kitchen helping to clean things up. Several of them, with soapsuds up to their elbows, were washing pots and pans. Just as I came into the kitchen to see how things were going, they paused, then in unison exclaimed, " 'The humble round of duties which women have come to regard as a wearisome task should be looked upon as a grand and noble work'!"

It was a memory gem we had drilled in Old Testament class the previous year.

Hannah, from whose experience this lesson is drawn (see *Patriarchs and Prophets,* p. 572), was one of the most devoted wives and mothers one would ever find. Her life illustrates that "there are opportunities of inestimable worth, interests infinitely precious, committed to every mother" (*ibid.*). Mothers such as Hannah, Jochebed, and Mary of Nazareth have had an influence so far reaching that eternity itself will never fully reveal the magnitude of their accomplishments. And yet most of their time was spent with that "humble round of duties which women have come to regard as a wearisome task"!

Notice again today's scripture. The expression "keepers at home" could also be translated "workers at home." There is no more important work. There is no work more grand and noble.

Someone once painted a picture of a kitchen in which angels were busily engaged in cooking and washing dishes. All was being done with such heavenly grace that you forgot that kettles are kettles and pans are pans, and noticed only how beautiful the lowly tasks can be.

A kitchen is indeed a place for angels. Thank God for the mothers, whether young women or older, who are exactly that!

THE TRAINING OF A PRINCE

The Spirit itself beareth witness with our spirit, that we are the children of God: and if children, then heirs; heirs of God, and joint-heirs with Christ. **Rom. 8:16, 17.**

Do you as mothers and fathers sometimes feel that your work is not important? Does the multitude of daily perplexities and cares sometimes cause you to lose sight of the things that really count?

Are there any little ones in your home, perhaps just a few weeks or months old? You know they are precious—but have you realized how precious?

"They are placed in our care to be trained," Heaven reminds us, "not as heirs to the throne of an earthly empire, but as kings unto God, to reign through unending ages."—*The Adventist Home,* p. 238.

How much thought and care should be given to the training of a prince or princess? Raymond S. Moore, who had opportunity to form an acquaintance with several members of the imperial family of Japan, shared with *Review and Herald* (Feb. 26, 1959) readers what was involved in the training of the crown prince. At the age of three he was placed under the care of highly trained retainers who would bring him up in a balanced, restrained environment, teaching him always that the best control is self-control.

This self-control was expected to govern every aspect of his life. He was educated in what to read, how to dress, and what to eat, as well as in the conduct and manners of a prince. Careful attention was given to the quality of music and entertainment. His responsibility to be an example to his fellow men was ever kept before him.

Are we as parents as careful to instill self-discipline into the hearts of our boys and girls? Do we teach them a sense of responsibility? "Nothing can take so strong a hold on the heart as the abiding sense of our responsibility to God. Nothing reaches so fully down to the deepest motives of conduct as a sense of the pardoning love of Christ."—*The Desire of Ages,* p. 493. Are we, through Christ, helping our children to develop this kind of motivation?

WHEN MOTHER ISN'T THERE

Put on then, as God's chosen ones, holy and beloved, compassion, kindness, lowliness, meekness, and patience. Col. 3:12, R.S.V.

Mrs. Billy Graham, in an article in the April, 1964, issue of *Decision* magazine, shared this illustration:

"France, according to a statement I came across recently, has had 69 kings, only three of whom were loved by their subjects. These three were the only ones who had been brought up by their own mothers. The rest had all been reared by tutors and governesses."—Page 8.

Compare this with the following thought from inspiration:

"Encourage the expression of love toward God and toward one another. The reason there are so many hardhearted men and women in the world is that true affection has been regarded as weakness. . . . If we wish our children to possess the tender spirit of Jesus, and the sympathy that angels manifest for us, we must encourage the generous, loving impulses of childhood."—*The Desire of Ages,* p. 516.

Who can do this like mother? If a mother must work, let her give special attention to kindness and affection when she is at home. And if at all possible, let her not work during her children's preschool years. The following poem, "When Mother Isn't There," vividly portrays how mother's absence can affect little ones:

Our house is not a home at all
    When mother isn't there.
It's just some rooms with furniture,
    And lonesome everywhere.

The things I eat don't taste the same;
    I don't know what to do.
The clock ticks louder, and my dog
    Looks awful lonesome too.

And when it's time to go to bed,
    Well, I don't even care;
Cause I don't feel like I am me
    When mother isn't there.
                —RUTH WILDON KELSEY

"I'D RATHER HAVE YOU"

Who is sufficient for these things? 2 Cor. 2:16.

Martha I. Johnson, writing in the *Moody Monthly* (Nov., 1965), tells of a mother who decided to give up her outside job in order to have more time to spend with her small daughter. "But remember, Rosemary," she said to her daughter, "I'll not be able to buy you nice dresses and pretty sweaters."

Replied the child, "I'd rather have *you*, Mommy."

The responsibility of being parents is the greatest responsibility there is. When we consider that our children are to be trained, as princes and princesses, to share a place with Christ on His throne, we exclaim, "Who is sufficient for these things?"

"The sphere of the mother may be humble," inspiration observed, "but her influence, united with the father's, is as abiding as eternity. Next to God, the mother's power for good is the strongest known on earth."—*The Adventist Home*, p. 240.

The father, though often gone, has the privilege of being a part of that influence. "I stopped to look into the face of my sleeping son the other night," a father wrote. "I had come home after a late appointment and had missed that last-moment-before-sleep experience we usually share together with God. I was deeply impressed that I need to look into this quiet face more often, less hastily, and realize the prize placed in my clumsy hands by an infinitely tender and patient Creator. For fourteen years this boy had been entrusted to his mother and me.

"Next I moved to another room where lay in guileless sleep my lovely little daughter, a full-of-life ten. Morning and evening we worship together as a family, yet those last few prayer and tuck-in moments are the 'whipped-cream,' the 'topping' to her day. And nearly always she clings to me 'longer than I have time.' "—*Review and Herald*, Feb. 26, 1959.

If these precious experiences get crowded out, what have we gained if we have two cars in the garage and a color TV in every room? The pressures of modern living—the *wants* sometimes adding greatly to the pressures of the *needs*—can rob us of the only things that really count. Heaven help us to put first things first!

"THE SHINING MOMENT"

I will give him unto the Lord all the days of his life. 1 Sam. 1:11.

A pastor told of staying at the farm home of a member of a rural New York church. He was especially impressed by the intelligence and good behavior of the only child in the home, a four-year-old boy. "Then I discovered," he said, "the reason for the child's charm.

"The mother was at the kitchen sink, washing the intricate parts of the cream separator when the little fellow came to her with a magazine. 'Mother,' he asked, 'what is this man in the picture doing?' To my surprise, she dried her hands, sat down in a chair, and taking the boy in her lap, spent ten minutes answering his questions.

"After the child had left I commented on her having interrupted her chores to answer the boy's questions, saying, 'Most mothers wouldn't have bothered.'

" 'I expect to be washing cream separators for the rest of my life,' she told me, 'but never again will my son ask me that question!' "—*Guideposts,* September, 1961, p. 20.

In publishing this incident, *Guideposts* gave it the heading "The Shining Moment." Such moments, once lost, are lost forever. Of the mother's work, inspiration declares: "No other work can equal hers in importance. She has not, like the artist, to paint a form of beauty upon canvas, nor, like the sculptor, to chisel it from marble. She has not, like the author, to embody a noble thought in words of power, nor, like the musician, to express a beautiful sentiment in melody. It is hers, with the help of God, to develop in a human soul the likeness of the divine. The mother who appreciates this will regard her opportunities as priceless."—*The Ministry of Healing,* p. 378.

Many are the opportunities to impart spiritual truth to the inquiring minds of little children. To each mother God says, "Take this son, this daughter, and train it for Me; give it a character polished after the similitude of a palace, that it may shine in the courts of the Lord forever."

PRAYER INSTEAD OF PUNISHMENT

I the Lord thy God will hold thy right hand; . . . fear not; I will help thee. Isa. 14:13.

Mother had been scolding eight-year-old Betty, and Betty was answering angrily. Mother was about ready to give a spanking, when suddenly she stopped. This isn't the way a Christian home should be run, she thought. Quietly slipping to her bedroom, she knelt by her bed and began to pray aloud, as was her custom. She asked God to forgive her for being so impatient, and prayed that she would be given wisdom to bring up her children in the way God would approve.

Before she was finished, Betty had knelt beside her. After mother's "Amen," Betty prayed, asking God to forgive her for being such a naughty girl, and to help her to do better.

"The rest of the day was sunshine," said Betty's mother.

"Isn't that better than much scolding and loud, angry words?" asks Martin T. Simon in the September, 1964, *Moody Monthly*. "Better than spankings, too, when it can be done!"

Mrs. White was the mother of four boys—Henry, James, Willie, and Herbert. Herbert died when but a few months old, and Henry at the age of sixteen. James and Willie grew to manhood. Along with her other responsibilities, Mrs. White encountered all the duties any mother faces, including that of correcting misdeeds. Concerning this she wrote:

"We should pray to God much more than we do. There is great strength and blessing in praying together in our families, with and for our children. When my children have done wrong, and I have talked with them kindly and then prayed with them, I have never found it necessary after that to punish them. Their hearts would melt in tenderness before the Holy Spirit that came in answer to prayer."—*Child Guidance*, p. 525.

On other occasions, when difficulties arose, she would tell the children that they would let things rest until evening. They would then discuss the matter calmly, finding a solution.

One can exercise this kind of discipline, and still be firm. Love becomes the ruling power, and the Holy Spirit has opportunity to influence hearts. Angels of heaven, too, will draw very near.

TAUGHT BY EXAMPLE

That our sons may be as plants grown up in their youth; that our daughters may be as corner stones, polished after the similitude of a palace. **Ps. 144:12.**

"Character is built at home during the first 17 years of the boy's life," said University of Southern California football coach John McKay. "How can we get him in his late teens and make basic changes? All we can do is to teach him how to play football."—Los Angeles *Herald-Examiner,* Jan. 25, 1965, p. D-1.

The coach's comments, reminiscent of the 1951 incident at West Point in which ninety cadets were expelled for cheating, were made after a similar incident at the Air Force Academy in Colorado. "You must remember," Sports Writer Melvin Durslag observed, "that the academy doesn't get kids until they are 18, by which time their makeup has been scarred by their elders, usually their fathers and mothers."—*Ibid.*

C. L. Paddock tells of a boy arraigned in juvenile court on a charge of theft. The judge, trying to get to the root of the matter, called in the father for a visit. The heartbroken father said he had done everything he knew how for his son—had encouraged him in hobbies, had bought woodworking machinery for him, and tried in every way possible to be a good father. He could not understand why his son would take something not belonging to him.

The judge asked if he might visit at the boy's home. He arrived on washday, and the mother was hanging out the clothes. One thing caught the judge's eye. Practically every towel on the line had the name of some hotel on it.—*Signs of the Times,* Sept. 19, 1950.

Today's scripture suggests that our homes be palaces where the sons are noble men and the daughters like princesses. "The youth are to be taught to look to Christ as their guide. They are to be taught lessons of forbearance and trust, of true goodness and kindness of heart, of perseverance and steadfastness."—*Counsels to Parents and Teachers,* p. 496.

These are traits taught not so much by words as by example. Let's pray that Seventh-day Adventist parents everywhere may be what they want their children to become!

A FATHER'S FOOLISHNESS

His sons made themselves vile, and he restrained them not. 1 Sam. 3:13.

A pastor was having problems with his two sons. Affable and easygoing, he had allowed his children to do pretty much as they pleased during childhood and youth. He had flattered himself that eventually his boys would pass over fool's hill and become responsible citizens. But it didn't work that way. The older the boys got, the worse they became. Skepticism, irreverence, selfishness, and rebellion grew progressively stronger. Religion, separated from wise discipline, became powerless to help them.

The influence of the father was constantly being counteracted by the misdeeds of his sons. Things finally got so bad that church members began to complain. The father, more shocked perhaps by the fact that his prestige had failed to silence the complaints than by his sons' conduct, mildly remonstrated with the boys, but to no avail. His sons couldn't care less about the damage they were doing. Their hearts had become as hard as the desert stones.

As two-year-olds Hophni and Phinehas could have been easily molded. At the age of six, either one with a small hand clasped in daddy's big hand, could have been led in the right way. As nine- or twelve-year-olds they would have profited greatly from wise discipline. But firm guidance was never given, the sons were never punished for misdeeds or taught self-denial, and unrestrained adolescence merged into profligate manhood. Even when their ways brought disgrace after disgrace upon the cause of God, the blind father continued to excuse and shield them. Things finally got so bad that a messenger from God charged the father with honoring his sons above the Lord (1 Sam. 2:29).

Would that such sinning against God and against children happened only in ancient times! But there are Elis everywhere today! And not only is the cause of God hurt, but the children themselves are robbed of happiness! "Every child that is not carefully and prayerfully disciplined will be unhappy. . . . There is a very great burden to be carried all through the life of a spoiled child."—*Child Guidance*, p. 213.

"THE MEANEST MOTHER"

A child left to himself bringeth his mother to shame. **Prov. 29:15.**

In the spring of 1970 an unusual open letter appeared in the Auburn, Washington, *Globe* (June 6, 1970). Here it is, somewhat abbreviated. Would you have entitled it, as did the writer, "The Meanest Mother"?

"As a child I had the meanest mother in the world. . . . When other kids ate candy for breakfast, she made me eat cereal, eggs, and toast. . . . My mother insisted on knowing where we were at all times. You'd think we were on a chain gang. She had to know who our friends were—and what we were doing. She insisted that if we said we'd be gone for an hour, that we would be gone for one hour or less. . . .

"I am ashamed to admit it, but she actually had the nerve to break the child labor laws. She made us work! We had to wash dishes, make all the beds, learn to cook and all sorts of cruel things. I believe she lay awake nights thinking up things for us to do.

"She always insisted on us telling the truth, the whole truth, and nothing but the truth. By the time we were teenagers she was much wiser, and our life became even more unbearable.

"None of this tooting the horn of a car for us to come running. She embarrassed us no end by making our dates come to the front door to get us. I forgot to mention, while my friends were dating at the mature age of 12 and 13, my old-fashioned mother refused to let me date until I was 15 or 16. She was mean!

"My mother was a complete failure as a mother. None of us has ever been arrested . . . or beaten a mate. Each of my brothers served his time in the service of his country . . . willingly, no protesting.

"And whom do we have to blame for this terrible way we turned out? You're right . . . our mean mother! We never got to take part in a riot, never burned draft cards or got to do a million and one things our friends did. . . . Using this as a background, I am trying to raise my children. . . . You see . . . I thank God He gave me the meanest mother in the world!

Signed: "Another Mother"

237

THE SECURITY OF A NO

He will command his children and his household after him, and they shall keep the way of the Lord. **Gen. 18:19.**

A group of teen-agers were coming into their Sunday school class. "Are you going to the lake with the other kids next Saturday?" someone asked.

"I'm not sure," the teen-ager spoken to replied. "I'm waiting for mom and dad to make up their minds. Are you?"

"I really don't want to. There was trouble the last time they went."

"I know," was the reply. "I just hope my folks say No."

The Sunday school teacher, busy with organizing her lesson, had not been paying much attention until this last remark. Looking up, she asked this teen-ager if she would mind repeating what she had just said. The girl hesitated, then said firmly, *"I wish my parents would say No more often."*

In the ensuing discussion it came out that these youth sometimes let group pressures influence them to do things that deep down inside they knew were wrong. They appreciated, though they ordinarily wouldn't be likely to say so, the security of a firm parental No. "It's really a relief to have a legitimate excuse," said a varsity basketball player.—*Christian Life,* May, 1964, p. 34.

Stated a monthly newsletter of the Royal Bank of Canada (May, 1958): "The truth is that children believe in parental discipline. A survey of 96,000 high school pupils in 1,300 schools in the United States revealed the clear-cut opinion that parents should carefully restrict their teen-age sons and daughters as to hours, frequency of dates, places of amusement, choice of associates, smoking and drinking."

Inspiration has counseled parents that youth—and it would be particularly true of early teens—often need "a wise, firm hand to point out the right way and to bar with counsel and restraint the wrong way" (*Testimonies,* vol. 5, p. 40).

Is this kind of help being given to the children and teen-agers in your home?

FINDING THE BECAUSES

How shall we order the child, and how shall we do unto him? Judges 13:12.

In his booklet *Discipline, Democracy, and You,* John Luther writes:

"Ideally, our children should know not only right from wrong, but *why* right is right and *why* wrong is wrong. Why should I tell the truth? Why shouldn't I steal? Why should I obey rules and laws? Why should I be tolerant? Why should I respect the rights of others? When a child—or an adult—appreciates the reasons *why* these things are right or wrong, he is far more apt to *do* what is right."

Addressing the 1969 Quadrennial Council for Secondary Education, Elder W. J. Hackett told of a father whose unfortunate attitude toward his son was: "Your job is to obey and not ask questions." Elder Hackett then read to the delegates this counsel:

"The education of children, at home or at school, should not be like the training of dumb animals; for children have an intelligent will, which should be directed to control all their powers. Dumb animals need to be trained; for they have not reason and intellect. But the human mind must be taught self-control."—*Fundamentals of Christian Education,* pp. 15, 16. Mentioning the large numbers of youth we are losing from the church, Elder Hackett then asked:

"Could it be that we are reaping the results of the kind of teaching and training we have all too often done? Why does it take us so long to learn that there is a better way?"

This "better plan of education" (*ibid.,* p. 18) is clearly portrayed by inspiration. The chapter in the book *Education* entitled "Discipline" would save us so many problems—and so many more youth for eternity—if we would follow *all* of it instead of hammering at youth with isolated statements about obedience. It does emphasize obedience—but it is an obedience based upon the enlistment of reason. Regulations are kept few and well-considered—and then enforced "with firmness, yet pleasantly and kindly" (*Counsels to Parents and Teachers,* p. 211).

As Mr. Luther puts it, we need to find the "becauses"—helping youth to see and appreciate the reasons for a regulation.

DON'T OVERDISCIPLINE

And, ye fathers, provoke not your children to wrath: but bring them up in the nurture and admonition of the Lord. Eph. 6:4.

An experienced teacher was discussing how much control should be exercised in an academy or college dormitory situation, and to what extent such control influences the spiritual experience of the dormitory residents. He suggested that the very worst spiritual experience would result from a situation where there is too loose a control. The next worst would be too tight a control. The ideal is a well-run program with moderate control.

The same is true in a family. Phillips translates today's scripture, "Fathers, don't overcorrect your children." *The New English Bible* puts it: "You fathers, again, must not goad your children to resentment."

There are parents who appear to be too blind to see wrongdoing when it does occur. But there is also another extreme— that of being too suspiciously watchful. "Children and youth are benefited by being trusted. Many, even of the little children, have a high sense of honor; all desire to be treated with confidence and respect, and this is their right. They should not be led to feel that they cannot go out or come in without being watched. Suspicion demoralizes, producing the very evils it seeks to prevent."—*Education*, pp. 289, 290. Far better than watching continually would be to preoccupy with good.

The object of discipline should be "training . . . the child for self-government" (*ibid.*, p. 287). The parent or teacher who does this will have the most lasting influence. "To the superficial observer his work may not appear to the best advantage; it may not be valued so highly as that of the one who holds the mind and will of the child under absolute authority; but after years will show the result of the better method of training." —*Ibid.*, p. 289.

IT CAN BE DONE!

Sanctify them through thy truth: thy word is truth. **John 17:17.**

Can children and youth be trained in such a way that pleasure or selfish attraction will not entice them to sacrifice principle? Can they develop such firmness that death itself would not cause them to vacillate?

We have the example of Shadrach and his young companions before Nebuchadnezzar's fiery furnace. We have the example of the youthful Joseph when a woman of Egypt, not once or twice but "day by day" (Gen. 39:10), used every enticement she could devise to try to get him to commit fornication. We have the example of the teen-age Daniel in the cafeteria line there at the University of Babylon.

Youth can be steadfast and true!

Consider the following statement as being fantastic encouragement:

"Only let the truth for this time be cordially received and become the basis of character, and it will produce steadfastness of purpose, which the allurements of pleasure, the fickleness of custom, the contempt of the world-loving, and the heart's own clamors for self-indulgence are powerless to influence."—*Testimonies,* vol. 5, p. 43.

If I were in a Bible class at this moment, I would ask the teen-agers which of these four things exert the greatest influence toward wrongdoing. The allurements of pleasure? The fickleness of custom? The contempt of the world-loving? Or their own heart's clamor for self-indulgence? It would provide a launching point for a good discussion, yet perhaps it matters little which is currently the strongest pull toward wrong. The truth of God, received and made the basis of character, will render any and all such pleasures and enticements powerless.

How is such training given? It would be profitable when you have the time to read the whole chapter from which this assurance is taken, a chapter in *Testimonies,* volume 5, entitled "Parental Training," pages 36-45. But in a sentence the matter could be summarized like this: "Children are what their parents make them by their instruction, discipline, and example."— Page 37.

241

WITH TRIPLE UNDERLINING

The wisdom that is from above is first pure, then peaceable, gentle, and easy to be intreated, full of mercy and good fruits. James 3:17.

We had been reading in senior Bible class the seven chapters in the book *The Ministry of Healing* that have to do with the home. Students who had personal copies of the book could, instead of writing reports, simply underline the statements that most impressed them.

As I scanned the books I noticed that one boy had triply underlined in red the caption under one of the pictures, which had been taken from the context. Here, italicized and within its context in *The Ministry of Healing,* is the sentence he had underlined:

"Perfect confidence should exist between husband and wife. Together they should consider their responsibilities. Together they should work for the highest good of their children. *Never should they in the presence of the children criticize each other's plans or question each other's judgment.* Let the wife be careful not to make the husband's work for the children more difficult. Let the husband hold up the hands of his wife, giving her wise counsel and loving encouragement."—Pages 393, 394. (Italics supplied.)

The students who did not own copies of the book were asked to write brief reports, in which they listed from each chapter two or three sentences that most caught their attention. This same sentence appeared in these reports more often than any other.

Evidently there is room for improvement upon this point!

Today's scripture also deserves triple underlining! The wisdom from above is peaceable, gentle, and easy to be entreated. It is full of mercy and good fruits—the fruits of the Spirit. The previous verse, James 3:16, notes that "where . . . strife is, there is confusion." There is no surer way of confusing the children than for the parents to fuss and disagree in their presence. If you ever catch yourself about to do so, remember the triple red line in that senior boy's copy of *The Ministry of Healing!*

HOW TO AVOID MANY OF OUR DIFFICULTIES

But let it be the hidden man of the heart, in that which is not corruptible, even the ornament of a meek and quiet spirit, which is in the sight of God of great price. 1 Peter 3:4.

The first six verses of 1 Peter 3 are addressed to wives, but verse four, urging that we put on the ornament of a meek and quiet spirit, is applicable to all of us! How many difficulties we would save ourselves at home and at work and at school if we would only do this! "By putting on the ornament of a meek and quiet spirit," notes inspiration, "ninety-nine out of a hundred of the troubles which so terribly embitter life might be saved."— *Testimonies,* vol. 4, p. 348.

This sentence is taken from a letter to a Brother and Sister F., which was published as part of the *Testimonies* and given the title "Self-Caring Ministers." Its counsel is primarily to the husband, a Seventh-day Adventist minister who at home was being "impatient, fretful, exacting." The writer frankly told this minister that before he was ready to manage a church he would first need to manifest the meekness of Christ in his home.

The statement of Jesus, "I am meek and lowly in heart" (Matt. 11:29), did not excite the admiration of His contemporaries. By the sophisticates of His time the word *humility* was often used contemptuously. For a Greek or a Roman to say that a man was humble meant that he was low or despised. And though Isaiah had so plainly stated that God dwells with "him . . . that is of a contrite and humble spirit" (Isa. 57:15), the Jews of Christ's time likewise despised humility.

One of the surest ways to become miserable is to become self-important. Do you know of a single self-important person who is happy? Alexander and Caesar are mentioned as men who "found it much easier to subdue a kingdom than to rule their own spirits" (*ibid.*). But where will one find Alexanders and Caesars—or self-caring husbands or wives or children— who have found happiness?

How wonderful it would be if "ninety-nine out of a hundred" of the things that embitter life were avoided! And they could be—if each member within a family would only put on "a meek and quiet spirit."

DON'T BE ANXIOUS

"Do not be anxious about tomorrow. . . . Let the day's own trouble be sufficient for the day." Matt. 6:34, R.S.V.

In his booklet, *Be Thankful for Your Troubles,* Robert R. Updegraff mentions that one of the most cheerful men he had ever known worked as plant superintendent in a large company. It was a high-pressure job with many headaches—yet this man never seemed worried or frustrated. One evening he was at this man's home for dinner. He knew that it had been a particularly trying day at the plant—one of those days when everything goes wrong—yet his host was most cheerful, making no mention of these difficulties. "It was a happy meal," Mr. Updegraff wrote. "Had I not known differently, I would have thought my friend hadn't a care in the world."—Pages 4, 5.

After dinner the two of them went out to look at the vegetable garden. Mr. Updegraff remarked to his host about his cheerfulness at the dinner table after such a difficult day. "I'll let you in on a little secret," he replied, grinning. "But don't tell my family." Taking his guest to the front yard, he pointed to a little copper beech tree by the front door.

"That's my private Trouble Tree," he explained. "Every night when I come home I mentally hang all the day's troubles on that tree. I say to myself, 'Hang there for the night. I'll pick you up when I start for work in the morning.'

"The funny thing about it," he continued, "is that half the time when I leave the house next morning I discover that most of what I thought were troubles when I hung them up have blown away in the night! Even the ones that are still hanging there aren't half as heavy or worrisome as they seemed when I came home the night before."

Suggests inspiration: "The father should do his part toward making home happy. Whatever his cares and business perplexities, they should not be permitted to overshadow his family; he should enter his home with smiles and pleasant words."—*The Ministry of Healing,* p. 392.

And whether you mentally have a "trouble tree" at the front door or not, you are invited to cast "all your care upon him" (1 Peter 5:8).

LEARNING TO LISTEN

He that hath ears to hear, let him hear. Matt. 11:15.

W. Lee Truman, having been told by a friend that "it is a rare person who even hears what you are saying," decided to test this theory at his wedding. "I simply shook hands in the reception line and stated that my grandmother died last night," he said.

"The majority of the guests," he went on, "looked me straight in the eye and said, 'Congratulations,' and the rest mumbled some of the other nice things people say at weddings. But not one heard what I was saying. My bride of 40 minutes or so, did hear me though, and she very sweetly kicked me in the shins."—Glendale *News-Press*, April 1, 1967, p. 4-A.

Have you ever been talking to someone, only to discover that they were not listening? Have you ever been telling someone something, and then noticed that he is looking beyond you as though his thoughts were a thousand miles away?

Jesus repeatedly used expressions similiar to our today's scripture. He, too, must have recognized the need for people to listen better. The chapter in the book *Education* entitled "The Sabbath" has a suggestion for helping children, and all of us, to get more out of the Sabbath services:

"In listening to the sermon, let parents and children note the text and the scriptures quoted, and as much as possible of the line of thought, to repeat to one another at home. This will go far toward relieving the weariness with which children so often listen to a sermon, and it will cultivate in all a habit of attention and of connected thought."—Page 252.

Why not try it next Sabbath?

And in our homes, and in faculty-student relationships, could we also do a better job of listening? Are there instances when a husband never really hears his wife? Are there parents who do not listen to their children? Could students do a better job of listening in class? And could teachers be more alert to hear and appreciate a student's viewpoint? "He that hath ears"—let him use them!

SCHOOLS OF THE PROPHETS

And these words, which I command thee this day, shall be in thine heart: and thou shalt teach them diligently unto thy children, and shalt talk of them when thou sittest in thine house, and when thou walkest by the way, and when thou liest down, and when thou risest up. Deut. 6:6, 7.

This scripture summarizes God's plan for the education of our children. His words are to be a natural part of all that we do. In our homes, as we converse together and as we come and go, God's words and works should be a continuous influence. Thoughts of God will thus be associated with all the actions and activities of our daily lives.

The same kind of influence should carry over into the educational experiences of our children. A non-Adventist Christian educator, addressing his words to the popular Protestant churches, wrote: "The right way for us as Christians would be to have the church teach our children secular knowledge. . . . It would be ideal for the church to teach its boys and girls everything they have to learn—arithmetic, reading, writing, etc.—and mix it all in with religion, helping the children to see that there is only one universe and one God, and that no two truths can ever contradict each other."—*Review and Herald,* Aug. 4, 1955.

In the providence of God Seventh-day Adventists have been able to establish this kind of educational program. The broad principles of God's plan have been outlined in Scripture. Then, to give us additional details for implementing this plan, we have been given books such as *Fundamentals of Christian Education, Education,* and *Counsels to Parents, Teachers, and Students.*

We can thank God every day of our lives for these books. If I had no other reason for believing in God and God's church than these three books, I would be fully convicted. The book *Education,* for example, was written in 1903. The author, though she never took an education course of any kind in her life, penned a book with principles far ahead of its time— principles still being discovered and proved true by the educational world. In the school year soon to open, the closer we follow these principles, the more God will be able to bless.

A STORM AHEAD

The south wind blew softly. . . . But not long after there arose against it a tempestuous wind. **Acts 27:13, 14.**

It was about the end of October, when severe storms could be expected in the Mediterranean. Paul, a prisoner aboard a Roman ship bound for Rome, urged the captain not to leave Crete. But "the south wind blew softly." One can picture a gorgeous sunset causing the Mediterranean to shimmer like gold. A few slow-moving clouds may have enhanced the sky, and the tropicallike south wind made for a sense of security and calm. Paul's warning was disregarded. "But not long after there arose . . . a tempestuous wind" (Acts 27:14). For fourteen days the tempest raged, until the ship was wrecked on the little island of Malta.

In 1969 our educational work accounted for a larger share of workers than any other phase of denominational activity— 31.9 per cent of our nearly 65,000 denominational employees. And the south wind, comparatively speaking, has blown softly. Though rising costs have caused concern, our schools have prospered. But let's not forget that "a tempestuous wind" lies just ahead. As the final crisis develops, our schools will be among our first institutions to be closed.

On June 30, 1969, the Vincent Hill School, in Mussoorie, India, closed its doors after fifty-eight years of service. The July 31, 1969, issue of the *Review*, reporting this closure, mentioned the increasing difficulty of securing visas and other problems. As I read the notice in the *Review*, my thoughts went ahead to that time when it may be Andrews University and Loma Linda that are being closed.

One of these days it will happen to all our schools—perhaps during a summer, or perhaps during a school year. If we could know, on that last September registration, that it would indeed be the last, would we be moved to seek the Lord with renewed earnestness? Would seeking an outpouring of God's Spirit be our foremost objective for whatever months remained?

Will this new school year be business as usual? Or will we most earnestly seek the Lord in our homes and on our campuses?

AT THIS VERY HOUR

Pray one for another. . . .The effectual fervent prayer of a righteous man availeth much. James 5:16.

Today, located all over the earth, the Seventh-day Adventist church has more than 5,000 colleges, academies, and elementary schools. The total enrollment in these schools is now approaching 400,000 children and youth.

Within the next two or three months all of these schools will be conducting a fall Week of Prayer. How wonderful it would be if at each school there could be an outpouring of God's Spirit greater than at any time in Seventh-day Adventist history!

One could scarcely ask for more evidence that "the end of all things is at hand" (1 Peter 4:7). Some September our schools will be opening for the last time. What could be of greater importance at this very moment than seeking for a continually greater outpouring of God's Spirit?

We need to be living in a spirit of intercession and prayer. We would like to suggest that we begin specifically to pray for the several hundred men who will be leading out in the academy and college Weeks of Prayer, and for the thousands of men and women who will be speaking in the elementary schools. Let's pray that God will lead the thoughts of these speakers, and that even as they prepare, the Holy Spirit will come upon them with Pentecostal power.

It would be well as we pray to remember Elijah's perseverance and faith—that faith which "reached out and grasped the promises of Heaven" (*Prophets and Kings,* p. 157). With God's children today, as with Elijah, "fervent prayer . . . availeth much." Let us, like him, claim God's promises, remembering this assurance:

"To us *today,* as verily as to the first disciples, the promise of the Spirit belongs. God will *today* endow men and women with power from above, as He endowed those who on the Day of Pentecost heard the word of salvation. *At this very hour* His Spirit and His grace are for all who need them and will take Him at His word."—*Testimonies,* vol. 8, p. 20. (Italics supplied.)

"LORD, INCREASE OUR FAITH"

Lord, Increase our faith. Luke 17:5.

In response to this request, "Lord, increase our faith," Jesus told His disciples, "If ye had faith as a grain of mustard seed, ye might say unto this sycamine tree, Be thou plucked up by the root, and be thou planted in the sea; and it should obey you" (Luke 17:6).

Jesus chose an illustration so difficult as to be absurd, and it is evident that He did not intend that His disciples go around removing trees and planting them in the sea. None of His miracles were of this nature. What He did want to convey is that in doing God's work, nothing is impossible. In Matthew 17:20 He used the illustration of moving mountains. Concerning this *The Desire of Ages* comments:

"When the mustard seed is cast into the ground, the tiny germ lays hold of every element that God has provided for its nutriment, and it speedily develops a sturdy growth. If you have faith like this, you will lay hold upon God's word, and upon all the helpful agencies He has appointed. Thus your faith will strengthen, and will bring to your aid the power of heaven. The obstacles that are piled by Satan across your path, though apparently as insurmountable as the eternal hills, shall disappear before the demand of faith. 'Nothing shall be impossible unto you.' "—Page 431.

Faith strengthens as one lays hold on God's Word. It increases as one exercises it. George Mueller, in praying for funds for the care of thousands of orphans, said that at first he would trust the Lord for ten dollars, then for one hundred dollars, and then for one thousand dollars. He observed that he would be able, if the need arose, to just as easily trust the Lord for a million dollars—though he would first quietly and carefully examine to see if what he was trusting for was something in accordance with God's word. "If I found that it was," he said, "the amount of difficulties would be no hindrance to my trust."

What are the obstacles to the finishing of God's work? Are we confronted with mountains of indifference and lukewarmness? Could not even these "disappear before the demand of faith" accompanied by Spirit-filled praying and preaching?

HIS INSTRUMENTS

The eyes of the Lord run to and fro throughout the whole earth, to shew himself strong in the behalf of them whose heart is perfect toward him. 2 Chron. 16:9, first part.

How strong is your faith? Do you as parents, as students, as faculty members believe that this new school year could become a year known everywhere as "the year of the Holy Spirit's power"? Would you be willing to become His instrument for helping bring about the mightiest manifestation of His grace ever seen?

A veteran teacher was leaving. "Ask what I shall do for thee, before I be taken away," he told one young man.

"I pray thee, let a double portion of thy spirit be upon me," the young man replied.

The request was granted. And when this young graduate, Elisha, began teaching in the schools of the prophets himself, "his words of instruction to the earnest groups of young men assembled were confirmed by the deep movings of the Holy Spirit."—*Prophets and Kings,* p. 240.

"The Holy Spirit loves to address the youth."—*Christ's Object Lessons,* p. 132. "The eyes of the Lord run to and fro throughout the whole earth," yes, and across every school campus, "to shew himself strong in the behalf of them whose heart is perfect toward him" (2 Chron. 16:9).

We suggested earlier this week that we should especially pray for an outpouring of God's Spirit upon those who will be leading out in the fall Week of Devotion on all our campuses. Let us today add another specific request to that one, praying that on every campus God will raise up young people through whom He can especially work as instruments in seeking a double portion of God's Spirit.

We need, O so much, the deep movings of God's Spirit on our campuses and in our churches. "It is the absence of the Spirit" that makes our efforts "so powerless" (*Testimonies,* vol. 8, p. 21). Even the shed blood of Christ is of no avail without the presence of the Holy Spirit (see *The Desire of Ages,* p. 671). Let us repent of every sin, and begin to pray most earnestly that on every campus God will be able to work mighty works in the salvation of souls.

CHRISTIAN EDUCATION'S FINEST HOUR

Behold, the darkness shall cover the earth, and gross darkness the people:
but the Lord shall arise upon thee, and his glory shall be seen upon thee.
Isa. 60:2.

"It is a terrible darkness that faces us now," wrote Columnist James J. Kilpatrick toward the end of the sixties, as violence erupted on campus after campus. Mentioning a "crude and filthy" publication from one campus, he asked, "How did it all happen? Where did the chain of blunders begin that led to this degeneracy of civilized values thus symbolized?"—The Seattle *Times,* April 27, 1969, p. 11.

Eighteen months earlier *Newsweek* magazine had noted "the swiftness with which all the old restraints are losing their force" —suggesting that the moral climate had changed more dramatically during the previous year "than in the preceding 50" (Nov. 13, 1967, p. 74). A follow-up report concerning morality told of a continued increase of sordidness in films, in novels, on the stage, and in advertising (*ibid.,* April 14, 1969, p. 67).

Inspiration forewarned of dissipation and corruption sweeping in "like an overwhelming tide" (*The Great Controversy,* p. 585). Said one of the *Newsweek* reports, "The floodgates have opened one by one, and the inundation is now a matter of fact, in the hinterlands as well as the big cities."

This very darkness is Christian education's hour of opportunity. People with standards and decency—and they still number millions—are perplexed by the degeneracy that has engulfed so much of society. Their concern gives Christian education its finest witnessing opportunity. The darkness, growing more dense, will make yet more striking the influence of modest, sincere, genuinely caring, Christlike young people.

In the church, before probation closes, the mercy, grace, and love of Christ "are to appear in full and final display" (*The Desire of Ages,* p. 680). The whole earth, wrapped as it is in the darkness of sin, and sorrow, and pain, is to be lighted with the knowledge of God's love.

May God make this school year Christian education's finest hour!

PUTTING FIRST THINGS FIRST

Be filled with the Spirit. **Eph. 5:18.**

This command of God is also a promise, for "all His biddings are enablings" (*Christ's Object Lessons,* p. 333). God is eager to fill us with His Spirit. Why, then, has this promise been so little realized? Is it because it has not been appreciated as it should be?

"All that the apostles did," we are encouraged to believe, "every church member today is to do."—*Testimonies,* vol. 7, p. 33.

But are we doing it? Think of the convicting power that attended Peter's preaching. Think of the miracles of healing that took place. Recall the boldness with which the believers witnessed—and how "the word of God grew and multiplied" (Acts 12:24). How is it today? How should it be today? "When the end of all things is at hand, should not the zeal of the church exceed even that of the early church? . . . Should not the power of God be even more mightily revealed today than in the time of the apostles?"—*Ibid.*

Is this what we are seeking above all else?

"With what are you and I most concerned?" asks Arnold V. Wallenkampf in the February 19, 1970, *Review.* "Are we more concerned with securing a comfortable home than in being filled with the Holy Spirit? . . . As a student, am I more concerned with getting good grades than with receiving the infilling of the Holy Spirit? . . . Are we more interested in getting new cars, new carpets for our homes, new furniture, than we are about being filled with the Holy Spirit? . . . What are you and I longing for most intensely? How earnestly do you and I really desire and long to be filled with the Holy Spirit?"

In the beginning of a new school year many things will compete for our attention, both at home and at school. That which is most important could easily be crowded out by things that in comparison are minor matters. The bestowal of God's Spirit has been called that blessing "which would bring all other blessings in its train."—*Testimonies,* vol. 8, p. 21. Will it be lost through neglect or indifference? Or can this school year truly become "the year of the Holy Spirit's power"? The answer depends on what you and I consider most important.

NO LIMIT

I will bless thee, and . . . thou shalt be a blessing. Gen. 12:2.

"There is no limit," declares inspiration, "to the usefulness of one who, by putting self aside, makes room for the working of the Holy Spirit upon his heart, and lives a life wholly consecrated to God."—*The Desire of Ages,* pp. 250, 251.

When Dwight L. Moody was converted at seventeen, he could barely read and write. He knew so little about the Bible that he searched the Old Testament for the Gospel of John. The first time he tried to say something at prayer meeting, a deacon told him that he could serve God best by keeping still.

Some time later, while in London, he was told: "The world has yet to see what God can do with and for and through a man who is fully . . . consecrated to Him." Moody was determined that in spite of his limited talents he would become that man. There was awakened in his heart a longing for God's Spirit—a longing which was ultimately to lead to an anointing with power.

It was following the Chicago fire that this anointing came. He had been sent to New York to raise funds. But his heart was not in this. He was crying all the time that God would fill him with His Spirit. And one day, in New York City, God did. "I cannot describe it," Moody said later. "I seldom refer to it; it is almost too sacred an experience to name. . . . I can only say that God revealed Himself to me, and I had such an experience of His love that I had to ask Him to stay His hand. I went to preaching again. The sermons were not different; I did not present any new truths, and yet hundreds were converted. I would not now be placed back where I was before that blessed experience if you could give me all the world—it would be as the dust of the balance."—WILLIAM R. MOODY, *The Life of D. L. Moody,* p. 149.

Heaven longs to see every son and daughter "filled with all the fulness of God" (Eph. 3:19). Seek not merely His blessing, but Him—putting self aside, and making room for the working of His Spirit upon your heart. Let your prayer be, "Lord, here am I; fill me."

WITHOUT MEASURE

He whom God hath sent speaketh the words of God: for God giveth not the Spirit by measure unto him. John 3:34.

What determines how much of God's Spirit a person will receive? Consider these words:

"The measure of the Holy Spirit we receive, will be proportioned to the measure of our desire and the faith exercised for it, and the use we shall make of the light and knowledge that shall be given to us. We shall be entrusted with the Holy Spirit according to our capacity to receive and our ability to impart it to others."—ELLEN G. WHITE, in *Review and Herald,* May 5, 1896, p. 273.

We will be entrusted with the Holy Spirit, then, according to (1) our desire for Him, (2) our faith, (3) our capacity to receive, and (4) our willingness and ability to impart.

"I will pour water upon him that is thirsty, and floods upon the dry ground," God promises (Isa. 44:3). Notice, again, inspiration's questions: "Why do we not hunger and thirst for the gift of the Spirit? Why do we not talk of it, pray for it, and preach concerning it?"—*The Acts of the Apostles,* p. 50. If we would, this earnest desire, combined with faith, would surely help prepare the way for a divine infilling according to our capacity to receive.

But what determines our "capacity to receive"?

We noted some months ago that "the power of love was in all Christ's healing, and only by partaking of that love, through faith, can we be instruments for His work."—*The Desire of Ages,* p. 825. As we pray for more of God's Spirit it may be that we should begin by praying for more of "the power of love." We need to sense "the power of love" flowing through us, a love that takes in even the most unlovely. When that love, itself a gift of the Spirit, is given without measure, we will have a capacity for a divine infilling of God's Spirit which is likewise without measure.

Such a love will be shared. We will not be able to hold our peace. And as we impart, our capacity to receive will be increased—"exceeding abundantly above all that we ask or think" (Eph. 3:20).

A FORETASTE

But this is that which was spoken by the prophet Joel; and it shall come to pass in the last days, saith God, I will pour out my Spirit upon all flesh. **Acts 2:16, 17.**

On the day of Pentecost Peter preached a sermon that resulted in the baptism of three thousand people. His opening text was the passage in the book of Joel which foretold an outpouring of God's Spirit. Our scripture today is a part of that passage, and is a promise that is to be again fulfilled just before the close of probation in a way that will be even "more abundant" (*Evangelism,* p. 701).

The passage in Joel specifically mentions young people. It has been on the campuses of our academies and colleges that some of the first stirrings of revival have begun to take place. This influence has often been first felt in our various schools. Early in the 1970-1971 school year a wonderful revival began on the campus of Andrews University. It started at a weekend retreat organized by the college students. Many decisions for Christ were made, and these youth upon their return to campus became a mighty influence on other students. During a chapel service held in the Pioneer Memorial church a student leader invited those who had been involved to share what had happened. Scores of students pressed forward to tell of what God had been doing. After the dismissal of chapel, hundreds of students remained for a service of praise and prayer and testimony. "It was so spontaneous," commented one student, "that you could powerfully sense the Holy Spirit's presence." Back in Washington, D.C., Autumn Council was in progress, and as Elder Robert Pierson, president of the General Conference, shared with the delegates what had been happening at Andrews he could scarcely keep back the tears of joy.

The following weekend, during Sabbath school, the college students shared their experience with the church. At the close of the eleven o'clock service more than a thousand people came forward to join in a renewed commitment to Christ. It was a little foretaste of far greater things yet to come. As the work of revival grows and spreads, the church will go forward with the power of Pentecost. Will *you* be a part of it?

255

A FLOOD TIDE

Behold, I send the promise of my Father upon you: but tarry ye . . . until ye be endued with power from on high. **Luke 24:49.**

The Holy Spirit is mentioned more than three hundred times in the Bible. "Christ, the Great Teacher, had an infinite variety of subjects from which to choose, but the one upon which He dwelt most largely was the endowment of the Holy Spirit."—*Selected Messages,* book 1, p. 156.

Are we doing the same? "What great things He predicted for the church because of this endowment. Yet what subject is less dwelt upon now? What promise is less fulfilled? An occasional discourse is given upon the Holy Spirit, and then the subject is left for after consideration."—*Ibid.,* pp. 156, 157.

These words were written in 1891. Are they still applicable? Are we giving our first and greatest attention to seeking "the endowment of the Holy Spirit"? Or does this matter still get too little attention?

M. G. Pearse tells an experience that illustrates our need. He says that he was standing on the east coast of England looking out upon the barges sitting immobile in slime and mud. It was useless for them to heave anchor or put up their sails. Had all the citizens of the land brought pots and kettles filled with water and poured it out upon this beach, it would have been to no avail. But as he watched, God turned the tide, and in swept the waters of the sea. The water flowed around the barges, the anchors were lifted, the sails hoisted, and the ships went forth out to sea.

Our greatest need is for God's Spirit to come in like that tide. And shouldn't it happen *now?* "Before the final visitation of God's judgments upon the earth," inspiration points out, "there will be among the people of the Lord such a revival of primitive godliness as has not been witnessed since apostolic times. The Spirit and power of God will be poured out upon His children."—*The Great Controversy,* p. 464.

Isn't it time for the church to receive the full measure of God's power? Shouldn't this school year, above all others, become "the year of the Holy Spirit's power"?

A STRIKING WITNESS

And the Lord shall make thee the head, and not the tail; and thou shalt be above only, and thou shalt not be beneath; if that thou hearken unto the commandments of the Lord thy God, which I command thee this day, to observe and do them. Deut. 28:13.

At the beginning of the 1968-1969 school year a letter from the department of education of the State of Washington was called to my attention. The research director from the office of the superintendent of public instruction was helping prepare a series of brochures to be entitled "Let's Share Innovations in Washington Education." The object of the series was to bring to light "new and promising things" being done in the schools of the State of Washington.

"Let us know what educational innovations you are pursuing, whether on a pilot or firmly established basis," the letter requested.

If our schools were truly patterned in every respect after the schools of the prophets, and if the great majority of our students were converted young people, what an opportunity an invitation like this might open up! Suppose we could have sent a copy of the book *Education* to this research director, with an invitation for him to spend a few hours or a day or two on an Adventist campus. Suppose that as soon as he arrived he could have sensed in the classrooms and shops and dormitories an unseen Presence—and that wherever he went on campus, he could have encountered genuinely converted youth, teachers truly following the methods of Christ, and evidences of the deep movings of God's Spirit.

Suppose a similar invitation could be sent to all the educators of a community or of a section of the country. Would not the increasing problems of secular campuses make the witness of a Christian campus an even more striking contrast?

God has given us a divine plan. He has blessed in our educational program. Tens of thousands of youth have found Christ and trained for service in Seventh-day Adventist schools. But we have not yet seen demonstrated all that Christian education might achieve.

Pray as schools open for another year that God's Spirit may lead.

WHY NOT TRY THE BLUEPRINT?

See, saith he, that thou make all things according to the pattern shewed to thee in the mount. Heb. 8:5.

Nearly seven decades ago the following words were written into our educational blueprint: "With such an army of workers as our youth, rightly trained, might furnish, how soon the message of a crucified, risen, and soon-coming Saviour might be carried to the whole world! How soon might the end come—the end of suffering and sorrow and sin!"—*Education*, p. 271.

That was in 1903! Why hasn't God's message been "carried to the whole world"? The one condition mentioned is for the youth of the church to be "rightly trained." Haven't they been? Wherein have we departed from the blueprint?

"True education," we are told, "is missionary training. Every son and daughter of God is called to be a missionary; we are called to the service of God and our fellow men; and to fit us for this service should be the object of our education."—*The Ministry of Healing*, p. 395. This does not necessarily mean going to a mission field, but it does mean that in whatever work we engage, our first interest will be to win others to Christ.

Is this the kind of training we have been giving? There has been taking place on some of our campuses a revival of interest in witnessing. Are we encouraging this spirit? Or has an overemphasis upon scholasticism sometimes blocked the way?

Could it be that we need to get back to the blueprint? What earthly architect in designing a skyscraper would allow deviations from his blueprint? What makes us think that the Master Architect in giving a blueprint for Christian education and designing as its objective a missionary training is any less careful?

Inspiration has cautioned against dividing life into two distinct periods—"the period of learning and the period of doing" (*Education*, p. 265). Students are, instead, to be given opportunity to engage in active service *while* learning, through various missionary activities. To what extent are we giving them these kinds of opportunities?

258

REVIEWING THE PATTERN

For I the Lord . . . will direct their work in truth. **Isa. 61:8.**

God is to be the Superintendent of Seventh-day Adventist education. "I the Lord . . . will direct," He says. Specifications for the kind of education He wants given are to be found in Scripture and in the several books provided through inspiration.

One year we gave a class of academy students opportunity to spend several weeks reading and underlining in the book *Counsels to Parents, Teachers, and Students.* (Note that it is counsels to *students* as well as to parents and teachers.) They enjoyed it immensely. We would read for a time, and then discuss together what we had found and underlined. These class periods developed some stimulating discussions. This was particularly true in sections such as "The Holy Spirit in Our Schools" and "A Missionary Training," as well as with chapters such as "Christian Discipline." Time and again as the students would come to things we are doing inadequately, or perhaps not at all, they would ask, "How come?"

It's a good question. What should one tell them?

The book *Counsels to Parents, Teachers, and Students* could contribute much to the spirit and success of this new school year if all of us—parents, teachers, and students alike—would spend some time studying and discussing the blueprint it presents. We would like to suggest that you read with a red and blue grading pencil in hand. When you come to something that in your local school (or schools) you are not doing at all, underline with a double red line. If it is being partly done, underline with a single red line. If being done well, underline in blue. Your book, like mine, will doubtless have considerable blue underlining—but also, far too many red lines!

Suppose that next Monday morning Jesus were to make a personal visit to your school. A student host and hostess show Him about. He visits the classes, observes the attitudes and appearance of the students, and the methods of the teachers. He notes with alert eye all the titles on the library shelves, and at the bookstore gives particular attention to the paperback section. His last stop is at the principal's or president's office. What recommendations might He make?

OUT INTO THE HIGHWAYS

Go out into the highways and hedges, and compel them to come in, that my house may be filled. **Luke 14:23.**

We have mentioned our review as a Bible class of the book *Counsels to Parents, Teachers, and Students.* In this study the students concluded that one of the areas where we fail the most in following the blueprint is that of doing missionary work as a part of the school program. We spent several days discussing the closing chapters of the book, all of which deal with various aspects of "A Missionary Training." The students noticed, in particular, this suggestion:

"It is necessary to their complete education that students be given time to do missionary work—time to become acquainted with the spiritual needs of the families in the community around them. They should not be so loaded down with studies that they have no time to use the knowledge they have acquired. . . . If a missionary spirit is encouraged, even if it takes some hours from the program of regular study, much of heaven's blessing will be given, provided there is more faith and spiritual zeal, more of a realization of what God will do."—Pages 545, 546.

By this standard, how many students graduate from an academy or college with a "complete education"?

At one day academy two afternoons a month were set aside for community involvement. The activities planned varied according to interests and grade level. In addition to temperance programs with Smoking Sam, and community service projects, efforts were made to contact every home in the community with appropriate literature. To pay for the literature, teachers contributed their Christmas bonuses, and the Home and School contributed an equal sum, which amounted to three hundred dollars. Then one day a student stopped by the Bible teacher's desk, handing him a check for three hundred dollars. It was money she had been saving for a trip to Europe, but she had decided to put it into the evangelism program instead.

It was a demonstration of self being forgotten "in earnest work to do others good" (*The Desire of Ages*, p. 641). Shouldn't we be seeing much more of this spirit? Wouldn't we, if we would follow more closely Heaven's plan?

TOASTING MARSHMALLOWS

Where there is no vision, the people perish. **Prov. 29:18.**

The magazine *Christian Advocate,* a Methodist paper, was launched shortly after the beginning of World War II. The first issue carried an article entitled "Toasting Marshmallows While the World Burns." The author, Paul D. Leedy, told of getting together a large group of Methodist youth. The program committee, in making preliminary plans, had considered what might be done to enlist the interest of more Christian young people. In their planning " 'they had settled upon the idea of a "social evening:" marshmallow roast and a hillside frolic, prefaced, of course, with a devotional service, for, after all, this was a "church" affair.' "

As to the success of their plans, he reported: " 'The evening was a wow! We had more young people than we had expected. They got into it in great fashion. Everything seemed to click. Those of us who were in charge went home with a glow of satisfaction in our hearts. We thought we had really "got somewhere." ' "

A few days later he received a letter which took them to task. Mr. Leedy, after some second thoughts, gave this evaluation: " 'What we had called a success was, in fact, a tragedy. We had had a marvelous opportunity that night. The most promising of our local Methodist youth were assembled in holy silence under a peaceful dome of starlit infinity. We had had a chance to inspire with a zeal to accomplish something really great for God. Instead, we sang lighthearted songs, listened to a speaker fumble with an inconsequential theme, and wisecracked together. Oblivious to the staggering responsibilities we faced, without a mention of the agony through which the rest of the world was passing, and indifferent to the great privilege of the hour, *we sat around and toasted marshmallows!'* "—Quoted in the *Review and Herald,* March 27, 1941, p. 2.

Has it ever happened on our campuses or in our churches? Social events, of course, have a place. But have we sometimes failed to put first things first? Just how will we begin that final school year? Will we come in September with a vision of finishing God's work? Or will we be toasting marshmallows?

261

SOMETHING MISSING

Seek ye the Lord while he may be found, call ye upon him while he is near: let the wicked forsake his way, and the unrighteous man his thoughts: and let him return unto the Lord, and he will have mercy upon him; and to our God, for he will abundantly pardon. Isa. 55:6, 7.

A young man throughout his academy years made it his "thing" to keep involved. He had a high opinion of himself— talking big, telling jokes, using profanity. He went out big for sports, and for extracurricular activities. Life was for fun. Yet something was lacking. "I would come back to the dorm on Saturday nights," he said, "after all the noise had died down and the jokes were over, and there was a gnawing inside. Something was missing."

In his senior year, during a Week of Prayer, he made a decision for Christ. That gnawing feeling was replaced by assurance and peace. He knew then what had been missing—the Saviour. "It was my senior year at the academy that saved my soul," he said.

"Of his fulness have all we received," wrote John, "and grace for grace" (John 1:16). That fullness satisfies the longing and emptiness of the soul—and day by day He imparts grace added to grace. We discover by personal experience what Paul meant when he wrote of being "filled with all the fulness of God" (Eph. 3:19).

Is there a void, an emptiness in your life, which nothing of the world has been able to fill? Jesus is the answer. Those who surrender their lives to Him find peace and joy. As we walk with Him, "we may be filled with His love, satisfied with His presence."—*The Desire of Ages,* p. 331. And this is only the beginning. Heaven will bring continual opportunities to know Him better and better—"and the more we know of God, the more intense will be our happiness."—*Ibid.*

Have you lost touch with Jesus? Seek Him again "while he may be found." Forsake your own ways, your own thoughts, and return unto the Lord. Let the Spirit of God fill you "with all the fulness of God." The more you experience of His presence, the more you will want. "More of Thee," will be your heart cry, to which He will answer, "Much more."

TO LIVE IS CHRIST

For to me to live is Christ, and to die is gain. Phil. 1:21.

When Paul wrote these words he was sitting in jail as a prisoner of Rome. He had no way of knowing what the future held. The capricious Nero could free him, or with a word could send him to his death—or he could let Paul just sit in jail. As it turned out, Paul, after a hearing, was finally freed. Knowing his days were probably limited, he used every opportunity for further witnessing. After a time he was again arrested—and this time he was indeed facing the executioner's sword.

But Paul, sitting there in jail, leaves the matter with God. His whole thinking is wrapped up in his Saviour. Every plan, every aspiration, is Christ centered. "To me to live," he said, "is Christ." "And to die"—well, it would seem but a moment, then the resurrection.

To me to live is —— How would you finish this statement? To live is what? Fame? Money? Pleasure? Carlyle B. Haynes suggests that you write your own version. Be completely honest and put down what for you would be real living.

Now, Elder Haynes asks, how would you finish the second part? *"To me to live is money; to die is* —— 'But,' you say, 'I cannot write "gain" after that! To die is *loss,* not gain. I shall leave it all. No, I cannot write "gain" after that.'

"To me to live is pleasure; to die is —— 'No, I cannot write "gain" after that. I do not want to think of death. I want my pleasure, my fun, my indulgence. Do not talk to me about death.'

"To me to live is fame; to die is —— Go ahead," Elder Haynes suggests, "finish it. *To die is* —— 'I cannot write it!' you say. 'To die is to perish, to be forgotten. What is fame when I am gone? I cannot write it.'

"No, my friend," says Elder Haynes, "you cannot write Paul's estimate of death after anything but Paul's estimate of life. If, by God's great grace, you can write, 'To me to live is Christ,' then you can write, 'To die is gain.' But not otherwise."— CARLYLE B. HAYNES, "Living for Christ," *Signs of the Times,* Dec. 23, 1952, p. 13.

To me to live is —— What is it for you, dear young friend, dear parent, dear reader or listener? What is it for you?

DOES THAT MAKE IT RIGHT?

There hath no temptation taken you but such as is common to man: but God is faithful, who will not suffer you to be tempted above that ye are able; but will with the temptation also make a way to escape, that ye may be able to bear it. 1 Cor. 10:13.

"All around me," a high school student told a reporter from *Look* magazine (March 10, 1960), "people cheat on everything and tend to think less and less about it. It's part of the high-school code. Most of my friends don't see that it matters."

Action magazine (September, 1968) states that a panel of high school students and teachers were asked about the prevalence of cheating in schoolwork. One student said it was definitely more than 85 per cent of the students who cheated regularly. A teacher commented that it depends on what kind of cheating you mean—if you mean things like copying homework or not reading the full book for a book report, it would be that high, but that if you mean just copying during tests, it wouldn't be.

Another student said there were only four or five of the kids she knew who didn't cheat. "I mean everybody does it," she exclaimed.

And among the education students at a State university, a secret test indicated that 32 per cent of these future teachers were cheating.

So a lot of people are cheating. But does that make it right?

A lot of people are lying, too. The same *Look* magazine article—a report of a survey conducted a number of years ago by twelve of that magazine's reporters—said that "nearly everyone interviewed also admitted to lying several times a day, mainly to 'avoid trouble,' to 'spare someone's feelings,' to 'keep my wife happy' or just to 'get along.' In a New York community, 60 per cent of the people interviewed said they lied to their spouses, and 50 per cent, to their children."

But does that make it right?

No one need be swept away by the "everybody's doing it" line. Today's scripture is our assurance that through Christ every temptation can be overcome. Christ is to be our example regardless of the crowd.

CONFESSING OUR SINS

If we confess our sins, he is faithful and just to forgive us our sins, and to cleanse us from all unrighteousness. **1 John 1:9.**

An eighth-grade girl, a Seventh-day Adventist in a public school, found that on a returned spelling paper she could have had a perfect paper except for having left off an "e" at the end of one word. She added the "e" and went to the teacher's desk.

"Isn't this word correct?" she asked.

"It certainly is," replied the teacher. "I wonder how I could have missed that!" She gave the point.

Said this student later:

"From the moment I added that letter 'e' to the paper, I could not pray. I knew that I was eternally lost. Through the first weeks of the summer I pleaded with the Lord to forgive me, but I had lost contact with Him. The little 'e' had completely blotted out His face. Over and over these words came to my mind, 'If we confess our sins, he is faithful and just to forgive us our sins, and to cleanse us from all unrighteousness.' "

Then she changed her prayer, promising God that when her teacher returned and school opened in September, she would acknowledge her wrong the very first day of school.

"What peace I had from that moment!" she said. "I knew I would never cheat again—and I never have." Telling her teacher was not easy, for this girl was the only Seventh-day Adventist in the school. But tell her she did.

We want God to work in a mighty way on our campuses and in our homes during this new school year. But are there some things we must make right before He can? Could there be a "little 'e' " in the way? Or some not-so-little things?

One thing is sure—if you harbor these sins, unconfessed and unforgiven, you are going to pay a terrible price. You will not be able to exercise faith in God, or to pray with confidence. A nagging sense of guilt will dog your steps, to eat away peace and joy and hope.

Why not make things right, and know joy again?

A TIME "OF POSITIVE PLEASURE"

Keep thy foot when thou goest to the house of God, and be more ready to hear, than to give the sacrifice of fools: for they consider not that they do evil. Be not rash with thy mouth, and let not thine heart be hasty to utter any thing before God. Eccl. 5:1, 2.

Are the religious services in your school, and the worships in your home, something to which children and youth look forward? Or are they dreaded?

Complaining about church services to which little thought had been given, a writer quoted in the November, 1965, *Moody Monthly* observed that "in the majority of our meetings there is . . . little sense of the divine Presence, no moment of stillness, no solemnity, no wonder, no holy fear."

Is it ever that way in our services? Velva Holt related the incident on a well-known TV broadcast in which a small boy was asked what his father did to earn a living. "My daddy is a preacher," he boasted.

"A preacher? And of what church?" he was asked.

"The Seventh-day Adventist," the boy quickly replied.

Then the master of ceremonies asked him to explain the difference between the Seventh-day Adventist Church and other churches. The boy thought a moment, then answered, "Our church is noisier than the others."

Today's scripture suggests that we come to God's house "ready to hear." As we do, reverence creates yet more reverence, and we will know that we are in the very presence of God.

Careful planning is a must too. Inspiration cautions that "unless constant care is exercised, and unless vitalized by the Spirit of God, the morning and evening service in the chapel and the Sabbath meetings will become dry and formal, and to the youth the most burdensome and the least attractive of the school exercises."—*Counsels to Parents, Teachers, and Students,* p. 502. The same thing can happen with family worships. We are urged to bring "all the pleasantness possible" into religious services. They are to be seasons "of positive pleasure" (*ibid.*).

May the vitalizing presence of the Holy Spirit and a quiet reverence make every worship experience a time "of positive pleasure"!

MORE ON DISCIPLINE

Whoso shall offend one of these little ones which believe in me, it were better for him that a millstone were hanged about his neck, and that he were drowned in the depth of the sea. Matt. 18:6.

We have mentioned that as we read the book *Counsels to Parents, Teachers, and Students* the students took note of the chapter entitled "Christian Discipline." It was their feeling in discussing it that we need to come closer to God's plan in handling discipline matters.

Today's scripture is quoted in that chapter, in this context: "Let Christ's methods be followed in dealing with those who make mistakes. Unwise actions, the manifestation of undue severity on the part of the teacher, may thrust a student upon Satan's battleground. Prodigals have been kept out of the kingdom of God by the un-Christlikeness of those who claimed to be Christians. 'Whoso shall offend one of these little ones which believe in Me,' Christ said, 'it were better for him that a millstone were hanged about his neck, and that he were drowned in the depth of the sea.' "—Page 266.

Speaking to parents as well as to teachers, inspiration states: "The youth will make many mistakes, and the teacher is never to forget to be compassionate and courteous. Never is he to seek to show his superiority. The greatest of teachers are those who are most patient, most kind."—*Ibid.*, p. 269.

Students likewise have a responsibility, as the same chapter mentions. Rules are necessary, and these the students should obey and support. At the same time, the wise parent or teacher will see to it that his rules are well chosen, reasonable, and few in number—and then, once made, enforced. And if an unwise regulation has been imposed, it is not the unpardonable sin to modify or abolish it.

The book *Education* also has a chapter on this subject, entitled "Discipline." We would find in reviewing these two chapters many suggestions that would be of help. Why not sit down some evening, pencil in hand, and underline as you read. Notice in particular the things you most need to apply in dealing with your children or youth. Then with God's help make whatever changes are needed.

267

TEEN-AGERS AND THEIR MONEY

But thou shalt remember the Lord thy God: for it is he that giveth thee power to get wealth. Deut. 8:18.

The Copely News Service, as reported in the Glendale *News-Press* (April 9, 1966), gave the results of a survey on how teen-agers spend their money. Seventy students were surveyed —thirty-five boys and thirty-five girls. Most of them were sixteen or seventeen years old. The boys had an average of $49.30 a month as spending money, the girls an average of $21.25.

Few of the seventy had savings accounts. Few paid any income tax. None had to worry about rent, insurance, or grocery bills. Most of the boys' dollars went for car upkeep, though quite a bit went for dates and presents also. The girls spent little on car upkeep; most of them didn't drive. The five girls who had their own cars all received them as gifts. The girls' major expenses were for such things as senior portraits or cheerleader outfits. The average teen-ager in this group owned about eight long-playing records that he himself had purchased. One boy reported buying 327 records. Major purchases reported by fellows, besides cars, included $300 for a guitar, $350 for drums, $250 for a car engine, $150 on trips. Seventy per cent relied on their parents for all or part of their income.

Only three of the girls gave a certain amount each month to their churches. None of the boys listed a church donation.

The major expense of most Seventh-day Adventist youth is probably Christian education. Most of them probably tithe. But how would the money spent on records, entertainment, dating, et cetera, compare with the offerings given?

Genuine revival influences our giving habits. At Andrews University a college girl told how in giving an offering she had always searched her purse for some coins. At the campus retreat in which Christ had come so close she decided it was time for a change, and gave money she had intended to use for other things. As she shared her experience, and told how God had blessed, it was evident that she had determined to adopt new giving habits.

268

". . . AND ASK, WHY NOT?"

The children of Issachar . . . were men that had understanding of the times, to know what Israel ought to do. 1 Chron. 12:32.

"Some men see things as they are, and ask, Why? I see things which never were, and ask, Why not?"

In our minds let's go back across the decades to an assembly in the Avondale School, in Australia. God's servant is speaking: "We need to realize that the Holy Spirit, who is as much a person as God is a person, is walking through these grounds."—*Evangelism,* p. 616.

Imagine the difference it would make if this divine Guest were granted full control on an academy or college campus.

The group of academy students who had opportunity to spend several weeks reading and discussing the book *Counsels to Parents, Teachers, and Students* were particularly impressed by the section entitled "The Holy Spirit in Our Schools." We discussed what might happen if we could prepare the way for the Holy Spirit to come to a campus the way He wanted to at the Battle Creek school. There would result, it was felt, a better faculty-student relationship, with a much greater love for one another and trust of one another by both groups. Wrongs would be made right, and differences put away. Lives would be changed, and conversions would take place. Religious services would be vitalized by the Holy Spirit. Prayer, anywhere on campus and at any time, would be natural.

Shouldn't we expect the Holy Spirit to come into our schools and churches with the same power as was manifest on the day of Pentecost? Could it be that on our campuses, as in our personal lives, we get so busy we leave too little room for the Holy Spirit? What would happen, asked these students, if we would allow more time for voluntary study and discussion groups, and Spirit-filled sessions for prayer and praise? What would happen if a genuine spirit of heart-searching and repentance could prevail? What would happen if seeking "a revival of true godliness" were to be made "our first work"?

God grant us men and women and youth who have "understanding of the times"—who, seeing "things which never were," will ask, "Why not?"

A LESSON FROM BATTLE CREEK

Now all these things happened unto them for ensamples: and they are written for our admonition, upon whom the ends of the world are come. 1 Cor. 10:11.

As we review denominational history it becomes evident that God set His hand following the 1888 General Conference to finish His work. As an emphasis on righteousness by faith brought new spiritual life to the church, God's servant wrote in 1892 that "the loud cry of the third angel has already begun in the revelation of the righteousness of Christ."—*Selected Messages,* book 1, p. 363. The following year there was a marked outpouring of the Holy Spirit upon our institutions at Battle Creek, and particularly at Battle Creek College. But unconverted hearts resisted this work, pronouncing it "excitement" and "fanaticism" (*ibid.,* p. 130), and God's Spirit was shut out.

Is there a lesson in this experience for us? What would happen if God's Spirit were to be poured out on churches or schools today to the same degree it was at Battle Creek? Would there be similar charges of "fanaticism"? At Battle Creek there were teachers who virtually said, "Thus far shalt Thou go with my students, but no farther. We need no enthusiasm in our school, no excitement."—*Counsels to Parents, Teachers, and Students,* p. 358. Would it be different today?

Inspiration gives no countenance to fanaticism—and in a February 6, 1894, article in the *Review* (see *Selected Messages,* book 1, pp. 129-143), in which Mrs. White discussed events at Battle Creek, she noted this danger. Whenever God works, she said, a counterfeit will also be seen, as the enemy attempts to "make of none effect the true work of God." But "by their fruits ye shall know them" (Matt. 7:20). We are entreated not to let counterfeits cause us to reject the true.

Had the Holy Spirit been welcomed at Battle Creek in 1893 instead of being "repressed and driven back," the revival there could have become an influence to the ends of the earth. The revelation of the righteousness of Christ could have swelled to a loud cry. But instead, the revival died. A fascination with amusements took its place. Did those so fearful of fanaticism join the shouting which accompanies sports events? One wonders . . .

NOT BY HUMAN WISDOM

Not by might, nor by power, but by my spirit, saith the Lord of hosts. **Zech. 4:6.**

When the Holy Spirit came with power to the Battle Creek campus in 1893 the thought was expressed by those who were resisting Him that "in school the time ought to be given to study, and that there was a time for everything—as if the hours devoted to common study were too precious to be given up to the working of the heavenly Messenger."—*Counsels to Parents, Teachers, and Students,* pp. 363, 364.

God's servant was in Australia at the time. She was shown what had happened, and was directed to write to the teachers at Battle Creek College. "Let me tell you what I know of this heavenly Guest," she wrote. "The Holy Spirit was brooding over the youth during the school hours; but some hearts were so cold and dark that they had no desire for the Spirit's presence, and the light of God was withdrawn. The heavenly Visitant would have opened the understanding, would have given wisdom and knowledge in all lines of study that could be employed to the glory of God. He came to convince of sin, and to soften the hearts hardened by long estrangement from God. He came to reveal the great love wherewith God has loved these youth."— *Ibid.,* p. 364.

The revival that could have helped bring about the fullness of the loud cry was squelched! The Spirit of God was grieved away. And today, almost eighty years later, the church is still sitting on the borders of the Promised Land.

Several communications were sent from Australia to Battle Creek, portions of which may be found in *Counsels to Parents, Teachers, and Students,* section entitled "The Holy Spirit in Our Schools." In reading this section one senses that the servant of God could scarcely find words with which to convey her indignation at the way God's Spirit had been treated.

How urgently we need to remember the truth expressed in today's scripture! At some place, at some time, the Spirit of God must be given full control of hearts and homes and churches and campuses.

How would *you* receive Him if He came in fullness of power today?

IN PROPER PERSPECTIVE

But the Counselor, the Holy Spirit, whom the Father will send in my name, he will teach you all things. John 14:26, R.S.V.

We speak in Seventh-day Adventist education of a balanced program—one that encompasses the intellectual, the physical, the social, and the spiritual. We emphasize, and rightly so, the importance of doing one's best scholastically, though somehow we haven't taught as well as we ought "the necessity and the power of application. Upon this," inspiration points out, "far more than upon genius or talent, does success depend."—*Education*, p. 232.

The increase of scientific knowledge has made the intellectual, to many people, seem more important than anything else. We may need to be reminded, as James R. Newman once put it: "It is not important to know everything. It is important only to know important things."

What are the most important things? Let us again consider that "education is a failure unless . . . the heart accepts the teachings of the gospel of Christ."—*Counsels to Parents, Teachers, and Students*, pp. 12, 13. If a son or daughter graduates without having found Christ, what has he gained even if he has a straight 4-point GPA?

"God wants our minds to expand" (Ellen White, *Review and Herald*, Feb. 18, 1890). What we too often forget is that the greatest educational influence among us is the Holy Spirit. Suppose you could bring onto campus the greatest men on earth. For whom would you ask? As you consider this question, just remember this: "God can teach you more in one moment by His Holy Spirit than you could learn from the great men of the earth."—*Ibid.* Wrote the servant of God, in the same *Review* article, "If divine power does not combine with human effort, I would not give a straw for all that the greatest man could do."

A converted heart is a motivated heart. The student who has found Christ not only has an increased capacity for understanding—he will also have a greater and more worthy motivation for wanting to learn. Shouldn't our first concern be to give the Holy Spirit the fullest opportunity to work? Shouldn't we, at home and at school alike, put first things first?

JUDGING THE HOLY SPIRIT

Wherefore I say unto you, All manner of sin and blasphemy shall be forgiven unto men: but the blasphemy against the Holy Ghost shall not be forgiven unto men. Matt. 12:31.

The Pharisees had just attributed the work of Christ to the power of Satan. Christ, in meeting these charges, spoke one of the most solemn warnings ever given. For us today, as we anticipate the outpouring of God's Spirit in the greatest measure that has ever been given, it is a warning particularly relevant. When men, through indifference or stubbornness, reject the workings of the Holy Spirit, they cut themselves off from the only power that can possibly help them.

It would have been interesting to have attended some of the faculty meetings at Battle Creek College back in 1893, when the Holy Spirit had come with power to that campus—and was being resisted. Perhaps what was happening was just ignored at those staff meetings. Perhaps it was business as usual. What a difference it could have made if the staff had dispensed with the usual order of business, prayed much among themselves, and discussed how they could have welcomed the Holy Spirit!

Instead, they were privately, and perhaps publicly too, judging the Holy Spirit. In her communications from Australia, Mrs. White noted that poor, finite mortals were passing sentence upon the work of the Holy Spirit just as the Jews had passed sentence upon Christ. "Let it be understood in every institution in America," she wrote, "that it is not commissioned to you to direct the work of the Holy Spirit, and to tell how it shall represent itself. You have been guilty of doing this. May the Lord forgive you, is my prayer. Instead of being repressed and driven back, as it has been, the Holy Spirit should be welcomed, and its presence encouraged."—*Counsels to Parents, Teachers, and Students,* p. 360.

It seems almost impossible to believe that what happened at Battle Creek could have happened! This was our leading denominational school! Yet the Holy Spirit was shut out. But let's not be too quick to condemn. What will our reaction be when He comes once again with power?

ARE YOU AFRAID OF THE HOLY SPIRIT?

And when he comes, he will convince the world of sin and of righteousness and of judgment. **John 16:8, R.S.V.**

"Have you not been afraid of the Holy Spirit?" the servant of God asked the teachers at Battle Creek who had shut out the Holy Spirit. "At times it has come with all-pervading influence into the school at Battle Creek, and into the schools in other localities. Did you recognize it? Did you accord it the honor due to a heavenly Messenger? When the Spirit seemed to be striving with the youth, did you say, 'Let us put aside all study; for it is evident that we have among us a heavenly Guest. Let us give praise and honor to God'? Did you, with contrite hearts, bow in prayer with your students, pleading that you might receive the blessing that the Lord was offering you?"—*Counsels to Parents, Teachers, and Students,* p. 363.

What were they afraid of? The context indicates that there was immorality "of every kind and degree" striving for the mastery on the campus. There was idle talk of the lowest kind. Would not the presence of the Holy Spirit have brought conviction and conversion to some of these students?

Our fear, perhaps, is of the consequences of complete surrender. We are afraid of what the Holy Spirit might do with us. We are afraid of being pushed into things we would rather not do. Yet how needless are such fears! The Spirit of God does not degrade—He elevates and refines.

It is the work of the Holy Spirit to convict of sin. A manifestation of His presence may lead to tears of repentance—but these are followed by "the sunshine of holiness." At Bible conferences where God's Spirit has been markedly present the transformations that have taken place have brought forth the fruits of the Spirit—love and joy and peace and goodness and faith. At one conference youth camp, where many lives have been changed, the camp is no longer thought of as simply a place for recreation. It possesses, instead, the sacredness of a place where many have found God.

There is no cause for fearing the Holy Spirit. Let us rather seek more and more of His presence in our lives and on our campuses!

FROM MINORS TO MAJORS

Thus saith the Lord of hosts; Turn ye unto me, saith the Lord of hosts, and I will turn unto you, saith the Lord of hosts. Zech. 1:3.

The work of rebuilding the Temple at Jerusalem had come to a halt. There had been many discouraging obstacles, and for more than a year nothing had been done. The exiles who had returned to Judea from the land of Babylon had become utterly discouraged. Forsaking the work of rebuilding the Temple, they sought to attain temporal prosperity. But everything seemed against them. Work as they might, they did not prosper.

The prophets Haggai and Zechariah were raised up to meet the emergency. Today's scripture is a summary of their message—a message urging the people to turn to the Lord. As the people responded, resuming work on the Temple, additional messages—messages of encouragement—came from the Lord. "Be strong, all ye people of the land, saith the Lord, and work: for I am with you, saith the Lord of hosts" (Haggai 2:4).

Would it not be the same today? The work of God, particularly in North America, has encountered a formidable obstacle in the secularism that prevails. Glen Greenwalt, one of the youth observers to the 1970 General Conference, wrote an evaluation of the meeting that was published in the North Pacific Union *Gleaner* of August 31, 1970. He noted that in his union the previous year's membership increase was 1.8 per cent, and that the church's national growth rate was 6 per cent less than that—"which," in his words, "shows that we really aren't growing." What has been the reason?

"Wherever the need of the Holy Spirit is a matter little thought of, there is seen spiritual drought, spiritual darkness, spiritual declension and death. Whenever minor matters occupy the attention, the divine power which is necessary for the growth and prosperity of the church, and which would bring all other blessings in its train, is lacking, though offered in infinite plenitude."—*The Acts of the Apostles,* p. 50.

Has there been a lack of spirituality in your church or on your campus? What have been the "minor matters" that have occupied the attention to the exclusion of God's Spirit? What changes can we begin to make?

275

WHEN 1844 IS REPEATED

Ye shall be baptized with the Holy Ghost not many days hence. Acts 1:5.

What would be the result in our homes and in our church and on our campuses if there were to be a fulfillment of today's scriptural promise now? There is to be, before the return of Christ, "a great reformatory movement"—"a reformation such as we witnessed in 1844" (*Testimonies,* vol. 9, p. 126). What would be the fruits we could expect if it came during this school year?

The 1844 experience is described in the book *The Great Controversy* in the closing pages of the chapter entitled "A Great Religious Awakening." Particularly vivid is the portrayal on page 369. The messages given, sent home by the power of the Holy Spirit, brought a conviction that few were able to wholly resist. Backsliders saw their worldliness and pride and selfishness, and sought the Lord with repentance and humiliation. The Spirit of God rested upon listeners, and sinners inquired with weeping, "What must I do to be saved?" Those who had been dishonest were eager to make restitution. The hearts of parents were turned to their children, and the hearts of children to their parents. The barriers of pride and reserve were swept away, and heartfelt confessions were made. Earnest labor was put forth for loved ones. Many wrestled all night in prayer for the assurance that their own sins were pardoned, or for the conversion of relatives and neighbors. The power of God was felt on old and young and middle-aged. Men sought their homes, after the meetings, with praises upon their lips, and the glad sound rang out upon the still night air.

We mentioned earlier this month the stirrings of revival on various of our campuses. At Andrews University, following a voluntary prayer session during the lunch hour, several college students were talking. "This spirit of revival that we have been seeing should be just the beginning," said one young man. "It must be," he added, "that God is preparing the way for something wonderful." And in one of the prayer groups a student had prayed, "O God, may the influence of revival be doubled, and tripled, and then multiplied a hundredfold." And when 1844 is repeated, it will be!

276

HIGHER AND STILL HIGHER

But when the Comforter is come, whom I will send unto you from the Father, even the Spirit of truth, which proceedeth from the Father, he shall testify of me. John 15:26.

It is the work of the Holy Spirit to testify of Christ. He is constantly seeking to draw the attention of men to the great offering that was made on the cross there at Calvary, that hearts may be convicted of the love of God. Then, as men yield to that love, He withdraws the affections from the things of this earth, and transforms them into the likeness of Christ. The cross of Christ is the most powerful of all appeals for a full surrender to Jesus. "If those who today are teaching the word of God, would uplift the cross of Christ higher and still higher, their ministry would be far more successful."—*The Acts of the Apostles,* p. 209.

Note the expression "higher and still higher." *Messages to Young People* speaks of that cross being planted "midway between earth and heaven" (p. 137). Can you picture it above your campus? Can you imagine, as you walk across campus, a cross planted "midway between earth and heaven"? Can you see, gloriously planted above the thousands of elementary church schools around the world, the cross of Christ? Can you see it above all our academies, and colleges, and universities?

Let it shine there, in wondrous splendor. Let nothing remove it. The cross of Christ is what should make Seventh-day Adventist schools distinctive. It is in the cross that we should glory. Glory not in buildings, nor in degrees, nor in large enrollments, nor in this or that department. Glory, rather, in the cross of Jesus Christ! It is as the cross is uplifted that true revival will come. It is as you accept the righteousness of Christ that you have a story to tell!

In the cross of Christ I glory,
　　Towering o'er the wrecks of time;
All the light of sacred story
　　Gathers round its head sublime.
　　　　　　　　　—JOHN BOWRING

A CHANGE OF RAIMENT

Behold, I have caused thine iniquity to pass from thee, and I will clothe thee with change of raiment. Zech. 3:4.

The vision of Joshua standing before the angel, as given to the prophet Zechariah, and recorded in Zechariah 3, is one of the most striking visions ever given—and is of special importance to God's people as they prepare for and enter into the final conflict.

Joshua, the high priest in Zerubbabel's time, was shown standing before the angel clothed in filthy garments. Satan stands at Joshua's right hand to accuse him.

Put yourself in Joshua's place. You stand there clothed in filthy garments. Satan, who has an accurate record of all your sins, boldly accuses you. He declares that God has no right to save you. Let's say your name is Jane. Satan's speech against you would go something like this:

"Is this Jane one of those who are to take my place in heaven, and the place of the angels who have joined me? She calls herself a Christian, but is she? Has she not loved herself more than she has loved God? Has she not frequently called attention to herself? Has she not loved the things of the world? Look at her filthy garments. Look at her sins, her pride, her vanity, her selfishness. Can God banish me and my angels, and yet save someone who has been guilty of the same sins? You can't do it, God, and be fair. Justice demands that this Jane die too."

What would you answer your accuser? All you would be able to do would be to point to your repentance and sorrow for your sins, claiming the mercy of a sin-pardoning Saviour. And your humility and contrition will be accepted. The accuser will be rebuked. It is Christ's royal right to save to the uttermost all who come unto God by Him. In the words of today's scripture, you will be given a change of raiment—even the spotless robe of Christ's righteousness.

This is the glorious, wonderful truth that is to be proclaimed as a loud cry. Humble, grateful hearts are to tell the good news everywhere. Christ is our righteousness. Accept His gifts, and rejoice!

278

FOR WHAT PURPOSE?

But thou, O Daniel, shut up the words, and seal the book, even to the time of the end: many shall run to and fro, and knowledge shall be increased. Dan. 12:4.

The journalist Hal Boyle once reported that "if the ocean highway had been paved, Christopher Columbus might have made it faster to America on foot. He averaged about 2.8 miles an hour by sail."

Why did man's inventive genius slumber for so many thousands of years? As Howard Weeks points out in the *Signs of the Times* of January 26, 1954, no one needed good communications more than did the ancient Romans with their far-flung empire. "Why," he asks, "could not they have discovered some of the principles of radio in their time as Marconi, one of their sons, did in our ours?" As for flight, he notes that few ages have produced minds as keen and inquiring as did the golden age of the Greeks. Why could not those minds have worked out the principles of flight or electronics?

Leonard C. Lee, discussing the same thing, suggested that "nothing has been invented that was not possible in Abraham's day. The Israelites could have drilled for oil in the desert and ridden into the Promised Land in jeeps."—*Ibid.,* March 1, 1955.

Yet through century after century man's inventive power lay dormant. Why has it been awakened in this our time?

A handful of early believers (there were 120 in the upper room) embarked on the stupendous task of taking the gospel to the then-known world of perhaps 100 million people within the Roman Empire. Had there been 1,000 disciples to begin with, it would still have been a ratio of only one believer to 100,000 people. Yet they did it! Paul could report, before his death, that the gospel had been preached "to every creature which is under heaven" (Col. 1:23).

Even with population explosions, how much swifter the believers of today could reach the whole world! Under the power of God the gospel could conceivably be called to the attention of every human being within a matter of weeks or even days! God grant us the faith to be ready when He moves!

279

AS SWIFT AS LIGHTNING

And the living creatures ran and returned as the appearance of a flash of lightning. Eze. 1:14.

We have long known that the final movements will be "rapid ones." And Paul assures us that the Lord will intervene to make "a short work" upon the earth (Rom. 9:28). But how rapid is *rapid?* How short is *short?*

Inspiration comments concerning today's scripture that "the bright light going among the living creatures with the swiftness of lightning represents the speed with which this work will finally go forward to completion."—*Testimonies,* vol. 5, p. 754.

We do not know just what means God will use. But there is scarcely a place anywhere too remote to have transistor radios today.

Elder H. M. S. Richards relates this story. In Europe some time ago a Seventh-day Adventist young man was brought to court for refusing to do ordinary work on the Sabbath. He declared to the court that the oath of loyalty that had been required of him forbade his breaking the Sabbath.

"How is that?" asked the judge.

The young man replied, "I was sworn in with a Christian oath, and therefore I cannot be under any obligation to violate the commandments of God and work on the Sabbath. One must regard God as the highest authority and obey Him first."

This witness was borne in a little courtroom in an obscure corner of the world, but the dispatches picked it up, with a description of the whole scene, and a report of the words spoken was carried by electro-magnetic waves to the presses of at least four continents, and millions read the testimony of the young man's faith.

Through instances such as these the whole world could quickly be made aware of the issues. And angels will also intervene. "God will employ agencies whose origin man will be unable to discern; angels will do a work which men might have had the blessing of accomplishing, had they not neglected to answer the claims of God."—*Selected Messages,* book 1, p. 118.

ALL INFATUATIONS FADE

Choosing rather to suffer affliction with the people of God, than to enjoy the pleasures of sin for a season. Heb. 11:25.

Within the Seventh-day Adventist Church and on every Christian campus there are young people who think that if they could just get away from the church they could really enjoy life. They see some of the things forbidden by the religion of Christ —the theater, dancing, social drinking, daring fashions, gay parties, drugs, premarital sex—and they imagine that if they could just be free to do these things, they would be happy.

But how many people do you know, young or otherwise, who in turning their backs upon Christ have found happiness? How many of them—after a few years' experience in sin, and after quietly reviewing the consequences of their decision—would recommend that you follow their example?

There is a certain infatuation about sin. Sin affords a kind of "pleasure"—"for a season." But though sin can entertain, it cannot satisfy. It can be very alluring in the future—but not in the past. In the words of Clovis G. Chappell, "Sin is only charming in the present or in the immediate future. It has no charm in the past. How fascinating is sin a moment before it is committed! How absolutely necessary it seems to our happiness! But when it slips into the past its pearly teeth become ugly fangs, its shapely hands become unshapely claws, its winsome tresses become writhing serpents. The sin of the future often seems as fair as an angel from heaven, but the sin of yesterday is as ugly as a fiend from hell."—*Sermons on Old and New Testament Characters,* p. 76.

All infatuations ultimately fade, leaving stark reality. Such reality can be terribly bitter, even in this life. And beyond is the inevitable awakening at the close of the millennium, when those who are lost will see what they have forfeited. As they stand outside the walls of the New Jerusalem, how desirable eternal life will then seem! "Oh, strange infatuation!" they will cry out. "I have exchanged peace, happiness, and honor for wretchedness, infamy, and despair."

God help us to weigh well our decisions now while probation lingers!

THE UNANSWERABLE QUESTION

What shall it profit a man, if he shall gain the whole world, and lose his own soul? Mark 8:36.

Two young men were talking about Jesus. One of them, a Christian, had been telling the other what it meant to him to know Christ, and what a privilege it was to serve Him. He suggested to his friend that he, too, would find great joy in accepting Christ as his Saviour.

"I'm thinking about it," his friend said, "but it would mean giving up several things; I am counting the cost."

"Have you ever counted the cost of *not* accepting Him and not serving Him?" asked the young man who was a Christian.

We are not always honest with ourselves when we think things through. We are apt to rationalize—we can talk ourselves into doing a lot of things that deep down in our hearts we know we shouldn't. But let every single one of us as we think about this be completely honest. Weigh carefully today's scripture. Give an honest answer to Christ's question.

Put into one scale Jesus Christ, and everything He means— peace, truth, the presence of the Holy Spirit, the joys of salvation, heaven, the friendship of God and of the angels. Into the other scale put every attraction the world can offer. Into the first scale put eternal life for yourself and for all those whom you might have been instrumental in saving. Into the other put the loss of your own soul and the loss of those whom you could have helped but didn't. Then "weigh for time and for eternity. While you are thus engaged, Christ speaks: 'What shall it profit a man, if he shall gain the whole world, and lose his own soul?' " —*Christ's Object Lessons*, p. 374.

What shall it profit? During the next few weeks there will be a fall Week of Devotion on all our campuses, followed by the fall Week of Prayer in our churches. Probably more prayers have ascended for a great outpouring of the Holy Spirit than at any previous time. Thousands of homes will be influenced by the decisions made by youth during the next few weeks. Let us pray that every single one of these Weeks of Prayer will be a time of the Holy Spirit's power. And let there be during this month much heart examination in our homes too.

FOR WHAT PRICE?

What shall a man give in exchange for his soul? **Mark 8:37.**

Elder H. M. S. Richards tells of a group of young men sitting around in a country store one evening telling what they did and did not believe. Finally, as the story has it, the leader of the group remarked that as far as he was concerned he would be willing to sign away all his interests in Christ and heaven for a five-dollar bill.

An old farmer happened to be in the store, and overheard the remark. "What did I understand you to say?" he asked.

"I said," replied the young man, "that for five dollars I would sign away all my interest in Christ, and so I will."

The old farmer drew out his leather wallet, took out a five-dollar bill and put it in the storekeeper's hand. Then calling for ink and paper, he said, "My young friend, if you will just step to the desk now and write as I direct, the money is yours."

The young man took up the pen and began, "In the presence of these witnesses, I, ..., for the sum of five dollars received, do now once for all and forever, sign away all my interest . . ." Then he stopped and dropped the pen, and with a forced smile he said, "Oh, I take it all back. I was only fooling."

For what price would *you* relinquish all your interests in Christ and heaven?

It has been argued that every man has his price. This is not true, but do you have a price? For what would you sell your soul? For what amount of money? For what indulgence? For what pet sin?

Are there those who relinquish heaven for even less than a five-dollar bill? For a few points dishonestly gained on a quiz, perhaps? One time at Glendale Academy a single black shoe turned up in lost and found. Several Bible references were written on the sole of the shoe—texts I recognized as being from a recent test. No one ever claimed the shoe. He gained, possibly, a few dishonest points.

But what a bargain!

What shall a man give in exchange for his soul?

TWO PATHWAYS STRETCHING BEFORE

Enter ye in at the strait gate: for wide is the gate, and broad is the way, that leadeth to destruction, and many there be which go in thereat: because strait is the gate, and narrow is the way, which leadeth unto life, and few there be that find it. Matt. 7:13, 14.

Jesus here speaks of two pathways—a narrow, upward way, and a broad downward road. There is no third.

The word *narrow* has an almost offensive sound. Youth call to mind some intolerant adult, some display of narrow-mindedness, and wish Jesus had not used this word in describing the way to life. But what is it that makes the upward way narrow?

"If you cling to any besetting sin you will find the way too narrow for you to enter. Your own ways, your own will, your evil habits and practices, must be given up if you would keep the way of the Lord. . . . Heaven's path is too narrow for . . . the play of self-centered ambition, too steep and rugged for lovers of ease to climb."—*Thoughts From the Mount of Blessing,* p. 139.

And what is it that makes the broad way broad? Is it not that you can take along just about any cherished sin, any bad habit, all your selfishness, all your pride, or anything else you can get by with? "There is room for every man's opinions and doctrines, space to follow his inclinations, to do whatever his self-love may dictate."—*Ibid.,* p. 138.

The road to success, in any worth-while endeavor, is narrow. The student who wishes to become a physician finds the way narrow. He cannot golf all afternoon, and watch TV all evening. Narrow is the way that leads to any worth-while achievement.

In landing a plane, narrow is the way. Billy Graham writes of a trip from Korea to Japan, through a rough snowstorm, with the ceiling and visibility at the Tokyo airport almost zero. The pilot had to make an instrument landing, with the man in the control tower guiding them in. "I did not want these men to be broad-minded," said Billy Graham. "I wanted them to be narrow-minded. I knew that our lives depended on it."—*These Times,* August, 1961, p. 5.

"SEEK THY SERVANT"

I have gone astray like a lost sheep; seek thy servant; for I do not forget thy commandments. **Ps. 119:176.**

It was our privilege while sponsoring the camping and hiking club at Glendale Academy to make several excursions annually. San Gorgonio, San Jacinto, Mount Whitney—we found occasion to climb them all. But a trip we had long talked about, and the one we waited the longest to make, was the pack trip into the Grand Canyon, which we have previously mentioned. No one in our group had ever hiked down into the canyon, and all we knew about its trails was what we had read. One description had told how there were places along the trail where a mule would sometimes stick his head out over a cliff, giving his startled rider a look straight down for more than a thousand feet. But we were planning on backpacking, not riding, and we were assured in any event that the hike is perfectly safe if one stays on the trail. But get yourself lost, we had read, and the canyon becomes a frightful monster, able to devour ten thousand like you in a single gulp.

In 1944 two Army pilots had had to bail out at night above the Grand Canyon. Seeing the lights of the village on the South Rim, they apparently thought themselves above a small town. To their horror they descended right on past the lights, dropping down, down, down onto the Tonto Platform some 3,000 feet below. It was three days before they were spotted by searchers, who then parachuted supplies to them—and it was with considerable difficulty that a rescue party was finally able to bring them out.

We lost no one on our trip, but hiking down into that vastness was a reminder of what it could be like to become lost. One thought was vividly impressed upon us—safety is found in staying on the trail. And so it is in following the upward pathway that leads to eternal life. Though narrow, it is safe—provided one stays on it. If through carelessness we do get off the trail, as David mentions in today's scripture that he had, let us not tarry in asking the Lord to help us find our way back. "Seek thy servant," David prayed. And God will. But we must want His help, and ask for it.

HE BIDS YOU COME—AND LIVE

Who shall separate us from the love of Christ? **Rom. 8:35.**

"Father, forgive them; for they know not what they do"—
this was the prayer Christ breathed as the soldiers were nailing
Him to the cross. Someone has computed that there are 21 billion billion atoms of nitrogen in a single breath. A newscaster
one Good Friday suggested that the 21 billion billion nitrogen
atoms from that breath with which Christ breathed this prayer
have since been completely diffused throughout the atmosphere, so that when we breathe it is possible we take in some of
those very same atoms. This newscaster concluded that it is literally true that nothing can separate us from Christ's forgiving
prayer.

One thing is certain—that prayer embraced us all. To all of
us forgiveness is freely offered. So often people stay away from
Christ because they do not feel good enough to come. And they
aren't. None of us are. But if we wait until we are good enough
to come to Jesus, we will never come.

Can you ever become better by your own efforts? Can a
leopard change his spots? "Then may ye also do good, that are
accustomed to do evil" (Jer. 13:23). If you are ever going to
come to Christ, you will have to come *just as you are.*

"I'm going to hell anyway, so why try?" a student said to one
of her friends. The devil delights to see us entangled in this
kind of hopeless despair. Do not let him get away with it! Remember again the parable of the prodigal son and how he was
received by his father. Just so will God receive us. "None are so
sinful that they cannot find strength, purity, and righteousness
in Jesus, who died for them. He is waiting to strip them of their
garments stained and polluted with sin, and to put upon
them the white robes of righteousness; he bids them live and
not die."—*Steps to Christ,* p. 53.

He bids you live! "I have blotted out," He says, "as a thick
cloud, thy transgressions, and, as a cloud, thy sins" (Isa. 44:22).
He will pardon you personally, individually. Come just as you
are! Don't let a devil's lie, or a friend's scorn, or some church
member's coldness, nor any of your sins keep you away! For
He bids *you* come—and live!

286

"HOW GREAT THOU ART"

Give unto the Lord the glory due unto his name; worship the Lord in the beauty of holiness. Ps. 29:2.

One summer it was our privilege to accompany a student group on a ten-day pack trip along the High Sierra "Loop" Trail that begins in Yosemite Valley and makes a fifty-mile circle up through the high country. We started by climbing up out of the valley on the north side, camping at Snow Creek there on the rim, and then at places such as May Lake and Glen Aulin. By Friday we were hiking along the Tuolumne River toward Tuolumne Meadows, where we were to spend the Sabbath. Our spirits were awed by all that we had seen. There had been so much to remind us of God—the sunrises and sunsets, the thunder that echoed among the mountain peaks during an occasional thunderstorm, the sparkling streams and rushing waterfalls, and the clearness of the starry heavens at night. As we hiked through a meadow of wildflowers, and within view of so much mountain splendor, someone began to sing, "How Great Thou Art."

If God is all that we say He is—and He is that, and more—should we not enter into His sanctuary with the same sense of awe? It is the King of kings into whose presence we are coming. "In every gathering for worship," inspiration observes, "there are more listeners than can be seen with the natural sight."—*Christ's Object Lessons,* p. 176. The angels of God are present, and the Holy Spirit is there. If our eyes could be opened to see the unseen, would not a great awe come over us?

One Sabbath morning a visitor to a church in the East Indies noticed a father and his little three-year-old boy enter the church. They walked up to the front to find a seat, and the little fellow sat down beside his father. Then the father bent over and whispered something to his son. Then they both bowed their heads for a moment of silent prayer.

How wonderful it would be if all of us would enter into God's house with the same sense of reverence! "Worship the Lord in the beauty of holiness," the psalmist invites. Let us, with thanksgiving and praise and a deep sense of the unseen, come reverently before Him.

287

GOING WITH THE FEW

But the path of the just is as the shining light, that shineth more and more unto the perfect day. **Prov. 4:18.**

On the High Sierra pack trip which we mentioned yesterday, we spent the first night in Yosemite Valley, having arrived late Sunday evening. We had heard that this famous valley has more than a million visitors a year, and we concluded as we tried to find space to roll out our sleeping bags that July evening that the whole million visitors must have decided to come the same weekend we had arrived.

During the night it began to rain. The showers continued to fall intermittently into the next morning. We decided to head for the high country anyway. We had arranged to rent seven burros, one for our three-year-old to ride, the others for pack animals. By noon we had the burros loaded, then shouldering our packs, started out. Clouds still hovered low over the valley, and groups of tourists watched as our block-long group of hikers and burros started along the trail up toward Mirror Lake and into Tenaya Canyon.

About an hour later we began to climb the Tenaya zigzags, a series of one hundred and forty switchbacks that take one to the rim of the canyon. We had not gone far until we left the crowds behind. During those ten glorious days up in the high country we met very few people. We enjoyed in almost complete solitude the adventures of the mountain trails. The meadows of blue lupine were all ours. The view from high ridges, the blueness of mountain lakes, the Milky Way seemingly almost close enough to touch, the endless variety of the wildflowers—these, too, were enjoyed apart from the crowds.

The crowd, we decided, is not interested in climbing. So it is also in spiritual things. "If you would climb the path of spiritual life, you must constantly ascend; for it is an upward way. You must go with the few; for the multitude will choose the downward path."—*Thoughts From the Mount of Blessing*, p. 138.

But like the high country, this is real living. You will be "with the few"—yet how wonderful the fellowship, and how joyous the living. Climbing takes effort and self-discipline—but it is worth it a thousand times over!

MAKING CHRIST AT HOME

That Christ may dwell in your hearts by faith; that ye . . . may . . . know the love of Christ, which passeth knowledge, that ye might be filled with all the fulness of God. **Eph. 3:17-19.**

At a number of Bible conferences we have used as a basis for the discussion groups the little book by Robert Munger entitled *My Heart—Christ's Home.* As Christ is invited to come into the life and make Himself at home, the first room He is shown into is the library, representing the mind. There is keen embarrassment on the part of the host as Christ notices some of the books and pictures. The offending books are replaced by the Scriptures, and the not-so-good pictures by a portrait of Christ.

They visit the dining room, the drawing room, the workshop, and the rumpus room. There are changes made in each room. Then, last of all, there is an upstairs hall closet. The closet, kept under lock and key, contains one or two little personal things that the owner certainly does not want Christ to see. It is an awkward moment, but the key is surrendered, and Christ removes the things that offend, bringing victory and joy.

It's a simple illustration, but it has provided launching pads for some good discussions about the meaning of having Christ within the heart.

Could you, without embarrassment, make Christ a guest in every part of your life? Would some changes be needed? Are there any upstairs hall closets that need attention?

When Christ is invited into the life, He brings with Him such wonderful love—"love . . . which passeth knowledge." We lose so much when we let some cherished sin in an upstairs hall closet rob us of His presence. He longs for us to experience what it means to "be filled with all the fulness of God." As we experience this love, this fullness, we will wonder how we could ever have been so foolish as to hold back on inviting Him to be the Master of our lives.

"To have the religion of Christ means that you have absolutely surrendered your all to God."—*Messages to Young People,* p. 30. Have you?

IF WITHIN MONTHS

Behold, now is the accepted time; behold, now is the day of salvation.
2 Cor. 6:2.

At the beginning of a recent school year we handed a slip of paper to each student in several Bible classes, and asked them to answer anonymously this question: "If you could know that Christ were going to come before the end of this school year, what would be the one change you would most need to make in your life?"

Several answered that the thing most needed would be for them to accept Christ as Saviour. Similar to this, and the largest single category, were the answers that had to do with endeavoring to win a loved one or friend to Christ.

A large number specified that the first change they would make would be in the kind of music to which they were listening. Several mentioned reading habits. With others it would be a change in TV habits. One person said he would need to make right some stealing. With another lying was the problem. Several answers had to do with problems of purity. A good many said they would spend more time in Bible study and prayer. Others indicated that they would have to quit dating non-Christians.

Though we had requested that each student put down only one item, several of them mentioned two, three, four or more changes that they would need to make.

What changes would *you* need to make?

When will we, in His strength, make these changes? "The age-old excuse is, 'There is plenty of time.' Illogical though it be, the excuse seems to be universal. Speak to a young man about God and his soul's salvation, and he will reply, 'There is plenty of time.' Speak about God to a middle-aged businessman, with the streaks of gray coming into his forelocks, and he will say, 'There is still plenty of time.' Speak to a tottering old man about eternity and the welfare of his soul, and with trembling voice he will answer, 'There is still plenty of time.' "—BILLY GRAHAM, *These Times*, September, 1970, p. 78.

"Behold, *now* . . . is the day of salvation"!

AN ANGEL'S MISTAKE

Except a man be born from above, he cannot see the kingdom of God. John 3:3, margin.

In Bible Doctrines class, when we are discussing the sinner's need of Christ, I sometimes relate a parable that I call, "When an Angel Made a Mistake." In this parable one of the angels accompanying Christ at His return catches up into the air by mistake a young man from Seattle—or Los Angeles, or wherever—who is a used-to-be Christian. We imagine that this young man, after dropping the church, became a space engineer and eventually achieved success in his chosen field. But he has cultivated the tastes of the world—its music, its entertainment, its attitudes. Before getting expelled from the academy he had studied about the second coming of Christ, but all that had faded into the background as he separated himself from Christ.

And now, unconverted, he is mistakenly caught up into space with God's people. He can't help being thrilled by the journey out past the galaxies to Orion. Yet even before they arrive he is very uncomfortable. At the New Jerusalem it gets worse. The buildings and scenery are tremendous. But the spirit of worship and praise is foreign to him. The anthems annoy him. He wishes he had brought some of his albums along. Nor can he understand the people. His selfishness cannot fathom unselfishness. His impurity cannot comprehend purity. The things they are interested in he couldn't care less about. He would do anything to get away from it all!

We do not finish the parable, but read from *Steps to Christ* this thought: "The sinner could not be happy in God's presence; he would shrink from the companionship of holy beings. Could he be permitted to enter heaven, it would have no joy for him. The spirit of unselfish love that reigns there—every heart responding to the heart of Infinite Love—would touch no answering chord in his soul. His thoughts, his interests, his motives, would be alien to those that actuate the sinless dwellers there. . . . Heaven would be to him a place of torture; he would long to be hidden from Him who is its light, and the center of its joy."—Pages 17, 18.

291

ALMOST ALL—OR ALL?

Ye shall seek me, and find me, when ye shall search for me with all your heart. Jer. 29:13.

One cannot be a partly surrendered Christian. We cannot be half the Lord's and half the world's. We cannot even be 98 per cent the Lord's and 2 per cent the world's. In the parable of the merchantman seeking goodly pearls, he not only located a pearl of great price—he "went and sold *all* that he had, and bought it" (Matt. 13:46). It is over the *all* that so many stumble.

Is God reasonable in asking for all our heart?

In our academy Bible Doctrines class, when we come to the plan of salvation, we generally read and discuss *Steps to Christ.* In connection with chapter five, entitled "Consecration," we discuss today's scripture. Oftentimes I illustrate it by telling the class a little bit about meeting and getting acquainted with the girl I married. I relate how the girls' dormitory at Union College had some date rooms just off the front parlor. It was there, one Saturday evening, that I asked her to marry me. "Suppose I had told her," I suggest to these Bible Doctrines students, " 'My darling, I love you very much, with all my heart in fact, well, that is with almost all my heart. I am reserving just a small per cent for another girl I used to date. But I love you with 98 per cent of my heart. Will you become my wife?' "

It doesn't take much imagination to know what her answer would have been.

Many who want to belong to Christ, who want to be saved, will be lost. "They do not make an entire surrender of their wrong habits. They do not die to self that Christ may live in them. Therefore they do not find the precious pearl. . . . Almost Christians, yet not fully Christians, they seem near the kingdom of heaven, but they cannot enter there. Almost but not wholly saved, means to be not almost but wholly lost."—*Christ's Object Lessons,* p. 118.

But what does God ask us to give up when He asks us to give up all? Is it not a sinful heart for Him to cleanse and purify? How could one ever be reluctant about something like that?

292

FREELY WILL HE PARDON

He that covereth his sins shall not prosper: but whoso confesseth and forsaketh them shall have mercy. Prov. 28:13.

J. R. Nelson tells of two little girls who attended the same Sabbath school, who sat side by side in church school, and who were baptized at the same time. A few years later one of these girls was happily serving with her husband in a mission land. The other girl was in a hospital waiting for death to erase from her memory a life of tragedy. When only fifteen she had suddenly disappeared from her home. Her parents tried in vain to find her. No one could understand what had happened. Why should such a beautiful girl, a member of the church, suddenly disappear?

Six years later she was discovered in a hospital. Her life, which had shown so much promise, was ruined. She shared what had happened. It all began with "little sins." "I covered up many of my sins," she confessed. She had started attending the theater and other public amusements, and soon was dating boys who were not Christians. "My father and mother and the church people didn't know what I was doing," she said. "They all thought I was being good when I wasn't. The worst thing about it all is that when I wanted to change I couldn't."

And she was only 21!

A men's magazine a few years ago displayed on its front cover a disrobed girl in a garbage can. It was an illustration for an article concerning the new morality, entitled, "The New American Woman: Through at 21." Sin is like that. It can take away everything decent, everything worth while. Its ravaged victims, "having no hope, and without God" (Eph. 2:12) are through before they even get a chance to live.

Are there things in your life that you are having to hide? Are there sins that need to be forsaken? "Let the wicked forsake his way, and the unrighteous man his thoughts," the Lord entreats. "Let him return unto the Lord, and he will have mercy upon him; and to our God, for he will abundantly pardon" (Isa. 55:7).

Let us do it while there is still time!

NOT REALLY SECRET

Thou hast set our iniquities before thee, our secret sins in the light of thy countenance. Ps. 90:8.

The story is told of an astronomer, who, to rest his eyes, turned his telescope from the heavens to the earth and focused it on a hilltop several miles away. On that hill was an orchard, and in it he saw two boys stealing apples. One was getting the apples, the other watching to make sure that nobody saw them. But though several miles away the astronomer could see them as plainly as if he had been right there in the orchard with them.

So it is with "secret sins"—for there are no truly *secret* sins.

God once sent a letter through His messenger to a girl who was indulging what she thought was a very secret sin. She knew what she was doing was wrong, but she had stifled the voice of conscience. In an attempt to help her realize that her sin was not as secret as she thought, the letter used this illustration:

"Would you, in the presence of your father, perform an impure action? No, indeed. But you do this in the presence of your heavenly Father, who is so much more exalted, so holy, so pure. Yes, you corrupt your own body in the presence of the pure, sinless angels, and in the presence of Christ; and you continue to do this irrespective of conscience."—*Testimonies,* vol. 2, p. 564.

This girl had been daydreaming about marriage. She loved to talk about boys, and had become bold and forward. This outward behavior was related to the secret sin with which she was corrupting herself. She was apparently a pretty girl, but spoiled, and had learned to deceive in order to get her way. She had become "vain, pert, and saucy."

Hopeless? Not at all. There would have been no point in writing to her if her case was hopeless. There is much help and encouragement in this letter, entitled "An Indulged Daughter," as you will find if you will turn and read it (vol. 2, pp. 558-565). It is frank, to the point, but designed to help her overcome. She could find, through a complete surrender to Christ, victory and happiness. The choice was hers. So also with us in dealing with our secret sins.

ECHOING ON AND ON

Every idle word that men shall speak, they shall give account thereof in the day of judgment. For by thy words thou shalt be justified, and by thy words thou shalt be condemned. Matt. 12:36, 37.

Several people were discussing new electronic devices. One mentioned that there had been talk of the possibility of a device being developed by which men could catch up with all the words said in the past, so that history could be heard all over again. They began to wonder. *Could it be true that all past words were traveling on somewhere in space, so that someday we could catch up with them and hear them again?*

What a thought!

It is after lights are out on a Friday evening in a college dormitory. Some fellows have gotten together in one of their rooms. The conversation is not one that they would have wanted the dean or any of their parents to hear. Their words, once spoken, are beyond recall. But are they also echoing on and on?

Several women in a boarding school community have gotten together to plan a social. After their work is finished the conversation becomes a kind of gossip about this person and that one. A recently expelled student is discussed at some length. As the misdeeds leading to expulsion are recounted, the tone is more of condemnation than of sorrow. After a while they break up and go home—but do their words live on?

A girls' dean has had to reprimand one of the monitors. The monitor, returning to her room, has plenty to say—things she would not want played back on a tape recorder. Finally she calms down, and goes to bed. But could it be that her angry words do not die? Could it be that they will echo on and on?

"The words we utter today," says inspiration, "will go on echoing when time shall be no more."—*Testimonies to Ministers,* p. 429.

"How can it be?" we exclaim. The *how* of it has not been explained, but the truth of it could not be more clearly stated. *The words we utter today will go on echoing when time shall be no more!*

"Set a watch, O Lord, before my mouth; keep the door of my lips" (Ps. 141:3).

BLOTTED OUT—OR "FOREVER FROZEN"

We shall all stand before the judgment seat of Christ. Rom. 14:10.

When Jack Ruby shot the accused assassin of President Kennedy, a TV camera there to get pictures of the intended transfer of the prisoner recorded the murder. A little later this film was played back to Jack Ruby. He watched himself committing murder. The March 16, 1964, issue of *Newsweek* also mentioned the expression of one of the attending officers. It was, said *Newsweek*, "forever frozen" on film.

The judgment is a sobering subject. We can argue that it is inconsistent with love, yet it really isn't, and no argument can change the fact that "we shall all stand before the judgment seat of Christ." Our shrugging it off doesn't alter the fact that God "will examine the case of each individual with as close and searching scrutiny as if there were not another being upon the earth" (*The Great Controversy*, p. 490). Unbelief does not change the fact that just as an officer's expression was "forever frozen" on TV film so "character is faithfully delineated in the books above."—*Ibid.*, p. 487.

There are three sets of books that will be used in the judgment—the book of life, the book of remembrance, and the record of sins. All of these, and the judgment now in progress, are described in the chapter in *The Great Controversy* entitled "The Investigative Judgment." The matter at stake is simply this—either our sins, if confessed and forsaken, will be blotted out of the book of death, or our names will be blotted out of the book of life. And if we are lost, and our names removed from the book of life, our sins will be "forever frozen" in the book of death.

As we discuss this in Bible class, the thought is sometimes expressed that if one had no other motive for wanting to be saved, just getting your sins blotted out so others wouldn't be able to examine that awful record would be a pretty good reason. And while that is not a sufficient motive, it is something to think about! How thankful we should be that the blood of Christ is still available to cleanse us from "all sin"—*if* we will bring these sins to the cross.

BECAUSE HE CARES

How precious also are thy thoughts unto me, O God! How great is the sum of them! Ps. 139:17.

When studying the doctrine of the judgment in Bible classes we sometimes get into some lively discussions. Here's an illustration that always sparks something:

"Suppose," I tell the class, "that your thoughts of the past twenty-four hours, unknown to you, had all been recorded on film. Suppose, further, that we were now to turn out the lights, start the projector, and have a playback right here during this class period for all to see."

Sometimes we remind the class of what Jesus said in the Sermon on the Mount about even our intentions being taken into consideration by Him. (See Matt. 5:28.) In *The SDA Bible Commentary,* Ellen G. White Comments, on Matt. 5:21-28, the messenger of God mentions that "God knows every thought, every purpose, every plan, every motive. The books of heaven record the sins that would have been committed had there been opportunity" (p. 1085).

This deeply troubles some. "It's hopeless! I'll never make it!" is sometimes the first reaction. But we need be troubled only as we cherish and excuse our secret sins. In Psalm 139 David wrote of God's infinite knowledge. "Search me, O God, and know my heart," he pleaded. "See if there be any wicked way in me." And right in the midst of his meditations is today's scripture thought. He found comfort in the fact that God does watch, and does care. It's like the text in Genesis 16:13, "Thou God seest me," which has also disturbed some. A little girl one time explained that this simply means that God loves us so much that He just doesn't want us ever to get out of His sight.

Any human body that harbors dangerous germs is inviting disaster. So it is with secret sins, even intentions of sin. God realizes this far better than we, and He would have us search our hearts and allow Him to remove these lurking evils because He does love and care.

We can thank Him that He does! May we, like David, throw open every chamber of the soul, inviting His presence to purify and cleanse.

IS THERE A DIFFERENCE?

So then every one of us shall give account of himself to God. **Rom. 14:12.**

An author, reporting the results of a nationwide survey on cheating, concluded that a kind of "moral relativism" seems to have replaced the moral certainties of the past. As for faking an insurance claim—"It depends on the amount." As for returning a lost wallet which you have found—"It depends on who owned it."

One year banks lost more than seven times as much cash to dishonest employees as they did to armed robbers. These employees, in most cases, would not have even thought of conducting an armed robbery. And millions of people who would never steal from an individual seem to have no compunctions at all about stealing from a company.

A teen-ager, in discussing cheating, expressed the opinion that circumstances make a difference. She may have studied hard for a test, but some things just don't come, so she copies just one or two answers from someone. Another student does not study at all, and gets help on almost every question. "But," she maintains, "I think there's a difference between the two."

But is it not still cheating?

In the words of another, "A slight deviation from truth, a little variation from the requirements of God, is thought to be, after all, not so very sinful. . . . But sin is sin."—*Testimonies,* vol. 4, p. 311.

Sin is sin. The question to be determined, then, is whether a little cheating, a little stealing, a little lying, is sin.

Knowing the Ten Commandments as we do, and knowing, as today's scripture so clearly states, that every one of us must give account of himself to God, we should be able to determine the answer to that one. Could you, with untroubled conscience, explain to God Himself that you have found nothing wrong with stealing just a point or two on a quiz? Could you slip a pat of butter under your bread in the cafeteria line, to avoid paying for it, and then go to your room and read with a clear conscience the commandment "Thou shalt not steal"?

What would you say in giving account of the matter to God?

CHEATING PROBE

The entrance of thy words giveth light; it giveth understanding unto the simple. Ps. 119:130.

The headline in the Los Angeles *Herald-Examiner* some years ago, following the resignation of one hundred and nine Air Force Academy cadets in consequence of their cheating, carried the words in black, screaming print, "CHEATING PROBE." The UPI story indicated that "institutional shortcomings" had contributed to the scandal.—Los Angeles *Herald-Examiner,* May 6, 1965, p. 1.

We would do well to examine whether or not anything within our methods of teaching contributes to cheating by youth of today. Some teen-agers think so. When asked, "What can teachers do to help alleviate the problem of cheating?" various suggestions were made.

"I think teachers should get together and make out their tests so that you don't have two or three tests a day," one student said. "This in itself causes cheating because you have to stay up late and study for all of them."

Another student felt that on the high school level too many teachers try to teach on a college level. A third expressed the opinion that "teachers should take some kind of refresher course where they learn how . . . to get across what they want to get across." A fourth student felt that grades should be replaced by some other kind of evaluation.

We have not been left in the dark concerning some of these things. Inspiration suggests, for example, that "the system of confining children rigidly to grades is not wise" (*Counsels to Parents and Teachers,* p. 177). The chapter in the book *Education* entitled "Methods of Teaching" contains excellent suggestions for teachers and parents alike. Memory work, the power to discriminate between right and wrong, personal attention to individual needs, the power of application, simplicity in teaching, enthusiasm, the matter of what's most important—these are some of the points covered. Our own "probe," perhaps, ought to include a review of our God-given blueprint. And though scholastic achievement is important, perhaps a greater spiritual emphasis would strengthen the scholastic.

"EYES FRONT, BUDDY"

Let thine eyes look right on, and let thine eyelids look straight before thee.
Prov. 4:25.

A student attending a school of technology where an honor system had long been held, had completed writing his examination. As he sat there, thinking over his work, his head turned inadvertently toward a neighbor. Immediately another student tapped him on the shoulder from behind and said, "Eyes front, buddy!"

Some people are of the opinion that the honor system will no longer work in this age of almost universal permissiveness. They argue that it "simply gives the green light to all crooks and cheaters, meanwhile penalizing every honest student in the room." Military academies have followed it, but with a number of much-publicized dismissals resulting from the violation of the system.

For the Christian student, or worker, there must be a personal honor system. He must determine that he will not cheat or steal no matter what everybody else is doing.

We like to pride ourselves on being able to think things through. The wise man suggests that we do exactly that. "Ponder the path of thy feet," he urges (Prov. 4:26). What is the price paid for a single point gained dishonestly?

One person told of a school where "nearly everyone had his pet system of fraud." Suppose you could develop yours—that you could make it clever enough that within a given semester you could gain fifty or a hundred or more dishonest points. What kind of price would you be paying?

Can you cheat on a quiz, or copy someone else's homework, and then pray? Could the prevalence of cheating, even in Christian schools, be a major reason why a lot of students are so lukewarm about Christ? How could you cheat and at the same time be enthusiastic about spiritual things?

Isn't it time that each of us develops our personal honor system? Shouldn't we determine that "integrity, unswerving integrity," will be the system we are going to live by?

CRUCIFIED AFRESH

They crucify to themselves the Son of God afresh, and put him to an open shame. Heb. 6:6.

The story is told of a man who dreamed that he arrived at Calvary just as Christ was being nailed to the cross. Coming up the pathway to the top of the hill, he could see the soldiers holding down Christ's hands and feet. Still another person had the hammer and nails, and had just knelt to drive the spikes, with his back toward the man coming up the path.

"Stop! Stop!" the new arrival cried out. The person driving the nails paused, and turned to look in the direction of the shouts. To his horror, the man in his dream saw his own face. It was he who was driving the nails into the palms of Christ's hands.

According to today's scripture the Lord Jesus can be and is still being crucified by professed followers today. When I checked on Hebrews 6:6 in the scriptural index to the writings of Mrs. White, I discovered that she has quoted this scripture in thirteen different places in her writings. Looking up these references, reading the context, and taking note of the things which crucify Christ afresh is an experience that leads to personal searchings of heart. Of the things mentioned, here are some examples:

(1) Using a holy office, as did Eli's sons, as a cloak for selfishness and sensuality, (2) a jovial minister in the pulpit, or one whose primary purpose is seeking praise, (3) married men receiving attention from women who are not their wives, (4) contention, strife, and lawsuits between brethren, (5) a life of continual ingratitude and rebellion.

Also mentioned as putting Christ to open shame, but without using the expression about crucifying Him afresh, were (1) conformity to the world, (2) joining hands with lovers of pleasure, (3) hasty suspension of students or dealing with them in an un-Christlike manner, and (4) loss of spiritual zeal and consecration.

Let no one look at a neighbor and judge him—there is sufficient reason for each of us to do some heart-searching of our own!

301

SORRY ENOUGH TO CHANGE

Blessed are they that mourn: for they shall be comforted. **Matt. 5:4.**

In discussing yesterday the things that "crucify . . . the Son of God afresh, and put him to an open shame" (Heb. 6:6), we omitted this comprehensive comment by inspiration: "By every sin Jesus is wounded afresh; and as we look upon Him whom we have pierced, we mourn for the sins that have brought anguish upon Him. Such mourning will lead to the renunciation of sin."—*The Desire of Ages,* p. 300.

Inspiration also uses this expression: "piercing the wounds of Christ afresh" (*Testimonies,* vol. 5, p. 243). The figure is a vivid one, but let us not, with squeamish stomach, turn away from a momentary contemplation of the consequences of our sin. The literal crucifixion would have been horrible to watch. Even in the restrained words of *The Desire of Ages* mention is made of how "the wounds made by the nails gaped as the weight of His body dragged upon His hands" (p. 760). It was not a pretty sight. And the thought that my sin, your sin, can figuratively open those wounds afresh is not a comfortable thought.

It is easy to lose a sense of the exceeding sinfulness of sin. Calvary is Heaven's estimate of its awfulness. We need to go there, and be convicted. We need to have deep feelings concerning sin. We need to be sorry that we so often re-enact Calvary—sorry enough to make some changes. "Such mourning will lead to the renunciation of sin."

That's our need—a renunciation of sin. The passage in Hebrews concerning crucifying Christ afresh has sometimes been misunderstood, because of the statement about its being impossible for those who have fallen away to renew repentance. It cannot mean that turning from Christ is the unpardonable sin. Who of us then could have hope? It is the *continued* deliberate sin, the *continued* hardening of the heart, that eventually makes repentance impossible. We can so grieve away the Spirit that we lose all spiritual care. But to realize that every sin wounds Christ afresh should lead to true sorrow, to genuine repentance. Such mourning "shall be comforted." The guilt—all of it—can then be left at the foot of the cross.

"BLACKER THAN I THOUGHT"

Stand in awe, and sin not: commune with your own heart upon your bed, and be still. Ps. 4:4.

"Sin," said Billy Graham, "is blacker than I thought."

There was blackness in Gethsemane. As Christ fell prostrate upon the ground "He felt that by sin He was being separated from His Father. The gulf was so broad, so black, so deep, that His Spirit shuddered before it."—*The Desire of Ages,* p. 686.

. The same blackness—if anything even more intense—overshadowed Calvary. As He hung on the cross, Jesus could not see through to His resurrection. He feared His separation from God would be eternal. So great was the agony of this separation that His physical pain in comparison was as nothing.

Could you have been there, standing by the cross just at noon, you would have found the whole crucifixion scene suddenly enveloped in literal blackness. From noon onward "there was darkness over all the land unto the ninth hour" (Matt. 27: 45). It descended with dramatic effect. Curses were broken off in the middle of half-uttered sentences. The people about the cross fell prostrate to the earth. Some, wailing with fear, attempted to find their way back to the city.

At three in the afternoon, the darkness lifted, except that it still enveloped the cross. "It was a symbol of the agony and horror that weighed upon His heart."—*Ibid.,* p. 754. "My God, my God," Jesus cried out, "why hast thou forsaken me?"

Had we been there through those three awful hours of darkness, and had we heard that despairing cry, would we be casual about sin? Could we take *any* sin lightly? Would we excuse any of our little deviations from God's will? Would we not conclude that all sin is blacker than we have thought?

We weren't at Calvary. But go there in the stillness of the night in your imagination and commune with your own heart. Stand there in the blackness. Try to sense, to understand, what is happening. Let your meditations impose upon you a restraining awe, that you "sin not."

THE AWFULNESS OF SEPARATION FROM GOD

The way of transgressors is hard. **Prov. 13:15.**

Throughout David's youth the Lord meant a great deal to him. As he watched his sheep there was spread before him a landscape of rich and varied beauty. About him trees swayed in the breeze, and streams flowed at his feet. In the distance the hills reached up toward the sky, and beyond in the far distance he could see the barren cliffs of the mountain wall of Moab. The sun flooded his world with light, and above all was spread the tender blue of the overarching heavens. It was here that he composed some of his psalms, and his voice was often heard in prayer and praise, as the Spirit of God came upon him. David knew what it meant to be close to God.

Let the scene change now to a time years later, and the matter with Bathsheba. How alluring was sin before it was committed! But what a price David immediately began to pay! There was the anxiety he must have felt as all his schemes for covering up his sin didn't work out. And surely there must have been some misgivings and a feeling of trapped desperation as he sealed the letter that would result in the murder of Bathsheba's husband! What were David's thoughts as he handed to Uriah that same sealed letter, and let his brave and trusted soldier bear back to the front his own death warrant?

How could David during the months that followed have possibly prayed? No longer was the Lord close to him. "My sin is ever before me," he wrote later (Ps. 51:3). And as he began to try to make things right with the Lord, he pleaded in anguish, "Cast me not away from thy presence; and take not thy holy spirit from me" (verse 11).

There is no emptiness like the sense of being separated from God. "The way of transgressors is hard"—terribly hard. The dull, awful feeling of separation from God is the most unendurable of all. When one has been so close to God and known so well the joys of salvation as David had, it's even worse.

Has sin separated you from God? Read the fifty-first psalm, and make it your own prayer. "Restore unto me the joy of thy salvation," David prayed. David's genuine repentance was accepted, as yours will be too.

PUTTING OFF THE WEIGHTS

Let us lay aside every weight, and the sin which doth so easily beset us, and let us run with patience the race that is set before us. Heb. 12:1.

What is "the sin which doth so easily beset us"? It varies, doubtless, according to individuals. But with a lot of us the so-called respectable sins are our greatest hindrance. We tend to look at the immorality, the violence, the drunkenness, all about us, with somewhat of a smug feeling. As parents or teachers we see the excesses of some youth, the carelessness, the hardness of heart, the apparent lack of morals, and decry their sinfulness, their lack of good taste or judgment. But hold it! Could we be making the same mistake Mrs. White was talking about when she wrote the following words?

"The drunkard is despised," she said, "and is told that his sin will exclude him from heaven; while pride, selfishness, and covetousness too often go unrebuked. But these are sins that are especially offensive to God; for they are contrary to the benevolence of His character."—*Steps to Christ,* p. 30.

Sin, any sin, is black. But could we conclude that the more contrary to the character of God something is, the blacker it is? Drunkenness is obviously contrary to God's ways. But let us say the drunkard makes no profession. Now let us consider the Christian. The Christian who is unforgiving, or proud, or self-important, has professed to be Christlike. Does not this make his sin the blacker of the two? And if you—professedly a Christian—are impatient or exacting in dealing with one of God's weaker children, isn't this extremely *unlike* Him? How black then is an uncharitable attitude?

Then there is selfishness. How contrary is it to the character of God? Little children often have a "me first" attitude. But how about the rest of us? Suppose someone announces after a Saturday night program that one hundred surplus watermelons are available without cost to anyone who wishes to pick up one as he leaves. There are two hundred families at the program. Would you wait and take what's left, if any?

What, again, are the sins that are "especially offensive" to God? Shouldn't *these* weights be forever put aside?

"BE THOU CLEAN"

And as soon as he had spoken, immediately the leprosy departed from him, and he was cleansed. Mark 1:42.

In Bible times leprosy was the "most dreaded" of all diseases. "Deep-rooted, ineradicable, deadly, it was looked upon as a symbol of sin."—*The Desire of Ages,* p. 262. Whatever the leper touched was unclean. Even his breath was considered polluted. He was shut away from society, from family and friends. His very presence was considered contaminating, and if anyone approached, he was required to cry out, "Unclean! Unclean!"

Leprosy has sometimes been called "the anesthetic disease," for in its earlier stages there is no pain, rendering it all the more deadly. Yet it gradually but surely consumes the body. The hair falls off, the nails loosen, decay, and drop off. Joint after joint of the fingers and toes shrinks up and eventually disappears. Gums, teeth, eyes, ears, nose, tongue, are all affected.

One time when Jesus was teaching by the lake, a leper watched from a distance. As he saw the lame and blind and paralytic being healed, faith strengthened in his own heart. Forgetting all restrictions, he pressed near. His decaying body, inspiration says, was "horrible to look upon"—and as he pushed through the crowd, people fell back in terror. Casting himself at the feet of Jesus, he cried out, "Lord, if thou wilt, thou canst make me clean." Jesus, laying His hand upon him, said, "I will; be thou clean." Immediately the leper's flesh became healthy, the nerves sensitive, the muscles firm. "The rough, scaly surface peculiar to leprosy disappeared, and a soft glow, like that upon the skin of a healthy child, took its place."—*Ibid.,* p. 263.

Our defilement from sin is like unto leprosy. Writes Isaiah, "The whole head is sick, and the whole heart faint. From the sole of the foot even unto the head there is no soundness in it; but wounds, and bruises, and putrifying sores" (chap. 1:5, 6).

Thank God, Jesus does not consider us untouchable! He is just as willing to put forth His hand and cleanse from sin as He was to cleanse the leper. If we desire it, we too can be healed.

VICTORY IS FOR TODAY

Thanks be to God, which giveth us the victory through our Lord Jesus Christ. 1 Cor. 15:57.

How long can one safely postpone gaining victory over his sins? Let's say you have a bad temper. Can you freely indulge in fits of anger this year, and find victory easier next year? Or let's say your problem is the indulgence of appetite. You eat too much, especially on Sabbath. Will victory be easier a year from now? Or take a habit that binds with even stronger chains of steel—that of impure thoughts and unholy deeds. How safely can one wait until next year or the year thereafter to overcome these things?

Suppose one goes along tolerating his sins, excusing them, intending to overcome someday, but never getting around to it. Then, unexpectedly, his probation is about to close, and he knows it. Can his character be changed by a last-minute death-bed repentance?

"Character cannot be changed when Christ comes, nor just as a man is about to die. Character building must be done in this life. We fear that repentance will come to the self-indulgent, tainted soul all too late."—*Testimonies to Ministers,* p. 430.

God gave an example of a man saved at the eleventh hour, the thief on the cross, so none might despair. But as someone has said He gave only one example, that none might presume.

Why not know the joy of victory now? Are not God's promises dependable *now?* He will not allow you to be tempted above what you are able to bear. The temptations that come to us are "common to man." Others have met these same temptations and overcome. So can you. "Resist the devil, and he will flee from you," James promises (James 4:7). "Draw nigh to God," he urges, "and he will draw nigh to you" (verse 8).

There is something for us to do. We must make things right with God, and if others have been hurt, with them. Then with God's help we are to make a determined effort to resist unholy impulses, reaching out in faith to exclaim, "Thanks be to God, which giveth us the victory through our Lord Jesus Christ" (1 Cor. 15:57). We can be, through Him, "stedfast, unmoveable" (verse 58).

GOD IS WONDERFUL!

This is the victory that overcometh the world, even our faith. 1 John 5:4.

When Pastor Vandeman was holding some meetings in Canada, a sixteen-year-old girl who was attending asked to talk to him. "I feel impressed that what you say is reasonable," she told him. "Do you think that I should take my stand for God?"

Before he could answer, she continued, "Now don't answer yet. Let me tell you my experience first. My mother was a Christian. She died when I was but ten years of age. My father didn't care for religion, and I have drifted into the world, and I have drifted seriously. Now suppose I take my stand for Christ? Suppose I step out and obey Him? Suppose I surrender to His claims—what then? Can I hold firm when I go home? When somebody takes me out for a date and temptation comes, how am I going to hold out?"

Pastor Vandeman, in talking to her, encouraged her to believe that as she opened her heart to the power of God, she could know that He would sustain her. That night she took her stand. "It was wonderful," related Elder Vandeman, "to see the new light in her eyes, the new expression which showed that God had visited her." She had determined, in simple trust, to give Jesus full control in her life.

Two weeks later Pastor Vandeman received a card from her. "God is wonderful!" she wrote. "I got home, and sure enough, the boys began to visit the home and I went out for a drive with a young man. I said to myself as I prayed, 'Lord, what will I do now?' And I turned to the young man at the wheel and said, 'Jim, I would like to tell you what a friend I have found in Jesus.' He turned and listened to every word I said, and tears streamed down his cheeks as he gave his heart to the Saviour that night." Several weeks later another card arrived. She wrote that Jim went off on a vacation and called her up the moment he returned. " 'Jean, I have been faithful. I'll never give it up.' "

"The two simple conditions of the life of victory are surrender and faith," someone has said. May we make that our experience—and be as great a blessing to others as was this sixteen-year-old.

THE GIFT OF A LIFE

For the wages of sin is death; but the gift of God is eternal life through Jesus Christ our Lord. Rom. 6:23.

When I was in college a vesper speaker gave a message based primarily on the book of Romans. He dwelt at some length on the sins from Romans 1 which are mentioned as deserving the death penalty. He had us take our Bibles and look at the list carefully, as given in the last four verses of the chapter. Some of the things we might have felt fairly complacent about—things like murder, haters of God, inventors of evil things. But then he dwelt upon yet other sins within the same list—covetousness, debate, pride, the breaking of promises, a lack of mercy. Of these too, Paul says, "They which commit such things are worthy of death" (verse 32).

By the time he had finished with Romans 1 we knew we were under the sentence of death. But then he went on to portray before us "the righteousness of God which is by faith of Jesus Christ unto all and upon all them that believe" (Rom. 3:22). The Spirit of God came very close as we realized anew that while the wages of sin is death, the gift of God is eternal life through Jesus Christ.

Moody once told of a mutiny within one regiment of the Austrian army. The decree went forth that every tenth man was to be shot. A young man and his father were in that regiment, standing side by side. As this young man looked down the line and counted, he could see that his father was one of the doomed tenth men. He thought of his mother, waiting for and needing her husband, and of his younger brothers and sisters. He reached over with his strong young arms and took his father by the shoulders and moved him into his place, and he stepped over into his father's place. When the order was given, the son stepped out and was marched off to be executed. He took his father's place and died for him.

That is exactly what Jesus has done for me! I sat there in vespers that evening, very much under the sentence of death. But Jesus has died in my place! How can I help loving Him? Could there be any gift greater than the gift of that life?

309

MORE THAN FORGIVENESS

Behold the Lamb of God, which taketh away the sin of the world. John 1:29.

One day in an academy Bible class I handed out slips of quiz paper to everyone and asked each student to indicate, anonymously, the one thing he considered to be his biggest problem. When I compiled the results, the list included things such as rules, not enough money, lack of friends, parents, teachers, school, et cetera. No one mentioned what is really youth's greatest problem—sin.

Many of you will recall that during the third quarter of 1970 the youth Sabbath school lessons were entitled "The One Indispensable Man." If you want to solve your biggest problem, Jesus is exactly that—indispensable. "Do you know of anyone besides Jesus who can effectively deal with sin?" one Sabbath school teacher asked his class. The nearly one hundred people knew of no one. There is no one else. Only Jesus.

And our sins "so easily beset us"! We need Jesus every single day. We need His forgiveness when we sin. We need His help and power to keep us from sinning.

"Behold the Lamb of God, which taketh away the sin of the world," John told the people. Jesus takes away, first of all, the guilt of sin. But He longs to do more than this for us—He also wants to take away our desire for sin! We will have temptations until Jesus comes. We will ever have to be on guard to keep the carnal nature from asserting itself. But it can be so much easier if we will let Jesus take away more and more of the desire for sin, so that as we gain new victories things that once tempted us will tempt no longer.

"The religion of Christ means more than the forgiveness of sin; it means taking away our sins, and filling the vacuum with the graces of the Holy Spirit. . . . It means a heart emptied of self, and blessed with the abiding presence of Christ. When Christ reigns in the soul, there is purity, freedom from sin. The glory, the fullness, the completeness of the gospel plan is fulfilled in the life. The acceptance of the Saviour brings a glow of perfect peace, perfect love, perfect assurance."—*Christ's Object Lessons,* pp. 419, 420.

RIGHTEOUSNESS IN HIM

But of him are ye in Christ Jesus, who of God is made unto us wisdom, and righteousness, and sanctification, and redemption. **1 Cor. 1:30.**

How many sermons have you heard that have made such an impression upon you that you will always carry that impact with you?

The message I remember most vividly was delivered by a district pastor to a small Oklahoma congregation of perhaps thirty or thirty-five people. When I was baptized at the age of sixteen I was for a time the only baptized Seventh-day Adventist in my family or in my school. One Sabbath the pastor used as his text today's scripture, emphasizing that portion which states that "Christ Jesus . . . is made unto us . . . righteousness." Whatever the spiritual perplexities were that were bothering me, this was just the emphasis I needed. It was such an encouragement and such a help that I shall probably always remember that sermon more vividly than any other I have ever heard.

I have wondered since how many more of the youth of the church who have left might still be with us if they could have had the righteousness of Christ more clearly presented to them. It was what I needed, and God in His mercy impressed our pastor to speak on that subject at just the right time. Wrote God's servant in the *Review and Herald* of November 22, 1892, "The theme that attracts the heart of the sinner is Christ, and him crucified. On the cross of Calvary, Jesus stands revealed to the world in unparalleled love. Present him thus to the hungering multitudes, and the light of his love will win men from darkness to light, from transgression to obedience and true holiness. Beholding Jesus upon the cross of Calvary arouses the conscience to the heinous character of sin as nothing else can do."

The time must come, and will come, when one interest will prevail, one subject swallow up every other—Christ our righteousness. Our thoughts and hearts are to turn to Him as the flower turns to the sun. He, "the Sun of righteousness" (Mal. 4:2), is to become to each of us "wisdom, and righteousness, and sanctification, and redemption."

DOES YOUR CHURCH HAVE A PROPHET?

And the dragon was wroth with the woman, and went to make war with the remnant of her seed, which keep the commandments of God, and have the testimony of Jesus Christ. **Rev. 12:17.**

Carlyle B. Haynes was holding evangelistic meetings in an Eastern city. He made it his practice during such meetings to have three sermons on the prophetic gift. His first study, on a Thursday night, examined the prophetic gift in the Old Testament. The following evening he gave the second study, in which he showed that the prophetic gift was a part of the New Testament, but did not end there, and could be expected to be manifested to the end of time. The third and final message, given Sabbath morning, was based on today's scripture, and showed how the Seventh-day Adventist Church possesses these two identifying marks of the remnant, in that it keeps all ten commandments and has the gift of prophecy.

One woman who had been attending the meetings, and who had already begun keeping the Sabbath, listened with intense interest to the first two of these messages. At the close of the second one she came to Elder Haynes and asked, "Do you have a prophet in your church?"

"What makes you ask that?" he replied.

"Because of your sermon tonight. I want your answer."

"My answer," he said, "is that we do have a prophet in our church."

"Then my search of a quarter of a century is ended," she continued, "and I praise God."

"Tell me what you mean," Elder Haynes invited. She explained that nearly thirty years before, she had become convinced from her study of Revelation 12:17 that God's end-of-time church would have the prophetic gift. At church after church she had inquired if they had this gift, only to be disappointed. Elder Haynes invited her to be sure to come the following morning to hear his talk on the prophet of the remnant church. She came and was thrilled by what she learned. Shortly thereafter she was baptized.

Shouldn't we, too, praise God for a church with the prophetic gift?

312

HER BIGGEST HANG-UP—ELLEN WHITE

Despise not prophesyings. Prove all things; hold fast that which is good.
1 Thess. 5:20, 21.

Carolyn Jones, writing in the October 27, 1970, issue of *Insight*, told of her personal "religious war." Carolyn, a senior at an Adventist college, had grown up in a Christian home. Her home life, her academy and early college years, were all experiences in rebellion. Finally, when she went back to college after a year out on her own, she decided to give God a chance. Of this experience she wrote:

"He started with my biggest hangup—Ellen G. White. I was in a class called Prophetic Gifts. First nine weeks covered the Old Testament prophets; then it was time to study Ellen White. I turned cold, but I promised myself to listen this once. So I listened with this mandate, 'God, if You can convince me this woman is a prophet like Daniel or John, I'll listen to what she says.'

"Don't ever challenge God—unless you are ready to lose. And all the while you're losing, He'll be opening your eyes to points of view that you thought you could never accept. By the end of the semester I was convinced. I started believing Ellen White's statements. Taking them for more than reprimands. God was slowly, slowly capturing me."

God invites us to prove, or test, the prophets. It was as a junior in high school in Oklahoma that I first encountered the name Seventh-day Adventist. In checking the encyclopedia in the school library, I discovered that Adventists had a prophet named Ellen G. White. The idea of a modern prophet was disconcerting. But not long after this the Voice of Prophecy sent me a book entitled *Behold the Man*. It contained numerous quotations from *The Desire of Ages*. I must get that book, I thought to myself. Then I was sent a copy of *The Impending Conflict*—a paperback from the closing chapters of *The Great Controversy*. The issues it revealed concerning the conflict between good and evil were fantastic beyond words. Yet there was something about these chapters that made me know they were true.

You owe it to yourself, if Mrs. White is your hang-up too, to at least test these writings. Then "hold fast that which is good."

THE STANDARD ONE TESTS BY

To the law and to the testimony: if they speak not according to this word, it is because there is no light in them. Isa. 8:20.

In testing a prophet there must be a standard to check against. Today's scripture makes clear what that standard is— the law of God and the Word of God—"if they speak not according to this word, . . . there is no light in them."

Does Mrs. White pass this test? Do her writings uphold the law of God? Search her writings from beginning to end, all twenty-five million words, and one does not find a single word weakening the authority of God's law. Yet there is no harsh legalism. The law is upheld as God's standard of righteousness, and Jesus is exalted as our means for attaining that righteousness.

But are there doctrines within the Seventh-day Adventist Church based upon what Mrs. White says rather than upon the Bible? I have found none. My initial introduction to the doctrines of the church was through the Voice of Prophecy correspondence lessons. Not once was Mrs. White quoted as an authority for anything. Nor have I in teaching academy Bible Doctrines classes ever needed to quote Mrs. White as the authority for what we believe.

In helping students to understand the relationship of her writings to the Bible, I sometimes use this illustration: One could take a comprehensive road map of the United States and easily travel from New York City to the Grand Canyon. Once you arrive there, though, a more detailed local map would mean much. We can think of the Bible as the comprehensive road map. The books of Daniel and Revelation, for example, give in broad outline what we can expect in these last days. Mrs. White's writings, and particularly the book *The Great Controversy,* bring out additional details concerning these things.

We could get along without this additional information concerning final events, and without all the encouragement given concerning education, health, Christian living, and many other subjects. And yet, as we are about to enter the final showdown of a six-thousand-year-long conflict, how wonderful to have this help!

"BY THEIR FRUITS"

Wherefore by their fruits ye shall know them. Matt. 7:20.

In a letter urging Seventh-day Adventists to get better acquainted with the writings of Ellen White, Elder H. M. S. Richards relates that as a boy he overheard his father talking with a man who was opposed to the Spirit of Prophecy. This man's mind was set against it; he would not listen to reason. Finally Pastor Richards' father said, "Just one question. Please answer honestly from the heart. When you read these books, are you a worse man or a better man?" "Oh," he said, "a better man, of course." Elder Richards' father replied, "Well, that settles it for me. That is all I wanted to know."

"Let the *Testimonies* be judged by their fruits," the author suggests. "What is the spirit of their teaching? What has been the result of their influence?"—*Testimonies*, vol. 5, p. 671.

The same standard can be used to test her life. During her seventy years of ministry she lived in New England, Michigan, Switzerland, Australia, and California. She was human, and there were plenty who watched her life with skeptical eyes. Any faults and inconsistencies would have been exposed with great satisfaction by her opponents, yet her life was singularly consistent.

One person who for a time was a skeptic was John Matteson, a Baptist minister who at the age of twenty-eight became a Seventh-day Adventist. While weighing the matter, he had accidentally overheard her praying when she was alone with her husband and children. Her childlike and earnest pleadings deeply impressed him, as did her home life. Later he wrote:

"In her home she did not betray the least sign of one who is exalted. She engaged in household duties, and appeared just as humble and social as one who had never spoken in public. When she spoke to the people, she manifested no human learning or art. No studied eloquence, nor gestures, nor display of education. But there was an earnestness, power, and yet simplicity, which told that she had been with Jesus and learned of Him."—*Review and Herald*, May 29, 1866.

Would that the same earnestness and power and simplicity might be seen in our lives today!

315

THE TEST OF FULFILLED PREDICTIONS

When the word of the prophet shall come to pass, then shall the prophet be known, that the Lord hath truly sent him. Jer. 28:9.

The work of Mrs. White was more a work of giving instruction and guidance than it was making predictions. Yet scattered throughout her writings are striking predictions that have been or are being fulfilled. The chapter in *The Great Controversy* entitled "The Impending Conflict," for example, has a remarkable prediction concerning the uniting of earth's major religions just before the end. When this was written, in 1888, nothing seemed more unlikely. But not now.

Among the most interesting predictions are those having to do with world events. Here, with the dates when made, are some examples:

In 1909: "In the visions of the night a very impressive scene passed before me. I saw an immense ball of fire fall among some beautiful mansions, causing their instant destruction."—*Testimonies,* vol. 9, p. 28.

Also in 1909: "They [government leaders] are struggling in vain to place business operations on a more secure basis."—*Ibid.,* p. 13.

In 1904: "Soon great trouble will arise among the nations—trouble that will not cease until Jesus comes."—*Review and Herald,* Feb. 11, 1904.

In 1894: "The Lord is removing His restrictions from the earth, and soon there will be death and destruction. . . . Those who are without God's protection will find no safety in any place or position."—*Testimonies,* vol. 8, p. 50.

In 1903: "A storm is gathering, ready to burst upon the earth; and when God shall bid His angels loose the winds, there will be such a scene of strife as no pen can picture."—*Education,* p. 180.

One cannot but be sobered by words such as these. How good it is to know that "He who is the King, the Lord of hosts, sitteth between the cherubim, and amid the strife and tumult of nations He guards His children still. . . . When the strongholds of kings shall be overthrown, when the arrows of wrath shall strike through the hearts of His enemies, His people will be safe in His hands."—*Thoughts From the Mount of Blessing,* p. 121.

THE LANGUAGE OF HEAVEN

Whosoever shall confess that Jesus is the Son of God, God dwelleth in him, and he in God. 1 John 4:15.

Mrs. White's favorite subject was the life and teachings of Jesus. She emphasizes over and over again "the grace and completeness of the Saviour." To her Christ was everything.

One of the tests of a true prophet is that he "confesses that Jesus Christ has come in the flesh" (1 John 4:2, R.S.V.). One need only read the book *The Desire of Ages* to know how fully Mrs. White does this.

Bert Rhoads relates that in his youth an elderly minister, not a Seventh-day Adventist, kidded him about believing the writings of "an old woman who had fits and palmed them off as visions." One day when he visited this minister he took a copy of *The Desire of Ages* along. After they had talked for a while, and there had been a period of silence, he asked his friend to listen while he read from *The Desire of Ages* the description of the birth of Jesus.

When he had finished, he asked, "Brother Jones, what do you think of that?"

The old man was in tears. "Those words," he said, "are the language of heaven!"

"Those are the words," he was told, "of that 'old woman who had fits and palmed them off as visions.'"

Deeply moved, he replied, "I can't help it. Those words are the language of heaven."—In *The Youth's Instructor,* Dec. 10, 1957.

As she wrote *The Desire of Ages,* she did so with a sense of awe and reverence, and with a feeling of, "Who is sufficient for these things?" The result was a book that was probably her literary masterpiece—a book in which the reader finds new truth, new beauty, every time he opens it. A prayerful study of its pages cannot but bring marked changes in one's Christian experience.

"Go forth," it is suggested, "with your hearts softened and subdued by reading of the life of Christ. Drink deeply of the water of salvation, that it may be in your heart as a living spring, flowing forth to refresh souls ready to perish."—*Colporteur Ministry,* pp. 126, 127.

THE TEST OF TIME

For the prophecy came not in old time by the will of man: but holy men of God spake as they were moved by the Holy Ghost. 2 Peter 1:21.

Today's scripture emphasizes that the true prophet is writing not personal opinion or private interpretation, but divine truth as given through the Holy Spirit. Only thus could the prophet's work stand the test of time.

Take the book *The Ministry of Healing,* for example. In 1905, when this book was published, the science of nutrition was just beginning to be developed. In many areas of medicine there was still the grossest ignorance. How could an impostor, with no medical training, have possibly selected out of the bewildering array of ideas only those that would stand the test of seven decades? How could any person, except by divine inspiration, have produced a five-hundred-page book which in every detail of nutrition and medicine would still be true thereafter?

Pastor George Vandeman, in *The Youth's Instructor* (April 12, 1955), shared an experience that came to his attention from New York City. A leading staff physician, later of Columbia University Medical School, was attending evangelistic meetings. He was so much in earnest he urged private study to prepare himself for baptism as soon as possible. At one such study the gift of prophecy was examined. At the close of the study he asked, "Do you have anything that this woman has written— anything that I can understand—something in my field of interest?" The pastor took from his library a copy of *The Ministry of Healing* and gave it to him.

For nearly five months the doctor studied the book. Finally he walked into the pastor's office and confessed the skepticism that he had had. How could a woman with no medical training presume to write a book dealing with medicine? But as he read and reread, it came to him—she had to be inspired! "That settles it, Pastor," he said. "That woman is of God. Why, Pastor, she has stated medical principles in that book far in advance of her time! She has made statements that the medical profession only *now* is discovering to be true! She is of God; there is no question about it!"

THE OBJECTIONS

I have written unto you, young men, because ye are strong, and the word of God abideth in you, and ye have overcome the wicked one. 1 John 2:14.

In Bible class one day a young man sitting at the very back of the room spoke up. He wanted the church to liberalize its standards. "Take the Sabbath," he said. "In most denominations they go to church in the morning, and in the afternoon they can go to a movie or to the beach and have fun." He felt he would enjoy religion more if he could do the same.

The Bible standards, in other words, were too strict.

A similar complaint is often made against the Spirit of Prophecy writings. Through the years, in academy Bible classrooms, I have probably heard all the objections against these writings. The most frequent one is that they are too strict.

Yet her writings hold up the same high ideals one finds in Scripture. "If you value the approval of God," wrote Paul, "fix your minds on whatever is true and honorable and just and pure and lovely and praiseworthy" (Phil. 4:8, Phillips). As a guideline for leisure-time activities, where could you find a higher ideal than this? How well would most TV programs pass this standard?

"I have written unto you, young men," says John, "because ye are strong." Are you strong by God's grace? Or have you become soft and compromising? "Love not the world," John urges in the very next sentence, "neither the things that are in the world. If any man love the world, the love of the Father is not in him." Let us get clear what John had in mind when he wrote this. He mentions "the lust of the flesh, and the lust of the eyes, and the pride of life." John's way of life is intended for real men and women, not for self-indulgent weaklings.

At the same time, neither the Bible nor the writings of Ellen G. White are full of don'ts. Try *Real Happiness Is* as an example. It is filled from beginning to end with encouragement and hope and love. There are cautions, just as there are in Scripture, but they are given in love. And it's the same in all of her writings.

THE PROPHET AS A PERSON

Elijah was a man of like nature with ourselves. James 5:17, R.S.V.

The messengers of God were just as real and just as human as you or I. Paul might well have stopped by your home for a pastoral visit. You could have had Amos over for dinner. You could have stopped on a street corner to chat with Jeremiah. Had you visited Isaiah's home you would probably have found his wife, a prophetess (Isaiah 8:3), busy with the children or perhaps in the kitchen fixing the evening meal. You might even have found Isaiah helping to set the table!

Had you visited the White home in 1859 you would have found them living in a little frame cottage in Battle Creek. Mrs. White would have been a woman of thirty-one, her husband thirty-seven. You would have met three boys—Willie, Edson, and Henry—ages four, nine, and twelve. Had your visit been on April 11 you would have found the day devoted to making a garden. In her diary for that day she wrote that she wanted "to make home . . . the pleasantest place of any" for her children.

There was often company for dinner. Conference time that same year found thirty-five at her home for dinner one day. The following day there was but one brief entry in her diary, "We were all much worn out."

She appreciated healthful recreation. One April she and some friends took a sailboat ride out through the Golden Gate onto the Pacific. She wrote, "The waves ran high, and we were tossed up and down so very grandly. . . . The spray dashed over us. . . . I never enjoyed anything as much in my life."

She loved the mountains, and the orchards, and all the beauties of nature. She was especially fond of animals. One of her granddaughters tells that a favorite memory of her grandmother was seeing her sitting out in the yard one morning, holding on her lap a number of little downy chickens that had been brought out for her to see. "I can still see her sitting there in the sunlight," this granddaughter has written. "The sun had come out, bright and cheery. She smiled and seemed so happy and relaxed and I was happy for her, because for a little while at least the burden was lifted—the burden of the work God had given her to do."—*Review and Herald,* July 31, 1958.

"TASTE AND SEE"

O taste and see that the Lord is good: blessed is the man that trusteth in him. Ps. 34:8.

One year in our academy Bible Doctrines class there was a student who seemed to hate the very thought of Mrs. White. We were discussing on one occasion the sinner's need of Christ, and I read a passage from *Steps to Christ* which emphasizes our need. "I don't believe that!" she bluntly exclaimed.

In the Bible class that she took the following year, we spent nearly a semester studying the Spirit of Prophecy books. For three weeks students read selections from the *Testimonies.* Sometimes we assigned a specific reading, but usually the students were free to read selections of their own choosing. Daily written reports included brief evaluations.

After finishing the project, this student wrote a report in which she mentioned how much she had resented Mrs. White. This resentment, she concluded, had been based mostly on hearsay. As she had read for herself, she found that her attitude had completely changed. What she had formerly despised she had come to appreciate.

If you have never eaten apples, I could lecture you endlessly about apples, and perhaps make you even hate the thought of the subject. But if you will take one and eat it, we can skip the lectures. So also with the Bible or Spirit of Prophecy writings. We must "taste and see" for ourselves!

The devotional readings during the first part of this year emphasized our need for a revival of Bible study, of prayer, of living faith, of witnessing. We would like to suggest now yet another revival—a revival of the study of the *Testimonies* and other Spirit of Prophecy books. Testimony Countdown has been a blessing to many. If each of us would continue with a personal Testimony Countdown study, and if we would take to heart the things we read, it would greatly change our lives, making it possible for God to pour out His Spirit as never before. Would you be willing for the rest of 1972, with these longer winter evenings, to spend half an hour a day with these books? God bless you as you do so!

TRY IT

Whoso is wise, and will observe these things, even they shall understand the lovingkindness of the Lord. Ps. 107:43.

What would it be like to get a letter from a prophet? Some of Paul's letters were to individuals. Suppose Paul were alive today, and that God should reveal to him some of your spiritual needs, your problems and conflicts. Would you be glad to get a letter from him? Would you take what it said to heart?

Mrs. White was often instructed to write to individuals. A number of such letters have been preserved in the *Testimonies* so that others with similar needs might benefit from them. You can find them readily as you leaf through the *Testimonies,* as they generally begin with a salutation such as "Dear Brother A," et cetera. They were written to all kinds of individuals, and deal with almost every kind of circumstance, as these few samples from volume 5 will illustrate:

"Dangers of the Young" (pp. 508-516) was written to a young denominational employee who was losing his way. It closes with a series of questions designed, if possible, to check his reckless course.

"Suitable Reading for Children" (pp. 516-520) is to an author. It includes the caution, "It would be well to give thought and careful study to whatever is to be immortalized in print."

"Advice to the Young" (pp. 520-529) was written to the students of South Lancaster Academy. Any student today would find it instructive and inspirational.

"God's Love for Sinners" (pp. 629-635) was written to a man who feared that he had committed the unpardonable sin. The whole letter radiates encouragement.

"A Letter" (pp. 621-628) is a reply to a man who had apparently written to Mrs. White concerning his decision to leave the church. In simple, moving eloquence she tries to get him to see the issues at stake.

Today is the Sabbath. Take time sometime today to open volume 5, or any of the others, and begin reading anywhere, whether letter or article. Underline those things that seem like God speaking directly to you. You will be so blessed that you will want to read some daily.

TIME TO START MOVING!

Ye have compassed this mountain long enough: turn you northward.
Deut. 2:3.

We have thought and prayed much about a revival of true godliness during these past months. Every such prayer God has heard, and every reaching out toward Him He has blessed. But until probation closes there remains the need for an ever more earnest seeking of the Lord. A sense of intense earnestness should take possession of us, as we thank God for what has been accomplished, and as we realize what yet needs to be done.

In today's scripture Moses reviews how the Lord had told him, after they had spent forty years in the wilderness, that they had been there long enough. It was time to set their face northward. It was time to move unitedly and concertedly toward Canaan.

The parallel scarcely needs to be drawn. "For forty years did unbelief, murmuring, and rebellion shut out ancient Israel from the land of Canaan. The same sins have delayed the entrance of modern Israel into the heavenly Canaan. In neither case were the promises of God at fault. It is the unbelief, the worldliness, unconsecration, and strife among the Lord's professed people that have kept us in this world of sin and sorrow so many years."—*Evangelism*, p. 696.

And the above words were penned in 1883!

Take a long hard look at the obstacles mentioned. There is unbelief. Do you really believe God could finish His work now? Do you want Him to? Or does it matter that much to you?

Then there is worldliness. And unconsecration. And strife. How can God work through us if these things are in our hearts? There needs to be among us, as there was on an earlier occasion in the tribe of Reuben, "great searchings of heart" (Judges 5:16). Until the latter rain comes in its fullness it will ever be true that "a revival of true godliness among us is the greatest and most urgent of all our needs. To seek this should be our first work."—*Selected Messages*, book 1, p. 121.

We have camped "long enough"! It's time to start moving!

REVIVAL LEADERSHIP

The God of heaven, he will prosper us; therefore we his servants will arise and build. **Neh. 2:20.**

Nehemiah is a Biblical example of how a single person, enthusiastically working in cooperation with divine power, was used of the Lord to bring about the seemingly impossible within a very short time.

The rebuilding of the walls of Jerusalem, delayed by the indifference of the people as much as by the opposition of enemies, apparently would never be finished. Then Nehemiah appeared on the scene. With firm and eager purpose, he threw himself into the work. "His holy purpose, his high hope, his cheerful consecration to the work, were contagious. The people caught the enthusiasm of their leader, and in his sphere each man became a Nehemiah."—*The SDA Bible Commentary,* Ellen G. White Comments, on Neh. 2:17, 18, p. 1137.

As things began to move there were those who laughed. The whole idea of a finished work seemed preposterous. Nehemiah simply answered, "The God of heaven, he will prosper us." As he went from worker to worker, he "encouraged the fearful, aroused the laggard, and approved the diligent" (*Prophets and Kings,* p. 639). His heart was constantly uplifted to God. "The God of heaven," he exclaimed again and again, "he will prosper us." His words were echoed and re-echoed along the wall, thrilling the hearts of the workers, encouraging them to believe that finally the apparently impossible was about to be done.

And within fifty-two action-packed, crisis-filled days, the task was finished!

"There is need of Nehemiahs in the church today," the Lord declares through His servant.—*Ibid.* And again: "We need Nehemiahs."—*Ibid.*

Let Nehemiahs arise, let their enthusiasm be caught by thousands of others, so that each in his sphere likewise becomes a Nehemiah, and the task that has lingered for so many decades could be finished through the power of the Holy Spirit in a very short time. Could God be calling *you* to become a Nehemiah?

A MAN OF PRAYER

And it came to pass, when I heard these words, that I sat down and wept, and mourned certain days, and fasted, and prayed before the God of heaven. Neh. 1:4.

When Nehemiah had first heard about the "affliction and reproach" (Neh. 1:3) that had fallen upon the work of God at Jerusalem, it sent him to his knees. He went apart, somewhere there in the royal courts of Persia, and "prayed before the God of heaven." And as he prayed, "his faith and courage grew strong. His mouth was filled with holy arguments. He pointed to the dishonor that would be cast upon God, if His people, now that they had returned to Him, should be left in weakness and oppression."—*Prophets and Kings*, p. 629.

The first chapter of Nehemiah records this earnest prayer, in which he confesses his sins and the sins of his people. It is as he is praying that a plan comes to mind, and he determines that if he can secure the consent of the king, and the necessary aid, he himself will undertake the task of rebuilding the walls of Jerusalem.

Four months passed before a favorable opportunity to make his request known presented itself. During these months, "in Nehemiah's seasons of retirement, concealed from human sight, many were the prayers, the confessions, the tears, heard and witnessed by God and angels."—*Ibid.*, p. 630. And when an inquiry from the king gave Nehemiah the opportunity to make his request, he first lifted his thoughts to Heaven in a silent prayer. "I prayed to the God of heaven," he stated (Neh. 2:4). "In that brief prayer Nehemiah pressed into the presence of the King of kings and won to his side a power that can turn hearts as the rivers of water are turned."—*Ibid.*, p. 631.

There are nine different places in the book of Nehemiah where record has been left of Nehemiah's going to the Lord in prayer. And thus it must be with those who today would exert an influence toward a revival of godliness. As with Nehemiah, let us confess our sins and unbelief. Let our prayers, too, be filled "with holy arguments." Let us seek Him with renewed earnestness, that He may work mightily for the finishing of His work and the honor of His name.

325

ENTHUSIASM AND HARD WORK

So we built the wall; and all the wall was joined together to half its height. For the people had a mind to work. Neh. 4:6, R.S.V.

As Nehemiah spoke to the people, urging them to arise and build, he spoke his words with power. He had seen the providences of God in his behalf, and he knew that with God's continued help the task could be finished. He put his whole heart into his appeal, and the people responded. "His hope, his energy, his enthusiasm, his determination, were contagious, inspiring others with the same high courage and lofty purpose."— *Prophets and Kings,* p. 638.

It is said that Betterton, a well-known actor of his time, was on one occasion dining with Dr. Sheldon, the archbishop of Canterbury. "Pray, Mr. Betterton," the archbishop said to him, "tell me why it is that you actors affect your audiences so powerfully by speaking of things imaginary." "My Lord," replied Betterton, "with due submission to your grace, permit me to say that the reason is plain: It lies in the power of enthusiasm. We on the stage speak of things imaginary as if they were real, and you in the pulpit speak of things real as if they were imaginary."

Inspiration, in relating this incident, suggests that we should speak of eternal things "with all the force and enthusiasm which a knowledge of their reality and importance can inspire" (*Education,* p. 233). The promises of God are sure. As we seek Him, He *will* manifest His presence. Let's have the faith to believe it, and let's say so with enough conviction that others will know that we believe it.

With enthusiasm must go persistence and hard work. Today's scripture mentions the rapid progress of the rebuilding of the walls of Jerusalem. Nehemiah attributes this to the people having "a mind to work." So it must be today. "Triumph always follows decided effort."—*Testimonies,* vol. 7, p. 30. And success, gained through persevering effort, promotes yet greater success.

Let us, then, have "a mind to work." If God's people would move forward as one, they could, in the power of God, move the world. Are we ready to do so? Are you?

THOUGHTFUL AND PRUDENT

And I said unto the nobles, and to the rulers, and to the rest of the people, The work is great and large, and we are separated upon the wall, one far from another. In what place therefore ye hear the sound of the trumpet, resort ye thither unto us: our God shall fight for us. Neh. 4:19, 20.

Back at the palace, as the doors of opportunity began to open, Nehemiah moved with prudence and forethought. Arriving at Jerusalem, he had "continued to exercise the same caution and prudence that had hitherto marked his course" (*Prophets and Kings,* p. 636). There would be no rashness, no zeal without knowledge, as he perseveringly pressed forward.

As the building got under way, the Samaritans at first simply ridiculed, then became more active in their plotting. Meanwhile, opposition arose from within. Some leading Jews became disaffected, and sought to discourage Nehemiah, complaining that "there is much rubbish; so that we are not able to build" (Neh. 4:10). Then other "Jews which dwelt by"—who had not been helping at all—gathered up reports from the enemies without and came to Nehemiah some ten different times to tell him what an impossible job he had undertaken (verse 12).

All this only inspired Nehemiah with greater determination. "We made our prayer unto our God," he said (verse 9). He also prudently established a watch day and night, with instructions that a trumpet be blown at whatever point danger might appear. "Be not ye afraid," he told the people (verse 14). The Lord would be with them in their efforts and give them victory over their enemies. "Our God shall fight for us," he assured them.

So today, as the church presses forward in a work of revival and reformation, there will be opposition—and perhaps more from within than without. There will be those who "put not their necks to the work of their Lord" (chap. 3:5). In every religious movement there are those who hold themselves aloof, who even ridicule the work being done. But the response of faith will ever be, "Our God shall fight for us"—"for God is in the work, and no man can prevent its ultimate success."—*Ibid.,* p. 645.

A WORK OF REFORM

So I said, "The thing that you are doing is not good. Ought you not to walk in the fear of our God to prevent the taunts of the nations our enemies?" Neh. 5:9, R.S.V.

"The grace of God," declares inspiration, "is always reformatory."—*Medical Ministry,* p. 226.

Thus it was in the work of Nehemiah. Even as the walls of Jerusalem were being rebuilt, there came to his attention the fact that there were those who were taking advantage of their poorer brethren by charging high interest rates. Some were men of wealth, whose support Nehemiah greatly needed, but he did not hesitate because of this. "The thing that you are doing is not good," he told them. He set before the whole congregation the requirements of God, urging that changes be made. And changes were made.

At a later time, after Nehemiah had been back in Persia for a while, he found when he returned that there had developed great carelessness concerning Sabbath observance, and widespread intermarriage with idolaters. Nehemiah first set about to correct the Sabbath problem. He then turned his attention to the unlawful alliances with heathen wives. Some of the offenders were men in high office, whose example would ruin the nation if it was allowed to continue. As Nehemiah sought to bring about changes, "there was a constant struggle with opposing elements, and only by fasting, humiliation, and prayer was advancement made."—*Prophets and Kings,* p. 674.

We, too, need to walk in the fear of God on these matters, for His name can be just as much dishonored today as in ancient times. "The grace of God," for us too, "is always reformatory." Revival must be accompanied by reformation if it is to be lasting. "Revival signifies a renewal of spiritual life, a quickening of the powers of mind and heart, a resurrection from spiritual death. Reformation signifies a reorganization, a change in ideas and theories, habits and practices. . . . Revival and reformation are to do their appointed work, and in doing this work they must blend."—*Selected Messages,* book 1, p. 128.

LIMITING GOD

Yea, they turned back and tempted God, and limited the Holy One of Israel. Ps. 78:41.

How can man limit God? Elder H. M. S. Richards relates an example, as told by Dr. F. B. Meyer. A revival meeting was dragging along. There were no signs of real revival, no success, until one evening an elder in the church arose and said, "Pastor, I don't believe there is going to be a revival here as long as Brother Jones and I don't speak to each other." Then he left his seat, went over to the other side of the church, and said, "Brother Jones, we have not spoken for five years. Let's bury the hatchet. Here's my hand."

A sob broke from the audience. Soon another elder arose and said, "Pastor, I have been saying mean things about you behind your back, and nice things to your face. Please forgive me."

Others stood up and confessed their wrongs, and the revival was on. The whole community was blessed and uplifted.

Probably the two biggest factors in limiting God, and hindering the finishing of His work, are differences between brethren and a lack of faith. Concerning the former, inspiration urges: "If there have been difficulties, brethren and sisters—if envy, malice, bitterness, evil surmisings, have existed, confess these sins, not in a general way, but go to your brethren and sisters personally. Be definite."—*Review and Herald*, Dec. 16, 1884.

How could we put into words the blessing that would come if *all* the obstacles were removed so that the power of God could be manifest more and yet more? We know a little of what He can do, but our hearts yearn for richer and still richer currents of divine power to flow.

What will you do, my fellow teachers? What will you do, beloved youth of God? What will you do, dear pastors and people? Will we enter into a yet fuller experience? The new school year is well under way. God has blessed, but there is so much more He could do if we would only become His instruments! "He longs to have you reach after Him by faith. He longs to have you expect great things from Him."—*Christ's Object Lessons*, p. 146. Will you? Do you?

"TO THEM THAT OBEY"

We are his witnesses of these things; and so is also the Holy Ghost, whom God hath given to them that obey him. **Acts 5:32.**

It has been suggested that obedience to the voice of the Holy Spirit includes yielding up every known sin and performing every known duty.

Lois Christian Randolph speaks of a retired minister whose Sabbath school class she visited whenever she could. One day he shared with his class how the Lord impressed upon him that he should obey the speed laws. "I confess," he told them, "that I have often driven too fast, especially when it seemed that I might be late for an appointment. I knew that other people should not drive over the speed limit. It was foolish and dangerous for them to do so, and was one of the principal causes of the many automobile accidents.

"But, for some strange reason I felt that it was safe for me to drive faster than the law allowed. I knew that I was a careful driver, sane and sober; I thought I was an expert at the wheel. I had never been involved in an automobile wreck in all of my thirty-eight years of driving. The first of this year I was taught to obey the traffic laws strictly. I had been earnestly praying for the Holy Spirit to come into my life that He might use me to help others. This had been the burden of my prayers for some time.

"Then, one day, as I was driving to the city, I began to go over the speed limit as I took a short cut. It was then that a voice spoke to me very distinctly. It said, 'You cannot expect to receive the Holy Spirit if you do not obey the laws of the land.' I slowed up immediately, and have found pleasure in obeying the traffic regulations since then."—*Come Up Higher,* p. 19.

Have you, like this pastor, been praying for more of the Holy Spirit to come into your life? What might be some of the things in your life that are obstacles to your receiving God's Spirit? Are you, too, driving too fast? Are there any known duties you have been neglecting? Are there any indulgences that need to be corrected? Are there any habits that need to be changed?

GOD'S INVITATION TO YOUTH

Let no one despise your youth, but set the believers an example in speech and conduct, in love, in faith, in purity. **1 Tim. 4:12, R.S.V.**

We have given attention in earlier devotional readings to the need for revival leadership, and to our need for modern Nehemiahs. So often, when we think of leaders like Nehemiah, we imagine that such men must come primarily from among the ministry. But not so. It is God's plan that each of us within our own sphere possess the qualities and influence of a Nehemiah.

Today's scripture is God's appeal to young men and young women—for He "has appointed the youth to be His helping hand" (*Christian Service,* p. 30). Those of you who are academy and college youth, it is to you that God says, "Set the believers an example." You are the ones who have the ardor, the generous devotion, the enthusiasm, to set the church on fire! It is you whom "the Holy Spirit loves to address"! It is to you that God is looking to "set . . . an example" in the changes that must come!

And changes there must be! It was in 1904 that the servant of God wrote: "In every church in our land, there is needed confession, repentance, and reconversion. The disappointment of Christ is beyond description."—*Review and Herald,* Dec. 15, 1904.

We have wandered in the wilderness far longer than ancient Israel. And if Christ's disappointment was "beyond description" in 1904, what must it be in 1972? He could at any time bring probation to a close—but so many, so very many, of His people would be unready. How much longer must He wait? How much longer *can* He wait? In every church, on every campus, "there is needed confession, repentance, and reconversion." God "is waiting"—waiting with such deep longing—"to inspire the youth with power from above" (*The Ministry of Healing,* p. 405).

Turn and read, in volume eight of the *Testimonies,* the chapter entitled "The Power Promised." "Plead for the Holy Spirit," the author urges. . . . "With your Bibles in your hands, say: 'I have done as Thou hast said. I present Thy promise, "Ask, and it shall be given you; seek, and ye shall find; knock, and it shall be opened unto you." ' "—Page 23.

"NOT AS MAN SEETH"

The Lord seeth not as man seeth; for man looketh on the outward appearance, but the Lord looketh on the heart. **1 Sam. 16:7.**

These words were spoken by God to a servant of His who had just made a serious misjudgment. Samuel, impressed by Eliab, thought he would surely be the Lord's choice. But God had a younger, humbler instrument in mind.

God has often worked that way.

If you were the Lord, looking for someone to serve as a prophet in these last days, would you have selected a seventeen-year-old girl? Consider for one thing the magnitude of the task. Out of the disappointment of 1844 there was but a handful of believers left—a handful that must become a mighty movement "to every nation, and kindred, and tongue, and people."

Honestly, now, would human wisdom have called a teenager?

God did. For "the Lord seeth not as man seeth." The Lord often acts in a way contrary to what man would do. Both Isaiah and Jeremiah were called at a time when God's people were almost bankrupt spiritually. Both were scarcely out of their teens, if indeed they even were. "Ah, Lord God!" exclaimed Jeremiah in protest, "behold, I cannot speak: for I am a child" (Jer. 1:6).

Human wisdom wouldn't have bothered to even ask him.

There were Daniel, taken captive at seventeen, and his three friends of about the same age. Through them a witness was given that was more far reaching than what the whole nation had been able to accomplish previously. There were Joseph in Egypt, and Timothy, and Mary the mother of Jesus. Would we have objected concerning these, as Saul said of David, "Thou art but a youth" (1 Sam. 17:33)?

What God appreciates is humility, and devotion, and ardor, and a susceptibility to the Holy Spirit. It is not talent that He is looking for, nor even experience, though both have a place. He wants above all else a willingness to be filled with His Spirit, and a childlike confidence and trust. Such an instrument any of us could become—if we would.

A "MARANATHA" ARMY

He which testifieth these things saith, Surely I come quickly. Amen. Even so, come, Lord Jesus. **Rev. 22:20.**

The word *Maranatha* is becoming an increasingly popular word among certain Adventist youth. The students at Forest Lake Academy, and then the youth throughout the State of Florida, have launched a share-your-faith program which they have entitled *Maranatha.* And early in 1970 seven thousand youth of the South American Division met in Brazil for a congress at which the theme was *Maranatha.*

What does the word mean? It is found only once in the Bible, in 1 Corinthians 16:22, and is an Aramaic word understood to mean "our Lord cometh." The *SDA Bible Dictionary* mentions that it seems to have been used as a Christian watchword with reference to the second coming of Christ. For a Christian to use this word as a greeting could be thought of as an expression of absolute confidence in the return of Christ. Some translations word it more as a prayer—"Our Lord, come!" or "Come, O Lord!"

Whether as a watchword or as a prayer it is an appropriate theme for Adventist youth. The Brazil youth congress, lasting for four days, had a different topic each day, one for each of the four "A's" in *Maranatha,* as follows:

First day: *Amar*—to love His return.

Second day: *Anunciar*—to announce His return.

Third day: *Apressar*—to hasten His return.

Fourth day: *Aguardar*—to await His return.

"God is pouring out His Spirit on the youth of South America," said Paul M. DeBooy in reporting this youth congress. He wrote that as he listened to their witness, he could truly say that *Maranatha* had become a personal experience in their lives.

All over the world a *Maranatha* army is forming. As the Spirit of God directs the movements, and the angels of God take the field, the work after all these years of delay *will* be finished and Jesus will come. "Even so, come, Lord Jesus!"

Maranatha!

WITH THANKFUL HEARTS

And Jesus answering said, Were there not ten cleansed? but where are the nine? Luke 17:17.

You remember the story—how that as Jesus entered a village, ten lepers from afar off cried out to be healed. Jesus did not immediately heal them, but sent them to show themselves to the priests. As they acted in faith upon His commission, they discovered when part way there that they were healed. One of them, a Samaritan, turned back and gave thanks. The other nine did not bother.

At the time of Christ leprosy was the most terrible of all diseases. "Its incurable and contagious character, and its horrible effect upon its victims, filled the bravest with fear."—*The Desire of Ages,* p. 262. It is hard to understand why nine out of ten victims, suddenly healed, would not even bother to say, "Thank You."

But how is it with us?

"Have any of us duly considered how much we have to be thankful for?" the servant of God once asked. "Do we remember that the mercies of the Lord are new every morning and that His faithfulness faileth not? Do we acknowledge our dependence upon Him and express gratitude for all His favors? On the contrary, we too often forget."—*Testimonies,* vol. 5, p. 315.

"Let us not," the same pen urges, "be like the unthinking nine, whose hearts were untouched by the mercy of God."—*Ibid.*

As we give thanks today, let's duly consider how much we do have to be thankful for. At a Bible conference being held at Sunset Lake in the State of Washington, a group of students were taking a walk about the lake. Someone suggested stopping to pray for the evening meeting. In a simple, earnest prayer one freshman girl said to the Lord, "Please help our hearts to be touched."

Wouldn't it be wonderful this Thanksgiving Day if we could receive a special outpouring of God's Spirit? Let us, like this freshman girl, ask God to touch our hearts. Then under the influence of the Holy Spirit let us fervently praise Him.

THE POWER OF PRAISE

I will bless the Lord at all times: his praise shall continually be in my mouth.
Ps. 34:1.

Following Friday evening vespers at most of our academies and colleges there is opportunity provided to gather for prayer bands. At Auburn Academy those desiring to stay for prayer bands generally remain in the chapel after the close of vespers. One year we were sometimes able to arrange to have two or three large bonfires in a field across from the chapel. At the close of vespers we would go over and gather around these bonfires, where we would sing for a while and then conclude by dividing into prayer groups.

Sometimes, particularly while we were in the chapel, we would take time for those who wished to do so to tell about an answer to prayer, or to mention some blessing received from God. More than once it almost brought tears of joy to listen to these brief sincere expressions of thankfulness.

We need to praise God more than we do. Such exercises drive back the power of Satan. They expel the spirit of griping and complaining. They increase faith. "It is for our own benefit to keep every gift of God fresh in our memory. Thus faith is strengthened to . . . receive more and more. There is greater encouragement for us in the least blessing we ourselves receive from God than in all the accounts we can read of the faith and experience of others. . . . Let us then remember the lovingkindness of the Lord, and the multitude of His tender mercies."
—*The Desire of Ages*, p. 348.

If we talk faith, we will have faith. Praise begets yet more praise. Why don't we, then, praise God more than we do?

Such a witness is particularly effective when coming from young people. One morning during Sabbath school at the White Memorial church in Los Angeles we asked several youth who had been greatly blessed at a Bible conference to simply share their experiences. Said one person afterwards, "You could just sense the presence of the Holy Spirit as these youth spoke."

"Whoso offereth praise," God says, "glorifieth me" (Ps. 50:23).

FOR THE HONOR OF CHRIST

And I looked, and, lo, a Lamb stood on the mount Sion, and with him an hundred forty and four thousand, having his Father's name written in their foreheads. Rev. 14:1.

During academy Bible Doctrines class, while we are studying the book of Revelation, the question sometimes is asked, "Just who are these 144,000?" We generally conclude in our discussions that they are people who have been translated "from among the living" (*The Great Controversy,* p. 649) as first fruits of the great harvest, and that in some manner they have become qualified to receive great honor.

The Youth's Instructor, back in 1956, related the story of the first woman to make the thirty-two-mile swim across Lake Ontario. Of the three swimmers who slipped into the water at Youngstown, New York, sixteen-year-old Marilyn Bell was the youngest. Both the other swimmers, though more experienced in long-distance swimming, gave up part way across. Marilyn Bell was the one who made it.

At times she had to battle six-foot waves, and once she shook off an eel that had attached itself to her foot. When it seemed at one time she could not go on, she was told by means of a blackboard that the other two had dropped out, and she took courage and kept on. After twenty-one hours in the cold dark waters she touched the sea wall on the Canadian side and stepped ashore as 250,000 people cheered.

She received an award of $50,000 plus other things, such as fur coats, furniture, vacation trips, and so on. But this five-foot-two-inch, freckle-faced high school girl said that her real reward was the knowledge that she had done it for the "honor of Canada."

So with God's youth. If it be their privilege shortly to stand with the 144,000 their one theme will be, "Worthy is the Lamb that was slain to receive . . . honor" (Rev. 5:12). Whatever their victories, these will have been through Him and for His honor.

What privileges and opportunities are opening up before us! Let all of us, for the honor of Christ, move forward in a work of repentance and revival and reformation now! "If God be for us, who can be against us?"

THE DREAM GOD DREAMS

But the Lord said unto me, Say not, I am a child: for thou shalt go to all that I shall send thee, and whatsoever I command thee thou shalt speak. Jer. 1:7.

For more than ten decades God has been waiting for His people to prepare the way for the outpouring of the Holy Spirit. Could we for a few moments dream the kind of dream God might dream as with deep anguish He considers His lukewarm people?

In God's dream we see being raised up on every campus, youth who have put self aside and who hunger and thirst for more and yet more of His Spirit. Upon their respective campuses they begin to meet together in small groups to pray—and as they pray, they catch a vision of the work's being finished *now!* They plead with God to help others to get a glimpse of the same vision, praying most earnestly for specific fellow students. Their persevering prayers bring souls to the cross. In cooperation with their self-sacrificing efforts Jesus moves upon hearts, and their numbers increase. Differences are put away, and hearts beat in unison, as believers are drawn together in close and tender fellowship.

Sincere witness for Christ is given in private and in public. Hearts are stirred and lives are changed. Each new participant seeks and wins yet others. The spirit of intercession grows. First things are put first, and even class time is taken for prayer and praise and witness. The influence spreads. The electrifying news is received that the same thing begins happening "in many places" (*Testimonies to Ministers,* p. 515). Fervent words of thanksgiving and praise are heard. The influence of revival spreads from the campuses to the churches. A growing flame, it encompasses the earth, spreading "like fire in the stubble" (*Selected Messages,* book 1, p. 118). Through wonderful workings of divine providence the gospel is finished.

Such is the dream that God looking down upon His youth might dream! Isn't it time for it to become more than a dream? Couldn't it become reality now, this very school year? If not now —we again ask—when? If not on your campus, in your church, where? If not you, who?

LENGTHEN THY CORDS

Enlarge the place of thy tent, and let them stretch forth the curtains of thine habitations: spare not, lengthen thy cords, and strengthen thy stakes. Isa. 54:2.

The message of God to His people in today's scripture is that our plans have been too limited, our vision too narrow. We need to greatly enlarge our program—lengthening our cords and strengthening our stakes.

Part of God's intervention for a swift finishing of His work will apparently be to allow persecution, which will purify the church. It wouldn't have to be persecution; the same purifying could take place through revival and reformation. But will it? The answer lies largely with us.

It is evident, in any event, that many apostasies will take place. In one vision the servant of God saw "company after company from the Lord's army" deserting and going over to the enemy. But at the same time "tribe after tribe from the ranks of the enemy united with the commandment-keeping people of God."—*Testimonies,* vol. 8, p. 41. This vivid portrayal is found in a chapter entitled "A View of the Conflict."

A "tribe," of course, is larger than a "company." In the words of inspiration, "The Lord will work so that the disaffected ones will be separated from the true and loyal ones. Those who, like Cornelius, will fear God and glorify Him, will take their places. The ranks will not be diminished. Those who are firm and true will close up the vacancies that are made by those who become offended and apostatize."—Ellen White manuscript 97, 1898.

Immediately following this terrible conflict the prophet John sees the victorious ones standing on Mount Zion, singing "a new song before the throne" (Rev. 14:3).

Let's not lose sight of the grandness of God's work nor of the glorious triumph awaiting those who are true and loyal. And as we anticipate this triumphant finish, let's have the vision to greatly lengthen our cords and strengthen our stakes.

A PREDICTION

And they went forth, and preached every where, the Lord working with them, and confirming the word with signs following. Mark 16:20.

"As we draw near to the coming of Christ, more and still more of missionary work will engage our efforts."—*Counsels to Parents, Teachers, and Students,* p. 532.

This prediction is within the context of instruction concerning the kind of education youth should be receiving. The time for its fulfillment surely is now! A number of programs, many of them initiated by students, are beginning to be developed. At the beginning of the 1970-1971 school year, for example, there were approximately one hundred student missionaries abroad, most of them serving for a full year. Cost of transportation there and back is provided primarily by student or youth groups, with food, lodging, and expenses while there provided by the mission. Concerning this student missionary program a report in the September 1, 1970, issue of the Lake Union *Herald* stated:

"Since the program began in 1959, 59 countries have requested student missionaries and have put them to work. The church's youth department expresses the opinion that this is one of the greatest youth-mission programs the church has ever conducted. And it all started with the youth themselves!"

Another program that also began with the youth themselves is the ACT student missionary program—or Adventist Collegiate Taskforce. Monte Sahlin first conceived the idea while a student on the La Sierra campus of Loma Linda University. The first summer three groups of four young people each served in underprivileged areas of Los Angeles, conducting day camps, giving Bible studies, and ministering to the needs of the people. Now ACT teams can be found in many metropolitan areas during the summer months—and oftentimes also do follow-up work into the school year as well.

Are we not at the point where the coming of Christ can scarcely be delayed any longer? Is it not time for this prophecy concerning missionary work to be fulfilled? Should not an enthusiasm for going out to seek souls be seen everywhere?

YOUTH WINNING YOUTH

So shall my word be that goeth forth out of my mouth: it shall not return unto me void, but it shall accomplish that which I please, and it shall prosper in the thing whereto I sent it. Isa. 55:11.

It has been estimated that in 1970 half the population of America was under 25 years of age. What are we doing to take Christ to the teen-agers of the world? What are we doing to win the teen-agers in our own community?

Youth, according to Billy Graham, are the most fruitful field for evangelism. During his Portland crusade of 1968 he said: "This generation of young people is far more religious-minded than the young people of 18 years ago when I was in Portland the last time. They are among the most religious young people in history. . . . I've just about given up on the older people, however."—Los Angeles *Herald-Examiner,* June 16, 1968, p. A-7.

One time when D. L. Moody was in Los Angeles preaching to a crowd of about ten thousand people, he asked everyone who was a Christian to stand. About five to six thousand people stood. "Now," he said, "I want everyone here who became a Christian before he was fifteen years of age to sit down." More than half of those standing sat down. He next asked those who had accepted Christ between fifteen and twenty to be seated— and more than half of those who had remained standing sat down. Mr. Moody continued until he reached the age of fifty, when there were only about twenty people still standing.

"My word," God promises, "shall not return unto me void." Is not this a promise we can claim as we seek to take God's Word to the teen-agers of our own community? "Educate the youth to help the youth," *Messages to Young People* suggests (p. 203). It need not take elaborate evangelism programs. "Thousands of hearts can be reached in the most simple way."—*Ibid.*

That "simple way" could be the sharing of your fellowship. Have you ever taken any of the earliteens or youth in your neighborhood along on an outing? After you have gained their friendship could you invite them to Sabbath school and then have them home for Sabbath dinner? Could missionary work become a family project in your home?

HIS PRESENCE BRINGS COURAGE

Why art thou cast down, O my soul? . . . hope thou in God: for I shall yet praise him for the help of his countenance. **Ps. 42:5.**

Do you ever become discouraged? David apparently did, until he turned his thoughts to God. As he determined to praise God he found hope and courage.

A very discouraged Christian stopped to pray. His heart was heavy. He was dejected and worried. Within his heart and life were many conflicts. But as he prayed he turned his eyes upon Jesus. The Spirit of God gave him new glimpses of the Saviour. The words of a hymn came to his mind, and he began to sing:

"Jesus, the very thought of Thee,
With sweetness fills my breast;
But sweeter far Thy face to see,
And in Thy presence rest.

"No voice can sing, no heart can frame,
Nor can the memory find
A sweeter sound than Jesus' name,
The Saviour of mankind.

"O hope of every contrite heart!
O joy of all the meek,
To those who fall, how kind Thou art!
How good to those who seek!
. . . . .

"Jesus, our only joy be Thou,
As Thou our prize wilt be;
In Thee be all our glory now,
And through eternity."
—BERNARD OF CLAIRVAUX

It was a radiant, courageous Christian who rose from his knees. As he paused he thought to himself, Now, what was my petition? What were my problems? They had vanished—lost in a hymn of praise!—DAVID LIN, *The Youth's Instructor,* Aug. 29, 1944.

Such is the power of song and of praise in dispelling discouragement! The marginal reading for today's scripture suggests that His presence is "salvation." May you find it true this day!

"A HEART LIKE THINE"

Therefore if any man be in Christ, he is a new creature: old things are passed away; behold, all things are become new. 2 Cor. 5:17.

A 16-year-old boy, in a letter to Billy Graham, told of the changes that came into his life when he accepted Christ. "In the morning," he wrote, "I now hum 'Lamb of God' instead of a rock 'n' roll tune. Instead of a rock 'n' roll song on the record player a hymn now plays. Instead of always reading sports magazines I read the Bible. In the place of beer I now have fruit juice. Instead of hate for my neighbors there is love. When I walk down a street now I can avoid a lustful look at a girl. There is a glow in my heart and for the first time in my life I have peace."

"If a man is in Christ," Phillips translates today's scripture, "he becomes a new person altogether—the past is finished and gone, everything has become fresh and new."

We understand, of course, that when the Bible speaks of "a new heart" (Eze. 18:31) the word *heart* is being used for the mind, the thoughts, the life. "To have a new heart is to have a new mind, new purposes, new motives. What is the sign of a new heart?—A changed life."—*Messages to Young People*, p. 72.

At the first Bible conference to be held in southern California, in the fall of 1966, the theme was "A Heart Like Thine." There was scarcely a person who attended whose life was not changed as the Lord Jesus came very close. Across the front of the new cafeteria where our meetings were held were the words, "A Heart Like Thine." None of those present will ever forget the influence of those words as we sang them, and as we prayed them.

"I want, dear Lord, a heart that's true and clean;
A sunlit heart, with not a cloud between.
A heart like Thine, a heart divine, a heart as white as snow;
On me, dear Lord, a heart like this bestow."
—G. JACKSON. Copyright Salvation Army Board.

"Create in me a clean heart, O God," David prayed; "and renew a right spirit within me" (Ps. 51:10). If you would know joy and peace, make this your prayer, too.

342

LOVING PURENESS OF HEART

He that loveth pureness of heart, for the grace of his lips the king shall be his friend. **Prov. 22:11.**

"When it comes to temptation," I asked a college student during a discussion time, "what in your opinion is the biggest problem area for Christian youth today?" This student thought for a minute, then replied, "Judging from what my friends encounter, and from what I know of my own struggles, it would be this matter of keeping the heart clean."

When Christ comes we will be standing in the presence of Someone who can see right into our heart. There can be no sensuality still lurking there. It is the pure in heart who shall see God—who shall stand unashamed before Him.

The battle to overcome sensuality of thought—and action— is one of the most difficult we face, for we find arrayed against us all the strength of the carnal nature plus all the influences of a society growing constantly more permissive. Now, as ever, "watchfulness and prayer are the safeguards of purity." "Keep thy heart with all diligence," the Scriptures urge: "for out of it are the issues of life" (Prov. 4:23). It is for this very reason that Christians choose to avoid some of the amusements popular in the world. Unless we avoid reading, seeing, or hearing that which suggests impurity of thought, the strongholds of the heart will be gradually but surely undermined.

"The young would not be seduced into sin," inspiration suggests, "if they would refuse to enter any path save that upon which they could ask God's blessing."—*The Great Controversy,* p. 622. We are to make the King of kings our Friend and our constant unseen Companion.

The religion of Christ does not make one prudish, repulsive, and unattractive, for its influence is to make the demeanor winning. It teaches us to "combine a high sense of purity and integrity with sunniness of disposition" (*Gospel Workers,* p. 122). Purity is associated, appropriately, with joy. Moral integrity and joyous living cannot be separated. It is the heart "that's true and clean" that is also "a sunlit heart, with not a cloud between."

CLEANSED—AND KEPT CLEAN

Purge me with hyssop, and I shall be clean: wash me, and I shall be whiter than snow. Ps. 51:7.

In the statement of Jesus, "Blessed are the pure in heart," the Greek word for pure is *katharos,* meaning "pure, as being cleansed." This suggests, as all of us know by painful experience, that the heart is not intrinsically pure. It must be cleansed. "Purge me . . . ," prayed David, "and I shall be clean." "Wash me," he pleaded, "and I shall be whiter than snow."

The cleansing agent is the blood of Christ. And then, once cleansed, we must "be aided by the abiding influence of the Holy Spirit, which will attract the mind upward, and habituate it to dwell on pure and holy things. And we must give diligent study to the word of God" (*Patriarchs and Prophets,* p. 460).

"Gird up the loins of your mind," Peter suggests (1 Peter 1:13). The thoughts cannot be allowed to wander to any subject the enemy may suggest. A group of four thousand student delegates from a federation of high schools once drew up what they called the "Teen-age Ten Commandments." One of these ten was, "At the first moment turn away from unclean thinking— *at the first moment.*"

That's the key—turning away *at the first moment.* You can't keep birds from flying over your head, but you can keep them from building nests in your hair! You can't keep thoughts of impurity from intruding—but you can refuse to toy with them or to welcome them. You can refuse to cherish them.

Probably there is nothing that blocks out the impressions of the Holy Spirit more quickly than sensuality. "Every impure thought defiles the soul, impairs the moral sense, and tends to obliterate the impressions of the Holy Spirit. It dims the spiritual vision, so that men cannot behold God. The Lord may and does forgive the repenting sinner; but though forgiven, the soul is marred. All impurity of speech or of thought must be shunned by him who would have clear discernment of spiritual truth."—*The Desire of Ages,* p. 302.

Why not pray, "I want, dear Lord, a heart that's true and clean."

ON CASTING STONES

He that is without sin among you, let him first cast a stone at her. **John 8:7.**

The time is early morning. The place is the Temple at Jerusalem. Jesus, seated there in the Temple, is talking to the crowd of people who have gathered about Him. Then out on the edge of the crowd hard, accusing voices are heard. A group of Pharisees and scribes, dragging a terror-stricken woman, press through the gathered multitude. "Master," they interrupt, "this woman was taken in adultery, in the very act. Now Moses in the law commanded us, that such should be stoned: but what sayest thou?"

They thought they had Christ. They knew of His willingness to forgive and expected that He would urge leniency. But if He did, they would accuse Him of despising the law of Moses. And if Jesus approved the stoning, they would accuse Him of usurping Roman authority.

The Saviour had apparently stood up as they had approached. He quietly surveys them for a moment. He knows that they themselves have led this woman into sin that they might lay a snare for Him. Now, ignoring them as though He had not heard, He stooped and began to write in the dust on the Temple pavement. Not to be put off, the hard-faced dignitaries press in closer, urging the matter. As their eyes look down to the pavement their accusations are stilled and their faces go pale, for written there in the dust are the guilty secrets of their own lives. The people, seeing the sudden change of expression, press forward to see what has caused their consternation.

Rising to His feet and looking directly at the accusers, Jesus says, "He that is without sin among you, let him first cast a stone at her." Again stooping, He continues His writing as these men, with downcast eyes, one by one steal away.

How often today those who are quick to accuse are in their own lives more guilty than those they condemn. God help us to remember that while correction must at times be given, "God sent not his Son into the world to condemn the world; but that the world through him might be saved" (John 3:17).

"GO, AND SIN NO MORE"

Neither do I condemn thee: go, and sin no more. John 8:11.

The woman taken in adultery and brought to Jesus had stood before Him with trembling and shame. She took His words, "He that is without sin among you, let him first cast a stone," as a death sentence. She did not even look up, but silently awaited her doom.

Can you put yourself in her place as she stood there? Can you sense the shame, the utter hopelessness and despair that she must have felt? And can you imagine the astonishment that must have come over her as she saw her accusers departing, speechless and confused?

After the Pharisees had left Jesus discontinued His writing on the Temple pavement and again stood upright. Looking at the woman He asked, "Woman, where are those thine accusers? hath no man condemned thee?" Upon her reply, "No man, Lord," the Saviour then said, "Neither do I condemn thee: go, and sin no more."

Again, put yourself in her place. Her heart is melted by His willingness to forgive, and she casts herself at the feet of Christ. With broken sobs she tries to express her grateful love, and with bitter tears she confesses her sins. "This was to her the beginning of a new life, a life of purity and peace, devoted to the service of God" (*The Desire of Ages,* p. 462). She became one of Christ's most steadfast and devoted followers.

Such is the power of forgiveness. While Christ does not excuse sin, He seeks not to condemn, but to save. Others may express contempt and scorn, but Jesus speaks words of comfort and hope. When others would stone, He reaches out a helping hand.

The story is told of an incorrigible soldier, who had driven his officers almost to despair. His superiors had used almost every punishment in the book. When he was once again brought in for a misdeed, the officers wondered what to do next. "He has never been forgiven," someone suggested. In an interview with the offender, an officer told him they were forgiving all his past offenses, and would hold nothing against him. This soldier wept. He was forgiven—and never again did he cause trouble.

SLOW TO ANGER

He that is slow to anger is better than the mighty; and he that ruleth his spirit than he that taketh a city. **Prov. 16:32.**

"The measure of a man," someone has said, "is the size of the thing it takes to get his goat."

How much does it take to make you angry?

"The highest evidence of nobility in a Christian," we read in *Messages to Young People*, "is self-control. He who can stand unmoved amid a storm of abuse is one of God's heroes" (p. 134). Can you?

"There is a wonderful power in silence," the same author suggests. "When impatient words are spoken to you, do not retaliate. Words spoken in reply to one who is angry usually act as a whip, lashing the temper into greater fury. But anger met by silence quickly dies away."—*Ibid.*, pp. 135, 136.

Psychologists tell us that outbursts of temper are most frequent in children between one and two years of age—and that such outbursts should decrease thereafter as a person grows into an adult. It doesn't necessarily work that way, however, for apart from Christ man often finds it impossible to truly rule his spirit. Even when from social pressures or other reasons an angered man holds back an outburst of temper, he may seethe inwardly.

True self-control is not control *by* self. It is control *of* self *by* Another. The peace and grace of Christ in the heart enable a man to pursue the even tenor of his way, neither elated by applause nor dejected by censure.

May God grant those of you who are teen-agers a double amount of His grace in developing self-control! Your example in patience and gentleness has never been more needed! May we suggest for your encouragement that you read in *Messages to Young People* the brief chapter entitled "Self-discipline," from which the above two quotations are taken (pages 134-136).

And no matter how often you fail, do not give up. Keep trying—never taking your eyes off your divine Exemplar!

THANKING GOD FOR DIFFICULTIES

We glory in tribulations also: knowing that tribulation worketh patience.
Rom. 5:3.

Have you ever asked God to make you a more patient person? Did you notice that often He answers your prayer by allowing some new tribulation to develop?

If you have, thank God for these difficulties! It won't be easy to do, but once you develop the habit of thanking the Lord every time something goes wrong, you have won a tremendous victory!

Patience, so charming in anyone, is especially so when manifested by a child or by a teen-ager. And it is in childhood and youth that the character is the most impressionable. It is then that the power of patience and self-control should be acquired.

A young woman who had met with a serious accident required some painful surgery that would necessitate many months of confinement in bed. When the doctor had finished his work, and was leaving, his youthful patient asked, "Doctor, how long will I have to lie here helpless?"

"Oh, only one day at a time," was his cheerful reply.

Thus it is with all our problems. God does not ask us to fret and worry about tomorrow. "My grace is sufficient for thee," He promises (2 Cor. 12:9). "As thy days, so shall thy strength be" (Deut. 33:25).

We would be stronger if we would pray more than we do. One time as two men were going to an appointment, it seemed they hit every red light. The man who was not driving began to fuss about all the time busy people lose waiting at stop lights. Shortly he noticed his friend was not paying any attention. "What are you thinking?" he asked.

"I was praying," his friend replied.

"What about?"

"For a friend," was the reply. "I have a prayer list. Every time I have to wait at a stop light, I pray for one person on that list."

Try it the next time you have to wait at a signal light!

KEEPING FRIDAY

Call the sabbath a delight, the holy of the Lord. Isa. 58:13.

There is something particularly special about Friday evening. The house has been cleaned, the baths taken, and you gather for sundown worship. Everything seems so relaxed, so different. You know that the angels of heaven are near.

Yet this Friday evening "specialness" can be lost through not being ready on time. A mother one Thursday pinned up the following two quotations in her kitchen:

"The Sabbath has not been kept. By some the work of six days has been carried into the seventh. One hour, and even more, has often been taken from the commencement and close of the Sabbath."—*Testimonies,* vol. 1, p. 150.

"We should jealously guard the edges of the Sabbath. Remember that every moment is consecrated, holy time."—*Ibid.,* vol. 6, p. 356.

Her two daughters, in the third and fifth grades, noticed these quotations. "Mother," asked one of them, "why did you pin up those cards near where you work?"

"Because I feel that for too long a time we have had what I might call a Friday flurry. We have not given ourselves any time to get ready in our minds for a quiet worship. There has been too much hurry near the beginning of the Sabbath."

One of the girls said that she almost dreaded Friday, though she loved the Sabbath. Said mother, "We are going to make some changes in our home. On Thursday evening we are going to wash our hair, and see that our shoes, stockings, and dresses are all ready for the Sabbath. Then on Friday morning we shall get up half an hour earlier so that you can help me get other things ready before you go off to school. That will give me a good start, and I'll have time to bake buns, cookies, or pie for the weekend."

The family did exactly that. Dad even did the vacuuming before he went to work. When the girls came home from school, everything was finished. "I like this way of keeping Friday," said both girls. All were ready one hour early to welcome the Sabbath.

IF CHRIST CAME TO CHURCH

Where two or three are gathered together in my name, there am I in the midst of them. **Matt. 18:20.**

The story is told of a pastor who, while preparing his Sabbath sermon, fell asleep. As he slept he dreamed that he was at church on Sabbath morning. The church was full, and just as he stepped up to the pulpit to begin his sermon, a stranger entered the sanctuary and slowly walked down the aisle, looking about carefully, as though he were noting the worshipers—how they were dressed and what they were doing. About halfway down the aisle someone noticed him and offered him a place to sit, which he quietly accepted.

The pastor sensed that the visitor's face had a deep intentness about it, as though he had lived much and known deep sorrow. As he delivered his sermon he became more and more conscious of this stranger listening to him. Following the benediction the pastor hurried to the foyer to meet the visitor, but he had already disappeared in the crowd. The minister then hunted up the man who had offered him a seat, asking, "Who was he?"

"Who was the stranger?" replied the parishioner. "Why, Pastor, don't you know him? That was Jesus of Nazareth . . ."

"Jesus of Nazareth!" The pastor couldn't believe it. A flood of questions poured into his mind. Perplexed and troubled, he murmured to himself, "The Lord whom I serve was observing and listening. What did He think of our sanctuary— its stained-glass windows, its costly organ? How was He impressed with the music, the robed choir? And what was I saying? In what spirit did I preach? What did He think of our worship today?"

In the midst of these troubled thoughts, the pastor awakened. It was all a dream. But what a dream!

If our eyes could see Jesus physically present in the audience, would we do anything differently in our Sabbath schools and church services? Would we study our lesson more earnestly if we knew He was to be in our class? If our scripture for today is true—and it is—shouldn't we consider that through the Holy Spirit He really is there?

THE BIG FOUR DIVERSIONS

Abide in me, and I in you. As the branch cannot bear fruit of itself, except it abide in the vine; no more can ye, except ye abide in me. John 15:4.

If you were the devil, what would be your best methods for separating a Christian from his Saviour? What devices would you use? There is a comment on page 71 of the book *Steps to Christ* which states that "it is Satan's constant effort to keep the attention diverted from the Saviour, and thus prevent the union and communion of the soul with Christ." What are the things he most effectively uses to take our attention away from Christ?

This is one of the most important questions we could possibly discuss. In Bible classes we generally spend a whole class period talking about it, and during the course of a school year we come back to it several times. We start our discussion with this next sentence from *Steps to Christ:*

"The pleasures of the world, life's cares and perplexities and sorrows, the faults of others, or your own faults and imperfections,—to any or all of these he will seek to divert the mind."—*Ibid.*

I list these four things on the board or on the screen of the overhead projector, then examine them. "Which of these four things," I ask the class, "would probably be the most effective in keeping the largest number of Adventist teen-agers from Christ?" Many conclude that it would be "the pleasures of the world." Others think it would be "your own faults and imperfections." And invariably there are those who are kept away by "the faults of others." We generally conclude that the devil is very effectively using all four of the methods listed above.

Which one would work the best on *you?*

"Do not be misled by his devices," the author urges. And how does one keep from being misled? By recognizing what the enemy is up to—and by turning our attention from self to Christ. The whole chapter from which these thoughts are taken, "Growing Up Into Christ," or, in *Real Happiness Is,* "Grow Up!" would be good reading for every teen-ager—and for all of us. Have you read it?

AS CHRISTMAS APPROACHES

There is that maketh himself rich, yet hath nothing: there is that maketh himself poor, yet hath great riches. **Prov. 13:7.**

I keep between pages 290 and 291 of the book *Counsels on Stewardship* a dollar bill that I use in discussing stewardship in our Bible classes. The word *dollar* is found twice in the section that makes up these two pages. After mentioning how much money is spent by youth "for self-indulgence and display, for that which they would have been just as happy without," this comment is made: "Every dollar which we possess is the Lord's. Instead of spending means for needless things, we should invest it in answering the calls of missionary work."

As Christmas approaches it would be well for us to remember that all of us would be "just as happy" without those things purchased for "self-indulgence and display." Let our gifts to one another be practical, with our largest gifts going to Jesus.

The second mention of a dollar is this one:

"Every penny should be carefully treasured. A cent seems like a trifle, but a hundred cents make a dollar, and rightly spent may be the means of saving a soul from death. If all the means which has been wasted by our own people in self-gratification had been devoted to the cause of God, there would be no empty treasuries."

The September 10, 1970, issue of the *Review and Herald* told of a plea that came to A. M. Bartlett, then president of the East Indonesia Union Mission. A tribal chieftain walked for days from a remote section of Indonesia to reach mission headquarters. He came to plead for a teacher. "There are ten thousand people up there waiting," he said. "If you could send us a teacher we would all become Adventists."

As we see so much being misspent, what can we say? There comes to us through the Holy Spirit this plea: "There should be no extravagance in building fine homes, in buying costly furniture, in indulging in worldly dress, or in providing luxurious food; but in everything let us think of the souls for whom Christ has died. . . . Let us save every dollar that can be saved, that the matchless charms of Christ may be presented before the souls of the perishing."—*Ibid.,* p. 298.

THE SACRIFICES PLEASING TO GOD

Do not neglect to do good and to share what you have, for such sacrifices are pleasing to God. Heb. 13:16, R.S.V.

The late Albert Schweitzer habitually traveled fourth class on the railroad. When someone inquired why he always insisted on such accommodations, with their discomfort, he quipped, "Because there is no fifth class."

The same spirit was manifested by the early pioneers. "The cause of God lay so near the heart of the pioneers in this message that they seldom took a meal at a hotel, even though the cost was but twenty-five cents each. But young men and women generally are not educated to economize, and waste follows waste everywhere."—*Testimonies*, vol. 5, p. 400.

The servant of God goes on to point out that while workers now "may not be called upon to deprive themselves of warm meals, as the early workers did in their itinerant life, they may learn to supply their real wants with less expense than they now think necessary" (*ibid.*). The suggestion is made that we study the history of the Waldensian missionaries, and "imitate their example of sacrifice and self-denial" (*ibid.*).

Are these words for a former generation? Or do they still have application in the affluence of the 1970's?

"If the Lord Jesus Christ came to our homes and churches today," asks an earnest Christian of another denomination, "would He approve the lavish manner of living of many of us? What would He think of the gleaming automobiles, the expensive and frequent vacation trips, the extravagantly-built homes, the consuming passion we have adopted toward what the Scriptures call 'the things of this world'?"—GUNNAR HOGLUND, "Are We Living Too Lavishly?" *The King's Business*, March, 1966, p. 22.

Jesus probably would not ask us to travel as Albert Schweitzer did; the swiftness of air travel is doubtless in His providence to speed His work. He would not likely ask us to eat cold meals like the early pioneers. But might He not have some very pointed inquiries about our use of His funds to purchase so many luxuries and indulgences? Would you be at ease if He came to your home?

DANGER FROM ABUNDANCE

Who gave himself for our sins, that he might deliver us from this present evil world, according to the will of God and our Father. Gal. 1:4.

A wild duck heading south decided to stop and spend the winter in a farmer's barnyard. He decided to take advantage of the farmer's corn and shelter, and remain with his newfound domestic friends.

The winter passed, and spring came, and with it the migrating birds. From the barnyard this duck heard the call of the wild fowl, and his heart beat faster. But as he flapped his wings to join his brothers in the sky, he found he could not rise. During the winter he had grown fat on the farmer's corn, and his wings could no longer lift him up into the blue heights. He rose a few feet and fell helplessly back to the earth.

Will it be that way with any of us as it comes time for the loud cry and God's glorious final witness? Can "this present evil world"—and its affluence—cause our hearts to be "overcharged with surfeiting" and "cares of this life" so that we will have lost the ability to dare and do for God?

"Our danger is not from scarcity," wrote inspiration even back in 1890, "but from abundance. We are constantly tempted to excess. Those who would preserve their powers unimpaired for the service of God, must observe strict temperance in the use of His bounties, as well as total abstinence from every injurious or debasing indulgence."—*Counsels on Diet and Foods,* p. 29.

The danger of affluence is not merely the hurtful indulgences it loads onto our tables. Our whole spiritual outlook is influenced as almost unconsciously we develop what is practically a mania for possessing more and more things.

There is a safeguard, however, and that safeguard is to follow the example of Christ in constant, unselfish giving. Every advantage we receive, materially or spiritually, will be prized as just one more opportunity to help and bless others. Like Paul, we will think of ourselves as debtors to all men, and every dollar we can possibly spare will be pressed into the work of hastening the return of Christ.

354

WHAT KIND OF EXAMPLE?

Be ye followers of me, even as I also am of Christ. 1 Cor. 11:1.

In North America alone there were some twenty-seven thousand workers employed by our conferences and institutions in 1970. Denominational employment is sometimes thought of as a kind of "sacrifice." I personally do not like to think of it that way. It is true that many of us could carry similar responsibilities in secular jobs, and make more money. But what we receive is adequate, if we are willing to limit our wants. And I would like to add as a personal testimony that I would not trade the joys of full-time church work for the highest paid secular job in all the world!

All of us as Christians are laborers together with God—as partners in "His great firm" (*Counsels on Stewardship*, p. 300). We could not ask for a finer Employer!

This partnership, along with its privileges, also carries a solemn responsibility, particularly as denominational workers, in how we spend our money. We of all Christians ought to be able to say to church members everywhere, "Be ye followers of me, even as I also am of Christ."

Gunnar Hoglund, an evangelical writer, tells of the disillusionment that came to him when, after contributing for years to a certain evangelical radio broadcast, he quite by chance happened to visit in the home of one of the staff members. "The house," he wrote, "was gaudy beyond description—expensive, filled from corner to corner with extravagant gadgetry and apparatus. Standing in the middle of this celestial palace, this showplace of opulence, my mind went back to letters which had come to my desk from this broadcast, exhortations to give, give, give—so the broadcast could keep on 'one more week.' A haunting question came to mind. Would the officials of this broadcast permit a photo of this home, this dream castle, to appear in one of their letters?"—"Are We Living Too Lavishly?" *The King's Business*, March, 1966, p. 23.

INFINITE GAIN

Gather my saints together unto me; those that have made a covenant with me by sacrifice. Ps. 50:5.

Some have had strange ideas as to what constitutes sacrifice. They itemize the things they "give up" to become a Christian— cocktails, dancing, smoking, the theater, various indulgences— and call it sacrifice. But when all these things are hurtful, spiritually or physically, how can dispensing with them be called a sacrifice? "The exchange we make in the denial of selfish desires and inclinations is an exchange of the worthless and transitory for the precious and enduring. This is not sacrifice, but infinite gain."—*Education,* p. 296.

So also when we deny ourselves color TV or extravagant automobiles or lavishly furnished homes in order to place more of the funds entrusted to us into the Lord's work. This self-denial is simply making the better investment—and it too is "infinite gain," not sacrifice.

What, then, is "sacrifice"? It must be when, like the early believers, we deny ourselves "even of necessary things in order to supply the needs of others" (*The Acts of the Apostles,* p. 343). It must be to follow the example of the widow, who cast of her "living" into the Lord's treasury. With her it was "all the living that she had" (Luke 21:4).

God is not unreasonable. He knows our need to supply life's necessities. But as we follow Christ's example, our heart will be so much in God's work that, while we will keep our homes and persons neat and attractive, we will use every dollar we can to further the gospel.

A professional man, an earnest Christian, was looking for a home for himself and his family. The real estate man who showed him about thought he should have a large and impressive home befitting, as he thought, his profession. He showed him such homes. "No," said this man, "when the Lord comes I do not want to be living in a house that costs that much."

What will it be worth to discover in heaven that funds we put into God's work have won others? Will self-denial be considered a sacrifice? Will it not then be seen, rather, as "infinite gain"?

WORSHIP WITHOUT SACRIFICE

If any man will come after me, let him deny himself, and take up his cross daily, and follow me. **Luke 9:23.**

According to the Religious News Service some years ago, *Social Welfare,* a magazine for Malayan youth published in Singapore, listed "worship without sacrifice" as one of the seven "deadly sins" of modern society. The other sins cited were politics without principle, wealth without work, pleasure without conscience, knowledge without character, business without morality, and science without humanity.

"Worship without sacrifice." Does it ever happen to us? Can our church become just a comfortable social organization to us? Can we attend for the social fellowship, and the status, and the "loaves and fishes" (or the punch), but without any zeal for evangelism?

Inspiration suggests that we should "cherish a spirit of sacrifice," spending "as little as possible" upon ourselves (*Testimonies,* vol. 9, pp. 130, 131). This is to be considered a privilege, something to "cherish"—not something to regard as a burden. "In every home there should be taught lessons of self-denial. Fathers and mothers, teach your children to economize. Encourage them to save their pennies for missionary work."—*Ibid.*

A spirit of self-denial does not come naturally to children. And all too often we strengthen their natural tendency toward love of display by unwise gifts and indulgences. Urges God's servant, "Parents, for Christ's sake do not use the Lord's money to please the fancies of your children. . . . Do not educate your children to think that your love for them must be expressed by indulging their pride, their extravagance, their love of display."—*Child Guidance,* pp. 134, 135.

Self ever clamors for indulgence—and the more it is pampered, the more it will demand. Jesus was being practical when He suggested that self-denial be made a "daily" matter. It's the little self-denials—the bottle of soda pop skipped, the between-meal candy bar omitted—that are sometimes the greatest victories. And if we would indeed follow the Saviour, we will cherish this privilege, and so will our children—making "duty . . . a delight, and sacrifice a pleasure."

TO GET—OR TO GIVE?

For ye know the grace of our Lord Jesus Christ, that, though he was rich, yet for your sakes he became poor, that ye through his poverty might be rich. 2 Cor. 8:9.

In addition to its many large towns and vast cities, India is reported to have more than one million villages. If Christ, at the time He was on earth, had begun to visit the villages of India, and visited one every day, He would not finish visiting all the villages of that country until sometime in the 2700's.

To what extent are these villages and their peoples your responsibility and mine?

" 'Go ye into all the world, and preach the gospel to every creature,' Christ has commanded His followers (Mark 16:15). Not that all are called to be ministers or missionaries in the ordinary sense of the term; but all may be workers with Him in giving the 'glad tidings' to their fellow men. To all, great or small, learned or ignorant, old or young, the command is given."—*Education*, p. 264.

God's servant then asks:

"In view of this command, can we educate our sons and daughters for a life of respectable conventionality, a life professedly Christian, but lacking His self-sacrifice, a life on which the verdict of Him who is truth must be, 'I know you not'?"—*Ibid.*

"A life of respectable conventionality"—youth have seen too much of this in too many of their elders. Palatial homes, luxurious boats, private pools, and expensive furnishings—all these luxuries affluence has made possible. Children brought up in indulgent luxury are not likely to settle for less as they choose careers.

And all the while, out there in India, are those one million villages. And the storm is gathering. The winds of Armageddon are about to be unleashed. Across the darkening clouds burns this question: "Can we educate our sons and daughters for a life of respectable conventionality, a life professedly Christian, but lacking His self-sacrifice?"

Can we?

358

ISN'T HONESTY THE BETTER POLICY?

Bring ye all the tithes into the storehouse, that there may be meat in mine house, and prove me now herewith, saith the Lord of hosts, if I will not open you the windows of heaven, and pour you out a blessing, that there shall not be room enough to receive it. Mal. 3:10.

How many of the tens of millions of churchgoers in the United States pay tithe? The Gallup poll, in a story released one Easter Sunday, estimated that "of the millions of adult worshipers who will flock to Easter services today, approximately three out of every 100 will represent families who believe in tithing."

How about Seventh-day Adventists?

One union conference president wrote that if all our people would return to the Lord their tithe "there would probably be sufficient money in the coffers to do everything that needs to be done." He estimated that probably not more than "about 60 per cent" of the professed people of God "really pay an honest tithe."

"I just can't afford to pay tithe," says one. This, perhaps, is one of the most commonly offered reasons given.

The excuse could be rephrased. "I can't afford to be honest."

It doesn't sound right, does it?

But suppose one is behind on his bills. Is he justified in attempting to pay off his debts before returning his tithes? Mrs. White, after she had spoken on tithing at the Sydney, Australia, church, was asked this same question. "Sister White, do you think my father should pay tithes?" a lady asked. "He has met with great loss recently, and he says that as soon as he cancels his debt, he will pay tithes."

Mrs. White quoted from Malachi 3, then said: "After such a statement, would I dare say to you, You need not pay tithes as long as you are in debt? Shall I tell you to be sure to pay all you owe any man, although you rob God to do so?"—*Counsels on Stewardship*, p. 92.

A "curse" rests upon those who rob God (Mal. 3:9). Would not an indebted person be foolish to take such a risk? As we approach the end of the year, shouldn't we review how we stand with God on this matter?

THE TWO CROWNS

Set your affection on things above, not on things on the earth. Col. 3:2.

"Money," said one news reporter, "is still considered the number one badge of success."

The whole drama could be portrayed as though upon a gigantic movie screen. The first scene is of "this earth, dark and gloomy." Looking closer, you see people moving about, some surrounded by angels of God, and others surrounded by evil angels. As you watch, two crowns come to view, one symbolizing eternal life, and the other earthly treasure. Within the second crown are jewels, gold, and silver.

As you continue to watch, a vast, clamorous crowd of people rush toward the earthly crown. Many of them seem almost "bereft of reason." There is shoving, crowding, trampling. The ones who manage to seize any of the treasures hold them fast. Others, wretchedly poor, look wistfully toward the treasures, then turn hopelessly aside as individuals who are stronger press ahead of them. Yet they do not give up. They are joined by many who are sickly, deformed, aged. Some fall dead while pressing forward, others die just as they take hold of the treasures. Dead bodies are everywhere. Everyone who reaches the crown and gains some of its treasures is loudly applauded.

Then you notice a second group. They look wistfully toward the heavenly crown, but seem to have no sense of its value. They reach languidly toward it with one hand, but with the other hand grasp eagerly toward the earthly.

You see a third group. Surrounded by angels, they are moving through the disorderly crowd toward the heavenly crown. Though ridiculed, they pay no attention. The closer they come to the heavenly crown, the clearer and brighter its light shines about them. Their faces seem to be transformed, resembling the angels.

An interpretation is scarcely needed. But one sentence concerning the majority of those within the first two groups stands out: "They fail of the earthly, yet while in pursuit of it, lose the heavenly."—*Testimonies,* vol. 1, p. 352.

AN ANGEL SENT TO HELP

He that is faithful in that which is least is faithful also in much. **Luke 16:10.**

One evening as a fourteen-year-old girl knelt to pray she realized that she had not been living as close to her Saviour as she should have been. She asked God to help her, though it seemed that her prayer was going no higher than the ceiling. But God did hear that prayer, for He sent an angel to that girl's grandmother, Mrs. Ellen White, with instruction for this girl and her younger sister, and for the family.

In her book *Stories of My Grandmother* Ella Robinson tells how her grandmother came over the next afternoon and read them the testimony that she had been given. There were instructions for the whole family, but as her grandmother read, fourteen-year-old Ella realized that much of the testimony was to her. There were suggestions concerning her need to be faithful in the duties of the home, heeding the suggestions made by her mother yet not waiting to be told what needed to be done. There was need for her to keep her room in neater order, to keep her bed made, and to be more careful in her work in the kitchen. "He that is faithful in that which is least," the testimony concluded, "is faithful also in much."

Part way through the reading Ella interrupted her grandmother to ask, "Did the angel say all those things, or did you think of them yourself as you were writing?"

"The angel talked with me in the night," her grandmother replied, "and I wrote down the message that was given to me for you and Mabel and for your parents."

As soon as she could, Ella fled upstairs to her room, buried her head in her pillow, and wept. Her thoughts were bitter and resentful. Then as a bolt of lightning she remembered! Hadn't she asked God the evening before for help? Hadn't God sent His angel in answer to her prayer? Yes. God *had* heard her! He *did* love her! He had sent a message of reproof *because* He loved her. Tears of repentance took the place of tears of rebellion, and she again knelt and thanked God for sending an angel to help her find her way back.

"GOD IS STILL LOVE"

Commit thy way unto the Lord; trust also in him; and he shall bring it to pass. Ps. 37:5.

The day before Christmas one year, the Los Angeles *Herald-Examiner* reported that Ronald Baker, who had run away from home in order to escape the surgery that would save his life, had returned home. It would be necessary for Ronald because of a cancerous tumor to have a leg amputated.

Seventeen-year-old Patty Hundley, who had undergone similar surgery some thirty months earlier, wrote Ronald a letter of encouragement. She had discovered at the age of fourteen that she would have to have her leg amputated above the knee to escape a slow death by cancer. It hadn't been easy. But she had been fitted up with an artificial leg, and graduated with her ninth-grade class. The day before she wrote to Ron she had gone skiing up at Big Bear. During the summer she said she swam almost every day. There were a lot of things she couldn't do, of course. She had to climb stairs a step at a time, and she could not run. "But the operation and having an artificial leg is not half as bad as it seems," she told Ron. "There are just a lot worse things that could happen."

Patty spoke of faith—of "something to fall back on." She concluded her letter, "Look to the future, and a full life, not the pain of the present. I know you will be brave and never regret your decision."

Charles Spurgeon was once talking to a farmer who had on his barn a weather vane with an arrow on which was inscribed the words, "God is love."

"What do you mean by that?" asked Spurgeon. "Do you think God's love is changeable? That it veers about according to the wind?"

"Oh, no," answered the farmer. "It means that in whichever way the wind blows, God is still love."

And so it is! No matter what our difficulties—God is still love! That is a truth we can always "fall back on." "Commit," then, "thy way unto the Lord; trust also in him."

DECEMBER 22

GOOD NIGHT

Blessed are the dead which die in the Lord from henceforth: Yea, saith the Spirit, that they may rest from their labours; and their works do follow them. Rev. 14:13.

The servant of God, writing to a family who had lost a child in death, cautioned them against dwelling upon their bereavement. The parents and others of the family had apparently given themselves up to unreasonable mourning and complaining. They were making themselves miserable and discouraged and were casting gloom upon others.

"The Lord is gracious, merciful, and true," she wrote to them. "He has permitted the one of your household band who was the most innocent and the best prepared to rest through the perils of the last days. Oh! do not shut up your souls against melody and joy, mourning as though there were to be no resurrection of the dead, but praise God that for her there is no more death, no more trial, no more sorrow. She rests in Jesus until the Life-giver shall call forth His sleeping saints to a glorious immortality."—*Testimonies,* vol. 5, pp. 313, 314.

The illustration is used of a father who made it his custom to tuck his daughter into bed at night. Whatever time of the night he would come in, he would always go in softly and tuck her in and kiss her good night. Sometimes she would partly awaken, and say, "Hello, Daddy," and he would say, "Good night, sweetheart."

There came the time she was to be married. He went in on that last night she would be under his roof, and he tucked her in. She put her arms around his neck and drew him close, and he put his arms around her and said, "My daughter," and she just said, "Daddy."

We can think of our heavenly Father the same way. If we are to sleep awhile before Jesus comes, He will tuck us in. He will watch over our resting place, and He will awaken us.

"The power of the truth," Mrs. White wrote to the grieving family we have referred to, "should be sufficient to sustain and console in every adversity. It is in enabling its possessor to triumph over affliction that the religion of Christ reveals its true value."—*Ibid.,* p. 314.

363

CALL HIS NAME JESUS

Call his name Jesus: for he shall save his people from their sins. Matt. 1:21.

I had been away at college for some months my freshman year, and Christmas vacation was approaching. I do not recall what the problem was but I was becoming discouraged, when I received a Christmas card from one of my younger brothers. Across the bottom of the card he had written, "Call his name Jesus: for he shall save his people from their sins." It was just the message I needed, and that verse of Scripture has been a favorite of mine ever since.

"Call his name Jesus."

There is power in that name. Speak it softly, reverently, in love and compassion—whether in prayer, or in witness to another person. Do you not sense the angels of God drawing near?

"For he shall save his people from their sins."

Is there anything you need more than you need this? Suppose you are in an accident and discover that you have but a few hours to live. Is there anything you would need more than forgiveness of sin?

Or suppose that within a few moments the air-raid sirens in your city should begin that undulating wail that warns that the real thing has happened. With perhaps fifteen minutes left, if the missiles are on target, is there any promise that could be more meaningful than the promise of salvation from your sins?

But probably neither of these eventualities is at the moment very likely. The next twenty-four hours and the ones after that and the ones after that will for most of us be very normal. But is there anything we will need more than we need Jesus?

There is no torture like the torture of a guilty conscience. There is no restlessness like the restlessness of a life separated from Christ. There is no emptiness like the emptiness of a soul from which Christ has been excluded. And only by Jesus can this torture be halted, this restlessness satisfied, this emptiness filled.

There is nothing else. Nothing at all.

Won't you let Him be the answer to your need today?

SO COMPLETELY WONDERFUL

Thanks be unto God for his unspeakable gift. 2 Cor. 9:15.

Sanford T. Whitman tells of an artist who one summer had gone to a home up on a ridge to paint the fantastic view one could see through the picture window. But the weather was against him. On the day of his visit the rising winds and gathering clouds brought rain. There was no view anywhere, and as the hours wore on, the artist became impatient. The owner of the home, a grandmother and a friend of the family, tried to dispel his gloom. "The day isn't over yet," she said, with an infectious smile. "Storms don't usually last long this time o' year. It may break away by evening. If it does, the sunset will be as beautiful as the day has been stormy."

It didn't seem possible. As evening drew on, the wind rose briefly, then died away. The rain ceased, and the sun broke through the clouds, descending with matchless splendor. The artist seized his palette and easel, dashed outside, and for a few moments worked furiously. Suddenly, he laid down his brush and colors. "I—I can't do it," he exclaimed. "I can't paint it. It's too big—too wide, too deep, too high."

He watched in silence. Finally, as the glory began to fade, he said softly, partly to himself and partly to the grandmother who was standing nearby, "I—I've never seen anything so completely wonderful. The air is so pure, the clouds so majestic. It's as you said it would be. The sunset is as beautiful as the storm was wild."

So it is with the love of God—a love so completely wonderful, so pure, so majestic, a love that would sacrifice so much to save sinful men. "Tongue cannot utter it; pen cannot portray it. You may meditate upon it every day of your life; you may search the Scriptures diligently in order to understand it; you may summon every power and capability that God has given you, in the endeavor to comprehend the love and compassion of the heavenly Father; and yet there is an infinity beyond. . . . Eternity itself can never fully reveal it."—*Testimonies,* vol. 5, p. 740.

But you can accept it—and invite others to accept it too.

NOTHING DULL HERE!

And the Word was made flesh, and dwelt among us, (and we beheld his glory, the glory as of the only begotten of the Father,) full of grace and truth. John 1:14.

In introducing his biography of the life of Christ, John goes back as far as he can go. "In the beginning was the Word," he wrote, "and the Word was with God, and the Word was God. He was in the beginning with God; all things were made through him, and without him was not anything made that was made" (John 1:1-3, R.S.V.).

"All things were made through him"—this world, this solar system, this galaxy, the billions of other galaxies. A single one of these galaxies contains upwards of 100 billion suns, and is so vast that for the total galaxy to make a single revolution, as it moves forward through space, takes 100 million years. Picture, if you can, the thousands of billions of these galaxies circling His throne. Picture Him, the King of kings, passing from world to world, from galaxy to galaxy, superintending the affairs of His vast realm.

Then be astonished, all peoples—this mighty God was made flesh and dwelt among us! "If it is only a dream," observes *The Interpreter's Bible,* "how wonderful a dream! But if it is true! If there is any chance that it is true, what then? Little wonder that Dorothy Sayers stares in bewilderment at people who assure her blandly that Christianity leaves them cold, as being a dull affair that bores them. Or that she is so confident that if they would read the gospel through just once and let it have its chance with them, they would be forced to admit, whatever attitude they might take up about it, that this is, out of sight, the most exciting and tremendous and amazing story that the world can ever hear."—Vol. VIII, p. 473.

It's true! We know it's true! He died—would have died for you alone. He arose from the dead. And He's returning to this same little speck of a world soon, perhaps within this very decade!

There is nothing dull here! This is the good news entrusted to you. It is yours—to tell the whole world! Will you? Are you?

TO SEE FOR OURSELVES

And they shall see his face; and his name shall be in their foreheads.
Rev. 22:4.

"Háve you ever wondered," asks George MacLean, "what Christ looked like? There is not a Christian on earth but has the conviction that he would know Jesus if ever he saw Him. But how do you really know? Was He tall or of medium height? Was His hair brown or black? Were His eyes blue, brown, or gray? Eighteenth-century artists portrayed Him looking as if He were in the last stages of some dreadful disease. Our modern artists show a more virile, manly conception of our Lord. Perhaps most of us imagine Him looking a lot like Sallman's *Head of Christ."—These Times,* June, 1961, p. 30.

In addition to the Gospels, we have three books from inspiration which sometimes mention little things that give us somewhat of a pen picture of what Jesus might have looked like. These are *The Desire of Ages, Christ's Object Lessons,* and *Thoughts From the Mount of Blessing.*

The first of these mentions that when Jesus came to this world "His glory was veiled, that the majesty of His outward form might not become an object of attraction" (p. 43). When John the Baptist introduced Him at the Jordan the people saw someone who "was apparently a simple personage, clad like themselves in the humble garments of the poor"—though at the same time "He impressed men with a sense of power that was hidden, yet could not be wholly concealed" (*ibid.,* pp. 137, 138).

He is described, as He taught in the Temple shortly before His death, as "the young Galilean, bearing no earthly honor or royal badge"—while about Him stood "priests in their rich apparel" (*ibid.,* p. 610). In another place, mention is made of His "youthful face, fresh with the sunlight of His Father's countenance" (*Christ's Object Lessons,* p. 19).

He still bears a human form, but when we see Him at His coming, His majesty will be no longer veiled. We must be there. If we miss that we have missed everything. We can only inquire once again, "What shall it profit a man, if he shall gain the whole world, and lose his own soul?" (Mark 8:36).

THINKING ABOUT GARDENS

And the Lord God took the man, and put him into the garden of Eden to dress it and to keep it. Gen. 2:15.

Winter has just begun, but it's not too soon to be thinking about gardens—of our own, if we have a place to plant one, and also of the Garden of Eden.

A beautiful description of our parents' Eden home is found in the book *The Story of Redemption.* One interesting thing it brings out is that the vines, which grew upright, were unlike anything man has seen since the fall of man. "The fruit was very large and of different colors; some nearly black, some purple, red, pink, and light green. This beautiful and luxuriant growth of fruit upon the branches of the vine was called grapes. They did not trail upon the ground, although not supported by trellises, but the weight of the fruit bowed them" (pages 21, 22). There were fragrant flowers everywhere, and lofty trees. In the midst of the Garden was the tree of life, with a fruit that "looked like apples of gold and silver" (*ibid.*, p. 22). As today's scripture mentions, it was the work of Adam and Eve to dress and keep this lovely Garden.

After Adam and Eve were expelled, the Garden of Eden remained on the earth until just before the Flood, when a divine hand removed it. It is now a part of the New Jerusalem, and by God's grace it will shortly be our privilege to walk along its pleasant paths.

Meanwhile, in gardens and flowers of this earth we have a reflection, though faint, of what Eden is like. Fortunate indeed are those children who can help with the care of flowers and plants. As children on an Oklahoma farm my brothers and sister and I would spend many pleasant moments looking through the seed catalogs, which usually came in January, planning what we would order and plant.

Our children if at all possible "should have a garden to cultivate, where they might find both amusement and useful employment. The training of plants and flowers tends to the improvement of taste and judgment, while an acquaintance with God's useful and beautiful creations has a refining and ennobling influence upon the mind."—*The Adventist Home,* p. 142.

BE ON YOUR GUARD

And take heed to yourselves, lest at any time your hearts be overcharged with surfeiting, and drunkenness, and cares of this life, and so that day come upon you unawares. Luke 21:34.

"Be on your guard—see to it that your minds are never clouded by dissipation or drunkenness or the worries of this life, or else that day may catch you like the springing of a trap." Thus Phillips has translated today's scripture.

I asked several academy Bible classes, "Which of these three things do you think will be the downfall of the largest number of church members?" Almost without exception the students indicated that they considered the cares and worries of this life to be the greatest danger.

What is it that keeps you from praying more than you do? What keeps you from going out and working to win others? It can be the television set, of course, and a lot of other things. But is it not more often "the cares of this life"? We become so involved in earning a living, in paying the bills, in keeping the children in school, in keeping up socially, and a hundred other things, that we have no time for God. Oh, we say a hurried prayer in the morning, sometimes—and salve our conscience with yet another few moments on our knees at night, but we don't really pray. It is just a mechanical going through the routine. And come Sabbath we are too tired even to think of doing any missionary work. As for taking a weekday evening to have some neighbors over for Bible studies, impossible! The house would have to be cleaned, et cetera.

The television set—the payments on it and on a lot of other things—may indeed be some of the pressure. It's things, things, and more things. Come when it will, the day of God will find many still struggling to keep up with the car payments, the Sears charge account, the payments on the furniture, and on, and on, and on—and still too busy to pray.

A failure to restrict our wants, living beyond our means, giving more thought to social standing than to soul winning—such can almost overwhelm one with unnecessary cares! God help us to begin now to free ourselves from every such entanglement!

"O ISRAEL, RETURN . . ."

And he spake a parable unto them to this end, that men ought always to pray, and not to faint. Luke 18:1.

"Prayer," someone has said, "is the most talked about and least practiced belief of the Christian church."

"I haven't prayed in years," an attractive girl told Miriam Wood, quietly, flatly.

"Oh, I don't mean that I haven't bowed my head at church or knelt at home during family worship. But I've just gone through the motions. I haven't really *prayed* since I was a child."

Surprised, Miriam Wood stammered the obvious remonstrances that crowded to her lips. "But you've been baptized— you've always attended denominational schools—you're a church member——"

The girl's level eyes met the eyes of Mrs. Wood. "What does that have to do with it?" she inquired softly.

The person who does not pray cannot possibly stand during the crises of the final hours of probation. No one will be able to depend upon the faith and devotion and prayers of another. Each must have a relationship of his own with Christ.

Those who exercise but little faith now, who pray spasmodically—if at all—will be in the greatest danger of giving in under the pressures of the impending Sunday legislation. "And even if they endure the test they will be plunged into deeper distress and anguish in the time of trouble, because they have never made it a habit to trust in God. The lessons of faith which they have neglected they will be forced to learn under a terrible pressure of discouragement. We should now acquaint ourselves with God by proving His promises."—*The Great Controversy*, p. 622.

If we have become careless about prayer, how do we restore the lost relationship? "Take with you words," Hosea suggests, "and turn to the Lord: say unto him, Take away all iniquity, and receive us graciously" (Hosea 14:2). God's sure promise is, "I will heal their backsliding, I will love them freely" (verse 4).

"O Israel, return unto the Lord thy God" (verse 1).

FULLNESS OF JOY

These things have I spoken unto you, that my joy might remain in you, and that your joy might be full. John 15:11.

A nineteen-year-old whose father had been involved in a gigantic stock exchange swindle said, "I feel like the unhappiest person on earth. I'm only nineteen. During my life I have had all the money I've wanted, but I hate it. It's the love of money that has put my father behind bars. Yet, I have tried everything else and there is not one solitary thing that I can find to make me happy. What can I do to find happiness?"

What would you have told him?

A European teen-ager—living in poverty, dressing in hand-me-downs, and milking ten cows a day for a dollar a week spending money—was discovered by Hollywood. At twenty-three she had homes in three countries, more cars than she could drive, and more suitors than she knew what to do with. Yet she spoke of her life as being empty. "I must do something to change my life," she said. "But what and how?" After a pause, during which she stared off into space, she continued, "I don't know. I really don't know."

What would you have told her?

Could you have told these people of Jesus and of the joy He brings into empty lives? Today's scripture speaks of a joy that is full. It is the joy of knowing Christ and of being clothed with His righteousness. The book *Steps to Christ* puts it this way:

"If we are clothed with the righteousness of Christ, and are filled with the joy of His indwelling Spirit, we shall not be able to hold our peace. If we have tasted and seen that the Lord is good, we shall have something to tell. Like Philip when he found the Saviour, we shall invite others into His presence."—Page 78.

This is the kind of witness needed—the witness of a personal experience with Christ. We need to tell others of "the attractions of Christ." And is not one of the greatest things about Him the fact that He was a friend of publicans and sinners?

God grant that you may possess fullness of joy this day!

A SPECIAL PROMISE

He shall feed his flock like a shepherd: he shall gather the lambs with his arm, and carry them in his bosom, and shall gently lead those that are with young. Isa. 40:11.

One spring vacation we had taken a group of academy and college students into a portion of the Grand Canyon known as Havasupai. Such a trip is no small adventure. Leaving Highway 66 at Peach Springs, Arizona, one travels northward over the plateau for about seventy miles on dirt and gravel roads. Then, parking your car, you hike fourteen miles down into the canyon to a camping area at Havasupai Falls. We had spent a couple of days down there swimming, hiking, and exploring, and were on our way out.

To avoid the heat, we waited till about four o'clock in the afternoon to start. After about ten miles, we decided to camp for the night and climb the final four miles, which were mainly switchbacks, early the next morning. But after supper some of the students wanted to go on up that night. I declined to give permission, but said they could get up as early as they wanted the following morning. Well, about two o'clock the next morning I was awakened by the realization that three of the academy girls had packed up and were about ready to leave. I had promised they could leave "early"—so I didn't stop them. But neither could I get back to sleep. Lying there under the Arizona sky, I mentally went through the Bible, seeing how many promises I could recall. It was an unforgettable experience.

The girls made it safely, of course. But I have thought of that experience, and of the anxieties we will have for loved ones during the time of trouble. Surely God will watch over them— but how much easier it will be for us if we know and can call to mind, even on the darkest night, the promises of God's Word.

Today's promise is particularly for just such a time. There will be those with small children and even babies during the time of difficulties ahead. God has promised to "gather the lambs," and to "gently lead" those with small ones. Let us hide promises such as this in our hearts, so that we will not walk in anxiety and fear.

Scripture Index

373

374